Fiscal Decentralization and Land Policies

Edited by

Gregory K. Ingram and Yu-Hung Hong

D1607396

LINCOLN INSTITUTE
OF LAND POLICY
CAMBRIDGE, MASSACHUSETTS

Library of Congress Cataloging-in-Publication Data

Fiscal decentralization and land policies /
edited by Gregory K. Ingram and Yu-Hung Hong.
p. cm.
Includes index.
ISBN 978-1-55844-178-1
1. Intergovernmental fiscal relations. 2. Land use—Government policy.
I. Ingram, Gregory K. II. Hong, Yu-Hung. III. Lincoln Institute of Land Policy.
HJ197.F57155   2008
333.77—dc22   2008008703

Designed by Vern Associates

Composed in Sabon by Achorn International in Bolton, Massachusetts.
Printed and bound by Puritan Press, Inc., in Hollis, New Hampshire.
The paper is Roland Opaque 30, an acid-free, recycled sheet.

MANUFACTURED IN THE UNITED STATES OF AMERICA

CONTENTS

ILLUSTRATIONS

Tables

Figures

PREFACE

Because it defines local governments' powers to raise revenues and to spend on local public goods, fiscal decentralization has important implications for land policies. The degree of fiscal autonomy, in turn, determines the authority local jurisdictions have to tax real property and influences their ability to manage urban growth and preserve the environment. The links between fiscal decentralization and land policies, however, are not explicit. To elucidate these connections, *Fiscal Decentralization and Land Policies* presents the main contributions to a Lincoln Institute conference that addressed the effects of decentralization on local policies. The conference, "Fiscal Decentralization and Land Policies," was held in Cambridge, Massachusetts, in June 2007. Conference papers examined decentralization experiences in developed and developing countries, including local public good provision, jurisdiction size, public school finance, local environmental policy, urban economic development strategies, local fiscal prudence, and income distribution.

Following Lincoln's practice, the conference encouraged cross-disciplinary and international dialogue on land policy issues. Accordingly, urban economists, public finance experts, regional and urban planners, and government officials were invited, as were policy analysts who have advised governments in developed and developing countries on the design and implementation of fiscal decentralization.

Three overriding themes emerged from the discussions at the conference and are discussed in the chapters of this book. First, analyses of decentralization effects on local service provision in selected industrialized and developing countries have yielded mixed results, with no firm evidence of either positive or negative net effects on populations. Second, fiscal decentralization affects local policies differently across sectors. For example, varying degrees of interjurisdictional competition in the United States do not seem to affect local environmental policies and economic development strategies significantly, but more centralized public school finance has altered financial and nonfinancial resource allocation across school districts in some states. Third, decentralization can have varying effects on land use policy and property taxation. For example, evidence strongly indicates that the size of the jurisdiction affects the stringency of land use regulations. The role of U.S. property taxes as an important source of local revenue also depends on the degree of centralization of local public school finance. This book offers extensive discussions on the complexities involved in assessing decentralization experiences and identifies research areas that need immediate attention.

We owe thanks to many people for their help in making the conference and this publication possible. We thank all the contributors for presenting their research and comments at the conference and for their efforts in revising what are now the chapters and commentaries of this book. We are also grateful for the assistance provided by our conference planning team, Vikram Bapat, Brooke Digges, and Rie Sugihara. Diana Brubaker assisted in getting the final manuscript into the proper format for copyediting. Last, but not least, our heartfelt thanks go to the editorial and design team, including Nancy Benjamin, Kathleen M. Lafferty, Emily McKeigue, and Vern Associates for their editorial expertise and professional help.

Gregory K. Ingram
Yu-Hung Hong

INTRODUCTION

1

The Nexus of Fiscal Decentralization and Land Policies

Gregory K. Ingram and Yu-Hung Hong

The study of fiscal decentralization has important policy implications for urban growth management, environmental conservation, and property taxation.[1] First, fiscal decentralization gives local governments powers to set local taxes and make local expenditures. Second, in many countries local governments also have powers to regulate land uses within the general guidelines set by higher authorities. These two powers can and do interact so that municipalities often make land use decisions while considering their fiscal effects. Hence, an understanding of the degree to which local and provincial governments can exercise power, make decisions about their revenues and expenditures, and are held accountable for outcomes is crucial for land policy research and education.

The devolution of power to subnational governments is controversial. Advocates claim that decentralization will increase both efficiency and equity in the public sector because it allows customization of public services to local preferences, promotes scrutiny by citizens of government expenditures, and encourages innovation through interjurisdictional competition (Oates 1972, 2006; Tiebout 1956). Critics are, however, concerned about a lack of local administrative capacity, potential corruption, and the risk of "elite capture" (McLure

We thank Diana Brubaker for her careful comments on the earlier draft of the chapter.

1. In principle, fiscal decentralization requires devolution of decision-making power to local governments to determine revenues and expenditures and to the citizens of municipalities to elect local public officials. Thus, in this chapter, decentralization means both fiscal and political decentralization unless stated otherwise.

1995; Prud'homme 1995; Sewell 1996). The importance and duality of the arguments on decentralization provided the rationale for the Lincoln Institute to hold a conference to discuss these issues in June 2007.

Aims and Themes

The conference goals were to review decentralization experiences in Organisation for Economic Co-operation and Development (OECD) countries and developing nations and to explore areas of consensus and disagreement among scholars and analysts on the opportunities and risks of decentralization. Three key themes emerged from the conference papers. The first theme concerns the extent and effectiveness of local service provision under decentralization. The evidence presented shows that the degree of decentralization (local government share of all government spending) has changed little since the 1970s in either OECD or developing countries. Moreover, results on the link between decentralization and effectiveness are mixed due to weak measures of decentralization across countries and the lack of data for disaggregate analyses. Some speakers asserted that country experiences have been too brief to realize the benefits of decentralization fully or that the objectives of decentralization vary significantly across cases, rendering a comprehensive evaluation difficult. Although most presenters agreed that countries will continue their decentralization efforts in the future, they disagreed on the implementation strategies and welfare implications of this trajectory.

The second theme focuses on the connections between decentralization and local policies, appraising how decentralization is related to jurisdiction size, public school finance, local environmental policy, and urban economic development strategy. Two studies showed that differences in the size of jurisdictions and in local control over the financing of local public schools have led to differences in the stringency of zoning policies across jurisdictions (smaller jurisdictions are more restrictive) and in the distribution of per student expenditure and average class size among school districts (property tax limits lowered per student expenditures and raised class sizes). In contrast, other empirical analyses of environmental regulation and economic development strategies found no strong evidence to support the notion of a "race to the bottom" caused by decentralization.[2] In sum, decentralization does matter; but its effects may not be consistent across all land policy areas.

Finally, the third theme addresses the effects of intergovernmental transfers on other issues such as local fiscal prudence and the association between decentralization and income distribution. Both issues pose major challenges to fiscal

---

2. See Oates and Portney (2001) for a summary of the debate related to the "race to the bottom."

decentralization. Similar to other empirical papers, results from cross-country comparisons are mixed because of theoretical and methodological issues. The consensus was to put more effort into refining the methods of evaluating decentralization reforms and designing institutional arrangements. Three speakers discussed new institutional arrangements to mediate the challenges to decentralization. Their proposals were mainly about redefining the boundaries of the public and private sectors to create a competitive environment in which efficient and equitable provision of local public goods is facilitated.

The conference papers in this volume are therefore grouped into sections relating to the three themes:

- Achieving decentralization objectives
- Decentralization, local governance, and land policy
- Emerging challenges and opportunities

Chapters 2 through 4 reveal the theoretical complexity and methodological difficulties involved in evaluating decentralization programs across countries. Chapters 5 through 9 analyze decentralization's effects on local policies. Finally, chapters 10 through 14 highlight challenges to decentralization and explore new institutional strategies for facilitating its implementation.

Achieving Decentralization Objectives

At the 2005 World Summit, many developing countries confirmed their commitment to design and implement national development strategies targeted to achieve the Millennium Development Goals (MDGs). Because more than 70 percent of the MDGs would be achieved primarily through subnational governments, decentralization is the predominant governance structure for delivering to the poor the basic services—public health, education, water and sanitation—that are critical to achieving these goals. Since the 1980s, as many as 75 countries have implemented decentralization policies as a means to ensure more efficient public service delivery and address poverty issues.

Decentralization has progressed in Central Europe and the Baltic states, where European Union accession has provided a strong incentive. In addition, decentralization is a high priority for many international aid agencies, such as the International Monetary Fund (IMF), United Nations Development Programme (UNDP), and the World Bank, which have all been actively involved in advocating and supporting decentralization reform in many countries.

Despite the overwhelming support for decentralization programs, there is little agreement among scholars and policy makers, and scant empirical evidence, as to whether the devolution of power to subnational governments actually increases or decreases their effectiveness in supplying public goods and raising own-source revenues. In chapter 2 Roy Bahl observes that the degree of decentralization has not changed. He reports that, from the 1970s through 2005, the average subnational government share of public expenditures in developing countries remained at about 13 to 14 percent of total public spending. For OECD countries, the percentages were also stable, ranging from 32 to 34 percent during the same period. Subnational government tax collections as a share of the total revenue in developing and OECD countries also experienced no drastic changes.

Bahl highlights two difficulties in assessing decentralization outcomes in less developed nations. First, decentralization is often a remedy for certain specific political or social problems rather than just a fiscal strategy. This duality complicates evaluation because matching theory with practice is difficult. Second, policy makers have given limited attention to the implementation of decentralization programs. Implementation is often flawed because governments do not fully recognize the benefits and costs of decentralization and the preconditions necessary for successful reforms. As a result of these oversights, decentralization in many countries has progressed slowly, with long time delays before benefits are realized. Bahl argues that it is too early to examine the full effects of decentralization.

In chapter 3 Paul Smoke examines local revenue generation under fiscal decentralization in developing countries. He finds that local capacity for generating own-source funds is rare due to a lack of attention to local politics. According to Smoke, public finance experts often use a narrow technical framework to analyze local revenues, thereby overlooking the political ramifications of reforms. For example, the sequence of implementing a viable reform has not been given due consideration. He suggests that local governments should first implement simple and politically acceptable changes and then follow them by more complex and controversial transformations. Tax increases or initiation of new levies must be associated with improvements in local service delivery. Classroom-based or on-the-job capacity building is also crucial. In sum, Smoke advocates a broader approach to local revenue reform: (1) the design of local revenue systems should include mechanisms for connecting with taxpayers; (2) local fiscal reforms should be contemplated, along with the larger decentralization and public sector reform agenda; and (3) more research on the political and strategic aspects of revenue reform is needed.

Responding to Smoke's challenge to the conventional fiscal analysis approach, Robert D. Ebel's comments take a more optimistic view on the issue. Although he agrees with Smoke that a narrow framework is often used to analyze local revenue reforms in developing countries, he believes that there are merits to the Western economic approach: it helps identify similarities between local revenue systems both in developed and developing countries and among developing economies. Ebel also cites examples in Central and Eastern Europe, where a broader framework has been applied successfully.

In chapter 4 Ehtisham Ahmad, Giorgio Brosio, and Vito Tanzi survey the related literature of decentralization experiences in selected OECD countries. Examining whether decentralization improves the performance of public educa-

tion and other local service provision, they review four areas: (1) productive efficiency; (2) regional convergence of service delivery; (3) preference matching; and
(4) decentralization and economic growth. They conclude that existing studies
fail to provide sufficient evidence to support the assertion that decentralization
improves effectiveness of service delivery. The main reason is the lack of linkage between expenditure and revenue assignments to local jurisdictions. Subnational governments are normally unable to raise enough own-source revenues
to finance unfunded mandates. Decentralization also does not seem to promote
regional convergence of service delivery, preference matching, and economic
growth. As Ahmad, Brosio, and Tanzi argue, these results may be due partly to
the limited implementation of decentralization reforms in some OECD countries
and partly to data and measurement problems.

Contrary to Ahmad, Brosio, and Tanzi's assessment, Paul Bernd Spahn in
his commentary argues that the outcomes of secondary education are positively
correlated with the level of decentralization in Spain. The findings of a cross-
country study on health care also indicate that decentralization seems to have
reduced infant mortality rates. These inconsistent results call for better methodologies and measures of decentralization in future empirical studies. One possibility is the case study method, which can elucidate the heterogeneity and specificity of decentralization effects in different countries.

Decentralization, Local Governance, and Land Policy

How does decentralization shape local governance? How does it thereby determine the incentive system for government officials to manage urban growth and
the environment and to finance local services? The contributors to chapters 5
through 9 analyze four issues—jurisdictional size, public school finance, environmental protection, and local economic development—that have direct and
indirect links to local land policy and land use.

William A. Fischel in chapter 5 argues that metropolitan areas with more
fragmented and decentralized government structures are more likely to have a
lower elasticity of housing supply than those dominated by large communities.
At the opposite end of the scale, metropolises with few large jurisdictions may
behave like monopolists and adopt overly stringent land use policies to boost
local property prices. Fischel's argument is that homeowners are easier to organize in smaller municipalities than in larger communities, lowering the transaction costs of enlisting voters' support for restrictive land use regulations, which
can maximize home values. In contrast, developers may have more influence
over local governments in metropolitan areas that are controlled by fewer and
larger municipalities because it is more costly to organize homeowners where
the number of parties involved is large. Fischel's findings are important for understanding how zoning restrictions across municipalities in the United States
vary by jurisdiction sizes.

Lee Anne Fennell comments that to reduce exclusionary zoning, it would be more promising to examine differences in the motivation of homeowners and developers to influence land use regulation rather than to examine variations in jurisdiction sizes. It seems more productive, she asserts, to align the interests of the two parties than to transform government structures. Fennell supports Fischel's proposal to establish a home-value insurance market that can compensate for adverse effects on homeowners' property values caused by new development.

One of the most controversial issues related to U.S. fiscal federalism is the financing of local public schools through property taxation. In theory, the system follows the principle of matching expenditures on public schools with preferences of local residents to pay property taxes for the services. If a home buyer wants a specific type of education for her children, she may buy a property in a neighborhood where the school system provides the desired education, financed by homeowners' property tax payments. Although this scheme may match preferences with expenditures and link the benefits of the services to costs, it is likely to lead to unequal access to quality education. Children of poor households that cannot afford to buy a home in affluent school districts may be excluded from their preferred school choices.

In response to this unintended outcome of fiscal federalism, movements have emerged to centralize the finance of education at the state level. In chapter 6 Daniel P. McMillen and Larry D. Singell Jr. examine two major measures— property tax limits and school finance reforms—and analyze how these policies affect real expenditures per student and average class sizes across school districts based on 1990 and 2000 data from 48 states. They find that the combined effect of property tax limits and school finance reforms led to a greater equalization of real expenditures per student across districts, with the 1990s policies having more profound distributional effects than did the policies implemented in the 1970s and 1980s.

McMillen and Singell also assess the effects of the two measures on real expenditures per student and average class sizes separately. In terms of real expenditures per student, the joint effect of property tax limits and school finance reforms led to a reduction in the number of districts with low expenditures, yet tax limitation alone increased the number of low-expenditure districts. The implication is that school finance reform provided a stronger impetus to equalize school expenditures by pushing spending across school districts toward the mean.

Regarding average class sizes, for policies implemented before the 1990s, both tax limits and school finance reforms made average class sizes more equal across school districts. In addition, school reforms (without tax limits) as adopted in the 1990s created more districts of similar average class sizes. In contrast, with no school finance reforms, the 1990s tax policies increased in the number of districts with large average class sizes. Overall, the estimates produced by McMillen and Singell indicate that centralization of public school finance in the United

States by means of property tax limits and equalization of school spending led to a more equal distribution of resources across school districts.

It is unclear, however, if the changes have improved social welfare because the heterogeneity of local preferences and the private responses to the reduction of educational spending were not incorporated into the analysis. In his commentary on chapter 6, Dennis Epple highlights the descriptive nature of the nonparametric analysis. He suggests that additional econometric analyses are needed to explain the observed changes in the distribution of educational expenditures and class sizes.

Some scholars are also concerned about subnational government effectiveness in setting environmental policy under decentralization (Jaffe at el. 1995; Levinson 1997; List and Gerking 2000; Oates and Portney 2001). Local governments may be too lax in establishing regulations to control pollution that can be exported to other jurisdictions. Moreover, municipalities may lower the standard of their environmental policy just to attract investment. In chapters 7 and 8 Shelby Gerking and Hilary Sigman, respectively, address the potential problems associated with decentralization of environmental policy.

Gerking analyzes the effect of state tax rates on the disposal of chlorinated solvent wastes in the United States. He finds that changes in the disposal costs of these chemicals as a result of increases in state tax rates did not have a significant impact on waste generation and disposal. Between 1988 and 2004, the disposal of chlorinated solvents decreased by 96 percent. For plants included in his study sample, the decreases were 78 percent during the same period. The reasons for the dramatic reduction were twofold: (1) the introduction of aqueous cleaners; and (2) increases in the recycling and reuse of the chemicals. As Gerking admits, these technological changes reduced the use of chlorinated solvents so greatly that it was difficult to identify any separate effect of the state tax rates. By examining data prior to the technological changes (1988–1990), Gerking found that firm decisions on the generation and disposal of chlorinated solvent wastes also did not respond to changes in state tax rates. Hence, he asserts that assigning to the states greater responsibility for regulating chlorinated solvent wastes had not resulted in inefficiency because waste disposal taxes had no effect on firm behavior.

In response to Gerking's analysis, Lawrence Susskind suggests another way of looking at the issue. Avoiding a race to the bottom, Susskind argues, involves civil society in environmental policy making and enforcement and a focus on innovation and technology sharing. Rewarding investors and stockholders who "green" their companies by recycling and using clean substitutes is also important. Debate on the governance structure of environmental protection should focus on these issues. Regulations are secondary, Susskind asserts.

In chapter 8 Sigman presents a cross-country analysis of the relationships between decentralization and environmental quality. She employs four measures in her study: (1) access to improved sanitation; (2) wastewater treatment; (3) ambient sulfur dioxide; and (4) the size of protected land areas. The results show no consistent effects of decentralization on environmental quality. Although decentralization seems to decrease access to sanitation, it increases the amount of land allocated to protected areas. In both cases, however, the estimated values of the coefficients used in Sigman's econometric model are not statistically significant.

Maureen L. Cropper, in her commentary on Sigman's analysis, finds the results surprising for two reasons. First, she expects that decentralization will increase sanitation access because it is a classic example of public goods that can be provided at the local level financed by households and firms that are direct beneficiaries of the service. Sigman's estimates indicate otherwise. Second, the environmental benefits of expanding land conservation areas may have spillover effects on adjacent jurisdictions; thus, in principle, local governments may not have the incentive to restrict land development, unless local politics induce homeowners to vote for excessive zoning, as Fischel describes in chapter 5. Again, Sigman's study implies that decentralization is positively correlated with the size of the preserved land. To explain these counterintuitive results, both Sigman and Cropper agree that better modeling and international data on environmental quality are needed. Besides, decentralization measures across countries are crude, which may in turn affect the results of the econometric analysis. Needed are greater international efforts to collect information about the net effect of decentralization on local environmental conditions across countries.

Similar to the decentralization of environmental policy, scholars and analysts also express concerns about the welfare effects of interjurisdictional competition on economic development under U.S. fiscal federalism. As taxing and spending powers are decentralized to state and local levels, subnational governments may offer tax breaks and public land at discount values to businesses to lure investment. Local economic development strategies—such as property tax abatements, subsidized financing for investment, job training, land concession, expedited incorporation, and quality public service provision—are often used to attract businesses and individuals, but it is unknown if these strategies are welfare enhancing. Sally Wallace discusses this topic in chapter 9.

Based on the survey of existing theoretical and empirical literature and specific case studies on automobile plant locational incentive packages in the Southeast, Wallace concludes that there is no hard evidence to prove that interjurisdictional competition has either enhanced or reduced welfare. Wallace emphasizes that most studies did not focus on measuring welfare changes or the opportunity cost of incentive packages. She suggests that a case study approach may be a more effective assessment method.

Jeffrey S. Zax found Wallace's assessment of existing studies convincing. He argues that many factors that some models do not take into consideration—such as peer effects—determine a firm's location. Besides, most studies employed a partial, rather than general, equilibrium analysis approach. In speculating on the distributional effects of interjurisdictional competition, Zax suggests that the major beneficiaries of the incentive packages may be the recipient firms and real estate owners. Any positive effects on workers in terms of better employment opportunities and higher wages are likely to be minimal.

Emerging Challenges and Opportunities

Managing intergovernmental fiscal relations and political and social development under decentralization can be challenging. Chapter 10 discusses intergovernmental transfers, and chapter 11 covers income distribution. Under fiscal decentralization, two major roles of central government are resource redistribution and financing of public goods that have large spillover effects. Both objectives can be achieved through intergovernmental transfers or grants. If central government grants are not predetermined and nonnegotiable, however, they may lead to fiscal excess at subnational levels. On one hand, transfers may induce local governments to spend more and incur more debt (the so-called deficit-bias hypothesis). On the other hand, fiscal shortfalls and indebtedness of grant-receiving jurisdictions may require central government bailouts, leading to the problem of soft-budget constraints.

In chapter 10 Luiz de Mello, using panel-based aggregate local government data from 13 OECD countries, examines the causal relationship between intergovernmental transfers and subnational jurisdictions' net worth. He found a stable, inverse relationship between current transfer receipts and local government net worth, implying that local indebtedness increases with more transfers from the center. In terms of causality, the results are mixed. Using dynamic fixed-effects estimators, de Mello discovered that transfers cause indebtedness, which supports the deficit-bias hypothesis. Moreover, other evidence also suggests that a deterioration of net worth is due to increments in current transfers. He argues that soft-budget constraints may be a problem in some OECD countries and recommends introducing tighter fiscal rules.

Ronald C. Fisher provides different interpretations of de Mello's results. He states that central government transfers may improve local fiscal conditions, thus lowering the cost of utilizing debts to finance infrastructure investment. Besides, matching grants for capital investment normally require local governments to cover a portion of the investment costs. Hence, it is perfectly rational for jurisdictions to use debts to finance local capital investment, and an increase in local indebtedness may not necessarily mean a lack of fiscal controls.

Another major challenge of fiscal decentralization is its effects on income distribution. Theoretical discussions have questioned whether decentralization increases regional disparities when subnational governments with different natural endowments compete for labor and capital. According to Jorge Martinez-Vazquez and Cristian Sepulveda in chapter 11, however, very little attention has been given to theoretical and empirical assessments of the effects decentralization has on household income distribution at the national level. In trying to identify the linkages between decentralization and income distribution, they conclude that it seems almost impossible to state their association a priori because of the numerous direct and indirect channels through which decentralization can improve or worsen income distribution. Martinez-Vazquez and Sepulveda also examine the relationship empirically, using data from 48 countries for the period from 1970 to 2000. They suggest that public expenditure decentralization exacerbates income inequalities in countries where the government's share of real GDP per capita is small. As the size of the government increases, decentralization begins to have a significant positive effect on income distribution.

Christine P. W. Wong comments on Martinez-Vazquez and Sepulveda's postulate as a major finding, provided their hypothesis can be verified. She points to a potential problem with the measure of decentralization used in their analysis: because expenditure decentralization is not always accompanied by revenue decentralization, relying on the former as an indicator to measure the degree of decentralization runs the risk of overstating the fiscal decision-making power of subnational governments. As in earlier chapters, Wong notes the inadequacy of fiscal decentralization measures across countries.

In addition to discussing the challenges of decentralization, chapters 12 through 14 explore several alternative institutional arrangements for future reforms. As discussed earlier, the traditional public school finance system under U.S. fiscal federalism has generated concern that the use of housing markets to ration resources and students to public schools may increase income and racial segregation. In chapter 12 Thomas J. Nechyba explores possible solutions, using a simulation model calibrated to the characteristics of New Jersey school districts in 1990. According to his simulations, centralizing public school finance reduces inequalities in per student expenditures across public school districts, as found by McMillen and Singell in chapter 6. Nechyba, though, argues that spending equalization can only be achieved at the expense of lower average school quality. When accounting for private school competition, his model predicts that centralizing public school finance will reduce the level of segregation across school districts because some households do not have to pay a high housing premium for public school when their school choice is separated from their housing decision. The problem in this scenario is that private schools have the competitive advantages of being able to "cream-skim" nonfinancial resources, such as better students and teachers, thereby lowering public school quality.

To solve this problem, Nechyba advocates a "choice-based" school resource rationing system in which students are assigned to both public and private schools based on an algorithm that includes parental preferences, "walk zones," and lotteries. This mechanism, Nechyba argues, can (1) retain the traditional role of residence-based admissions by including walk zones as one of the assignment criteria; (2) foster the matching of students to schools by incorporating parental preferences into the decision; and (3) minimize cream-skimming by providing public funds only to the private schools that are willing to participate in this choice-based rationing system. This proposal's major implication is that school financing will become more centralized, relying more on state income and sales taxes rather than local property taxes as revenue sources. Decisions about the design of the algorithm that defines priority classes for school allotments can be retained at the local level, however.

Responding to Nechyba's proposal, Helen F. Ladd asks how race may factor into the model, an issue Nechyba discusses briefly in the concluding section of his chapter. Ladd also adds another interesting dimension to the discussion by describing school systems in other countries where private schools are entitled to public funds and public schools are encouraged to charge fees. She cautions that the devolution of school operational authority to the district level should only be implemented with a careful consideration of local capacity.

In chapter 13 Robert H. Nelson describes an important change in local governance structure under the U.S. federal system. There has been a rapid increase in the number of residence-based, voluntary community associations (CAs) formed by private developers to supplement municipal services and regulation. According to Nelson, about half of the new housing units between 1980 and 2000 were subject to the governance of a CA. In 2007, 20 percent of the U.S. population (or 60 million people) lived in CAs, whereas the 1970 estimate was only 1 percent. If this trend continues, Nelson argues, CAs may transform the traditional functions of local government. Future municipal responsibilities may be more regional in scope. They may include, for example, supplying water and sewer services, fire protection, citywide crime prevention, arterials, rapid transit systems, courts of law, and other public goods with significant economies of scale. Some aspects of land use regulation and the provision of microservices, such as garbage collection, street cleaning, and neighborhood security, will be undertaken by CAs.

What facilitates this change? Nelson asks. Could the growing private governance of neighborhood be integrated into the traditional local government structure? Nelson proposes a transaction-cost framework for analyzing these questions. He hypothesizes that CAs may have a comparative advantage over the traditional municipalities to minimize the transaction costs of (1) fine-tuning voting rules for matching local services with resident preferences; (2) negotiating for dispute resolutions at the neighborhood level; (3) controlling aesthetics; and (4) transferring the management responsibilities of the commons from one contractor to another. In contrast, municipalities can collect taxes and enforce statewide standards of land use regulation and local service provision more effectively than CAs.

Commenting on Nelson's trajectory, Robert W. Helsley raises two issues related to the transfer of municipal responsibilities to CAs. First, as CAs take over some existing municipal functions, the public sector may partially withdraw from the provision of local services. Helsley argues that residents who are neither high-demanders nor low-demanders of local services will be worse off because they are presented with the choices of either over- or underprovision of public goods. Second, maintaining one community's security by gating can divert crime to other neighborhoods, which may, in turn, encourage all other communities to gate. The result may be overgating and subsequent welfare loss.

As discussed in chapters 7, 8, and 9, interjurisdictional competition under fiscal decentralization may give local governments the incentive to lower their environmental policy standards or grant businesses with lucrative tax exemptions and favorable land deals so as to attract investment. Although these strategies seem sensible for individual jurisdiction, the aggregate effects of this type of competition are not always welfare enhancing. In chapter 14 Clifford F. Zinnes proposes an innovative approach to shaping interjurisdictional competition in which all players know the rules and rewards of the game in advance to engender a "race-to-the-top" competitive environment. Zinnes calls it prospective interjurisdictional competition (PIJC). In applying PIJC to organize intergovernmental fiscal relations under decentralization, a central government can be perceived as a donor that provides funds to local jurisdictions for specific reform purposes or provision of local services. To ensure efficiency, central authorities set goals and the corresponding tasks for achieving the targets. They also establish indicators for measuring outcomes, specify all monetary and in-kind rewards, and offer technical assistance. The final step is to design the tournament by identifying municipalities that are willing to participate and defining the time frame. In PIJC the central government does not dictate how each jurisdiction will achieve outcomes. Instead, calibrating the task selection, scoring method, and reward structure will become the major components of the central government's grant project.

Unlike the contracting approach, the PIJC approach needs only a set of tournament instructions when policy goals and the related tasks are determined. The decision to participate in the tournament and how to achieve the preordained objectives will be left to each jurisdiction. It is assumed that autonomy and explicit rating systems and rewards would stimulate local initiatives to cooperate. Intensive project monitoring for compliance required in the conventional approach would be replaced by the scheduled publicity of participants' performance throughout the tournament. In a situation in which scarce resources need to be allocated to best performers who are unknown to a central government or foreign donor, the PIJC promoted by a tournament would reward a limited number of contestants for achieving the best possible outcomes based on a set of predefined assignments.

José Roberto R. Afonso and Sérgio Guimarães Ferreira caution the general applicability of the PIJC approach to developing countries. They indicate that the idea is mainly designed to improve the management of foreign aid for donor organizations, such as the World Bank and the United States Agency for International Development, and that there are major differences between intergovernmental transfers and foreign aid. First, in most countries, intergovernmental transfers are earmarked and linked to central government tax revenues. Changing the current system of grant allocation to a tournament system may face strong political resistance. Second, the tournament approach cannot be used to allocate cost-sharing grants whose purpose is to help local governments provide social services to the population. If poor regions have to compete with developed areas for this central assistance, they will be in a disadvantageous position. It is the less developed jurisdictions that need more help from the center.

Conclusions

The contributions in this volume support three major findings. First, the analyses of decentralization's impacts on public service provision have yielded mixed results, with no consistent evidence of either positive or negative net effects on populations in industrialized and developing countries. Arguments generated from studies that employ the currently available measures of decentralization are not robust across nations. Additional empirical research to improve measures of the degree of decentralization is needed to inform the analysis of decentralization's effects.

Second, each chapter provides interesting specific insights on how decentralization (or centralization) may affect local policies. On the performance of particular sectors, the availability of different interest groups to shape local policies varies with jurisdictional sizes and leads to varying degrees of restrictiveness in land use regulation. Centralizing local public school finance has important implications for the allocation of financial and nonfinancial resources across school districts. Interjurisdictional competition under decentralization does not seem to have significant effects on local policies for environmental protection and economic development. Although some issues related to these studies remained unresolved, identifying the problems and suggesting the diagnosis should be instrumental for future local policy research and education.

Third, the findings of decentralization's impacts on selected local policies also have important bearings on land use policy and property taxation. Because the size of the jurisdiction that controls land use may affect the stringency of related regulations, the allocation of land use controls across levels of government—counties and municipalities—is critical to development outcomes. Similarly, decisions on the governance structure and financing of local school expenditures will determine whether the property tax can remain a major source of local revenue in the United States. These research areas are important because improved understanding of how decentralization affects local governments and policies in different countries is necessary to formulate land policy and design local fiscal reforms.

REFERENCES

Jaffe, A. B., S. Peterson, P. Portney, and R. Stavins. 1995. Environmental regulation and the competitiveness of U.S. manufacturing: What does the evidence tell us? *Journal of Economic Literature* 33:132–163.

Levinson, A. 1997. A note on environmental federalism: Interpreting some contradictory results. *Journal of Environmental Economics and Management* 33:359–366.

List, J. A., and S. Gerking. 2000. Regulatory federalism and environmental protection in the United States. *Journal of Regional Science* 40:453–472.

McLure, C. E., Jr. 1995. Comment on "The dangers of decentralization" by R.
    Prud'homme. *World Bank Research Observer* 10:221–226.
Oates, W. 1972. *Fiscal federalism.* New York: Harcourt Brace Jovanovich.
———. 2006. The many faces of the Tiebout model. In *The Tiebout model at fifty:
    Essays in public economics in honor of Wallace Oates,* W. A. Fischel, ed., 21–45.
    Cambridge, MA: Lincoln Institute of Land Policy.
Oates, W. E., and P. R. Portney. 2001. The political economy of environmental policy.
    Discussion Paper 01–55. Washington, DC: Resources for the Future.
Prud'homme, R. 1995. Dangers of decentralization. *World Bank Research Observer*
    10(2):201–220.
Sewell, D. O. 1996. "The dangers of decentralization" according to Prud'homme: Some
    further aspects. *World Bank Research Observer* 11:143–150.
Tiebout, C. M. 1956. A pure theory of local expenditures. *Journal of Political Economy*
    64(5):416–424.

ACHIEVING DECENTRALIZATION OBJECTIVES

2

Opportunities and Risks of Fiscal Decentralization: A Developing Country Perspective

Roy Bahl

Since the 1980s, the rhetoric of fiscal decentralization has taken root in developing countries. Most developing countries now place the strengthening of subnational government on the development policy agenda. Despite all the pronouncements, plans, and even political promises, however, there has been no rush to grant state and local governments significant taxing powers and increased expenditure autonomy. Perhaps economic conditions have not been right for countries to adopt all-encompassing decentralization schemes, perhaps political freedoms were too new in some cases, or perhaps the idea still takes some getting used to. Whatever the reason, signs that countries are now ready to move forward with implementing fiscal decentralization continue to appear.

Many analyses attest to the efficacy of fiscal decentralization as a policy strategy.[1] Most existing research focuses on evaluating decentralization experiences from around the world and looks for the links between theory and practice. Much less attention has been given to implementation strategies (Bahl 1999b). This chapter offers some guidelines for both design and implementation—beginning with a discussion of the rationale for fiscal decentralization—by analyzing objectives, opportunities, and risks that should lead the design of a decentralization program.

---

1. Among them are Bahl and Linn (1992); Bahl and Martinez-Vazquez (2006a, b); Bird and Vaillancourt (1998); Dillinger and Webb (1999a, b); Litvack, Ahmad, and Bird (1998); and Tanzi (1995).

What Is Fiscal Decentralization?

"The empowerment of people by the empowerment of their local governments" is offered here as a working definition of fiscal decentralization. The key term is "local government." Fiscal decentralization is about a central government passing budgetary authority to subnational governments through the power to make taxing and spending decisions. In this chapter, fiscal decentralization means transferring fiscal power to any level of government below the center, such as states or provinces, cities or districts, and even fourth-tier local governments.

What is not included in this definition of fiscal decentralization? The deconcentration of decision making and service delivery powers within a ministry would not count. Deconcentration decentralizes administration and management, and even some decision making. Although deconcentration could be used to gain inputs about needs and demands particular to a local area, higher-level government retains the dominant voice in local planning committees, even when elected local officials are given a seat on such committees. Deconcentration of this kind does not empower the local population. Nor would we count the delegation of service delivery powers to community interest groups or nongovernmental organizations (NGOs). Although these units may be locally based, they are not empowered by vote of the entire community, nor are they accountable to the local population. To be sure, the community-centered, informal organization approach can enhance the probability of successful decentralization by providing a lobby voice for local interest groups. Often, it can enable an otherwise disenfranchised group to gain a voice in governance. In no way does it substitute for representative local government, though. Another version of "private decentralization" would allow community groups (neighborhoods) to select their own package of public services. In developing countries, this approach might draw significant resources away from the local government budget and compromise its ability to allocate resources according to voter preferences.[2]

One gray area to consider is where subnational governments are not elected, as in China. In this case, local populations cannot use the vote to hold central officials accountable. Subnational governments, however, are empowered with some budgetary discretion, and the appointed political leadership does respond

---

2. In some higher-income countries, the decentralization of decisions regarding collective goods might extend even further, as it has with private community associations in the United States. These associations, governed by officers elected by the community group, ensure that the preferences of very small groups of homeowners are honored by covenants. Approximately 20 percent of the U.S. population now lives in some form of community association. Nelson (see chapter 13) argues that these community associations are fast replacing traditional local governments in parts of the United States as the unit responsible for delivering some local services. Governments in some less developed countries are attracted by the community development model. In Pakistan, for example, community groups exercise a degree of control over a share of the budgetary resources of the general local government.

to local preferences. In fact, China is a good case in point. In the significant intergovernmental fiscal reforms enacted since the 1980s, the central government was constrained in its choices by the need to appease the coastal provinces (Bahl and Martinez-Vazquez 2006b). Moreover, provincial-level officials regularly act in the self-interest of their provinces, such as by enacting protectionist policies, even when provincial policies might compromise national objectives.

A second gray area is the case of local governments with limited budgetary discretion. In many developing and transition countries, central governments limit local revenue powers and impose expenditure mandates to such an extent that even elected local governments become little more than spending agents of higher-level governments. Still, these local governments do have some discretion, they are technically accountable to the local population who elects them, and they have the potential to assume a greater degree of autonomy.

Why Fiscal Decentralization? The Rhetoric

There seems to be no uniform rhetoric about why a nation should adopt a fiscal decentralization strategy. The justification varies from country to country, and, not surprisingly, it usually matches up well with the problems the country is facing. Fiscal decentralization is often more a remedy than a development strategy. Russia's fiscal decentralization looks very much like one designed to head off separatist movements, and South Africa's transfer of decision-making power to more than 800 local governments is exactly what one would expect in the aftermath of apartheid. Advantages and disadvantages aside, various advocates see decentralization as primarily an economic, political, social, management, or even military strategy. The way these national leaders see it will drive the way they design it, which also explains why the rhetoric in support of fiscal decentralization is so varied and perhaps even why there is such a gap between the rhetoric and the reality of successful decentralization.

Many would like to believe that fiscal decentralization is an effective economic development strategy. Intuitively, the argument appears reasonable. The government closest to the local or regional economy is in the right position to decide matters such as the best regulatory environment for local business, the right infrastructure investments to make, the proper structure of taxation, and, in general, the enabling environment best suited to develop the local economy. Lady Ursula Hicks had this argument in mind in her 1961 book, *Development from Below*. Martinez-Vazquez and McNab (2000) develop the interesting point that the possible effects of decentralization on economic development are indirect, that decentralization directly affects technical efficiency, income inequality, and corruption, which, in turn, affect economic growth. The search for empirical evidence on the relationship between decentralization and economic development has not been conclusive, however (Davoodi and Zou 1998; Lin and Liu 2000; Martinez-Vazquez and McNab 2000; Zhang and Zou 1997, 1998).

The growing number of countries with democratically elected governments clearly has stimulated interest in decentralized government. Those interested in the politics of nation development would argue that this factor has been paramount in stimulating at least the rhetoric of and probably the demand for fiscal decentralization. It is not all rhetoric. Elected politicians at the subnational government level push hard for some powers to shape budgets, although they are much more enthusiastic about having power to spend than they are about having power to tax.

Centralization may be an inefficient management approach, especially in large countries. Fiscal management—that is, supervision of some part of the budgetary affairs of every subnational government—can become costly and lead to poor public service outcomes. It is especially troublesome in large countries. A relatively few central officials cannot make the important fiscal decisions for every local government on a case-by-case basis. There are too many complications, too many special circumstances, for this approach to be viable. China and India have populations in excess of one billion, and China has 58,545[3] subnational governments and India 237,687.[4] Brazil has a land area in excess of 8.4 million square kilometers, and Indonesia comprises 17,500 islands, of which 6,000 are inhabited. How could Russia, a country with 11 time zones, be managed efficiently from Moscow by a relatively few senior officials? As late as the mid-1990s, though, the budget of each of the 89 regional governments was being approved in Moscow on the basis of face-to-face negotiations. Some form of decentralized governance would seem an imperative in large countries.

The problems with centralized control are not limited to large countries. Even in small nations, poor transportation and communications networks can make the national capital very remote. In Nepal, for example, many of the 4,053 local governments are several days' journey from Kathmandu.

Fiscal decentralization is a strategy that sells because people want different things from their local governments. Centralization, on the other hand, implies a degree of uniformity in government services and in revenue raising. Enforced uniformity creates resentment, however, and various regions within countries have pushed hard for autonomy to choose a package of services that better fits their demands. Countries with variations among regions in language (India, Sudan), ethnic background (Indonesia, Nigeria), or climate and terrain (Russia) are usually good candidates for fiscal decentralization. Even countries that are relatively homogeneous in population mix and climate may be pressured for different service standards in urban and rural areas, or in regions with different economic bases.

---

3. China has 151 prefectures and 185 prefecture-level cities; 1,903 counties and 279 county-level cities; 56,027 townships, towns, and city districts.

4. India has 3,609 urban local bodies, 474 zilla parishads in rural areas, 5,906 panchayat samitis, and 227,698 gram panchayats.

Another explanation of the increased demand for fiscal decentralization in recent years is the improved management and administrative capacity of local governments. In the past, the issue with local governments was their inability to deliver services effectively or to manage money. Although many of the same criticisms are leveled today, many local governments are "growing up" in terms of their management and administrative abilities. Affordable microcomputer systems, improved education, and the greater relative attractiveness of employment in the subnational government sector have all contributed to this change. Indonesia's local governments have taken on significant increases in expenditure responsibility, South Africa's urban local governments are nearly self-sufficient in financing their budgets, and the state governments in Brazil and Argentina play important roles in their federal systems. When subnational governments feel ready, they bring pressure for more fiscal autonomy.

Some attribute the current interest in decentralization to the consideration that the time for local autonomy has come. Local elections, improved administrative capacity, and "local nationalism" have made the demand for fiscal decentralization irresistible. If it is not given in a formal way, local autonomy may be achieved through "backdoor" approaches. A good example is Chinese local government officials who were denied formal taxing powers but who levied informal (often illegal) taxes that were kept in off-budget accounts. Local governments did take on more fiscal autonomy on the revenue and the expenditure side in response to a demand for local services that higher-level governments were unwilling to fund. This backdoor approach, however, created inefficiencies in how the funds were raised and in spending from segmented, extrabudgetary accounts (Bahl 1999a; Wong, Heady, and Woo 1995). It may be far better to structure a program of fiscal autonomy than to have it taken on an ad hoc basis.

Perhaps the most compelling argument has to do with service delivery. The level and quality of local public services provided in most developing countries is poor. "The job is not getting done anyway, so let's try another approach" is an argument that gets a great deal of sympathy and support. In many camps, there is a belief that more local control over expenditure decisions can make things better. Intuitive arguments support this belief. Subnational governments are best positioned to determine the location of capital investments. They can recognize benefits, they may better manage the performance of employees working at the local level, and they have a greater stake in maintaining local public capital. Local voters feel more likely to be "heard" by local politicians and bureaucrats than by central politicians and bureaucrats.

Finally, decentralization may be a part of the strategy to hold countries together or may be a strategy for nation building. Some nations have been formed out of unnatural partners and have dissolved when the opportunity arose, such as Czechoslovakia and Yugoslavia. In cases such as Indonesia, South Africa, and Russia, the fall of strong central regimes has prompted a call to move governance away from the central level and has stimulated fiscal decentralization initiatives.

Other troublesome partnerships have played to special autonomy measures in attempts to hold the country together, as in Nigeria and Sudan. Even in the case of reunifications as in Vietnam, Germany, and China–Hong Kong, decentralization plays an important role.

The Benefits

The design of a program of fiscal decentralization that has a chance for success must move from rhetoric to an identification of the potential benefits and costs of this policy and to the possibilities for realizing these benefits and costs. The main reason the rhetoric of fiscal decentralization has not been translated into a widespread growth in the relative importance of local government finance is that the benefits and costs have not been properly understood or accepted. Implementation plans for fiscal decentralization are almost always flawed.

EFFICIENCY GAINS
Rhetoric is necessary to popularize the concept of decentralization and perhaps make it more politically acceptable. It is, however, often based on impressionistic evidence. What is needed in the national debate about fiscal decentralization is a more structured approach to capturing the benefits of fiscal decentralization.

What are the major advantages to be captured? The first, and most important, is the welfare gains that come from moving government closer to the people. This economic efficiency argument drives the thinking of most economists who work on this subject (Musgrave and Musgrave 1984; Oates 1972). The argument is straightforward. Let us assume that people's preferences for government services vary, for example, because of religion, language, ethnic mix, climate, or economic base. Let us assume further that people living within a country or even a city have sorted themselves so that those with like preferences live in proximity. If subnational governments respond to these preferences in structuring their budgets, decentralization will result in variations in the package of services delivered in different regions. People will get what they want, so the welfare of the population will be enhanced.

Under the same circumstances, but with a centralized system, service provision would be more uniform and people in different regions would get less of the service mix they want. The potential benefits from decentralization, then, include (1) more accountability on the part of government officials because they are responsible for service delivery to the local population who elected them; and (2) more willingness on the part of the local population to pay for services because they get what they want.

For advocates of fiscal decentralization, this scenario is the primary argument. True believers can point out that successful fiscal decentralization at once attacks several problems that face developing countries: revenue mobilization, innovation in economic decision making, accountability of elected officials, capacity development at the local level, and grassroots participation in governance.

This view of the benefits of decentralization makes it easy to believe that welfare gains exist even if they cannot be measured.[5] Whether the conditions necessary are in place to capture these benefits is another story. Even if gains do materialize, are they large enough to warrant the possible disruption of the national public financing system?

To capture the gains from fiscal decentralization, a number of conditions must be met. First, regional and local legislatures must be accountable to the regional/local population. If local political leadership is elected, does the electorate have the information and willingness to exercise the vote to ensure accountability? If these political leaders are appointed rather than elected (as in China), do they see their political success as being related to the satisfaction of the local population? The middle ground is a type of parliamentary system whose leaders are elected by and possibly more accountable to the party than to the local population.

Second, the chief officers of the regional/local government must be accountable to their legislature. If they are appointed by the center/state, their first accountability will be to a higher level of government, and local programs may not be delivered according to local preferences. The mayor's directive about enforcement of property tax penalties for failure to pay may have a hollow ring if the chief local tax collector is appointed by the state or central government.

Third, subnational governments should have some independent taxing powers. Provincial and local governments should have the ability to set at least the tax rate. This power is important if the local population is to hold the political leadership accountable. Local voters will subject politicians to a much tougher test if voters pay for services than if services are financed primarily by a transfer from the center.

Fourth, subnational governments should be responsible for some important government services. The issue here is that the local voters should care about the quality of services delivered. In most cases, states and provinces are assigned services that affect the quality of people's lives, so this criterion is satisfied. In the case of local (third-tier) governments, this assignment of important responsibilities is not always the case. When local governments are given responsibility for little more than housekeeping functions, the local population will be less likely to raise strenuous objections about the quality of services delivered.

Fifth, subnational governments should have adequate discretion over the level and composition of expenditures. If a higher-level government mandates

---

5. Indirect evidence that the efficiency gains are being captured includes increased satisfaction with local public services, changes in the mix of service provided to better satisfy local preferences, electoral results, and increased compliance with local taxes and user charges.

the expenditures, the subnational government has little ability to respond to citizen preferences. Excessive mandates can be a major impediment to fiscal decentralization. In some cases, mandates are necessary for achieving overarching social goals, such as guaranteed quality of education or equalization in the distribution of resources among local (third-tier) governments.

The efficiency gains that might be captured with fiscal decentralization are far from automatic. A structure must be in place to allow the subnational government to capture these gains. In fact, these necessary conditions are often missing.

REVENUE MOBILIZATION

In developing and transition economies, state and local governments are assigned relatively little independent taxing power. The higher-level government may fear the tax base competition, the prospect that increased state and local government tax collections will be accomplished at the expense of lower central government taxes.

That decentralization can increase overall revenue mobilization in a country by broadening the aggregate tax base is, in fact, a more reasonable hypothesis. If this hypothesis is correct, subnational government taxes would not be raised at the expense of reductions in central-level taxes. In addition, the claim of subnational governments on central revenues via intergovernmental transfers would be reduced by increased revenue mobilization at the subnational government level.

The argument behind this hypothesis is that subnational governments have the potential to reach the traditional income, consumption, and wealth tax bases in ways that the central government cannot. Typically, central governments rely on a combination of company income tax, individual income tax, value-added tax, and excise taxes. In most developing countries, however, these taxes have a high entry threshold. Small firms and most individuals are "underrepresented" in the tax base. In fact, local governments can broaden the overall tax base with a variety of tax instruments and administrative measures, and they do so in many countries.

In developing and transition countries, most individual income taxes are collected through withholding from workers in the formal sector. The threshold is set high enough that only a small fraction of the population is included in the tax net. In Indonesia, a country with a population of more than 200 million, the income tax base includes only about 1 million people. Even when their income is above the threshold, self-employed workers often escape taxes because of administrative difficulties, and overall collection rates tend to be quite low. The problem is identifying self-employed workers (informal sector) and determining their tax liability. The self-employed taxpayers play "catch me if you can," and the central government often sees the cost of the chase to be greater than the revenue rewards. Local governments, though, with a better knowledge of the local economy, can identify the tax base more easily. Given the paucity of local government resources, the revenue returns are potentially lucrative. Subnational government payroll taxes, levied in a simple way, can augment the national revenue take. These taxes might be justified as a kind of user charge for the provision of local public services.[6]

The company income tax is usually focused on large firms. In market economies, smaller firms are covered, but typically under an alternative form of company tax. In transition economies, private businesses and collective enterprises—very rapidly growing sectors—are often outside the tax net for administrative reasons.

The value-added tax (VAT) has a very high threshold and typically excludes most enterprises from the tax base. Most VAT revenues are collected from a small number of firms, and it is administratively inefficient to focus heavily on the "hard to tax" for the little revenue they generate. The situation in Guatemala, where 97 percent of VAT revenues are collected from one-third of the VAT-paying firms (Bahl, Martinez-Vazquez, and Wallace 1996), is not atypical. These high thresholds for central taxes, however, leave a significant taxable capacity unreached. Ample taxing room can be found in this situation. Subnational governments may levy a variety of taxes on the sales or assets of these companies, or even charges for the privilege to operate. Included are asset taxes on businesses, property taxes, gross sales taxes on small firms, and narrow-based retail sales taxes.

In general, the high thresholds set for central government taxes can be attributed to two factors. First, the lack of familiarity with the local tax base makes it very difficult to identify the small taxpayers and to maintain a tax roll. Second, the revenue gains from bringing small taxpayers into the net are small. A local government policy analyst, however, might propose another view. The analyst might point out that the local governments do have familiarity with the local tax base. They oversee a variety of licensing and regulatory activities, and they track property ownership and land-based transactions. They have ample opportunity to identify businesses in their community and gain some knowledge about the real property assets and scale of operations. A convincing case could be made that the potential revenue from these activities may be quite large when compared with the overall size of the local government budget.

In particular, a strong case could be made for the real property tax as a local government revenue source. Familiarity with the tax base gives local governments a comparative administrative advantage, and it offers the opportunity to connect tax payments to the benefits of local services provided. In addition, central governments often do not want this tax. Further, the property tax can, in theory, give local governments access to a large and growing tax base. Still, elected officials may be hesitant to levy such an unpopular tax on the local voting population.

---

6. Subnational governments often fail to gain access to broad-based taxes for two reasons: (1) the center is unwilling to give up or share the revenue base; and (2) the subnational government is wary of taking on responsibility to enforce these taxes.

REGIONAL BALANCE

Another argument posits that if fiscal decentralization goes far enough, a better size distribution of regions (cities) would result. The traditional theory of migration holds that an individual's decision about movement, say from a rural to an urban area, is determined by his or her assessment of the probability of finding employment in the urban versus rural area and by the difference in the expected wage. Business and individual location decisions are driven by the quality of public services available and by the cost of these services.

A problem in developing countries is that local governments, even in large metropolitan areas, are often financed primarily by intergovernmental transfers rather than local taxes. The tax price for local services in these cities is therefore low. If local governments were forced to raise a greater proportion of their own revenues, the marginal cost of living in cities (and probably in higher-income regions) would rise because residents and businesses would now pay the marginal cost of service provision. If the tax disparities among regions, and among urban–rural places, grew large enough, presumably some urban migration would be discouraged. Whether migration to more prosperous regions and to cities could be discouraged to any significant degree by greater tax and user charge differentials is a question that calls for more research.

NATION BUILDING

When citizens participate in their own governance, as in a decentralized system, a greater measure of national stability may be achieved. In countries where the ethnic or religious mix of the population has created divides, the threat of disharmony, or even civil war, is present. Part of this problem is due to different preferences for public services, and part is due to the desire for more self-governance.

Fiscal decentralization can offer a compromise between the status quo and secession in such cases. By enabling some degree of regional autonomy, the central government might satisfy the demand for more control over public services. This local autonomy might be achieved by a federal structure of government (Nigeria, India) or by special local autonomy laws (Indonesia, Philippines).

The Costs

The limited growth in fiscal decentralization may be explained by the costs of giving up the considerable advantages of fiscal centralization. It has long been argued by public finance theorists that fiscal policy to address stabilization and growth issues, and distribution policy, can be more effectively managed by central governments. Whether subnational government fiscal decisions seriously compromise the effectiveness of central government policy in these areas is controversial.

STABILIZATION POLICY IS NOT PROTECTED

Developing and transition economies are by their very nature unstable. Developing countries often depend on a small number of primary exports (agricultural or mineral). A change in world market prices can have devastating effects on such a country. Movements in world economic conditions can slow the rate of economic growth of "vulnerable" countries. World recession, for example, could slow the rate of foreign investment, reduce the demand for exports, discourage tourism, and so forth. Smaller countries are especially vulnerable. Their economies tend to be the most exposed, and even a natural disaster (hurricane, earthquake, drought, or epidemic such as AIDS) can have lasting and disastrous effects.

This volatility in economies is transmitted to the public sector, and it can even be magnified. Swings in world interest rates and real exchange rates directly determine the real cost of servicing foreign debt, sales taxes respond automatically to swings in consumption, and public expenditures move with inflation and unemployment. The Inter-American Development Bank (1997, 113–114) makes the interesting points that indirect tax revenues in Latin American countries are 2.5 times more volatile than in industrial countries and that public expenditures are four times more volatile. Faced with this potential for instability, central governments believe that, to implement effective stabilization policy, they must control a substantial portion of total government revenues and expenditures. The ministry of finance in virtually all countries would like to control (1) the tax rate and the tax base of all major taxes; (2) expenditure assignment and determination of the level of expenditures; and (3) borrowing by local governments. How can a program be put in place to control inflation and the size of the deficit when a significant percentage of national spending and taxation is in the hands of subnational government politicians who do not have a vested interest in pursuing stabilization policy? The situation is exacerbated when the subnational governments do not face a hard budget constraint and when they have borrowing powers.[7]

Central governments would like the flexibility to respond quickly to changes in the economy so as to raise taxes or cut expenditures to deal with a deficit, for example. If the government is locked into a fixed share of revenue allocated to local governments, the ability to cut the deficit by reducing expenditures is significantly reduced. The pressures from the International Monetary Fund (IMF) and the World Bank for more austere economic policy to bring about internal or external balance usually requires maintaining an acceptable level of the fiscal deficit and limiting the level of domestic credit. In a truly decentralized economy, both targets are more difficult to achieve than in a centralized economy. Decentralized countries are not inherently more unstable than centralized countries.

---

7. See Bahl and Linn (1992), Prud'homme (1995), Spahn (1997), Tanzi (1995), and Ter-Minassian (1997) for more detailed discussions. These papers show that there is anything but agreement on this point.

Whatever the degree of inherent instability of a country, the ability to control the fiscal sector would seem more limited in the decentralized system.

Finally, does borrowing by subnational governments compromise macroeconomic stability in developing countries? The case of Brazil, where state-level debt contributed to a national fiscal crisis and forced central government intervention, is the example most often mentioned (Ter-Minassian and Craig 1997). The problem, according to some, was an unwise decision to rely on market discipline to control the issuance of debt.

On the other hand, borrowing by subnational governments has not compromised the fiscal position in many other countries where it is allowed. This situation usually is attributed to the imposition of some form of control—either rule-based or direct administrative controls—over state and local government borrowing.

INFRASTRUCTURE INVESTMENT MUST BE CENTRALLY DIRECTED
Capital is short in most developing and transition countries, and subnational governments have a low savings rate. Some would argue that the net result of fiscal decentralization, then, could be a shift of resources from central governments that have higher rates of savings and investment to provincial and local governments that spend at a greater rate on consumption goods and services. With this conclusion, fiscal decentralization could therefore lead to a lower rate of spending on infrastructure, and national growth could be harmed.

Three points should be made. First, local governments have been assigned functions that are consumption-intensive (primary schools, provision of safe drinking water), and these expenditures contribute to economic growth. Second, even if there were a local preference for capital spending, central mandates (particularly for subnational government wage and salary levels) may drive the budgets of lower-level governments toward consumption spending. Finally, subnational governments lack access to revenues adequate to generate capital financing.

Another line of thinking poses that, in developing countries, national priorities for capital investment should trump those that conform to local government choices. The national government is interested in investments in infrastructure that have regional and national benefits, such as irrigation, national (interstate) roads, and power. State governments, especially large states in large countries, focus on capital investments with regional benefits, such as highways, universities, and hospitals. Local governments, on the other hand, are expected to place more emphasis on projects with local benefits, such as markets, small area water supply, municipal buildings, and recreation areas. Those interested in maximizing economic growth would argue that the big national infrastructure projects should dominate. Advocates of fiscal decentralization argue that overall welfare will be increased if local governments play a role in project selection. Also, a fear persists that local governments either cannot, or will not, build their facilities to proper standards and that they will not maintain them at adequate levels. The case for provincial involvement in capital project selection is stronger in countries where the provinces are large and have stronger service delivery capability.

EQUALIZATION POTENTIAL IS GREATER UNDER
REVENUE CENTRALIZATION

Most developing and transition countries are characterized by significant inter-regional disparities in income and wealth. Poor regions within a country typically have a low taxable capacity and a high level of expenditure need. It usually falls to the central government to do something about equalizing the resulting fiscal disparities. One of the most common methods of addressing these disparities is a system of equalization transfers.

Revenue centralization provides a greater potential for equalization. In countries where the claim of local governments on the overall tax base is small, the central government can create a larger pool of funds for allocation among local governments on an equalizing basis. Just because the central government has more funds to allocate, however, does not necessarily mean that it will allocate these funds on an equalizing basis. In fact, most countries do very little equalization through their grant systems.

The decentralization of both revenue-raising power and expenditure responsibility can be a counterequalizing policy in developing countries. When local governments are given taxing powers, or more expenditure responsibilities and some borrowing authority, the higher-income places are best positioned to take advantage of these newfound powers. They have the fiscal capacity to tax and usually have a better ability to collect taxes, the technical ability to deliver more public services, and the repayment potential that enables borrowing to finance capital improvements. Under a fully decentralized fiscal system, one would expect a growing gap in well-being between rich and poor regions. This argument is more a hypothesis than it is based on hard research, in part because richer places always seem to do better, whether located in centralized or decentralized countries. Those who have studied the issue, however, tend to support the hypothesis that decentralized tax assignment leads to larger fiscal disparities because it allows local governments with a stronger taxable capacity to make use of their comparative advantage.

CENTRAL GOVERNMENTS ARE MORE COMPETENT

The superior ability of central governments to deliver public services and collect taxes is another argument for centralization. Central competency is believed to be superior for a number of reasons. It can be argued that the best and brightest government officials are drawn to that level where their opportunity for advancement is greatest. Moreover, they are drawn to "where the action is," and central governments in developing countries account for 85 percent of all government expenditures. Perhaps most important is that central officials have significant experience doing the job of service delivery and tax collection, and they are often well up the learning curve from local government employees.

On the other hand, no hard-and-fast evidence exists that central governments can deliver services for all functions at a lower cost or higher quality than can local governments. The experience in Indonesia offers perhaps the best form of transition. Central government employees who were already involved in providing the services were transferred to the jurisdiction of local governments and the quality—and cost—of these public services did not suffer.

CENTRAL GOVERNMENTS ARE LESS CORRUPT
Another argument against stronger local government is the corruption that is bred from the "closeness" between elected local politicians and the local political power structure. Both Prud'homme (1995) and Tanzi (1995) present this view. Another line of reasoning, making the same point, is that the probability of successful stealing is increased by weakening central authority and monitoring. Various students of corruption place the blame on the greater number of contacts with public officials in developing countries, on lower-paid public officials having more incentive to steal than higher-paid central officials, and on voters at the local government level who have not yet learned to use their power to monitor and discipline their employees.[8]

The case that corruption and decentralization are inherently linked is, arguably, weak, however. Certainly, no good empirical evidence supports this contention. As suggested by Guess, Loehr, and Martinez-Vazquez (1997), the perception that fiscal decentralization and corruption are related may reflect only that localized corruption is more transparent.

Empirical work on the relationship between decentralization and corruption is inconclusive. Fisman and Gatti (2002), for example, find that corruption is lower in more decentralized countries; Treisman (2000) finds corruption to be higher in federal than in unitary countries.

Sequencing Fiscal Decentralization

The success or failure of fiscal decentralization in developing countries results as much from implementation as from program design. In particular, when introducing decentralization policies and administration, sequencing is key.

Bahl and Martinez-Vazquez (2006b) have argued that there is an optimal pattern of sequencing that is applicable for most countries. Even before beginning the implementation, two prerequisites are necessary for success: a rule of law and an existing deconcentration of public service delivery. The former makes it possible for subnational governments to protest violations of the decentralization law, even those committed by the central government. The latter makes it possible to shift central employees to local status without having to train a new force of local public employees.

The sequencing of decentralization should begin with two important steps (figure 2.1). The first is to hold a national debate about decentralization, possibly in the context of an election or the report of a national commission. It is better to deal with objections up front, or else the national debate could disrupt

---

8. For a good review, see Martinez-Vazquez, Arze del Granado, and Boex (2007).

Figure 2.1
Sequencing Fiscal Decentralization: A Normative Approach

| Step 6: Monitor, Evaluate, and Retrofit |
| Step 5: Implement the Decentralization Program |
| Step 4: Develop the Implementing Regulations |
| Step 3: Pass the Decentralization Law |
| Step 2: Do the Policy Design and Develop a White Paper |
| Step 1: Carry Out a National Debate on the Issues Related to Decentralization Policy |
| The Platform: Deconcentration, Rule of Law, etc. |

Source: Bahl and Martinez-Vazquez (2006b).

program implementation after it is under way. National discussion should culminate in a policy paper on fiscal decentralization that lays out the goals of the program and the strategy for achieving it. These steps make up the road map for the decentralization program. The policy paper would include matters such as the assignment of expenditure responsibilities, the nature of the intergovernmental transfer system, and the revenue-raising powers of subnational governments. Going forward without a policy guideline would be tantamount to adopting a "make it up as we go" strategy.

Based on this road map, the decentralization law can be written. This key document of the program will guide all else that is done in the implementation process. Although the law must contain the key features of the program, it must not be too specific because legal drafting cannot accommodate all the realities of administration that will arise.

The administrative phase begins with developing the implementing regulations that accompany the decentralization law. For example, the law may specify an equalizing grant program, but the implementing regulations may specify the exact formula to be used in distribution. The implementing regulations must conform with the decentralization law. If there are no implementing regulations, or if they are not clearly written, policy making would implicitly fall into the hands of bureaucrats. With these implementing regulations in hand, the program can be brought on line.

A final step in the process is to provide for monitoring and evaluation. Fiscal decentralization programs emerge and change over time, sometimes due to poorly formulated policy and sometimes due to the changing needs of the country. It is important to have in place a process for fine-tuning the structure. This process of gradual reformulation underlines the reasons why it is dangerous to include too much detail about decentralization in the constitution.

One problem with the stepwise approach to implementing decentralization proposed here is that it makes the process very transparent and vulnerable to criticism. It also requires time, especially at the stage when the program is being formulated, which gives the opposition time to organize their objections and their constituency. Another approach is simply to push ahead before opponents can get organized and to get the law written and adopted. The hope in this strategy, as was the case in the big-bang decentralization in Indonesia, is that once the law is written, there will be no turning back.

Is Fiscal Decentralization a Development Elixir?

It is easy for advocates to get enthusiastic about fiscal decentralization. It offers the opportunity to improve service delivery, increase the rate of revenue mobilization, involve citizens more closely in the process of governance, and help resolve conflict within disaffected regions.

In fact, fiscal decentralization is not a panacea for economic development problems. The potential effects are real enough, but developing economies often do not have the economic, institutional, and administrative wherewithal to capture these benefits. Moreover, the costs of decentralization can be too high for developing economies.

Countries around the world have moved only slowly toward the adoption of decentralized intergovernmental fiscal systems. Despite the advantages, no hard evidence shows a strong trend toward fiscal decentralization. Based on IMF *Government Finance Statistics*, which is one of only a few comparable data sources available, the subnational government share of public expenditures has remained at about 13 to 14 percent in developing countries since the 1970s.[9] The rather remarkable stability in the subnational government expenditure share is reported in table 2.1 for developing countries and for Organisation for Economic Co-operation and Development (OECD) member countries.

These results are not all surprising. The costs of decentralization are extremely high for less developed countries. Subnational government finance is

---

9. Here, decentralization is measured as the subnational government share of total government expenditure in the country, that is, subnational government expenditures in the numerator and total central plus subnational government expenditures in the denominator.

Table 2.1
Fiscal Decentralization Indicators

	1970s		1980s		1990s to 2000s		
	Developing Countries	OECD Countries	Developing Countries	OECD Countries	Developing Countries	OECD Countries	Transition Countries
Subnational government tax as a share of total government tax	10.68 (43)	17.91 (24)	8.87 (33)	18.18 (23)	10.61 (28)	18.39 (21)	22.41 (23)
Subnational government expenditure as a share of total government expenditure	13.42 (45)	33.68 (23)	12.09 (41)	31.97 (24)	12.97 (54)	32.68 (24)	30.32 (24)

Note: Sample sizes are in parentheses.
Source: Bahl and Wallace (2005, 91).

a type of luxury good whose benefits come only slowly to low-income countries. The political costs are also very high. Central bureaucracies are firmly entrenched, often since independence, and difficult to move. Even at the local level, the traditions of central control seem inviolate. Local voters, at whom these benefits are aimed, often have not yet learned enough about their power.

What to make of all this divergence between the rhetoric and the outcomes? Is decentralization an interesting idea that just hasn't caught on? Perhaps not. The trends presented in table 2.1 are deceiving. The period studied coincides with the introduction and growth of value-added taxes in developing countries. Because the VAT is such a revenue productive central government tax in most countries, the existence of a "flypaper effect" suggests that there would have been an increased share of spending at the central level. That subnational governments held a constant share of expenditures is evidence of continued support for decentralization as a development strategy.

Two other dimensions of fiscal decentralization make its success difficult to evaluate. First, the primary objectives may vary from country to country. Holding off dissolution may have driven the Russian design, whereas involving new voters in governance may have been paramount in South Africa. A global evaluation of fiscal decentralization programs is likely to be less accurate than a series of country case studies. Second, program design may be flawed in some countries, and implementation is always complicated. The result is that fiscal decentralization goes slowly, and its effects take time to show up.

REFERENCES

Bahl, R. 1999a. *Fiscal policy in China: Taxation and intergovernmental fiscal relations.* San Francisco: The 1990 Institute.

———. 1999b. Implementation rules for fiscal decentralization. *Public Budgeting and Finance* 19(2):59–75.

Bahl, R. W., and J. F. Linn. 1992. *Urban public finance in developing countries.* New York: Oxford University Press.

Bahl, R., and J. Martinez-Vazquez. 2006a. Fiscal federalism and economic reform in China. In *Federalism and economic reform: International perspectives*, J. S. Wallack and T. S. Srinivasan, eds., 249–300. Cambridge: Cambridge University Press.

———. 2006b. Sequencing fiscal decentralization. World Bank Policy Research Working Paper 3914, Public Sector Governance Group. Washington, DC: World Bank.

Bahl, R., J. Martinez-Vazquez, and S. Wallace. 1996. *The Guatemalan tax reform.* Boulder, CO: Westview Press.

Bahl, R., and S. Wallace. 2005. Public financing in developing and transition countries. *Public Budgeting and Finance*, Silver Anniversary Edition, 83–98.

Bird, R. M., and F. Vaillancourt, eds. 1998. *Fiscal decentralization in developing countries.* Cambridge: Cambridge University Press.

Davoodi, H., and H. Zou. 1998. Fiscal decentralization and economic growth: A cross-country study. *Journal of Urban Economics* 43(2):244–257.

Dillinger, W., and S. B. Webb. 1999a. Decentralization and fiscal management in Colombia. Policy Research Working Paper 2122, Latin American and Caribbean Division. Washington, DC: World Bank.

———. 1999b. Fiscal management in federal democracies: Argentina and Brazil. Policy Research Working Paper 2121, Latin American and Caribbean Division. Washington, DC: World Bank.

Fisman, R., and R. Gatti. 2002. Decentralization and corruption: Evidence across countries. *Journal of Public Economics* 83:325–345.

Guess, G. M., W. Loehr, and J. Martinez-Vazquez. 1997. Fiscal decentralization: A methodology for case studies. Consulting Assistance on Economic Reform II: Discussion Paper 3. Cambridge, MA: Harvard Institute of International Development.

Hicks, U. 1961. *Development from below.* Oxford: Clarendon Press.

Inter-American Development Bank. 1997. *Latin America after a decade of reforms.* Washington, DC: Inter-American Development Bank.

Lin, J. Y., and Z. Liu. 2000. Fiscal decentralization and economic growth in China. *Economic Development and Cultural Change* 49(1):1–22.

Litvack, J., J. Ahmad, and R. Bird. 1998. *Rethinking decentralization.* Washington, DC: World Bank.

Martinez-Vazquez, J., J. Arze del Granado, and J. Boex. 2007. *Fighting corruption in the public sector.* Amsterdam: Elsevier.

Martinez-Vazquez, J., and R. McNab. 2000. Fiscal decentralization and economic growth. International Studies Program Working Paper. Andrew Young School of Policy Studies, Georgia State University, Atlanta.

Musgrave, R., and P. B. Musgrave. 1984. *Public finance in theory and practice.* 4th ed. New York: McGraw-Hill.

Nelson, R. H. 2008. Community associations: Decentralizing local governments privately. In *Fiscal decentralization and land policies,* G. K. Ingram and Y-H. Hong, eds., 332–355. Cambridge, MA: Lincoln Institute of Land Policy.

Oates, W. E. 1972. *Fiscal federalism.* New York: Harcourt Brace Jovanovich.

Prud'homme, R. 1995. The dangers of decentralization. *World Bank Research Observer* 10(2):210–226.

Spahn, P. 1997. Decentralized government and macroeconomic control. Infrastructure Notes FM-12. Washington, DC: World Bank.

Tanzi, V. 1995. Fiscal federalism and decentralization: A review of some efficiency and macroeconomic aspects. In *Annual World Bank Conference on Development Economics,* M. Bruno, and B. Pleskovic, eds., 295–316. Washington, DC: World Bank.

Ter-Minassian, T., ed. 1997. *Fiscal federalism in theory and practice.* Washington, DC: International Monetary Fund.

Ter-Minassian, T., and J. Craig. 1997. Control of subnational borrowing. In *Fiscal federalism in theory and practice,* T. Ter-Minassian, ed., 156–174. Washington, DC: International Monetary Fund.

Treisman, D. 2000. *Decentralization and the quality of government.* Washington, DC: International Monetary Fund.

Wong, C. P. W., C. Heady, and W. T. Woo. 1995. *Fiscal management and economic reform in the People's Republic of China.* Hong Kong: Asian Development Bank / Oxford University Press.

Zhang, T., and H. Zou. 1997. Fiscal decentralization, the composition of public spending, and regional growth in India. Development Research Group Working Paper. Washington, DC: World Bank.

———. 1998. Fiscal decentralization, public spending, and economic growth in China. *Journal of Public Economics* 67(2):221–240.

3

Local Revenues Under Fiscal Decentralization in Developing Countries: Linking Policy Reform, Governance, and Capacity

Paul Smoke

*A*s many developing countries have pursued fiscal decentralization reforms in recent years, local government revenue enhancement has received considerable attention. Public finance specialists have elaborated well-defined and broadly used principles for selecting and designing own-source revenues. It is clear from the empirical literature, however, that even where such advice has been followed, local revenue generation has rarely met expectations. Indeed, much of the literature documents frustrating underperformance (Ahmad and Tanzi 2002; Bahl and Linn 1992; Bardhan and Mookherjee 2006; Bird and Vaillancourt 1998; Ebel and Taliercio 2005; Ebel and Yilmaz 2003; Litvack, Ahmad, and Bird 1998; Prud'homme 1995; Shah 1994, 2004; Smoke 2001; Tanzi 2001; Ter-Minassian 1997; World Bank 2001, 2005).

This chapter argues that the often limited success with local revenue generation in developing countries results, at least in part, from the mainstream analytical framework that dominates how reform is approached. Public finance experts continue to focus on overly narrow and technical fiscal factors, paying insufficient attention to the broader political and institutional context in which reform must take place. A brief review of key elements of the mainstream fiscal decentralization approach is followed by a consideration of how moving beyond it could promote and sustain improved local revenue performance.

Given great variations in structures, functions, and performance across and within regions and countries, it is misleading to speak authoritatively about "local governments in developing countries" as a single group.[1] Reforms appropriate for established, capacitated, economically dynamic urban governments in a more advanced developing country may be irrelevant for weak, poor rural councils recently created in a least developed country. Although illustrative examples are provided throughout this chapter, it is impossible to cover the diversity of experience or to generalize beyond some basic points.

Conventional Fiscal Federalism Wisdom and Experience: A Condensed, Selective Review

The typical starting point for considering local revenues is to determine the specific sources permitted by constitutional, legal, or administrative provisions in a particular country (Litvack, Ahmad, and Bird 1998; Bahl 2000a; Bahl and Martinez-Vazquez 2006; Ebel and Taliercio 2005; Rodden, Eskeland, and Litvack 2003; Shah 1994, 2004; Smoke 2006a). Local revenue generation ultimately depends on establishing a broader enabling environment for decentralization, including the legal status of local governments, their specific rights and functions, and their degree of autonomy. Certain elements of the national legal framework not specific to decentralization may also affect revenue generation. Property rights, for example, set parameters for property tax policy and administration. Legal provisions for local political mechanisms are also important. Although they do not directly determine revenue design, they do influence the extent to which local governments are accountable to their constituents in how they raise and spend public resources.

Fiscal federalism principles for assigning revenues to local governments are fairly well defined.[2] Developing countries often broadly follow these principles. Thus, central governments typically attempt to assign to local governments revenue bases that are, for example, relatively immobile and do not compete seriously with central tax bases. There are, however, examples of local taxes that violate key principles, such as the infamous South Asian *octroi*. This productive,

---

1. This diversity is a theme throughout the fiscal decentralization literature. A number of volumes focus on individual countries, including Alm, Martinez-Vazquez, and Indrawati (2004) and Bahl and Smoke (2003). Some are regional specific and somewhat interdisciplinary, including Bird and Vaillancourt (1998), Burki, Perry, and Dillinger (1999), Smoke (2003a), Wunsch and Olowu (2003), and World Bank (2001, 2005). Others are cross regional, including Ahmad and Tanzi (2002), Bardhan and Mookherjee (2006), and Smoke, Gomez, and Peterson (2006).

2. Fiscal federalism is introduced in Oates (1972) and revisited in Oates (1999). Other work, some revenue specific, includes Bahl (2000a), Bird (1999), Ebel and Taliercio (2005), Litvack, Ahmad, and Bird (1998), McClure and Martinez-Vazquez (2000), Shah (1994), and Ter-Minassian (1997). Critiques include Prud'homme (1995), Smoke (2001), and Tanzi (1996, 2001). Recent literature on "second-generation" fiscal federalism includes Oates (2005) and Weingast (2006).

but inefficient, tax on interjurisdictional commerce is also used in various forms
in other parts of the world.

LOCAL REVENUE SYSTEM DESIGN: PRINCIPLES AND REALITY
Although local revenue design principles may seem to be straightforward, challenges arise when they are applied in the real world (Bahl 2000a; Bahl and Linn
1992; Bird 1999, 2001; Ebel and Taliercio 2005; Ebel and Weist 2006; Shah
1994; Taliercio 2005). Key principles and illustrations of practice are only outlined here, but references to more complete discussions are provided.

Own-source revenues, over which local governments exercise an element
of control, should cover budgetary needs to a reasonable degree of adequacy as
per the well-known "finance follows function" principle. In reality, revenue adequacy is difficult to determine given common problems with insufficient clarity,
inconsistency, and incomplete adoption of functional assignments. In addition,
the well-accepted inherent advantage of central governments in revenue generation often promotes central claims on the most productive sources; a greater
role than some analysts might like for intergovernmental transfers; and a tendency for local governments to use numerous unproductive, and even unofficial,
sources (Lewis 2003b, 2005; Prud'homme 2003; Taliercio 2004, 2005).

Local revenues are also expected to be elastic, growing at least in proportion to the local economy and expenditure needs. Adequate elasticity, however,
is elusive, due both to the types of revenues that are typically decentralized and
to the failure of local governments to take actions needed to ensure base growth,
such as revaluing and indexing property assessments.

Local revenues are expected to be efficient and equitable. Efficiency comprises both minimizing distortions of economic decisions made by individuals
and firms (that result, for example, from selectively differentiated property assessment ratios and rates) and ensuring correspondence between payments and
benefits (by, for example, limiting tax exporting). In fact, local revenue systems
often compromise efficiency through choice of potentially problematic instruments, such as turnover taxes; differential treatment for specific policy objectives, such as favorable property tax rates to spur development in target areas;
poorly developed or enforced rules, which may facilitate political manipulation of tax burdens; and adoption of local taxes with "exportable" burdens
(although not all economists oppose this practice). At the local level, there is
more concern with horizontal equity (equal treatment of equal individuals and
firms) than vertical equity given the potential spatial inefficiencies created by local redistributive taxation. Equity, however, can be problematic no matter how
it is defined because local taxes often fail to cover all sectors, and preferential
treatment of certain taxpayers or groups commonly results from tax regulations
and weak or selective administration.

One of the most coveted principles of local revenue generation is the need
to provide local governments with a degree of fiscal autonomy over a share of

revenues sufficient to create a connection in the minds of local voters between the revenue generation and service delivery actions of local elected officials. In reality, the degree of autonomy is often limited by an unwillingness of central government to share power or concerns about local capacity. In addition, local governments may not take advantage of autonomy because they do not know how to do so or they do not want to take responsibility for revenue generation.

It is often recommended that local revenue systems be designed for consistency with other elements of the national fiscal system, including central revenues, intergovernmental transfers, and subnational borrowing systems. Relevant policies include, for example, limiting redundant taxation and embedding incentives for local revenue generation in transfer and lending mechanisms. Inconsistencies in the fiscal framework, however, are not uncommon, with poor harmonization of taxes used by central and local governments, weak incentives for revenue generation in transfer programs (Bahl 2000b; Bird and Smart 2002; Schroeder and Smoke 2003; Shah 2006a), and failure to enforce repayment of local government loans from central government lending mechanisms (Friere and Peterson 2004; Peterson 2000).

Beyond pure fiscal concerns, local revenues are expected to be administratively feasible. The most common prescription is to adopt appropriately simple rules and procedures that are consistent with often weak local capacity and also limit the potential efficiency and equity effects of differential treatment. Administrative feasibility, however, is often compromised by pursuing non-revenue-raising objectives and adopting poorly defined or unduly complex procedures (Bird and Wallace 2003; Ebel and Taliercio 2005; Lewis 2006; Mikesell 2002, 2007; Taliercio 2004, 2005). Also desirable is political feasibility, which is framed in terms of using revenues that are less lumpy or visible (e.g., small payments over time versus large lump sums), that are transparently defined, and that create taxpayer confidence in fair tax administration. In reality, political feasibility is often difficult to determine and achieve in developing country environments where citizens are not used to receiving or paying for services. In addition, politically feasible revenues may be problematic in other ways.

OBSTACLES TO EFFECTIVELY APPLYING THE PRINCIPLES

Relatively weak performance relative to fiscal principles results from a number of factors. First, there are well-known technical trade-offs and complexities inherent in these principles. Certain tax bases, such as sales, turnover, and property, may be potentially productive and buoyant, but they are also difficult to administer, especially where capacity is weak. The above-noted *octroi* is also often productive and buoyant but inefficient. Some efficient revenue sources, such as user charges, may be seen as inequitable. Thus, objectives must be prioritized. A related problem is a common lack of appropriate and reliable information for good revenue policy design and administration.

Second, national politics obviously support or undermine appropriate fiscal decentralization policy.[3] Politics significantly influence which functions and revenue powers are decentralized, how they relate to the larger fiscal architecture, the degree to which the center grants genuine autonomy, and the process and support structures that enable local governments to assume new responsibilities. In many cases, reluctance to decentralize reflects an unwillingness of the center to relinquish functions and resources, but subnational government empowerment can also be used strategically to consolidate power for a single dominant party or the current regime.

Third, national institutional actors that elaborate local revenue powers, design operational procedures, and provide technical and capacity-building support to local governments may not have sufficient capacity to meet their obligations. They may also be uncooperative or antagonistic to each other (Cohen and Peterson 1999; Litvack, Ahmad, and Bird 1998; Smoke 2007; Smoke and Lewis 1996). Battles between ministries of finance and local government, for example, can result in incomplete or inconsistent policies that complicate local assumption of powers.[4] Even within a ministry of finance, aspects of fiscal reform—local revenues, transfers, and lending—may be under different departments that function independently or competitively, resulting in a failure to resolve important policy matters or inconsistency in formal policies and procedures.[5]

Fourth, the role of international development agencies should not be overlooked in developing countries.[6] Although such agencies have arguably modified their behavior over time, they long supported primarily technical approaches to revenue reform, irrespective of whether these approaches were politically and institutionally workable. There is also some tendency to draw on the positive experiences of industrialized and transition countries, recommending reforms that may be more difficult for many developing countries, particularly outside of major urban centers, to implement successfully, such as complex computer-based valuation models for property taxation.

---

3. The national politics of decentralization are discussed to varying degrees in Bardhan and Mookherjee (2006), Bird and Vaillancourt (1998), Burki, Perry, and Dillinger (1999), Cohen and Peterson (1999), Eaton (2002, 2004), Litvack, Ahmad, and Bird (1998), Manor (1998), Smoke (2007), Smoke, Gomez, and Peterson (2006), Willis, Haggard, and Garman (1999), and Wunsch and Olowu (1990, 2003).

4. In Uganda, for example, the Ministry of Finance and the Ministry of Local Government separately developed local financial management systems. Similar situations have occurred between the Ministry of Finance and the Ministry of Home Affairs in Indonesia.

5. In Indonesia, for example, bureaucratic battles within the Ministry of Finance have been a major factor in obstructing property tax decentralization and subnational borrowing reform.

6. Many references cited in this chapter touch on donor approaches to supporting decentralization, sometimes with specific reference to fiscal decentralization and revenue reform. Some emphasis on donor behavior and coordination is found in Romeo (2003) and Smoke (2000).

Fifth, revenue generation at the local level is inherently political. How local governments use their revenue powers—depending on where local political power really lies—may, for example, overtax or undertax businesses relative to individuals or particular sectors relative to others, creating both behavioral distortions and inequities. Under certain political power scenarios, high levels of autonomy may lead to massive capture by local elites or exploitation of certain groups. Without adequate development and enforcement of a local government framework and adoption of appropriate accountability relationships beyond simple elections, local populations may not be capable of securing their "preferences" from local politicians, which is the basis of fiscal decentralization.

Common Local Revenues, Key Challenges, and Standard Policy Responses

Fiscal decentralization experts often recognize these constraints on implementing local government revenue principles. Their response to these realities, however, has on the whole been fairly limited. Before considering how to advance thinking and practice, it is useful to review a few of the most common developing country local revenues, problems experienced in using them, and standard recommended policy responses. The focus here is primarily on revenue policy and administration reforms, with the political dimension treated more fully below. It is important to emphasize that specific reforms that have worked in some countries will not be applicable everywhere, but the general strategies and principles involved can often help analysts to think about how to improve the situation in a variety of environments.

PROPERTY TAXATION

The property tax, often seen as a mainstay of local revenue, is known to suffer from design and administration problems that are often particularly severe in developing countries (Bahl 1979; Bahl and Linn 1992; Bahl, Martinez-Vazquez, and Youngman 2008; Bird and Slack 2006; Dillinger 1992; Franzsen 2003; Kelly 1993, 2000, 2003; Lewis 2003a; Oates 2001; Rosengard 1998). First, some developing countries, in pursuit of policy or political goals, tax certain types of property more heavily than others through higher assessments and rates. In the case of business properties, for example, this practice could lead to relocation or shifting the tax burden through higher prices to the very residents that differential treatment is trying to protect; alternatively, exporting could occur. A central policy recommendation is to reduce or eliminate differentials in assessment ratios and tax rates on different classes of property. This practice limits incentives for tax avoidance and evasion, such as attempts to have property classified differently, to seek special exemptions, or to subdivide plots.

Second, problems associated with the complexity and infrequent application of valuation procedures, such as inefficiencies, inequities, and stagnant tax bases, are well known and pervasive. There has been a movement to adopt simplified mass assessment procedures that use a limited, standard set of land and building characteristics, with some evidence of improved yields and lower administration costs. In addition, provisions to revalue at regular intervals and to index between valuations can improve revenue buoyancy.

Third, collection long received less attention than valuation reform in developing countries. Indonesia's property tax reform in the late 1980s and 1990s was among the first to replace a valuation-led strategy with collection-led reform (Kelly 1993). This reform was justified by the argument that improved valuation would have a limited impact on yields without improved collection. Key elements of collection-led reforms include legal provisions that broadly define liability, permitting renters to deduct property tax payments from rent; steps that improve taxpayer convenience, such as more accessible payment points and simpler procedures; and enhanced enforcement, such as higher penalties for nonpayment and seizure of properties in default.

Fourth, conventional property tax administration requires considerable information: on parcels and characteristics of land, owners and users, assessments, billing, and collection. This severe problem has been tackled in various ways, such as by trying to reduce the amount of information required (mass appraisal as noted above); by using and coordinating with existing sources of data; and by improving the use of technology to record, update, and manage information for tax administration.

OTHER COMMON LOCAL REVENUE SOURCES

Beyond the property tax, user charges and business-related fees are among the most common local revenues in developing countries. Experts generally agree that user fees are often under- and inappropriately utilized (Bahl and Linn 1992; Bird 2000; Bird and Tsiopoulos 1997; Crane 1994; Whittington 1991). The case for their use is powerful, including improvement of the consumption-cost connection and the enforcement benefits of being able to exclude nonpayers. There are also challenges, however, such as choosing among pricing schemes with different implications for cost recovery and efficiency, administrative and political barriers to collection, reluctance or inability to raise charges over time, and equity concerns about how charges affect the poor.

Recommendations must be made in terms of the context of specific sectors and countries, but evidence that people are willing to pay something for services if adequate quality and reliability are maintained, and successful reform experiences, suggest general approaches. There has been movement to simplify and be more transparent about charge structures. Raising charges incrementally seems more acceptable than large increases. Cost recovery can be improved while offsetting equity concerns through various means—use of alternative service technologies in low-income areas (e.g., communal water taps), appropriate price discrimination schemes (to reflect community standards or variations in price elasticities of demand), and adopting flexible ways to cover prohibitive service "entry costs" (e.g., water system connection), among others. Collection can also be improved under certain conditions through contracting third-party agents (e.g., private firms for network services and community organizations for local services).

In developing countries, business-related taxes and fees can be productive in absolute terms and with respect to total local revenues (Bahl and Linn 1992; Bird 2001). Perhaps most widespread are business licenses and market fees, but problems are common. License fees often duplicate fees charged by higher-levels agencies (such as a ministry of commerce) that are more likely to be paid. In addition, the fee structure often seems arbitrary, with no clear justification for differences in fees across professions or merchants, and widely varying charges across jurisdictions that could induce movement of economic activity. Finally, enforcement is commonly inconsistent, due to both administrative weaknesses and political interference.

Recommended reforms include giving local governments sole access to licensing and requiring fee structures based on clear standards, often according to a centrally defined allowable range of fees. A commonly cited example of good practice is the single-business permit in Kenya, which grants to local governments exclusive rights to levy and collect business licenses but sets national guidelines intended to improve efficiency and equity (Devas and Kelly 2001).

Some subnational revenue options tend to be less universally used or relevant, primarily for intermediate tiers (states, provinces, regions) or large urban areas (Bahl and Linn 1992; Bird 2001; Shah 1994). Motor vehicle taxes and licenses, for example, can be productive and structured to promote efficiency and to target wealthier people. Natural resource taxes can also be lucrative. They are generally collected and shared by the center or are relatively easy to collect. With some exceptions, however, motor vehicle and natural resource taxes are normally reserved for higher tiers or heavily defined and regulated by the center.

Another exceptional example of productive local taxes is the regional services council levy, a payroll and business turnover tax in South Africa. It is a major source, but primarily benefits urban areas. Potentially problematic, it can harm businesses, undermine tax bases, and adversely affect equity if raised too high or passed to consumers (Bahl and Solomon 2003). Similarly, Uganda uses the graduated personal tax, an unusual hybrid of a pay-as-you-earn income tax, a presumptive income tax, a wealth tax, and a poll tax. It is poorly designed and implemented, and politically contentious, but outside of Kampala, the revenue-diversified capital, it accounts on average for 70 percent of local revenues (Smoke 2002). Despite recognized concerns with such sources, their revenue productivity discourages reform, unless they can be replaced with a source that is revenue neutral or more productive.

Some analysts frustrated with poorly performing traditional local taxes make the case for a different approach. They argue that the property tax is costly and difficult to administer and that even a well-administered version cannot finance major social expenditures. Moreover, subnational business taxes are often poorly structured and administered. These realities have generated calls to adopt subnational value-added taxes (VAT) or business-value taxes, a VAT levied on the basis of income (production, origin) rather than consumption (destination) (Bird 1999, 2001, 2005). A subnational VAT can be complicated, but there are ways to mitigate likely problems. Such taxes will not work for small- or low-capacity local governments, but proponents argue that a dual approach could be taken. Smaller local governments could use (in conjunction with user charges) business licenses, such as the Kenyan single-business permit mentioned earlier. Regional and metropolitan governments could use the business-value tax.

Although positive reforms have been realized, and useful proposals to strengthen local yields have been advanced, weak revenue generation and poorly designed subnational revenue systems remain among the most prominent flaws of decentralization in developing countries. Even where progress has been made, it is more common for individual local revenues to be improved than for broader systemic reform that has greater potential for major impact.

Neglected Aspects of Local Revenue Reform: Politics, Governance, and Implementation

Many of the constraints on local revenue reform outlined above are recognized both in the academic literature and in practice. For example, analysts commonly identify trade-offs inherent among local revenue principles and try to help policy makers understand options available to them and the implications of each choice. They also typically emphasize the importance of developing good frameworks as well as sound systems and procedures through which to implement local revenue policies.

On the other hand, beyond vague discussions of the need for "political will," analysts often deal superficially with political and institutional dimensions of revenue generation, perhaps the most important factor constraining performance. In addition, limited attention is paid to local revenue policy implementation beyond recognizing that administrative systems and capacity to operate them must be built. This point is particularly important given that, in many developing countries, the desired system identified by using normative revenue principles is often not easily or quickly attainable. Moreover, a potentially close link exists between political and institutional constraints and implementation. If the latter is approached strategically, a good revenue system might be built gradually over time in a way that responds to, and helps to overcome, constraints.

POLITICS, GOVERNANCE, AND FISCAL BEHAVIOR
The academic literature across various disciplines includes several approaches to the political economy of taxation (Addison and Levin 2006; Bräutigam 2008; Moore 2004, 2007; Sabates and Schneider 2003; Schneider 2003; Therkildsen

2001). Broadly speaking, the authors attempt to explain the composition and level of taxation, and, to varying degrees, how they are related to state structure, capacity, and the relationship between the state and civil society. Main approaches include the traditional public finance approach, which focuses on understanding the effects of taxation on economic development and other public goals; a taxpayer approach examining how ideology, value, and culture influence willingness to pay and compliance; a political institutions approach that uses historical analysis to explain state capacity and tax system development; a crisis-based approach that considers how war and conflict drive tax expansion and modernization; and a fiscal contract approach, which analyzes how revenue-maximizing governments "negotiate" with payment-minimizing taxpayers by offering state-provided benefits. Some literature focuses on issues related to decentralization. For example, a study of 68 countries found that politically decentralized regimes tax citizens less than more centralized regimes, but it did not disaggregate national and subnational revenue levels (Schneider 2003). Aspects of these various analytical approaches are relevant for local taxation.

There is also a more general (non-taxation-specific) empirical literature on how national political institutions and contextual factors affect the behavior of elected officials and outcomes that result from state action. Limited work on decentralization examines various relationships between government structures, governance measures, and outcomes.[7] This literature, however, often takes either a "macro" perspective, focusing on cross-national comparisons, or a "micro" perspective, focusing on particular cases. Comparative econometric studies document broad patterns, and case studies illustrate details of complex relationships among politics, governance, and decentralization (Ahmad and Tanzi 2002; Bardhan and Mookherjee 2006; Bird and Vaillancourt 1998; Cheema and Rondinelli 2007; Smoke, Gomez, and Peterson 2006). The comparative studies, however, do not capture key details of structural design or political variables, and their broad findings provide a weak basis for concrete reforms. Case studies, on the other hand, vary in focus and in the way they collect and use evidence, so their broader relevance is also unclear. Much practitioner literature leans toward prescriptive advice and "snapshots" of cases that illustrate this advice with relatively limited consideration of if and how to replicate or modify it elsewhere (UNCDF 1999, 2006; UNDESA 2005a, 2005b; UNDP 2000, 2004; USAID 2000; World Bank 2000, 2004). Both the academic and the practitioner literatures on the relationship between politics/governance and outcomes tend to focus primarily on expenditures and service delivery rather than revenue generation.

---

7. Recent political science literature is reviewed in Hoffman and Gibson (2006). Some relevant economics literature is reviewed by Martinez-Vazquez and McNab (2006), who find evidence of a bidirectional and temporal relationship between fiscal decentralization and democratic governance.

THE POLITICAL DIMENSIONS OF LOCAL REVENUE GENERATION

The politics of local revenue reform can be critical, a fact recognized to some extent by much of the literature referenced in this chapter. At the national level, even with agreement to assign revenue sources to local governments, efforts to limit the autonomy with which they are executed are common. Many decentralization frameworks, for example, devolve the property tax, but onerous regulations and arbitrary central interventions can undermine local autonomy and limit productivity.[8]

The greatest political obstacles to local taxation are often found at the local level. Although property tax, for example, is considered to be a good local tax, it is very visible. It is not hidden in income deductions or purchase prices, and known inequities in administration can create local resistance. Concentration of land ownership and a stark division in developing countries between the rich and elite, on one hand, and the poor and marginalized on the other hand, also complicate the use of this tax. Cultural traditions and ethnic loyalties can lead to politicization of revenue-generation activities in ways that undermine tax yields and taxpayers' sense of fair treatment. For example, taxing land or livestock can be contentious in some situations, and residents from the same ethnic group as the tax collector may be treated favorably. Enforcement can be arbitrary or politicized, even if a local government has reasonable capacity. Perhaps most fundamental is that local residents may be unwilling to pay if they do not believe that they are getting adequate services or those that they want.

The preceding discussion highlights that politics is at the core of local revenue generation. Indeed, fiscal federalism assumes some means for local governments to discern citizen preferences and be responsive to them in how revenues are raised and used.[9] The normative, technical approach to local revenue analysis, however, barely addresses governance and accountability reform beyond promoting elections and recognizing the need for transparent, rule-based procedures and taxpayer appeal mechanisms. Without significant governance mechanisms and a willingness and ability of local residents to use them, local revenue generation is likely to remain limited.

---

8. Some degree of regulation by the central government is justified. Without it, substantial local variations in tax base definition, assessment ratios, or tax rates can create problems and complicate local tax effort comparisons needed for national policy design and enforcement in a particular country. Such regulation, however, must be defined in a way that limits political manipulation.

9. Useful reviews of decentralization and governance from various perspectives, none particularly focused on revenue generation, are provided in Blair (2000), Cheema and Rondinelli (2007), Crook (2003), Manor (1998), Olowu (2003), Ribot (2004), Ribot and Larson (2005), Schneider (1999), Shah (2006b), Shah and Thompson (2004), Tendler (1997), and Wunsch and Olowu (2003).

Some key local governance instruments, such as credible and competitive elections, are obviously not within the local fiscal realm, and they are in any case a blunt instrument for improving accountability. Other mechanisms, however, such as town meetings, oversight boards with private-sector and nongovernmental organization (NGO) representatives, participatory planning and budgeting, and social auditing of local resource use have been widely explored. These mechanisms can be useful in promoting public understanding both of how revenue sources are defined and levied and of how the proceeds are being used for local expenditures. Improved political mechanisms, more broadly based participation, and better local services can alleviate political obstacles to more effective use of local taxes (Blair 2006; Commins 2006; Manor 2007; Platteau 2006). Some authors have argued that a closer relationship between local governments and citizens through such processes can help to develop local social capital (de Mello 2002).

There are at least three important caveats to these broad claims. First, accountability mechanisms can be just as "technical" as fiscal mechanisms. For example, rules and processes for participatory budgeting or planning, including how they treat local revenue generation, can be well articulated to meet normative principles, but what matters is how they are applied. If participation is token or noninclusive, broad improvements in service coverage, quality, and willingness to pay local taxes should not be expected. If such mechanisms are captured by political and economic elites—even powerful but nonrepresentative citizen groups or NGOs—their effect will be limited or different than intended. In some countries, particularly for highly local or village decision-making processes, participation is mandatory or requires a minimum involvement of underrepresented groups (e.g., a certain percentage of women), but such rules do not automatically make participation meaningful.

Second, the use of accountability mechanisms requires a degree of awareness, capacity, and interest on the part of citizens. Local budgets or participatory forums may be available to the public, but people may not know it and may not know how to access, interpret, or use them. Similarly, mechanisms to appeal property tax assessments or local business license fees will not be effective if people do not know about them or face barriers in using them, such as lack of appropriate knowledge, poor access to advice, or intimidation.

Third, only limited empirical evidence provides specific guidance on how to incorporate political considerations in analyzing local revenue reform. There are, however, a few studies that provide useful insights into the political nature of local revenues in particular countries, such as why residents comply with or evade local taxes. In Tanzania, for example, local tax compliance is positively related to factors such as ability to pay and the (perceived) probability of prosecution, and it is negatively related to oppressive tax enforcement, taxpayer harassment, and weak satisfaction with public services (Fjeldstad and Semboja 2001). Although that study suggests that unduly harsh treatment may backfire, a more focused study of the same country found that some element of coercion enhances local government revenue performance. The ability to enforce depends on the power and capacity of local governments and the insulation of revenue collection from direct influence by elected councilors (Fjeldstad 2001).

In South Africa poor compliance in service charge payment is commonly blamed on poverty and a sense of entitlement to national subsidies. Recent research, however, finds that although inability to pay is important, there are great variations in compliance within and between communities with similar socioeconomic characteristics (Fjeldstad 2004, 2005). A key factor is the extent to which citizens perceive local governments to be acting in their interest, which includes their level of satisfaction with services provided and a sense that other citizens pay a fair share. Similar sentiments emerge from a survey in Uganda. Only 11 percent of respondents believed that local tax payments were substantially used to improve services; 46 percent said to some extent, and 32 percent saw little service benefit (Kjaer 2004, 2005). A strong majority of respondents—75 percent—indicated a willingness to pay more if local governments did more for the community.

In Senegal tax compliance decreased substantially after collection was devolved to local councilors (Juul 2006). Compliance was greatest for foreigners and newcomers, who used payment as a way to be recognized as community members and to block attempts by local elites to deny them their civil rights. Reasons for noncompliance included lack of service provision and weak general confidence in local authorities. In contrast, evidence from the city of Porto Alegre (Brazil), famous for pioneering participatory budgeting, used local participatory mechanisms to mobilize support for tax reform and compliance (Schneider and Baquero 2006). Throughout the 1990s, tax avoidance decreased and revenue collection increased impressively. From 1989 to 2004, local tax effort increased 338 percent, which far exceeded economic growth, and the revenue increase occurred during a time when intergovernmental transfers were also rising rapidly.

Other studies document how the structure of local revenues influences the way local politicians use them. For example, a study of local budgets from Tanzania and Zambia found that local governments devote a larger budget share to public service delivery as local taxes increase (Hoffman and Gibson 2006); a higher share of local resources from intergovernmental transfers and foreign assistance, however, is associated with a larger budget share for employee benefits and administrative costs. Also relevant is how revenue distributions within a local government can be distorted by local politics. Education allocations in Uganda, for example, often did not reach intended end-users (schools) over a five-year period. Schools received on average only 13 percent of allocations, with the bulk captured by local officials (Reinikka and Svensson 2004). Within local governments, the great variations in percentage of allocation realized suggest that certain schools had power to claim more of what they were due. Such a situation should be expected to influence willingness to engage in local affairs and to pay local taxes.

Some evidence also suggests that commonly recommended revenue reforms can be sidetracked by unanticipated behavioral adjustments. Recent work on private collection of local taxes in Uganda, for example, finds that such efforts can improve revenue growth and stability (Iversen et al. 2006). Revenue leakage, however, may remain significant: it is merely shifted from the collection point (the collector–taxpayer transaction) to the district administration (the contractor–local government transaction). Although not local specific, recent research on the Uganda Revenue Authority, which was established to reduce corruption, finds that behavior of individual actors in the revenue collection system substantially depends on the interests of social groups to which they belong (Fjeldstad 2006). In effect, social relations can undermine formal bureaucratic structures and positions. Thus, technocratic reforms supported by donors and halfheartedly or opportunistically (in search of other objectives) embraced by local bureaucrats do not adequately recognize that progress in tax administration depends on stimulating changes in the behavioral culture of the civil service. Even with major changes in structures and procedures, reform does not happen easily.

The empirical literature is difficult to synthesize. Not only is it limited, but the focal issues being studied vary, the authors employ diverse methods, and the studies are generally based on only one or two countries. In addition, factors underlying documented behavior are not always well explored. One conclusion, however, is reinforced by this empirical work—the nature and quality of local governance are likely to significantly affect how local revenue is generated and used, as well as how citizens perceive and react to local government fiscal behavior.

IMPLEMENTATION

In recent years increased attention has been given to implementing and sequencing fiscal decentralization (Bahl and Martinez-Vazquez 2006; Burki, Perry, and Dillinger 1999; Ebel and Weist 2006; Falleti 2005; Litvack, Ahmad, and Bird 1998; Shah and Thompson 2004; Smoke 2006a, 2000b, 2007; Smoke and Lewis 1996). With one exception (Ebel and Weist 2006), this literature does not specifically focus on local revenues, but the basic approaches to thinking about implementation are relevant. Even the best-designed local tax on a high-value base may not be productive unless care is given to how it is implemented. Local governments need to develop good procedures and capacity to use them. At the same time, citizens and businesses must learn to pay taxes, which means being satisfied that local governments are being responsive and treating them fairly.

Decentralization (including local revenue) implementation comprises both national and local dimensions and can be accomplished in a variety of ways. At the national level, on one extreme, national framework implementation becomes the responsibility of individually acting central ministries and local governments. They must adjust to the new framework, develop capacity for their role in it, and adopt its provisions. This approach might be called "sink or swim." On the other extreme, a central government might pursue a highly managed process for gradually implementing the framework provisions according to criteria. Under such an approach, nothing is automatic, and the framework is implemented according to central decisions. This approach might be called "paternalistic."

Neither of these extremes makes sense in most developing countries. The "sink or swim" approach would work well only where central ministries are likely to comply with decentralization mandates, the discipline of a hard budget constraint is institutionalized, local governments have a minimum capacity, and citizens have enough power and experience to hold local governments accountable. A purely "paternalistic" approach, however, is also problematic. In many developing countries, some subset of local governments is capable of responsibly managing their fiscal affairs, and they should not be hampered by central control over assumption of their legal rights, including those related to autonomous revenue generation (Bahl and Smoke 2003; Smoke 2004).

Compromise is possible through objective differentiation among local governments. Those with certain capacities can, essentially, be left to "sink or swim," whereas others might more gradually assume responsibilities and be targeted with evolving capacity building and technical assistance as they move toward autonomy. Under such an asymmetric, "developmental" implementation strategy, the target systems may be the same, but the path to attaining them need not be. The danger, of course, and the reason many analysts have reservations about this approach, is that politicized, subjective assessment of which local governments are ready to do what, can undermine the process. As a result, local governments might be brought into the reform effort at a level inconsistent with their capacity, and some may be stalled at early stages of reform that leave them with limited authority and autonomy. Such problems, however, can be managed if the process is appropriately defined and implemented; moreover, given how poorly other approaches have performed in developing countries, it is at least worth considering a more strategic process.

If properly conceived, local revenue reforms can be linked to broader efforts to build capacity, including governance, and they can be structured to improve performance progressively. The central government has considerable leverage, with the possibility of using access to rights, resources, and technical assistance to encourage adoption of new revenues and procedures, accountability mechanisms, and other local reforms. Using such leverage implies that, at least to some extent, local autonomy in developing environments should be earned. High levels of local autonomy in the absence of a minimum of capacity to assume functions responsibly and some degree of accountability to local citizens are a well-documented recipe for poor performance. At the same time, in some cases local officials may be able to undermine central controls: because the center does not have the capacity to monitor them, because local officials are powerful, or because they are able to raise local revenues through extrabudgetary means that escape central detection. In addition, central agencies must have the capacity and disposition to design and implement fair controls in the first place. In short, this path is difficult to follow and would need to be carefully explored and structured.

The specific situation will also differ among developing countries that are at different stages of reform. Some countries already have a local revenue system that they are trying to improve. Others are transferring portions of a centrally managed system to local governments, sometimes along with staff. In still other cases, new revenues are being created for new local governments. Such differences in the nature of the system—along with the political and institutional factors outlined above—should inform the strategy that would be developed in a particular country.

At the local level, the notion of an implementation strategy takes on a different meaning. Even the most capable local governments may need to selectively implement local revenue reforms that require major changes in the nature and level of what residents pay for local services. Simple and more politically acceptable reforms could be undertaken before more complex or controversial ones, which could be phased in later. For example, in places where movement to full property valuation is intended and current valuations are low, assessment ratios could be phased in and related to specific improvements in service delivery. Similarly, to avoid harsh equity effects, undesirable changes in service use, or administrative and political resistance, user charges could move gradually toward cost recovery. New systems and procedures could be tested through pilot programs, allowing for improvements before wider adoption.

Institutional innovations can also be used to help overcome some of the constraints discussed earlier. Adoption or tailoring of citizen engagement and oversight mechanisms can facilitate public acceptance of local tax reforms, as some of the empirical work reviewed above suggests, and public education campaigns may promote improved citizen awareness and compliance. User committees for specific services have sometimes been strategically used to connect citizens to local government service delivery and associated revenue generation, although they have also bypassed and undermined local governments in some cases (Manor 2004). Working with community groups on service delivery and revenue generation for local services such as trash collection can be productive and benefit both local governments and the community groups.

It is also worth noting that capacity building, a key to implementation, is usually treated in a perfunctory, boilerplate way (Green 2005). Local revenue experts recognize the need for capacity building so that local government employees can manage revenue generation effectively, and training and technical assistance are often provided. Capacity building, however, can be "supply driven" (by the center) or "demand driven" (by local governments). In addition, training can be "classroom based" or "on the job." Many developing countries continue to focus on traditional supply-driven classroom training. Anecdotal evidence and a growing consensus suggest that "on the job" training specifically demanded by local governments for particular tasks they are currently implementing is a better way of developing and retaining skills. Thus, having a general course at a training institute on property valuation or determining costs to calculate user charges may be less useful than, or should at least be supplemented by, "on the job" training provided as local revenue administration employees are undertaking these functions. Although not strictly a local revenue issue, how capacity building is handled may well affect the ability of local revenue administrators to perform effectively.

POSSIBLE STRATEGIC ROLE FOR ALTERNATIVE MECHANISMS

Most of the discussion here focuses on the standard mechanisms of fiscal decentralization used in formal intergovernmental systems. In least developed countries with weak local governance traditions, a number of alternative funding mechanisms have been used to improve the climate for general decentralization (Romeo 2003; Smoke 2007). These improvements can be made in ways that promote responsible fiscal behavior and even stimulate local revenue generation.

International donors have long supported various special funding mechanisms for local governance, such as community development funds, microproject funds, small-town development funds, and social funds. These initiatives have been taken primarily in least developed countries or in poor areas of better-off developing countries. Typically, the resources (which may be on or off budget) finance local development projects identified through dedicated planning, budgeting, financial management, and participatory processes. If local governments are new, or not yet operational, these processes can pilot mechanisms that support the development of formal local government procedures. If local governments exist but are weakly accountable, temporary separation of these processes from regular planning and budgeting can partially insulate them from common local government financial problems, such as resource leakages or disbursement delays. These mechanisms can help to build local governance and technical capacity, although they often ignore how to deal with recurrent revenues for operating and maintaining the facilities they finance. They can also become counterproductive if they are not eventually integrated into formal local government systems.[10]

Perhaps most directly relevant for present purposes is the Local Development Fund, or LDF (UNCDF 1999, 2006). It differs from the other funds noted above in two key respects. First, it provides local governments not with project-specific funding, but with a block of funds that function like an unconditional

---

10. This point is particularly true for social funds, which often provide resources to local NGOs and community-based organizations as well as local governments. Formal links to local government can be planned, and these mechanisms can enhance local capacity and governance where democratic decentralization has not been formally adopted. See Romeo (2003) and Tendler (2000) for a discussion of social funds.

transfer, subject only to procedural and legal controls. A participatory resource programming process requires local prioritization of activities within a resource envelope—the essence of true planning and budgeting—rather than developing a list of projects that local governments apply for without guaranteed funding. Second, LDF funds can be partially used for recurrent expenditures, and they often include requirements or incentives for local governments to generate their own revenues. This approach can begin to create in the minds of citizens a linkage between paying for and benefiting from collective services and a culture of civic engagement.

Strategically Bridging the Technical and Political Aspects of Local Revenue Generation

All local revenue reforms in developing countries bridge technical and political matters to some degree. There is often a strategic element as well. Many technical aspects of reform discussed earlier, such as simpler and more transparent property valuation, incrementally raising assessment ratios or user charges, or convenience-enhancing payment mechanisms, are a strategic response to political constraints on revenue compliance, even if they are not framed in this way. Most of these reforms, however, involve procedural changes, falling short in building a stronger direct connection between local governments and the citizens who are expected to pay local revenues. Most of them are also partial and ad hoc, focusing on a single problematic aspect of the local revenue system that may not be sustainably fixable without attention to other matters.

Sometimes a more limited approach is the best that can be done given political realities, and it is often, but not always, better than nothing. Given the common and pervasive weaknesses in local revenue performance, however, it is worth thinking more broadly and carefully about how to approach reform. Although there are no "best practice" cases to draw upon, there are elements of "potentially better approaches" embedded in some cases, examples of which appear throughout this chapter. It is also useful to think about how national and local governments in a particular country have collectively attempted to improve local revenues. The cases of Kenya and Cambodia are instructive.

CENTRAL COORDINATION AND LOCAL CONSULTATION: IMPROVING LOCAL GOVERNMENT REVENUES IN KENYA

Although local government performance has long been dismal and token reforms have been common (Smoke 1993, 1994), recent developments have pushed Kenya to more serious action (Smoke 2003b; Steffensen, Naitore, and Tideman 2004). Intergovernmental fiscal reforms began in the late 1990s through a joint Ministry of Finance (MOF) and Ministry of Local Government (MLG) effort. Evolving political pressures provided an opening. Improved cooperation between these two key central agencies was facilitated by a change in senior MOF leadership and the (only partly intentional) deployment of motivated, well-placed technical staff and advisors in both agencies.

A key early step was the nearly simultaneous abolition of the problematic local authority service charge (LASC) and institution of the local authority transfer fund (LATF) to replace lost LASC revenues. The LASC was essentially a revamped version of the graduated personal tax, the poorly structured and contentious revenue source noted earlier in reference to Uganda. The LASC demise was generally welcomed, and its replacement by a transfer did not much affect local revenue autonomy because the LASC structure and rates were nationally regulated. The LATF involved several improvements in the Kenyan context. In addition to setting aside a share of the national income tax for local governments, a special treasury account was created to protect LATF funds, a broad-based advisory committee including nongovernmental actors was formed to manage the transfers, and clear fund disbursement rules were issued and generally enforced.

Perhaps the greatest LATF innovation is linking it to adoption of broader reforms being promoted through a larger local government reform program outlined below. Although LATF is allocated through an objective, transparent formula, portions of these allocations can be withheld if local governments do not meet specific reform program conditions, such as adopting streamlined budgeting guidelines. Some have criticized this program as an infringement on local autonomy. Others see it as strategic. Proponents of this latter view do not believe that the central government should control how legally empowered local governments spend their resources (beyond legitimate use of conditional transfers for national priorities). Instead, they argue that it is reasonable in developing country environments for the center to require local governments to adopt basic procedures and processes that help improve transparency and accountability, especially where local accountability mechanisms taken for granted in the West often do not exist and civil society is relatively weak.

The MOF/MLG alliance has also been promoting local revenue improvements and better financial management. The above-noted harmonization of central and local business licenses through the single-business permit provided a productive local revenue with some discretion in setting rates and guidelines to reduce erratic treatment of businesses within and across jurisdictions. More attention is now being given to poorly administered property rates, which have great unmet potential. The Rates Administration Management System, which initially involves updating fiscal cadastres and adopting appropriately simple computer-assisted mass appraisal systems, is being piloted, and the Integrated Financial Management System is being developed to enhance procedures and incentives for recurrent and capital budgeting, cash-flow management, and financial control. There are some broadly strategic aspects to Kenya's reforms. The finance elements outlined above have been reasonably well conceived and coordinated. They are embedded in a broader set of reforms promoted by the Kenya Local Government

Reform Program (KLGRP), which pilots local fiscal and institutional structures as well as efforts to build local accountability and capacity. The KLGRP involves an element of negotiation regarding specific reforms participating local governments will undertake in a given year; thus, they can be held responsible to the terms of their agreement. At the same time, certain procedural reforms are expected of all local governments. The funds provided through the LATF, for example, must be programmed through a Local Authority Service Delivery Action Plan, which requires citizen participation and other formalized procedures. Technical assistance and capacity building are targeted to specific tasks at hand, rather than relying fully on the traditional system of standardized classroom learning at the Government Training Institute. Many participating councils have improved services and revenue generation. The quality and effects of participation have not yet been well evaluated, but this effort is the first documented attempt in Kenya to link governance mechanisms to local government finance reforms (Republic of Kenya 2005).

At the local level, only limited study of revenue performance has been conducted. Elite capture has long been a problem in Kenya, but the return to a multiparty system and growing pressures from dissatisfied businesses and citizens seem to be slowly improving accountability in some places. Documented experiences of citizen input into local fiscal decisions include local government negotiations with chambers of commerce and civil society groups, such as market merchant associations and NGOs, over increases in property taxes, market fees, or user charges, usually in connection with promised road maintenance, market improvements, or other service enhancements. Such practices are a step toward including governance in local revenue development processes. Another promising sign is increasing activity of the Association of Local Government Authorities of Kenya in advocating for citizen participation, providing training for such participation in local government decision-making processes, and supporting neighborhood and resident associations.[11]

Kenya is no model of good intergovernmental fiscal performance, either generally or with respect to local revenue generation, and it is also not known for being strong on local governance. Many problems remain in the overall public fiscal system: a stark bifurcation between a deconcentrated provincial administration system connected to the national budget and the semiautonomous local government system, generally poor linkages between planning and budgeting, and budget execution weaknesses, among others. After decades of inaction or blockage, however, central and local governments are taking limited steps to make the system work better. Some of these efforts have potential broader relevance for other countries with elements of a local government system already in place.

---

11. More information on these activities can be found at www.algak.net.

STRATEGIC GRADUALISM: CREATING A LOCAL REVENUE SYSTEM IN CAMBODIA

Cambodia's deconcentrated administrative system fell into disrepair during decades of postcolonial civil war and turmoil.[12] A peace accord in 1991 ended major hostilities, and elections for a new national government were held in 1993. The groundwork for the local government system was laid by donor experiments. A postconflict resettlement, reconciliation, and service delivery program initially funded by the United Nations was transformed into a local institution-building and governance program in the late 1990s. This process of transformation was facilitated by piloting the adoption of the LDF model described above, which set up basic institutional structures and procedures to plan, finance, and deliver simple local services. Based on the success of this experience, the country began a formal, modest process of decentralization to elected governments at the commune (subdistrict) level in 2002.

The early focus of decentralization in Cambodia was on building political credibility and basic technical capacity, so it was not particularly driven by the conventional principles of fiscal decentralization. No major functions or revenues have been devolved, and local governments rely almost exclusively on intergovernmental transfers. The transfers, however, are structured such that local citizens participate in deciding how to use them and must make a contribution toward activities financed by them. This process familiarizes residents with the concept of paying for services they want and forces them to think about how to raise funds from the community.

With a basic system in place, policy discussions have turned to formal functional and revenue assignment. On the revenue side, four possibilities are being explored. First, certain provincial revenues are being considered for reassignment or sharing with communes, including business licenses and market fees. Second, commune authority to impose user charges for services they deliver is likely to be formalized. Third, transforming the local contributions made by commune residents to partially fund former LDF-financed infrastructure projects into a betterment levy is under consideration. Finally, discussions are beginning on designing a property-based tax to the communes. A process for considering these proposals is currently being developed.

Property taxation has particularly significant revenue potential and involves key political dimensions. Initial reform proposals also include interesting strategic elements. The 2001 decentralization law assigns the property tax to communes, but discussions on implementation have moved slowly, for at least two reasons. First, property-related data are limited. Land registration is problematic, with many competing claims, inconsistent cadastral maps in the few areas

12. This section is drawn from the limited available literature on decentralization in Cambodia, including Blunt and Turner (2005), Smoke (2006b), Smoke and Taliercio (2007), Turner (2002), and World Bank (2003), and the author's personal experience there since 1995.

where they exist, and no generally functioning ownership dispute adjudication system. Property sales information is considered unreliable, including the data used for a provincial land transfer tax. Progress in dealing with these problems has been minimal.

Second, despite the legal mandate, the property tax is politically contentious. Senior politicians, including the prime minister, have publicly attacked it. This reaction results in part from the typical political reluctance to tax constituents, but there is a historical dimension as well. Citizens in rural areas associate property taxation with a reviled agricultural tax imposed during the Vietnamese occupation that followed the removal of the Khmer Rouge regime. Perhaps more important is that many citizens were getting no public services until recently and would surely not associate payments to local administrations with benefits. The emerging commune governments are gradually changing this situation, but expenditures remain small and centrally financed. Improvements to date have by no means eliminated opposition from politicians and bureaucrats to adopting a property tax, particularly as the country enters a new electoral cycle.

Two recent developments suggest that property taxation may get back on the agenda after commune elections in 2007 and national elections in 2008. First, the commune governments are increasingly strapped for recurrent revenues. Second, the central government is under growing pressure to ensure that the nascent local governments have enough resources to deliver basic services. Some recent tentative research on commune revenue options suggests the high revenue productivity of even a very low property-based tax relative to current commune revenues. The once recalcitrant tax department in the Ministry of Economy and Finance seems willing to consider property taxation as part of the national Public Financial Management Reform Program, and some local government officials are increasingly open to the idea.

At the same time, given all of the constraints, it seems unlikely that a "typical" property tax is feasible in the near future, even in urban areas. The modest proposal on the table—intended to ease political concerns and take account of the weak state of information and administrative capacity—is to frame a new property-related revenue source in a simple way as a general user charge. If local governments can charge for a specific service, they would be encouraged to do so, but there would also be a commune service levy (CSL) introduced as a general source of revenue. The CSL is proposed to be based on a few very simple characteristics of land and property, with appropriate variations, for example, between urban and rural areas.

A number of proposed features of the CSL are intended to deal with specific constraints. First, its proceeds could be dedicated to functions prioritized in participatory planning and budgeting exercises, likely reducing public opposition. Second, steps could be taken to alleviate onerous administrative challenges. Commune councils could assist with land dispute adjudication; in the absence of another credible mechanism, some have already assumed this function, and the central government seems to accept their decisions. In addition, self-declaration of the land and property characteristics on which the CSL would be based could help to surmount massive data deficiencies. Communes are small so that it would be difficult to dramatically misreport data. In some areas with more advanced civil society development, emerging citizen watchdog groups could play a role and serve as a model for other areas. The Ministry of Lands is piloting a GIS-based land information and registration system that is operational in about 40 of the 1,621 communes. Locally self-reported data could feed into and be checked against this system.

Progress in adopting these proposals to date has been limited, but policy discussions have raised awareness about options and generated some enthusiasm for reform. The need to enhance local revenues will only continue to grow. Details clearly need to be worked out, but momentum is gathering to pilot a simple, politically sensitive system that could lay the foundation for developing a true property tax in the future. This specific aspect of reform—as well as the general approach that Cambodia has taken to decentralization and local fiscal reform, which includes a number of strategic elements—is likely to facilitate moving to the next level in local revenue development. It could also provide useful ideas for developing local revenues in poor, weakly capacitated countries or in underdeveloped areas of other developing countries.

Is a Broader Approach to Revenue Reform Really Possible?

Local government revenues are considered to be a core requirement of fiscal decentralization. Successful local revenue generation, however, has been elusive. Unexceptional performance seems to be the norm in developing countries. Considerable attention has been paid to this problem, but much of it has been directed toward the development of policies, structures, and procedures that are primarily intended to meet normative technical standards of revenue design and administration. The politics of local revenue generation have received considerably less attention, even though they are probably the most fundamental determinant of good performance. Enough is known from empirical research and the casual observations of those engaged in the field to be sure that politics and governance matter. Less is known about exactly how they matter and how to take them into account in an operationally productive way in general and under particular circumstances. In addition, although there are often tactical aspects of revenue design and attention is typically given to capacity building, the implementation of local revenue reform has not been given the degree of deliberate, integrative, and strategic consideration that it merits.

At some level, it is legitimate for fiscal experts to focus on technical aspects of revenue system design and leave the politics and implementation to others. Such experts have particular training, which influences how they think about local revenue generation, what their specific interests are, and what they feel they have to contribute. In addition, those working on local revenue policy have often been hired for specific tasks by a government or donor agency. Even academics may have access to relevant data and policy makers only through a contract to provide specific policy advice. It is also important to recognize that the influence of outsiders on some constraints is invariably limited. Analysts can inform policy debate, but they rarely have much direct influence over political and bureaucratic behavior in the design and implementation of local revenues at either the national or the local level. Still, these challenges and limitations do not excuse ignoring factors that commonly prevent the potential benefits of technically well-conceived reforms from being realized.

A few general recommendations can be suggested. First, the design of local revenue systems should specifically pay attention to mechanisms for connecting with taxpayers. A great deal of knowledge and experience on citizen participation and local governance are available to draw on, but very little of it focuses on revenue generation. Second, greater effort can be made to consider how to implement local revenue reforms more strategically in the context of the larger decentralization and public-sector reform agenda. Some possible tactics were suggested above, but this topic merits much more careful and systematic consideration. Third, more formal research on the political and strategic aspects of local revenue reform is clearly needed. Such work could push our understanding of local revenue generation to a new level and have great relevance for the future design and implementation of local revenue systems in developing countries.

REFERENCES

Addison, T., and J. Levin. 2006. *Tax policy reform in developing countries.* Copenhagen: Ministry of Foreign Affairs.

Ahmad, E., and V. Tanzi. 2002. *Managing fiscal decentralization.* Oxford: Routledge.

Alm, J., J. Martinez-Vazquez, and S. M. Indrawati. 2004. *Reforming intergovernmental fiscal relations and the rebuilding of Indonesia.* Cheltenham, UK: Edward Elgar.

Bahl, R. 1979. *Taxation of urban property in less-developed countries.* Madison: University of Wisconsin Press.

———. 2000a. How to design a fiscal decentralization program. In *Local dynamics in an era of globalization,* S. Yusuf, W. Wu, and S. Evenett, eds., 94–100. Oxford: Oxford University Press.

———. 2000b. *Intergovernmental fiscal transfers in developing countries: Principles and practice.* Urban and Local Government Background Paper 2. Washington, DC: World Bank.

Bahl, R., and J. Linn. 1992. *Urban public finance in developing countries.* Oxford: Oxford University Press.

Bahl, R., and J. Martinez-Vazquez. 2006. Sequencing fiscal decentralization. Policy Research Working Paper 3914. Washington, DC: World Bank.

Bahl, R., J. Martinez-Vazquez, and J. Youngman, eds. 2008. *Making the property tax work: Experiences in developing and transitional countries.* Cambridge, MA: Lincoln Institute of Land Policy.

Bahl, R., and P. Smoke, eds. 2003. *Restructuring local government finance in developing countries: Lessons from South Africa.* Cheltenham, UK: Edward Elgar.

Bahl, R., and D. Solomon. 2003. The regional services council levy. In *Restructuring local government finance in developing countries: Lessons from South Africa*, R. Bahl and P. Smoke, eds., 127–172. Cheltenham, UK: Edward Elgar.

Bardhan, P., and D. Mookherjee, eds. 2006. *Decentralization and local governance in developing countries: A comparative perspective*. Cambridge, MA: MIT Press.

Bird, R. M. 1999. *Rethinking tax assignment: The need for better subnational taxes*. Washington, DC: World Bank.

———. 2000. *User charges in local government finance*. Washington, DC: World Bank Institute.

———. 2001. *Subnational revenues: Realities and prospects*. Washington, DC: Fiscal Policy Training Program, World Bank Institute.

———. 2005. A new look at local business taxes. *State Tax Notes* 36(9):685–698.

Bird, R. M., and E. Slack. 2006. The role of the property tax in financing rural local governments in developing countries. International Tax Program Paper 0608. Joseph L. Rotman School of Management, University of Toronto.

Bird, R. M., and M. Smart. 2002. Intergovernmental fiscal transfers: International lessons for developing countries. *World Development* 30(6):899–912.

Bird, R. M., and T. Tsiopoulos. 1997. User charges for public services: Potentials and problems. *Canadian Tax Journal* 45(1):25–86.

Bird, R. M., and F. Vaillancourt, eds. 1998. *Fiscal decentralization in developing countries*. Cambridge: Cambridge University Press.

Bird, R. M., and S. Wallace. 2003. Is it really so hard to tax the hard-to-tax? The context and role of presumptive taxes. International Tax Program Paper 0307. Joseph L. Rotman School of Management, University of Toronto.

Blair, H. 2000. Participation and power at the periphery: Democratic local governance in six countries. *World Development* 28(1):21–39.

———. 2006. Innovations in participatory local governance. Paper prepared for the 2007 World Public Sector Report. New York: United Nations Department for Economic and Social Development.

Blunt, P., and M. Turner. 2005. Decentralization, democracy, and development in a postconflict society: Commune councils in Cambodia. *Public Administration and Development* 25(1):77–85.

Bräutigam, D. 2008. Taxation and state building in developing countries. In *Capacity and consent: Taxation and state building in developing countries*, D. Bräutigam, O-H. Fjeldstad, and M. Moore, eds., 1–33. Cambridge: Cambridge University Press.

Burki, S. J., G. Perry, and W. Dillinger. 1999. *Beyond the center: Decentralizing the state*. Washington, DC: World Bank.

Cheema, G. S., and D. Rondinelli, eds. 2007. *Decentralized governance: Emerging concepts and practices*. Washington, DC: Brookings Institution.

Cohen, J. M., and S. Peterson. 1999. *Administrative decentralization in developing countries*. Boulder, CO: Lynne Reinner Publishing.

Commins, S. 2006. Community participation in service delivery and public accountability: Advancing the MDGs. Paper prepared for the 2007 World Public Sector Report. New York: United Nations Department for Economic and Social Development.

Crane, R. 1994. Water markets, market reform, and the urban poor: Results from Jakarta, Indonesia. *World Development* 22(1):71–83.

Crook, R. 2003. Decentralization and poverty reduction in Africa: The politics of local-central relations. *Public Administration and Development* 23(1):77–88.

de Mello, L. R. 2002. Can fiscal decentralization strengthen social capital? Working Paper 00/129. Washington, DC: International Monetary Fund.

Devas, N., and R. Kelly. 2001. Regulation or revenues: An analysis of local business licenses, with a case study of the single-business permit in Kenya. *Public Administration and Development* 21(5):381–391.

Dillinger, W. 1992. *Urban property tax reform: Guidelines and recommendations.* Washington, DC: World Bank.

Eaton, K. 2002. *Politicians and economic reform in new democracies: Argentina and the Philippines in the 1990s.* University Park: Pennsylvania State University Press.

———. 2004. *Politics beyond the capital: The design of subnational institutions in South America.* Palo Alto, CA: Stanford University Press.

Ebel, R., and R. Taliercio. 2005. Subnational tax policy and administration in developing economies. *Tax Notes International* 37(1):919–936.

Ebel, R., and D. Weist. 2006. *Sequencing subnational revenue decentralization.* Washington, DC: World Bank.

Ebel, R., and S. Yilmaz. 2003. Fiscal decentralization in developing countries: Is it happening? How do we know? In *Public finance in developing and transition countries: Essays in honor of Richard M. Bird,* J. Alm and J. Martinez-Vazquez, eds., 101–120. Cheltenham, UK: Edward Elgar.

Falleti, T. 2005. A sequential theory of decentralization: Latin American cases in comparative perspective. *American Political Science Review* 99(3):327–346.

Fjeldstad, O-H. 2001. Taxation, coercion, and donors: Local government tax enforcement in Tanzania. *Journal of Modern African Studies* 39(2):289–306.

———. 2004. What's trust got to do with it? Non-payment of service charges in local authorities in South Africa. *Journal of Modern African Studies* 42(4):539–562.

———. 2005. Entitlement, affordability, or a matter of trust? Reflections on the non-payment of service charges in local authorities. In *Trust in public institutions in South Africa,* S. Askvik and N. Bak, eds., 85–100. Aldershot, UK: Ashgate.

———. 2006. Corruption in tax administration: Lessons from institutional reforms in Uganda. In *International handbook on the economics of corruption,* S. Rose-Ackerman, ed., 484–511. Cheltenham, UK: Edward Elgar.

Fjeldstad, O-H., and J. Semboja. 2001. Why people pay taxes: The case of the development levy in Tanzania. *World Development* 29(12):2059–2074.

Franzsen, R. 2003. Property taxation within the Southern African development community. Working Paper. Cambridge, MA: Lincoln Institute of Land Policy.

Friere, M., and J. Peterson, eds. 2004. *Subnational capital markets in developing countries: From theory to practice.* Oxford: Oxford University Press.

Green, A. E. 2005. Managing human resources in a decentralized context. In *East Asia decentralizes: Making local government work,* 129–153. Washington, DC: World Bank.

Hoffman, B. D., and C. C. Gibson. 2006. Fiscal governance and public services: Evidence from Tanzania and Zambia. Working Paper. Department of Political Science, University of California San Diego.

Iversen, V., O-H. Fjeldstad, G. Bahiigwa, F. Ellis, and R. James. 2006. Private tax collection—remnant of the past or a way forward? Evidence from rural Uganda. *Public Administration and Development* 26(4):317–328.

Juul, K. 2006. Decentralization, local taxation, and citizenship in Senegal. *Development and Change* 37(4):821–846.

Kelly, R. 1993. Implementing property tax reform in developing countries: Lessons from the property tax in Indonesia. *Review of Urban and Regional Development Studies* 4:193–208.

———. 2000. Property taxation in East Africa. Working Paper. Cambridge, MA: Lincoln Institute of Land Policy.

———. 2003. Property taxation in Indonesia: Challenges from decentralization. Working Paper. Cambridge, MA: Lincoln Institute of Land Policy.

Kjaer, A. M. 2004. Institutional history or quid-pro-quo? Exploring revenue collection in two Ugandan districts. Paper presented at the American Political Science Association Annual Meeting, Chicago, August 2–5.

———. 2005. Accountability and the graduated tax in Uganda. Paper prepared for Second Meeting on Fiscal Decentralization. Copenhagen: Kommunernes Landsforening.

Lewis, B. 2003a. Property tax in Indonesia: Measuring and explaining administrative (under-) performance. *Public Administration and Development* 23(2):227–239.

———. 2003b. Tax and charge creation by regional governments under fiscal decentralization: Estimates and explanations. *Bulletin of Indonesian Economic Studies* 39(2):177–192.

———. 2005. Indonesian local government spending, taxing and saving: An explanation of pre- and post-decentralization fiscal outcomes. *Asian Economic Journal* 19(3):291–317.

———. 2006. Local government: An analysis of administrative cost inefficiency. *Bulletin of Indonesian Economic Studies* 42(2):213–233.

Litvack, J., J. Ahmad, and R. Bird. 1998. *Rethinking decentralization in developing countries*. Washington, DC: World Bank.

Manor, J. 1998. *The political economy of democratic decentralization*. Washington, DC: World Bank.

———. 2004. User committees: A potentially damaging second wave of decentralization? *European Journal of Development Research* 16(1):192–213.

———. 2007. Strategies to promote effective participation. Paper prepared for the 2007 World Public Sector Report. New York: United Nations Department for Economic and Social Development.

Martinez-Vazquez, J., and R. M. McNab. 2006. The interaction of fiscal decentralization and democratic governance. In *Decentralization in Asia and Latin America: Towards a comparative interdisciplinary perspective*, P. Smoke, E. J. Gomez, and G. E. Peterson, eds., 15–40. Cheltenham, UK: Edward Elgar.

McClure, C. E., and J. Martinez-Vasquez. 2000. *The assignment of revenues and expenditures in intergovernmental fiscal relations*. Washington, DC: World Bank.

Mikesell, J. L. 2002. *International experience with administration of local taxes: A review of practices and issues*. Washington, DC: World Bank.

———. 2007. Developing options for the administration of local taxes: An international review. *Public Budgeting and Finance* 27(1):41–68.

Moore, M. 2004. Revenues, state formation, and the quality of governance in developing countries. *International Political Science Review* 25(3):297–319.

———. 2007. How does taxation affect the quality of governance? *Tax Notes International* 47(1):79–98.

Oates, W. 1972. *Fiscal federalism*. New York: Harcourt Brace Jovanovich.

———. 1999. An essay on fiscal federalism. *Journal of Economic Literature* 37:1120–1149.

———, ed. 2001. *Property taxation and local government finance*. Cambridge, MA: Lincoln Institute of Land Policy.

———. 2005. Towards a second-generation theory of fiscal federalism. *International Tax and Public Finance* 12(4):349–373.

Olowu, D. 2003. Local institutional and political structures and processes: Recent experience in Africa. *Public Administration and Development* 23(1):41–52.

Peterson, G. 2000. Building local credit institutions. Urban and Local Government Background Paper 3. Washington, DC: World Bank.

Platteau, J-P. 2006. Pitfalls of participatory development. Paper prepared for the 2007 World Public Sector Report. New York: United Nations Department for Economic and Social Development.

Prud'homme, R. 1992. Informal local taxation in developing countries. *Government and Policy* 10:1–17.

———. 1995. The dangers of decentralization. *World Bank Research Observer* 10(2):201–220.

———. 2003. Fiscal decentralization in Africa: A framework for considering reform. *Public Administration and Development* 23(1):17–27.

Reinikka, R., and J. Svensson. 2004. Local capture: Evidence from a central government transfer program in Uganda. *Quarterly Journal of Economics* 119(2):679–705.

Republic of Kenya. 2005. *Guidelines for the preparation, implementation and monitoring of local authority service delivery action plan (LASDAP)*. Nairobi: Ministry of Local Government.

Ribot, J. 2004. *Waiting for democracy: The politics of choice in natural resource decentralization*. Washington, DC: World Resources Institute.

Ribot, J., and A. Larson, eds. 2005. *Democratic decentralization through a natural resource lens*. Oxford: Routledge.

Rodden, J. A., G. S. Eskeland, and J. Litvack, eds. 2003. *Fiscal decentralization and the challenge of hard budget constraint*. Cambridge, MA: MIT Press.

Romeo, L. 2003. The role of external assistance in supporting decentralization reform. *Public Administration and Development* 23(1):89–96.

Rosengard, J. K. 1998. *Property tax reform in developing countries*. Boston: Kluwer Academic Publishers.

Sabates, R., and A. Schneider. 2003. Taxation perspectives: A democratic approach to public finance in developing countries. Seminar Report. Brighton, UK: Institute of Development Studies, University of Sussex.

Schneider, A. 1999. Participatory governance for poverty reduction. *Journal of International Development* 11(4):521–534.

———. 2003. Who gets what from whom? The impact of decentralization on tax capacity and pro-poor policy. Discussion Paper. Institute of Development Studies, University of Sussex, Brighton, UK.

Schneider, A., and M. Baquero. 2006. Get what you want, give what you can: Embedded public finance in Porto Alegre. Working Paper. Institute of Development Studies, University of Sussex, Brighton, UK.

Schroeder, L., and P. Smoke. 2003. Intergovernmental transfers in developing countries: Concepts, international practices, and policy issues. In *Intergovernmental transfers in Asia: Current practice and challenges for the future*, Y-H. Kim and P. Smoke, eds., 20–59. Manila: Asian Development Bank.

Shah, A. 1994. The reform of intergovernmental fiscal relations in developing and emerging market economies. Policy Research Working Paper 23. Washington, DC: World Bank.

———. 2004. Fiscal decentralization in developing and transition economies: Progress, problems, and the promise. Policy Research Working Paper 3282. Washington, DC: World Bank.

———. 2006a. A practitioner's guide to intergovernmental fiscal transfers. Policy Research Working Paper 4039. Washington, DC: World Bank.

———. 2006b. Corruption and decentralized public governance. Policy Research Work Paper 3824. Washington, DC: World Bank.

Shah, A., and T. Thompson. 2004. Implementing decentralized local governance: A treacherous road with potholes, detours, and road closures. Policy Research Working Paper 3353. Washington, DC: World Bank.

Smoke, P. 1993. Local government fiscal reform in developing countries: Lessons from Kenya. *World Development* 21(6):901–923.

———. 1994. *Local government finance in developing countries: The case of Kenya.* Oxford: Oxford University Press.

———. 2000. Strategic fiscal decentralization in developing countries: Learning from recent innovations. In *Local dynamics in an era of globalization*, S. Yusuf, W. Wu, and S. Evenett, eds., 101–109. Oxford: Oxford University Press.

———. 2001. *Fiscal decentralization in developing countries: A review of current concepts and practice.* Geneva: United Nations Research Institute for Social Development.

———. 2002. Fiscal decentralization in East and Southern Africa: A selective review of experience and thoughts on moving forward. Prepared for IMF Conference on Fiscal Decentralization. Washington, DC: International Monetary Fund.

———. 2003a. Decentralization in Africa: Goals, dimensions, myths, and challenges. *Public Administration and Development* 23(1):1–17.

———. 2003b. Erosion and reform from the center in Kenya. In *Local governance in Africa: The challenge of decentralization*, J. Wunsch and D. Olowu, eds., 211–230. Boulder, CO: Lynne Reinner Publishers.

———. 2004. Expenditure assignment under Indonesia's decentralization: A review of progress and issues for the future. In *Reforming intergovernmental fiscal relations and the rebuilding of Indonesia*, J. Alm, J. Martinez-Vazquez, and S. M. Indrawati, eds., 77–100. Cheltenham, UK: Edward Elgar.

———. 2006a. Fiscal decentralization policy in developing countries: Bridging theory and reality. In *Public sector reform in developing countries*, Y. Bangura and G. Larbi, eds., 195–227. London: Palgrave-Macmillan.

———. 2006b. Cambodia's nascent decentralization: From donor experiment to sustainable government system? In *Decentralization in Asia and Latin America: Towards a comparative interdisciplinary perspective*, P. Smoke, E. J. Gomez, and G. E. Peterson, eds., 63–87. Cheltenham, UK: Edward Elgar.

———. 2007. Fiscal decentralization and intergovernmental relations in developing countries: Navigating a viable path to reform. In *Decentralized governance: Emerging concepts and practice*, G. S. Cheema and D. Rondinelli, eds., 131–155. Washington, DC: Brookings Institution.

Smoke, P., E. J. Gomez, and G. E. Peterson, eds. 2006. *Decentralization in Asia and Latin America: Towards a comparative interdisciplinary perspective*. Cheltenham, UK: Edward Elgar.

Smoke, P., and B. Lewis. 1996. Fiscal decentralization in Indonesia: A new approach to an old idea. *World Development* 24(8):1281–1299.

Smoke, P., and R. Taliercio. 2007. Aid, public finance, and accountability: Cambodian dilemmas. In *Peace and the public purse: Economic policies for postwar state-building*, J. Boyce and M. O'Donnell, eds., 55–84. Boulder, CO: Lynne Reinner Publishers.

Steffensen, J., H. Naitore, and P. Tideman. 2004. *A comparative analysis of decentralization in Kenya, Tanzania and Uganda. Report to the World Bank*. Copenhagen: Nordic Consulting Group.

Taliercio, R. 2004. Administrative reform as credible commitment: The impact of revenue autonomy on revenue authority performance in Latin America. *World Development* 32(2):213–232.

———. 2005. Subnational own-source revenue: Getting policy and administration right. In *East Asia decentralizes: Making local governments work*, 107–128. Washington, DC: World Bank.

Tanzi, V. 1996. Fiscal federalism and decentralization: A review of some efficiency and macroeconomic aspects. *Proceedings of the 1995 Annual World Bank Conference on Development Economics*, 295–316. Washington, DC: World Bank.

———. 2001. Pitfalls on the road to fiscal decentralization. Global Policy Program Working Paper 19. Washington, DC: Carnegie Endowment for International Peace.

Tendler, J. 1997. *Good government in the tropics*. Baltimore: Johns Hopkins University Press.

———. 2000. Why are social funds so popular? In *Local dynamics in an era of globalization*, S. Yusuf, W. Wu, and S. Evenett, eds., 114–129. Oxford: Oxford University Press.

Ter-Minassian, T., ed. 1997. *Fiscal federalism in theory and practice*. Washington, DC: International Monetary Fund.

Therkildsen, O. 2001. Understanding taxation in poor African countries: A critical review of selected perspectives. *Forum for Development Studies* 28:99–123.

Turner, M. 2002. Whatever happened to deconcentration? Recent initiatives in Cambodia. *Public Administration and Development* 22(3):353–364.

UNCDF. *See* United Nations Capital Development Fund.

UNDESA. *See* United Nations Department for Economic and Social Affairs.

UNDP. *See* United Nations Development Program.

United Nations Capital Development Fund. 1999. *Taking risks*. New York: UNCDF.

———. 2006. *Delivering the goods: Building local government capacity to achieve the Millennium Development Goals*. New York: UNCDF.

United Nations Department for Economic and Social Affairs. 2005a. *Decentralized governance*. New York: UNDESA.

———. 2005b. *Participatory planning and budgeting at the subnational level*. New York: UNDESA.

United Nations Development Program. 2000. *The impact of participation in local governance: A synthesis of nine case studies*. New York: UNDP.

———. 2004. *Decentralized governance for development: A combined practice note on decentralization, local governance, and urban/rural development*. New York: UNDP.

United States Agency for International Development. 2000. *Decentralization and democratic local governance handbook*. Washington, DC: USAID.

USAID. *See* United States Agency for International Development.

Weingast, B. R. 2006. Second generation fiscal federalism: Implications for decentralized democratic governance and economic development. Background Paper for the Decentralization and Democratic Local Governance Handbook. Washington, DC: United States Agency for International Development.

Whittington, D. 1991. A study of water vending and willingness to pay for water in Nigeria. *World Development* 19(2):179–198.

Willis, E., S. Haggard, and C. Garman. 1999. The politics of decentralization in Latin America. *Latin American Research Review* 34(1):7–56.

World Bank. 2000. *World Development Report: Entering the 21st century*. Washington, DC: World Bank.

———. 2001. *Decentralization in the transition economies: Challenges and the road ahead*. Poverty Reduction and Economic Management Paper. Washington, DC: World Bank.

———. 2003. *Integrated fiduciary assessment and public expenditure review for Cambodia*. Washington, DC: World Bank.

———. 2004. *World development report: Making services work for the poor*. Washington, DC: World Bank.

———. 2005. *East Asia decentralizes: Making local government work*. Washington, DC: World Bank.

Wunsch, J., and D. Olowu. 1990. *The failure of the centralized state: Institutions and self-governance in Africa*. Boulder, CO: Westview Press.

———, eds. 2003. *Local governance in Africa: The challenge of decentralization*. Boulder, CO: Lynne Reinner Publishers.

COMMENTARY
Robert D. Ebel

To expand on themes that are developed in Paul Smoke's thoughtful and well-documented treatment of the topic of local revenue and fiscal decentralization in developing countries, several points can be made. First, local tax policy not only matters, but, indeed, goes to the essence of decentralization. Second, although the limitations of a "narrow" approach are present in much of the literature and practice, this approach clarifies some important similarities between the conventional "Western" economics and the economics of the developing world. Third, a convergence of conceptual knowledge and practice has led to several cases in which the "broader" framework Smoke calls for has met with success. Finally, as a system of governance characterized by self-determination and devolution of power, the payoff for getting decentralization "right" can be high in terms of improving the human condition.

Why Revenue Policy Matters

The importance of tax policy in decentralization is grounded in the theorem that the set of governments closest to the citizenry can adjust budgets in a manner that best leads to the delivery of a set of public services that reflect local, community preferences (Oates 1972). Improving efficiency is the focus. Once the public sector intervenes, the efficiency logic implies some form of fiscal decentralization. The argument is that because of spatial considerations, local governments are best situated to establish budgets that match the benefits and costs of local goods and services (in technical jargon, the "matching" or "benefits" principle). To satisfy those conditions, the local collective decision makers (e.g., citizens acting through their governments) must be allowed to exercise own-source taxation and be in a position to do so. This requirement is the essence of fiscal decentralization.

The Basic Framework

Smoke rightfully stresses the dissimilarities across countries, such as differing economic and demographic structures, institutions, cultures, and traditions; geography; and access to technology and information. These differences do matter, but so do the similarities. Key among them are the fundamentals of the open economy that a subnational (e.g., local) jurisdiction cannot effectively restrict the flow of goods and services across its borders by erecting barriers such as tariffs, quotas, and import licenses, nor can it control cross-border movements of capital and labor. There are also political similarities, including the reaction "from below" to extensive central control and the fiscal expediency of the soft-budget constraint whereby central governments ease their own strained finances by shifting responsibilities "downward." Such governments then seek to negotiate some level of central-to-local intergovernmental transfer to avoid the short-term local fiscal imbalance and dependence on the center (Kornai 1992).

Need for a Broader Model

The "localization" revolution that has come to characterize the twenty-first century is defined by the way countries respond to the converging forces of diversity and similarity (World Bank 2000). In developing an intergovernmental system, some countries have done well, others badly. What has led to getting it "right" is, as Smoke points out, the development of a more extensive model than the "narrow and technical framework." This broader model is apparent in the experience of many "transition" countries of Central and Eastern Europe as they have moved from a system of Soviet-style centralization through a sorting out of spending responsibilities and revenue roles among types of governments. The traditional analysis of decentralization examines the fiscal functions of subnational and central governments in terms of their respective (and largely separate) roles in allocation, distribution, and stabilization (Musgrave 1983). The successful, postsocialist model has been broadened to include the reform of public-sector pricing, the privatization of state-owned assets, and a role for local governments in providing important parts of the safety net such as family assistance, social welfare, and, in some cases, pensions and employment. In some countries, decentralization has become a strategy for nation building (Bird, Ebel, and Wallich 1995; Pallai 2003).

Another important development has been the willingness of policy makers and practitioners to draw on the experience of developed countries in adopting (as Smoke discusses) a system of asymmetrical decentralization whereby the features that make a nation diverse are treated differently. The growing list of successful systems—Belgium, Bosnia-Herzegovina, Canada, China, Germany, India, Indonesia, the Philippines, Spain, Switzerland, and, if it can hold on, Sudan—attests to the potential of an asymmetrical approach (Bird and Ebel 2007).

Does Revenue Decentralization "Work"?

A growing body of empirical evidence suggests that there is a high payoff for a reform program that includes a focus on the importance of revenue autonomy. For example:

- Developed countries are associated with mature systems of decentralization and varying degrees of fiscal autonomy (Akai and Sakata 2003). Conversely, the dismal macroeconomic record of central command and control under communist regimes has been well documented (Bird and Banta 2000; Dunn and Wetzel 2002).

- It is expected that if decentralization enhances efficiency, it should be associated with economic growth. Indeed, evidence suggests that this relationship does exist with respect to revenue decentralization. Martinez-Vazquez and McNab (1997) reach this conclusion with respect to per capita income. By defining the decentralization variable both restrictively and broadly in terms of revenues (broad includes unrestricted grants), Ebel and Yilmaz (2003) reach a similar conclusion with respect to per capita output. A similar finding is reported in Meloche, Vaillancourt, and Yilmaz (2004), who conclude that decentralization of expenditures, combined with centrally controlled revenues, is an obstruction to growth.
- On the matter of macrostability, there is econometric evidence for the Central European model that subnational revenue autonomy improves the fiscal position of subnational governments, but that a reliance on central-to-local transfers may worsen that fiscal position (Ebel and Yilmaz 2003).

Smoke is correct that there needs to be rethinking of decentralization approaches for developing countries. He is also correct to take the next step and stress the importance of building capacity, not only human capacity, but also institutional and organizational capacity. That said, reform in developing countries will take time. To paraphrase Kornai (1992), change in governance is not only a change in systems, but a precondition for that change.

REFERENCES

Akai, N., and M. Sakata. 2002. Fiscal decentralization contributes to economic growth: Evidence from state-level cross-section data for the United States. *Journal of Urban Economics* 52(1):93–108.

Bird, R. M., and S. Banta. 2000. Fiscal sustainability and fiscal indicators in transition countries. In *Transition economies and fiscal reforms*, A. Shapleigh, F. Andic, and S. Banta, eds. Washington, DC: United States Agency for International Development.

Bird, R. M., and R. D. Ebel. 2007. *Fiscal fragmentation in decentralized countries: Subsidiarity, solidarity and asymmetry*. Cheltenham, UK: Edward Elgar.

Bird, R. M., R. D. Ebel, and C. Wallich. 1985. *Decentralization of the socialist state*. Washington, DC: World Bank.

Dunn, J., and D. Wetzel. 2000. Fiscal decentralization in former socialist economies: Progress and prospects. *Proceedings of the 92nd Annual Conference on Taxation*, 242–250. Washington, DC: National Tax Association.

Ebel, R. D., and S. Yilmaz. 2003. On the measurement and impact of fiscal decentralization. In *Public finance in developing and transition countries: Essays in honor of Richard M. Bird*, J. Martinez-Vazquez and J. Alm, eds., 101–120. Cheltenham, UK: Edward Elgar.

Kornai, J. 1992. *The socialist system: The political economy of communism*. Princeton, NJ: Princeton University Press.

Martinez-Vazquez, J., and R. McNab. 1997. Tax reform in transition economies: Experience and lessons. International Studies Program Working Paper 97-6. Andrew Young School of Policy Studies, Georgia State University, Atlanta.

Meloche, J-P., F. Vaillancourt, and S. Yilmaz. 2004. Decentralization or fiscal autonomy? What really does matter? World Bank Policy Research Paper 3254. Washington, DC: World Bank.

Oates, W. E. 1972. *Fiscal federalism*. New York: Harcourt Brace Jovanovich.

Pallai, K., ed. 2003. *The Budapest model: A liberal urban policy experiment*. Budapest: Open Society Institute.

World Bank. 2000. *World Development Report: Entering the 21st century*. Washington, DC: World Bank.

4

Local Service Provision in Selected OECD Countries: Do Decentralized Operations Work Better?

Ehtisham Ahmad, Giorgio Brosio, and Vito Tanzi

oes decentralization "improve" local service provision? This policy question is a key one for Organisation for Economic Co-operation and Development (OECD) countries as well as for developing countries. This chapter focuses on the effect of decentralization on service delivery in selected OECD countries. It considers the effectiveness and economic efficiency of decentralization measures, as well as issues of equity, surveys the existing literature, and draws some tentative conclusions from the information available.

Although efficiency in service provision is a focal concern of economists—and citizens—it is not always the main goal of decentralization. In many OECD countries, decentralization arose from political (regional) demands for autonomy, not from efficiency considerations. Citizens may be ready to trade lesser efficiency for government closer to home (as in the case of Belgium or Switzerland).

The empirical literature on efficiency issues focuses more on developing, rather than on OECD, countries. In developing countries decentralization has been encouraged by external donors and international organizations that have an interest in the outcomes, especially in terms of efficiency and, often, equity as well.

Verifying the outcomes and results of policies is a difficult exercise. Only the more advanced OECD countries have moved toward performance budgeting, France being the latest to do so. In the absence of a performance budgeting framework, an approximation may be attempted to evaluate outcomes. Required, however, is a defined, appropriate methodology and supporting information that may not be readily available.

Therefore, it is useful to identify key analytical issues, survey the literature, and examine results critically. Methodological and substantive conclusions may then be drawn that could guide a research agenda in both OECD and developing countries. These conclusions could also be useful to donors and international agencies in designing and evaluating the effectiveness of essential public services at the local level.

Decentralization and Service Delivery

Decentralization may be understood as a process through which the role and importance of the subnational government are expanded. This expansion can take place through three main different processes, which are not necessarily in actual or suggested order of sequence.

POLITICAL DECENTRALIZATION
OECD countries are characterized by democratic institutions at all levels. In this context, political decentralization means devolution of political authority or of electoral capacities to subnational actors. Typical examples are the popular election of governors and mayors[1] (previously appointed by local councils or by central authorities), constitutional reforms that reinforce the political autonomy of subnational governments, and electoral reforms designed to augment political competition at the local levels.

FISCAL DECENTRALIZATION
Fiscal decentralization involves a transfer of expenditure responsibilities to lower-level local governments, financed by a combination of own and other sources of revenues, including transfers. The manner in which responsibilities are assigned—for example, by unfunded mandates or by earmarked or tied transfers—may reduce the "effective autonomy" of the local governments. Similarly, without own-source revenue at the margin, the local governments may lack incentives for proper accountability because they might be able to leverage the federal government or pass on the consequences of their actions to other jurisdictions (see Ahmad and Brosio 2006; Ambrosiano and Bordignon 2006).

REGULATORY DECENTRALIZATION
Regulatory decentralization does not imply an appreciable transfer of financial resources or assignments, although its effect may be considerable for citizens (such as regulation of car emissions). Pure regulatory decentralization is much less frequent than fiscal decentralization. In fact, substantial centralization of

---

1. Popular election of the heads of the executive of all levels of government is considered to be the most important component of the recent decentralization process in Italy because it increased the stability of subnational governments and increased, through expanded political legitimacy of mayors and governors, their bargaining power vis-à-vis the central government.

regulations has taken place, particularly in environmental, health, and even financial policies.

Both fiscal and regulatory decentralization imply transfer of some decision-making power over public (fiscal) or private (regulatory) resources from the central to the subnational governments. Recognition that this shift in decision-making power is essential to decentralization is crucial to identifying and using proper indicators of fiscal decentralization. For example, a simple reassignment of health expenditure from the central to regional budgets does not imply per se an increase in the degree of decentralization if it is not accompanied by the transfer of some decision-making power relating to this expenditure to subnational levels.

If the reassignment is financed by tied transfers, regional budgets would show a higher amount of expenditure, but because regions have to follow centrally set instructions for the use of these resources, no decentralization takes place. Regions act simply as hierarchical subordinated agents of the central government.[2] Conversely, there can be real decentralization even if the share of regional expenditure or revenues does not change, but only if more decision-making power concerning the existing resources is devolved to regions. This situation poses a difficulty for empirical work because the extent to which a spending assignment can be treated as a local responsibility depends on the financing arrangements, in particular whether tied transfers are involved.

DECENTRALIZATION IN OECD COUNTRIES

OECD countries present practically every conceivable model of intergovernmental relations, ranging from highly decentralized federal systems, as in the United States, Canada, and Switzerland, to highly centralized unitary state systems, as in Ireland, Greece, and Portugal, and some of the new European Union (EU) member states, such as Hungary, without traditions of relatively strong subnational governments. Between these polar models are recently created regional systems, as in France, Italy, and Spain, and unitary states with traditions of strong local government, as in the Scandinavian countries.

In recent decades, reflecting increasing democratic trends, most OECD countries have experimented with decentralization reforms, but addressing different motivations (as described below). A few have embarked on ambitious decentralization processes requiring constitutional revisions. Most notable have been the federalization of Belgium and the regionalization of Spain, Italy, France, and the United Kingdom. While Italy is quite decentralized, the Constitutional Reform of 2001 is yet to be fully implemented. Noticeable decentralization reforms have also been introduced in Mexico in the 1990s, although the process there is far from complete.

---

2. Deconcentrated spending assumes that there is full information on subnational operations, without which tied transfers could degenerate into spending others' moneys without adequate supervision.

Decentralization has also taken place in all of the new Eastern European EU member nations. Poland, Slovakia, and the Czech Republic have also introduced a regional level of government. Decentralization initiatives have been more hesitant in Asian OECD countries (Yagi 2004).

A few countries, including Denmark, recentralized their system of territorial government. In Denmark higher education, and hospital management—the chief responsibilities of the counties—have been transferred to newly created regions. The Danish example follows a trend in health care in Scandinavia. Although hospitals have been transferred to new and single-function regional entities, the role of municipalities in primary care has been strengthened (Rico and Léon 2005). See table 4.1 for information on decentralization trends.

The motivation to decentralize often reflects complex and not always transparent political debates. In most cases, decentralization is a long, multistep process, carried out by changing political coalitions, that affects various layers of government differently.

In Italy, for instance, decentralization since 1993 has successively involved (1) the devolution of taxing powers to municipalities and regional governments; (2) the popular election of mayors and of provincial and regional governors; (3) the devolution of important expenditure responsibilities and legislative functions to regional governments; and (4) the elimination of many central government controls on subnational units. These reforms—some of which are constitutional—have been implemented by both center/left and center/right coalitions and have reflected pressures applied by regionally based political movements.

France has taken a similar path. Decentralization reforms there were started in 1982 (during a socialist presidency) with the devolution of functions and the creation, in 1984, of the decentralized public service, the *fonction publique térritoriale*, which administers local functions. The powers of the prefects (appointed by the central government) vis-à-vis subnational governments have shifted from control to support. Since 1986 regional councilors have been popularly elected. Following the 2001 budget reforms that led to the introduction of performance budgeting, the 2003 constitutional reform (sponsored by a center/right government) aimed at increasing the role of subnational governments by introducing the subsidiarity principle, involving both policy and fiscal autonomy (Documentation Française 2007).

Spain has almost completed a transition to a regional or quasi-federal system. The process was set in motion by the 1978 constitution that granted a high level of autonomy to the historical nationalities of Navarra, the Basque region, and Catalonia, while recognizing the right of the other regions to attain a similar level of self-government (Garcia-Milà and McGuire 2002; Moreno 2002). Spanish decentralization has been typically asymmetric, thus providing a good basis for empirical analyses of decentralization's effects. Also in Spain, decentralization has been promoted by both conservative and socialist governments.

One common motivation for decentralization is a central government's desire to share with other levels the rising political costs of governance of complex

Table 4.1

Main Traits of Evolution of Intergovernmental Relations in Selected OECD Countries

Countries	Share of Subnational Spending on General Government Spending, 1985 (%)	Share of Subnational Spending on General Government Spending, 2001 (%)	Main Traits of Intergovernmental Relations	Recent Reforms
Australia	n.a.	43.3	Federal system	Value-added tax administration by center with all revenues distributed to the states
Austria	28.4	28.5	Federal but highly federally regulated system	Constitutional convention recently fostered debate on constitutional reform of intergovernmental relations
Belgium	31.8	34.0	Federalization based on linguistic divides	Transformed from unitary to federal state
Canada	54.5	56.5	Federal system	Asymmetries (Quebec)
Germany	37.6	36.1	Federal system with extended concurrent responsibilities	
Mexico	n.a.	n.a.	Federal system with high political and low fiscal decentralization	Fiscal and regulatory decentralization since late 1980s, with devolution to states of basic education (1992) and health care (1996)
Switzerland	n.a.	67.4	Federal system	
United States	32.6	40.0	Federal system	
France	16.1	18.6	Regional	Regulatory, fiscal, and political decentralization
Italy	25.6	29.7	Regional	Fiscal, regulatory, and political decentralization
Spain	25.0	32.2	Regional, quasi-federal system	Completed transition toward a regional system

(*continued*)

Table 4.1
(*continued*)

Countries	Share of Subnational Spending on General Government Spending, 1985 (%)	Share of Subnational Spending on General Government Spending, 2001 (%)	Main Traits of Intergovernmental Relations	Recent Reforms
United Kingdom	22.2	25.9	Regional	Introduction of regional government in Scotland and Wales
Czech Republic	n.a.	30.0	Quasi-regional	Regionalization 2000
Denmark	53.7	57.8	Unitary system with strong municipal government	Recentralization of higher education and health since 2006
Finland	30.6	35.5	Unitary system with strong municipal government	
Greece	4.0	5.0	Typical unitary	
Japan	46.6	40.6	Typical unitary	
Luxembourg	14.2	12.8	Typical unitary	
Netherlands	32.6	34.2	Quasi-regional	
New Zealand	n.a.	n.a.	Typical unitary	
Norway	34.6	38.8	Unitary system with strong municipal government	
Poland	n.a.	33.3[a]	Unitary	Political and fiscal decentralization with emphasis on the local level
Portugal	10.3	12.8	Unitary	Asymmetric regionalization of islands
Slowak Republic	n.a.	n.a.	Unitary	Recent creation of regions
Sweden	36.7	43.4	Unitary system with strong municipal government	Devolution of responsibilities in education to municipalities
Turkey	22.2	25.9	Unitary	
Average	28.0	34.0		

n.a. = not available.
[a] This figure is for 2005.
Sources: Unless otherwise noted, qualitative information derives from OECD (2002) and from papers quoted in the text.

systems. Increasing efficiency is a motivation for decentralization in France and, partly, in Italy. In Spain decentralization has been a response to aspirations of strong historic communities. In Italy the economic divide between rich and poor regions led to a demand for autonomy from the former. The goal of equity has led to an expansion of public spending. The results have been a greater reliance on redistributive transfers and a higher tax burden that is resented by voters in the rich regions.

Federalization in Belgium and regionalization in the United Kingdom derive exclusively from historical, linguistic, and cultural divides. In Eastern European countries, decentralization has been sponsored by the EU and by international organizations, replicating the pattern observed in many developing countries, in which the consolidation of democracy, efficiency, and improved governance are dominant concerns. The EU, however, does not sponsor a particular model of decentralized governance.

In the Scandinavian countries, decentralization and subsequent recentralization have been driven largely by efficiency concerns. In Mexico decentralization was also seen as a reaction to seven decades of virtual single-party, "centralized" rule. Although the political power of state governors has grown, on the fiscal side spending functions remain unclear, states lack effective revenue tools, and the transfer system is opaque.

Demands from local elected officials and bureaucrats for more power and autonomy are important. Many OECD countries have long-standing traditions of decentralized government and thus strong constituencies in favor of decentralization.

Outcomes can be examined within single countries where local jurisdictions have achieved varying degrees of autonomy (asymmetries). Or, it is possible to observe different countries with different degrees of decentralization. Proper analysis requires adequate data on outcomes, efficiency, and distributional considerations. Governments take time to adjust policies and assignments; hence, a full evaluation of the outcomes of devolution would require assessments over a long time frame.

Outcomes of Decentralization

Traditional, normative approaches to decentralization were based on the assumption of benevolent government, in the Musgrave tradition of public finance. Questioning this premise has led to a more positive political economy approach, as described below.

TRADITIONAL APPROACHES
Traditional approaches on the effectiveness of the delivery of services have dealt largely with allocation aspects, employing Musgrave's terminology. In this view, decentralization is expected to effect positively on preference matching and on production efficiency.

Preference Matching   Policies devolved to lower-level governments are expected to better match the preferences of the residents of these governments than
policies by higher levels. This advantage was formulated initially by Hayek (1945).
While analyzing the effect of knowledge on society, Hayek stressed that local governments possess better access to local preferences and, consequently, have an
advantage over the central government in deciding which provision of goods and
services would best satisfy citizens. The advantages of decentralization for preference matching, however, have been disputed (Breton 2002) on the grounds that
higher-level governments are quite capable of matching services to preferences,
whereas lower levels may lack incentives and capabilities of doing so effectively
(Tanzi 2002). Important theoretical contributions have been made based on the
new political economy approaches (see Lockwood 2006; Seabright 1996).

Production Efficiency   Services and policies are expected to be more efficiently
provided at lower levels of government. Such provision would require that the
same outcomes require fewer inputs or, alternatively, that the same quantity of
inputs produces more output and better outcomes. Decentralization is posited to
operate through the production function by reducing waste and corruption, and
by searching for innovative techniques. An important part of the literature on
federalism stresses its virtues as a laboratory for innovation in government. Better outcomes can be achieved when more effective policies are introduced. This
argument has often been used when comparing the outputs of centralized school
systems with those of decentralized school systems. Using Bradford, Malt, and
Oates's (1969) terminology, direct production will be changed, whereas desired
outcomes remain the same when decisions are taken locally. Production efficiency can be impaired when economies of scale are important, although the
effect of the latter may be substantially reduced by separating provision from the
production of goods or services (outsourcing, contracts with other levels).

     Under a more modern political economy approach, inter- and intrajurisdic-
tional competition would be important in ensuring effective outcomes (Lockwood 2006).

Regulation Poses a Constraint   The potential benefits of decentralization
may be reduced by stipulations in constitutions or national legislation, or by
regulation. The scope for preference matching may be reduced from the imposition of uniform standards of service delivery; or through introduction of constraints on the use of inputs, such as for education, a minimum or maximum size
of classes; or through restrictions on the choice of policies. Stringent constraints
may arise for health care, such as prohibitions on subcontracting services to the
private sector. Similarly, in the education sector, obligations may be imposed for
different purposes, such as to preserve the responsibilities assigned to teachers'
and parents' boards.

     On the other hand, the benefits of decentralization can be increased by con-
comitant central government policies. Thus, examination of similar assignments

in two different circumstances may yield different evaluations of decentralization, posing difficulties for empirical research.

POLITICAL ECONOMY APPROACHES

Political economy, or positive, approaches to decentralization take into account the incentives faced by different "players," including governments and their associated politicians and officials. These incentives are affected principally by the interactions between policy instruments—in particular, the design of transfers and revenue assignments—as well as the extent to which there is full information on the sources and uses of funds at each level of subnational government. We examine these issues in turn.

Interlinkages Between Revenues and Transfers   Political economy approaches emphasize subnational accountability. As argued in Ahmad and Brosio (2006) and Ambrosiano and Bordignon (2006), it is difficult to achieve accountable subnational service delivery without own-source revenues at the margin for the subnational governments. Given indivisibilities in tax administration, the result could be varying capabilities for subnational administrations in their prospects for generating own-source revenues (Breton 2002). Indeed, with the exception of the United States, Nordic countries, and Switzerland, subnational governments in OECD countries exercise relatively limited taxing powers in general (particularly with respect to control over rates as well as overall contributions to financing subnational spending); see table 4.2. The low averages hide considerable variations of own-source revenues as percentages of total local financing within countries because the smaller and weaker local governments tend to have relatively low capacities to implement what little is assigned to them.

Here, then, is a role for the central/federal government to play in the design of transfers. Excessive reliance on special-purpose transfers negates subnational autonomy. Properly designed equalization or untied transfers should reduce the central/override of subnational preferences, yet evidence suggests that the magnitude of central equalization transfers may have an effect on incentives (e.g., the case of Sweden; see below).

Transparency and Public Expenditure Management Requirements   Transparency is critical for the full implementation of "competition" and constraints on the behavior of local governments. It is also important in informing local electorates about the performance of their government in relation to local expectations as well as in relation to those in neighboring jurisdictions. Timely, accurate, and standardized information is also critical for the central/federal government to maintain macroeconomic stability. Unfortunately, many local governments in OECD countries and other parts of the world have less than complete generation of information on decentralized operations. This lack of information makes the decentralization process prone to "capture" or misuse and also makes it difficult for the central government to conduct macroeconomic policy. The need for

Table 4.2
Subnational Government Taxing Powers in Selected OECD Countries, 1995

	Subnational Government Taxes Related to:		Discretion to Set Taxes[a]	Summary Indicator of Taxing Power[b]
	Total Taxes	Gross Domestic Product		
Sweden	32.6	15.5	100.0	15.5
Denmark	31.3	15.5	95.1	14.7
Switzerland	35.8	11.9	92.4	11.0
Finland	21.8	9.8	89.0	8.7
Belgium	27.9	12.4	57.9	7.2
Iceland	20.4	6.4	100.0	6.4
Japan	24.2	6.8	90.3	6.1
Spain	13.3	4.4	66.6	2.9
New Zealand	5.3	2.0	98.0	2.0
Germany	29.0	11.1	12.8	1.4
Poland	7.5	3.0	46.0	1.4
United Kingdom	3.9	1.4	100.0	1.4
Netherlands	2.7	1.1	100.0	1.1
Austria	20.9	8.7	9.5	0.8
Portugal	5.6	1.8	31.5	0.6
Czech Republic	12.9	5.2	10.0	0.5
Hungary	2.6	1.1	30.0	0.3
Norway	19.7	7.9	3.3	0.3
Mexico	3.3	0.6	11.2	0.1

Note: The countries are ranked in descending order according to the value of the summary indicator of taxing powers.
[a] The figures show the percentage of the total taxes for which subnational governments hold full discretion over the tax rate, the tax base, or both the tax rate and the tax base. A value of 100 designates full discretion.
[b] The summary indicator is the product of the ratio of subnational government taxes to GDP and the degree in the discretion to set taxes. Thus, it measures subnational government taxes with full discretion as a percentage of GDP.
Source: Ambrosiano and Bordignon (2006), based on OECD data.

standardized reporting and accounting, and timely information flows, is now increasingly emphasized in the literature on accountable governance (see Ahmad, Albino-War, and Singh 2006).

The Empirical Literature

In evaluating the potential benefits, it is clear that decentralization can be promoted by different motivations. Furthermore, different institutional, or even political, conditions may play significant roles in determining the outcomes of service provision. Before describing the few empirical studies that provided relevant information for OECD countries, it may be worthwhile to address some issues that have a bearing in evaluating the conclusions of these studies.

Economists tend to focus on efficiencies. These considerations are, for example, the focus of Hayek (1945) and Oates (1993). They implicitly assume that the primary motivation for initiating or developing a process of decentralization should be the promotion of efficiency or, even, as Oates argues, economic growth. Given a well-working democratic process, good governance, and adequate statistical information that would be a component of an effective public expenditure management system at the local level, a better matching of preferences and use of resources would be expected to result in a higher level of service provision and efficiency. Unfortunately, the world tends to be more complicated than economists assume.

Fiscal decentralization is an eminently political process. Political processes are rarely driven exclusively by purely economic considerations. The promotion of economic efficiency infrequently leads countries to initiate decentralization. In most countries, not just in OECD nations, fiscal federalism, or fiscal decentralization, is prompted by the desire of residents of some regions to increase their independence from the national government so as to achieve a greater say in the economic, political, and cultural decisions that affect them. The use of Basque language was significantly boosted by the help of tax incentives and spending provided by the government of the Basque region, which could hardly be considered an efficiency-enhancing policy. Thus, the desire for differentiation—rather than economic efficiency—often plays a determining role. The more culturally or ethnically identified the population of a region is, the greater the likelihood that the region will push harder for decentralization.

Political motivations for fiscal decentralization have been obvious and central in most of the OECD countries that in recent years have chosen to pursue decentralization policies. In France the cultural differences of the population of Corsica and of its non-European territories clearly played a major role. In Spain regions with distinct cultural and linguistic characteristics, such as Catalonia and the Basque Country, were at the forefront of the political movement for decentralization. In Italy the push toward fiscal federalism came mainly from the Northern League, a political party with strong regional roots that at times considered its members to belong to an ethnically distinct group (the Lombards). In the United Kingdom the Scots played a leading role. In Canada the province of Quebec and its French-speaking population threatened to secede and create an independent state. All these cases imply that the economists' motive for fiscal decentralization— the search for the efficient use of public resources—is not likely to be the original impetus to decentralize. Therefore, the connection between decentralization and enhanced service provision should not be expected to be close.

Decentralization extends greater control over spending and other decisions to subnational governments. This control may result in increased levels of subnational spending or in a reallocation of existing spending. Greater spending raises the question of how to finance the increases. Reallocation challenges the degree to which local spending decisions can be allowed to diverge from nationally established norms. Such norms inform education standards, access to, or procedures for, health services, pensions, public assistance, or other functional categories of public spending, categories accounting for a large share of total public spending in most countries. These norms and expenses are at the base of universal public programs that have led to sharply increased public spending since World War II. It is thus easy to see why problems often arise between national and subnational governments. These problems are magnified by a dynamic world in which new technologies and new views about the role that the state should play in the economy are always changing. These changes must be reflected in revised policies. The elasticities with respect to time of various categories of public spending, and particular taxes, will diverge, implying the need for ongoing adaptation of the national and subnational roles. Adaptation can come about through constitutional amendment (as in Italy and Brazil) or through reinterpretation of the constitution and the passage of new laws. When this adaptation is complex, major difficulties may arise.

Political arrangements about fiscal federalism or decentralization in general are essentially contracts between the political representatives of national and subnational governments. As in the case for all legal agreements that extend into the future, these contracts cannot specify and anticipate possible developments that may require rewriting of the original contract. For this reason, unless the occasional rewriting of the contracts is relatively simple and possible, a powerful referee to help settle future disputes is needed. In the case of the United States, the nature of the existing arrangements between the states and the federal government is reinterpreted by the Supreme Court, in the absence of difficult-to-make constitutional changes. The Court's decisions are not challenged. In other cases in which a powerful referee is absent, constitutional changes are required, and they are never easy.

In most decentralized countries, efficient and broadly accepted mechanisms for reducing frictions and settling disputes between national and subnational governments are not available. It is thus much more difficult to accommodate the changing needs of particular regions. These frictions can create tensions and, at times, even lead to terrorist movements.

When different regions that are part of the federal state have broadly similar per capita incomes and taxable capacities so that horizontal imbalances in fiscal resources are not significant, it will be easier for the national governments to delegate some responsibilities or mandates to the regions (or other subnational institutions) for particular categories of public spending. Such delegation will give the latter a better chance to match expenditures with local preferences. When, in addition, tax bases can be transferred to the local governments and there are no significant economies of scale in the administration of the transferred taxes, fiscal decentralization will have a greater chance of success, which is broadly the U.S. situation.

Regions, though, may vary significantly in per capita incomes and taxable capacities, and there could be significant economies of scale in the administration of taxes. In this case, fiscal decentralization will require the national government to tax richer regions and transfer financial resources to the poorer ones. These transfers are easier politically when they take place implicitly within a unitary country in which particular expenditures (education, health, unemployment compensation) are made within a system in which subsidies from richer to poorer regions are largely buried in administrative budgets. In some countries, such as Italy, decentralization has been spearheaded by the citizens of rich regions who complained that too large a share of their incomes was being taxed away to subsidize less productive, or less hardworking, individuals in poorer regions. Making the transfers explicit, in a decentralized setting, could make them less likely, thus endangering the redistributive role of the state and the maintenance of uniform national standards.

Tax administrations are likely to be characterized by economies of scale because of the large fixed costs that they require for buildings, equipment development of particular procedures, and so forth. In a complex world with modern taxes, small tax administrations are unlikely to be efficient. Furthermore, when they operate in small geographic areas, where tax administration employees and taxpayers both reside and have friends and relatives, interpersonal relations are likely to be important. Familiarity is often a major ingredient for the development of practices that diverge from arm's length. In other words, corruption is often more likely to develop at the local level than at the national level. It has been a common assumption on the part of public finance experts who observe the tax system in the United States that corruption has been rare in the (national) Internal Revenue System, whereas cases of corruption have been more frequent at the local level. Similar considerations apply to other actions such as those of zoning boards and areas of outsourcing such as garbage collection. When local governments are relatively small and when administrators and citizens are close because of family, friendship, community, or other ties, it is more difficult to put relationships at arm's length.

Local tax administrations can also suffer from the mobility of employees, financial capital, and economic activities. It is easier for employees to move within the same country than across national borders. Those who move may be the ones with the greatest taxable capacity. Given that important services such as health and education can now be bought from many sources in different places, taxpayers may choose to be in the locales with lowest taxes and buy health and educational services at the most convenient place. Thus, the argument that high taxes correspond to better services for the specific individual does not carry much weight. Even in well-working federations, such as the United States, tax competition is a major issue. Here, though, it is tempered by the full exchange of information on taxpayers that exists between the national government and the governments of the states. This efficient exchange of information on taxpayers is not common between governments. For all these reasons, the relationship between fiscal decentralization and efficiency in the use of fiscal resources should not be expected to be particularly close.

SUMMARY OF THE LITERATURE

A number of papers discuss decentralization outcomes in industrial countries[3] or provide international comparisons. The cross-country studies are generally constrained by limited availability of comparable data to use a reduced-form relationship between decentralization and efficiency.[4] Assessments for single countries can, potentially, overcome the control variables issue and provide firmer results. Many studies use data from different sources, mainly budgets, administrative sources, and household survey data. Assessments based on household data in particular illustrate a promising avenue of research. A typical model of the demand and supply of locally provided public goods, which serves to illustrate some of the key concepts of allocation and production efficiency, is presented in the appendix.

The empirical literature on decentralization and efficiency can be arranged in four distinct groups. The first and largest group of studies refers to decentralization and production efficiency.

The second group refers to preference matching and decentralization. Preference matching is important for OECD countries considering the importance of cultural and ethnic motivations for decentralization. Relatively few papers address this issue, however, and most consider it jointly with growth issues.

A third and smaller group of papers relates decentralization to convergence of service delivery levels. According to this literature, decentralization should decrease convergence when heterogeneity of preferences and disparities of economic conditions prevail. This theory, however, does not imply that centralized provision ensures uniformity of levels. For example, in Italy major differences can be observed among regions at different levels of development in their actual levels of centrally provided services, such as tax administration, education, health, or postal services. These differences may reflect neglect by national politicians, slack, and bureaucratic capture in deconcentrated agencies. It is expected

----

3. Several papers are on Spain, which provides excellent opportunities for testing theories about the effect of decentralization (some are summarized in table 4.3 and discussed below). First, Spain has experienced an important process of fiscal decentralization since the reestablishment of democracy and the constitution of 1978. Second, the timing of decentralization has not been equal for all Autonomous Communities (AC). Some ACs have assumed devolved responsibilities earlier than others, thus allowing researchers to examine decentralization effects with reference to two distinct samples: one with decentralized and the other with still centralized responsibilities.

4. The dependent variable is usually a comparable but simple indicator of policy outcomes, whereas decentralization is represented by fiscal indicators based mostly on the relative shares of central and subnational governments in total national public expenditure, revenue, or both.

that decentralization could bring convergence, particularly if accompanied by introduction of uniform standards and effective transfers.

Finally, a large fourth group of papers examines decentralization and growth. Although it is difficult to argue that overall economic growth could depend on decentralization, one of the crucial goals pursued by local politicians is the promotion of growth in their areas, which may have an effect on overall growth. The origins of the literature linking decentralization to growth can be traced to Oates (1993), who argued that the gains from decentralization should also apply to a dynamic framework of economic growth because centrally determined policies do not adequately consider local conditions in the provision of public goods and services, such as those regarding infrastructure and education. It is argued that economic growth might accelerate with decentralization if more resources go to public investment; health and education policies are better targeted to growth, and, in sum, the result is more growth. In other words, local preferences are growth oriented. A simpler approach focuses mostly on productive efficiency. The main hypothesis is that if decentralization promotes more efficient use of resources, it should also result in higher rates of growth for the entire economy.

A number of arguments question positive links between decentralization and growth. For example, decentralization could work against growth if it discourages big investment projects with growth-conducive spillovers across regions. It may discourage the production of genuine public goods. Moreover, political objectives may emphasize equity more than growth: elected politicians want results within their terms in office.

Production Efficiency   The main contributions to this issue of production efficiency are listed in table 4.3. Barankay and Lockwood (2007) examine the relationship between educational outcomes and decentralization in Switzerland. They demonstrate that (1) it is possible to overcome most of the problems associated with information constraints; and (2) decentralization does, in fact, contribute to improved outcomes. In Switzerland responsibility for education has always been cantonal, although the federal government equalizes across cantons. Cantons can devolve some expenditure responsibilities to their local governments, and they effectively do so. It is thus possible to observe different degrees of decentralization in education between cantons.

Educational outcomes in the study are measured by the number of 19-year-olds that pass the final exams (*Maturité*) to enter universities.[5] The index of

---

5. Some problems should be noted in applying this measure of outcome. Cantons are mostly responsible for upper-secondary education, whereas local governments are fully responsible for primary education. Their expenditure and policies are thus effecting minimally on *Maturité*. To partially account for this fact, Barankay and Lockwood (2007) relate results at *Maturité* to the degree of decentralization in the years when the concerned students were enrolled in primary schools, but clearly the main effect on *Maturité* derives from years spent in secondary education. Finally, there is no federal intervention in exams that could ensure uniformity of criteria.

Table 4.3
Summary of Literature on Productive Efficiency and Convergence

Author(s)	Countries	Period	Dependent Variable	Decentralization Index	Main Results
Ahlin and Mörk	Sweden	1989–2000	Convergence in per student spending and teacher-pupil ratio	Regulatory variables	Little evidence on convergence
Balaguer-Coll, Prior, and Tortosa-Ausina	Spain (1,315 municipalities)	1995–2000	Output of local services	Range of responsibilities (regulatory and fiscal)	Decentralization increases efficiency
Barankay and Lockwood	Switzerland (26 cantons)	1982–2000	Education attainment	Fiscal and regulatory: local on cantonal expenditure controlled for regulatory powers	Decentralization increases efficiency
Cantarero and Pacual Sanchez	15 EU member countries	1993–2003	Infant mortality ratio and life expectancy at national level	Fiscal decentralization: local on total expenditure	Decentralization improves outcomes
Crivelli, Filippini, and Mosca	Switzerland (26 cantons)	1996–2001	Expenditure and input measures for health	No specific decentralization index	Huge disparities associated with decentralization and federalism
Jakubowski and Topińska	Poland (local governments)	1999–2003	Various variables referring to education	Fiscal regulatory decentralization	Mixed results
Jiménez and Smith	Canada (10 provinces)	1979–1995	Infant mortality rate	Fiscal decentralization	Decentralization reduces infant mortality
Montero-Granados and de Dios Jiménez	Spain (17 autonomous communities)	1980–2001	Life expectancy at birth and infant mortality	Regulatory (before and after devolution of responsibilities)	No clear convergence: regions with low levels improve, but greater dispersion of outcomes emerges
Robalino, Picazo, and Voetberg	High-income countries, Spain	1970–1995	Infant mortality ratio	Fiscal decentralization: subnational on total national expenditure	Positive effect declining with increases of GDP
Salinas Peña	Spain (50 provinces)	1980–2003	Survival rate: proportion of students in last course of compulsory education who have access to noncompulsory education	Regulatory (before and after devolution of responsibilities)	Decentralization is associated with positive outcomes

decentralization is measured by share of education expenditure by the local governments in each canton over the sum of local and cantonal expenditure for education. In other words, the index shows the degree of education expenditure within each canton:

$$D_{ct} = \frac{LE_{ct}}{LE_{ct} + CE_{ct}},$$

where D_{ct} is the index of canton c in year t, LE_{ct} is the sum of education expenditure in all counties of canton c in year t, and CE_{ct} is education expenditure at the cantonal level in year t.

The use of a purely fiscal variable, such as the expenditure share, entails the risk that it does not adequately represent the degree of effective autonomy of local government. To solve the problem, Barankay and Lockwood (2007) examine cantonal regulations in four crucial areas for education: (1) appointing teachers; (2) determining pay levels for teachers; (3) granting teachers' incentives; and (4) organizing the structure of school. Apparently, decentralization of expenditure is closely associated with higher local decision-making power, especially for teachers' incentive pay. Local government expenditure for education is mainly for teachers' salaries. Thus, when the number of teachers or the pay levels increase, the degree of decentralization also varies within cantons. Secondly, variation in expenditures for teachers' salaries is induced by changes in the size of the student population. If it increases, local government will have to provide more teachers because cantons impose minimum class sizes. Also, changes in student numbers induce changes in the indicator of decentralization. Variations in outcomes can thus be meaningfully associated with changes in decentralization if the number of students does not affect outcomes.

Finally, Barankay and Lockwood (2007) regress for 20 years (1982–2002) the *Maturité* results on their chosen index of decentralization after adding a number of variables that control use of inputs and canton and year-fixed effects. Results show that educational attainment is positively and significantly related to the degree of decentralization. The absolute effect of decentralization is also substantial. According to the estimate, if the decentralization index increases by 10 percent, the share of students obtaining the *Maturité* increases by 3.5 percent. Thus, cantons seem to play an important role in ensuring effective outcomes.

It should be noted, however, that since the paper was written, the system of transfers in Switzerland has been reformed. The authorities believed that the previous system, in which transfers are linked to variables under the control of cantons, provided an incentive to increase costs, thereby generating macroeconomic inefficiencies.

Salinas Peña (2007) conducted a similar analysis of Spanish schools. Spain provides, through its asymmetric regionalization, a unique opportunity for checking the outcomes of decentralization. The central government has retained the responsibility for defining the structure of, and setting national guidelines and standards for, education policies, leaving other competencies to the regions. Peña uses as an indicator of outcomes the share of students who complete postsecondary education (*Bachillerato*) in relation to those enrolled in the last year of compulsory education, assuming that a high level of educational quality will induce students to stay at school. Typical variables explaining educational outcomes, such as family income or the size of classes, are used for control purposes, although a few dummies are used to distinguish between regions that acceded to education responsibilities in different years. The fiscal discipline of regions is controlled via the introduction of the surplus/deficit in the regional budget. Different specifications of the chosen model are tested. The results reveal some problems referring to the control variables, most of which do not show the expected sign. Decentralization is positively and significantly correlated with the survival rate in two out of three specifications. Earlier decentralized regions, however, are at the same time those with a higher per capita income. Because income is also a determinant of the survival rate, the link of the latter with decentralization is somewhat blurred. The dependent variable is also correlated positively with fiscal discipline, supporting a basic tenet of decentralization theory: the benefits of decentralization are also dependent on the quality of decentralization.

Distributional Effects   The use of household surveys facilitates assessment of the access of poor and disadvantaged individuals and of the personal characteristics of users. When combined with fiscal and administrative data, household surveys can potentially allow for an examination of both efficiency and equity. Jakubowski and Topińska (2006) use this methodology to evaluate the results of decentralization on education and health care in Poland.

Decentralization has been more extensive in the former sector. Local governments, *gminas*, have taken on increased responsibilities for preschool and primary education since the early 1990s. Central government still regulates teacher qualifications, contracts, and salaries; supervises schools; defines curriculum; and accepts textbooks. Local governments (and provinces, *powiats*, in the case of secondary education) own schools and, in principle, are responsible for the way educational services are provided. In practice, their rights are importantly limited by laws, decisions of the Ministry of Education, and high autonomy of school principals. After 1999, almost all funds for public education were transferred to *gminas* through a block grant. On average, central transfers finance 70 percent of education expenditure, with the rest covered by own sources of revenue.

The effect of decentralization is evaluated from distinct points of view. First, the availability of service for kindergartens (derived from administrative data) decreased—the percentage of *gminas* with kindergartens fell from 82 percent to 78 percent (73 percent to 66 percent in the case of rural *gminas*). More importantly, many *gminas* closed their kindergartens with some of them completely eliminating the provision of such services in their area. As a result, variation between *gminas* relating to preschool accessibility increased overall, but with some dramatic regional differences.

Second, household survey data are used to explore more closely the effect of decentralization, using before-and-after comparisons linking preschool enrollment rate to per capita expenditure and a poverty indicator. As expected, the higher the spending of *gminas*, the higher the probability of sending a child to a kindergarten. There is neither an appreciable higher access for the poor households nor a better use of expenditure as a result of the comparisons, however.

The results differ somewhat for primary and lower secondary schools. The authors observe that after decentralization there is a lower variation between *gminas* relating to expenditure per student. They attribute this finding to (1) the new grants, based on objective costs rather than historical costs; (2) increased efficiency from reorganization of the school network; and (3) shifting of resources from unregulated preschools to other levels of education, subject to stricter central regulations.

Further analysis of primary education shows that expenditure per pupil increased in constant terms, after an initial decline, which would imply that no efficiency benefits are derived from decentralization. Household surveys also allow for an analysis of the effect of decentralized policies, specifically of local expenditure on poor families relative to rich families. The study on Poland also shows that decentralization has not had an appreciable effect on the poorest: the share of local public expenditure on education devoted to the advantage of the poorest quintile of the population is unchanged over the centralized system.

Jiménez and Smith (2005) try to trace out the effect of decentralization on health care outcomes proxied by infant mortality, with reference to Canada during the period 1975 to 1995. Among Canadian provinces, infant mortality shows higher variation than life expectancy. First, the authors attempt to check the production efficiency of decentralization with a single-step model, where infant mortality is regressed on a decentralization index and a number of control variables. Second, they proceed to estimate a two-step model. In the first step, provincial expenditure for health is regressed on the index of decentralization and on a number of control variables, such as transfers from the central government, private-sector expenditure, birthrates, and the like. In the second step, the authors proceed again to check the effect of decentralization on infant mortality by substituting actual provincial expenditure for education with an estimated one. The purpose of the two-step exercise is to control the effect of decentralization on preference matching and then to proceed to control the efficiency effect.

The results show a negative and significant relationship between infant mortality and the decentralization. More specifically, reduction of mortality is closely dependent on provincial expenditure on health: roughly a 1 percent increase in provincial expenditure on health stimulated a 3.8 percent reduction in infant mortality.

Unfortunately, the reliability of the results is reduced by the indicator of decentralization used, which is based on the provincial share of total health care in that province.[6] By not controlling for the effective subnational decision-making power, the index shows mostly the propensity to spend for health by a provincial government and its municipal governments. Moreover, as federal expenditure in each province is not a substitute for subnational expenditure, its relative size is not an indicator of degree of decentralization of expenditure.[7]

Balaguer-Coll, Prior, and Tortosa-Ausina (2006) examine a sample of Spanish municipalities during 1995 and 2000. They attempt to estimate the effect of decentralization on typical municipal services, that is, those that constitute the backbone of any decentralized system. The study tries to evaluate the gains in productive efficiency brought by decentralization by using a nonparametric estimate of the efficiency frontier. The study links inputs used—more specifically municipal expenditure—to a number of indicators of municipal output, such as the waste collected and surface of public parks, and then selects the most efficient units. The authors distinguish between (small) municipalities with less responsibilities and medium and large municipalities with extended responsibilities. After controlling for the operation of scale economies, municipalities with wider responsibilities should be ahead in the decentralization process. The results show that average efficiency is higher for large and medium-sized municipalities and that the differences tend to grow larger over time (a proxy for increased decentralization).

Robalino, Picazo, and Voetberg (2001) provide one of the few cross-country studies for industrial economies. In their empirical model, they regress infant mortality on the ratio of expenditure managed by local governments relative to that managed by the central government. They also introduce a few control variables, which refer to institutional capacity, such as political and civil rights, and corruption. These variables allow the authors to control the quality of political institutions. Without reference to the actual use of inputs, however, one cannot perform a thorough assessment of production efficiency (with the partial exemp-

---

6. The indicator is represented by the following formula:

$$D_{pt} = \frac{MEH_{pt} + PEH_{pt} + SSF_{pt}}{MEH_{pt} + PEH_{pt} + SSF_{pt} + FEH_{pt}}$$

where MEH_{pt} is health expenditure by all municipalities in year t, PEH_{pt} is provincial expenditure for health in the same year, SSF_{pt} is security funds by provincial expenditure, and FEH_{pt} is the federal government expenditure in the same province in the same year t.

7. Consider a numerical example. In province A subnational expenditure for health is 80 and federal 20. In province B the same numbers are 10 and 90. The indicator will have a value of 0.8 in A and of 1.0 in B. It means simply that subnational governments in province A spend more for health than the corresponding governments in province B. This increased spending could be compensated by lower expenditure for education, but it is not referred per se to any difference in decentralization. On the other hand, federal expenditure is for native Canadians, military personnel, inmates of federal penitentiaries, and the Royal Mounted Police, which has no relationship with decentralization.

tion of GDP). The sample of low- and high-income countries is not specified. The results show that outcomes are positively correlated with decentralization. They also show that the marginal effects of decentralization diminish as GDP increases. This finding, if validated with other empirical evidence, would be an interesting result. It would mean that when countries grow, their institutional capacity increases, and thus the advantages of decentralization are likely to vanish because the presumed differences between central and local management of public affairs disappear.

Cantarero and Sanchez (2006) provide a similar analysis for 15 EU countries. Their results, however—positive association between outcomes in health and decentralization—are weakened by, among other factors, their use of nationwide indicators.

CONVERGENCE OF SERVICE PROVISION ACROSS AREAS

A small but increasing number of studies analyze convergence across areas of levels of service provision. Empirical observation seems to confirm the theory for health care in Switzerland, one of the most decentralized countries of the world. With respect to health care, the role of the federal government is limited to funding of health care to poor people (federal expenditure is 20 percent of total national health care) and to the definition of basic packages of health insurance (Crivelli, Filippini, and Mosca 2007). Provision of health care shows huge disparities between cantons, whether measured in terms of expenditure, use of inputs, or outcomes, such as differences in mortality rates amenable to absence of timely and effective care (Crivelli, Filippini, and Mosca 2007). Decentralization, if it is not accompanied by the imposition of strict national standards on service levels and if substantial equalization grants are not provided, will increase disparities in levels of service delivery. Montero-Granados and de Dios Jiménez (2007) do not provide an analytical framework, but they test the convergence hypothesis with reference to the Spanish regions in the health sector. Health care is provided by a national health system funded (with the exception of Navarre and the Basque Country) by general taxation and small user copayments. Standards are determined by the central government, whereas regional authorities are responsible for planning, organization, and management of health care and are provided with a centrally determined block grant allocated according to an unadjusted capitation formula. The authors use two measures of convergence derived from the literature on growth: the sigma (σ) convergence and the beta (β) convergence. The first measure is based on changes of standard deviation over time. When variation declines, there is more homogeneity of outcomes, or of behaviors. According to the second measure, convergence increases when laggard regions improve more quickly than more advanced regions.

Outcomes of health care include life expectancy at birth and infant mortality, whereas decentralization is measured by access of regions to health responsibilities. The authors also use a host of variables, other than decentralization, that are expected to affect outcomes. The results show convergence taking place at the extremes. That is, less developed regions improve faster than more advanced regions, although in the middle there is a big increase in variation. These results are open to interpretation. One could say that decentralization fills the most optimistic expectations because the difference between the rich and the poor regions are leveled and, at the same time, individual (middle) regions adjust to their preferences. One can also argue that the results confirm that there is little to expect in terms of homogeneity from decentralization.

Ahlin and Mörk (2007) analyze the effect on convergence in the Swedish education sector of different stages in decentralization. Sweden took three major steps to decentralize its education system. In 1991 formal responsibility for compulsory, upper-secondary, and adult education was moved to the local government level. Teachers were transferred to municipalities, but salaries, as well as curricula and national evaluations, were still determined centrally. Distinct specific grants for education, such as for books and school facilities, were unified into a single specific grant. In 1993 all sector-specific grants—such as those for education, health, and social protection—were unified into a single block grant, giving municipalities, the freedom, for example, to move resources from education to social protection (or vice versa). In 1996 teachers' wage setting was moved to municipalities, and a new block grant system was introduced, based on revenue and cost equalization. Note that since 1992 the central government introduced public funding for independent schools, thus generating more competition between public and private education. Convergence is analyzed with reference to two typical input indicators: per-pupil spending and teacher-pupil ratio. Ahlin and Mörk (2007) show that no appreciable change has taken place in the pattern of per-pupil spending, although variation in the teacher-pupil ratio has decreased over time. The authors explain the surprising result (challenging traditional theory) in terms of the strategic interactions between local politicians— local choices are constrained by neighboring municipalities' choices. They do not control for the varying equalizing effect of different systems of grants, however. Subsequent regression analysis shows that, with decentralization, higher reliance on own-source revenues had an effect on per-pupil expenditure, but it may have been neutralized by the equalization grants. Thus, the power ceded to local governments by decentralization of responsibilities may have been offset by the ability of the central government to influence local choices through the allocation of grants.

Preference Matching   The empirical literature on industrial countries exclusively devoted to preference matching is still relatively small. In fact, most studies link preference matching with growth, as illustrated in table 4.4. A well-structured and accurate analysis is provided by Strumpf and Oberholzer-Gee (2002) with reference to regulation of the liquor sales in the United States between 1934 and 1970. In 1933 the Prohibition Act was repealed, and the states were made responsible for liquor control. States then chose between centralized/statewide regulation or devolution of regulation to their local governments (counties, municipalities,

Table 4.4

Decentralization: Preference Matching and Growth: Summary of Selected Papers

Author(s)	Countries of Reference	Period of Reference	Fiscal Variables of Reference	Growth Variables of Reference	Decentralization Index	Main Results
Akai and Sakata (2005)	U.S. counties	1993–2000	n.a.	GDP growth rate	Fiscal with emphasis on tax autonomy	Growth is positively related to tax autonomy, specifically nonbailouts
Arze del Granado, Martinez-Vazquez, and McNab (2005)	45 developed and developing countries	1973–2000	Ratio of education and health expenditures to total public expenditures	n.a.	Fiscal decentralization	Likely increase of expenditure for health and education
Ebel and Yilmaz (2002)	19 OECD countries	1997–1999	Public sector's expenditure share of GDP	GDP growth rate		
Faguet (2004)	Bolivia (sample of municipalities)	1991–1996	Investment for education, water and sanitation, watershed mgt.	n.a.	Fiscal decentralization	Increased spending in poorer areas
Jin and Zou (2002)	17 industrial and 15 developing countries	1980–1994	Subnational, national, and aggregate government size: the ratio of total expenditure at corresponding level to GDP	n.a.	Fiscal and regulatory decentralization	Increase of subnational expenditure and reduction of national expenditure
Solé-Ollé and Esteller-Moré (2005)	Spain (44 provinces)	1977–1998	Investment in roads and education	n.a.	Fiscal and regulatory decentralization	Better adaptation of investment to local needs
Thiessen (2000)	26 mainly developed countries	1975–1995	Annual growth rate of real gross fixed capital formation (as indicator of physical investment)	Growth rate of per capita GDP, total factor productivity growth	Fiscal decentralization	Growth initially increases but then declines with decentralization
Thiessen (2003)	14 and 21 high-income OECD countries	1973–1998	Average annual investment share in GDP	Log difference GDP per working-age person; Average annual total factor productivity growth	Fiscal decentralization	Growth initially increases but then declines with decentralization

n.a. = not available.

95

and towns). Initially, seven states prohibited sale of package liquor, whereas among nonprohibitionist states 20, and later 34, devolved regulation to their local communities, where the issue was decided in local elections.

Strumpf and Oberholzer-Gee (2002) construct, and test with regression analysis, a model predicting that decentralization of regulation would be observed in states with huge heterogeneity of preferences on liquor sales, whereas centralization should prevail with less extreme disparities. The test is conducted in two sequential stages. The first stage refers to counties (3,100) where the tastes of the decisive voters are estimated using variables that, according to the literature, should influence attitudes toward liquor, such as religious affiliation and socioeconomic variables. Tastes will predict the policy—wet or dry—adopted by the community. The second stage refers to states and is based on regression of decentralization of policy with two measures of within-state taste heterogeneity. The results show that the states with more heterogeneous preferences have been more prone to decentralize.

Arze del Granado, Martinez-Vazquez, and McNab (2005) provide specific empirical testing of preference matching, also with reference to developing countries. More precisely, they analyze the effect of fiscal decentralization on the provision of publicly provided private goods, such as health and education. The analysis is based on 45 developed and developing countries between 1973 and 2000. The dependent variables are the share of local health and education expenditure on total local expenditure, whereas the independent variable is the share of local total government expenditure. The results show that decentralization brings about an increase of the share of these two categories of expenditure, but the generality of the findings may be questioned. Because there is no evidence—only a general presumption—that more expenditure for health and education means effectively in every country better adaptation to local preferences, more spending for these two sectors could simply be because these sectors are the ones where decentralization has taken place.

Faguet's study (2004) looks at preference matching in a developing country, Bolivia. It assesses how decentralization affects the composition of local expenditure by sector in line with citizens' preferences and does not address the growth effect. Although there are problems derived from the budget information used, the studies exert considerable effort in singling out local preferences for expenditure. This effort has been challenged, however, especially concerning the effectiveness of local service delivery in general, given the overall levels of dissatisfaction with the process, unspent monies, and inefficiencies in spending that have been stressed by donors and international agencies, as well as the authorities. A fundamental rethinking of the decentralization process is under way in Bolivia.

Solé-Ollé and Esteller-Moré (2005) analyze the effect of decentralization on the pattern of investment in roads and education facilities from 1977 to 1998 in Spain. Their paper is well constructed, although it is not strictly a test of preference matching, but rather an efficiency test of spending decisions. The main focus of the analysis is, in fact, testing, if after decentralization investment decisions have been more closely targeted to effective needs, such as more road construction in congested areas and more school construction in areas with higher student population growth, and if investment activities have become more cost conscious. The results show that, with decentralization, the regional allocation of investment in these two sectors has become better adapted to local conditions and needs, thus showing a higher level of efficiency than under the previous centralized regime.

Decentralization and Growth   Although there is a great deal of empirical literature on the link between decentralization and growth, there appears to be consensus that any relationship is relatively weak. Breuss and Eller (2004, 11) have provided a good survey of the main results.

The empirical literature refers to samples across countries, as in Thiessen (2000, 2003) and Ebel and Yilmaz (2002), and to distinct countries, such as in the papers by Behnisch and Stegarescu (2003) on Germany and by Feld, Kirchgässner, and Schaltegger (2004) on Switzerland. The empirical findings are mixed. Negative findings are more frequent for European countries and with a longer-term perspective.

In this chapter, we limit our consideration to the studies of Thiessen (2000, 2003), which are mostly devoted to OECD countries. The relationship between decentralization and growth is represented by a bell-shaped curve, meaning that when countries move from low to medium levels of decentralization, growth accelerates, but higher decentralization will reduce growth. Part of this explanation derives from the positive effects on capital formation resulting from decentralization. The key variables used, however—average rate of growth from 1973 to 1998 and average indexes of fiscal decentralization—raise a few doubts about the results even after other variables that affect growth are controlled for. In the case of Italy, most decentralization reforms were introduced in the 1990s, but growth declined in that period, whereas lower decentralization and higher growth characterize the previous years. Ireland has the highest rate of growth, but it has always been a highly centralized country. Norway has promoted some recentralization, but its high growth rate is due to oil. Japan is close to Ireland in the sense that no change toward decentralization is observable, but economic growth had declined there in the second half of the period.

Convergence and Divergence in Regional Rates of Growth   When countries decentralize, less developed regions fear losing in terms of growth, with less support from the central government. At first view, this view looks reasonable, although increasing divergence may be attributed to the peculiarities of the decentralization process. Akai and Sakata (2005) provide good analytical and empirical analysis for the United States. They distinguish between two different concepts and effects of decentralization. The first refers to decentralization of resources. The presumable effect of decentralization is to increase disparities among regions. Here the effect of decentralization will arise mostly through the expenditure multiplier. The second concept refers to decentralization as a commitment device. Decentralization occurs when subnational governments rely on their own sources of revenue with a hard budget constraint. In this case, regional efficiency in spending and self-reliance will be increased, with likely positive effects on growth. Akai and Sakata test their model with reference to an unspecified number of U.S. counties from 1993 to 2000. They also use a number of appropriate control variables to take into account many of the factors that affect growth. The results show that decentralization, as a commitment device, has a significant effect on the reduction of regional disparities in growth. The results by Akai and Sakata are confirmed by Rodriguez-Pose and Bwire (2003) with a detailed analysis of a group of five OECD countries, Germany, Italy, Mexico, Spain, and the United States, plus India.

The exploration of a link between purely regulatory decentralization and growth is also an important one. When subnational, particularly regional, governments are empowered with growth-related responsibilities, there are clearly new potentialities to foster growth, but regional growth-inducing policies can be construed at the expense of other regions. There are worries—for example, in Italy—of excessive regional regulation in growth-related sectors, such as the environment, health, and labor. These issues have been initially explored by Weingast (1995), who maintains that a federal system is market preserving if it has three characteristics: (1) subnational governments have primary regulatory responsibility over the economy; (2) a common market is ensured, preventing the lower governments from using their regulatory authority to erect trade barriers against the goods and services from other political units; and (3) the lower governments face a hard budget constraint; that is, they have neither the ability to print money nor access to unlimited credit. Weingast and others (e.g., Cao, Qian, and Weingast 1997; Lin, Tao, and Liu 2003) have made extensive empirical analyses of market-preserving federalism theory with reference to China. Unfortunately, similar studies for other—specifically OECD—countries are still missing. Again that may have been the case during the early years of the economic reforms, but increasing inequalities and other potential constraints are likely to have changed the composition of the "growth engine" in recent years.

Conclusions

Despite the often proclaimed benefits of decentralization for enhanced service delivery, efficiency, convergence, and growth, the evidence is at best inconclusive. The survey of the theoretical and empirical literature suggests the following conclusions that may have far-reaching policy conclusions:

- In theoretical terms, the claims that decentralization enhances service
  delivery fail to recognize the joint nature of the spending and revenue constraints, and lower levels of administration are likely not to have adequate

own-source revenues for effective hard budget constraints, nor the budgeting and reporting infrastructure to make decentralization effective.

- There is relatively poor evidence to characterize effective changes over time, using comparable administrative and household data sets—for OECD or developing countries—although this lacuna is now beginning to be addressed.
- Links between decentralization and growth, convergence, efficiency, and the like are tenuous.
- Claims for improvements in developing countries may be due to the general development process and growth; linkages with decentralization are also tenuous. What evidence exists weakens even further as countries develop.

APPENDIX

Let us introduce the standard model for the demand of a publicly provided good, g.[8] There are two regions, A and B, with homogeneous preferences inside. Region A has a higher per capita income, y, than region B. Explicit consideration of differences in income conditions will help clarify convergence issues in service delivery. Region A also has a higher voting population ($N_A > N_B$). This difference is sufficient to ensure that region A's preferences will translate into national choices when a decision concerning the whole country has to be made. The citizens' preferences over g and a composite private good, x, are represented by

$$(1) \qquad u = u(g) + v(x).$$

The total cost C of supplying the publicly provided good is

$$(2) \qquad C = c(N, g),$$

with $c'_N \geq 0$ and $c'_g > 0$, while $p = c/N$ is the per capita average cost of one unit of g. For the sake of simplicity, we assume that the production of g is subjected to constant returns to scale, but that cost depends on the degree of rivalry, γ, and on population, N. More specifically, for pure public goods, where γ = zero, the average per capita cost decreases with the population. For private goods, where $\gamma = 1$, the total cost is proportional to the population, and the average cost is independent of the population. Thus, $p_N \leq 0$.

Concerning rivalry, we simply assume that p increases with γ; thus, $p_g > 0$. The cost of providing g is financed through a proportional income tax (or a bundle of taxes producing a total revenue that is proportional to income, y).

---

8. See Brosio, Cassone, and Ricciuti (2002).

Total tax payments by individual voters are therefore ay, where a is the tax rate, chosen by the median voter. For individuals, the budget constraint is

(3) $x = y - ay,$

whereas the government budget constraint is $cg = aY$, where Y is the total aggregate income. Letting $t = Y/N$ be the per capita tax base, the budget constraint becomes

(4) $pg = at.$

Thus, individuals maximize their utility, U, by choosing the level of g, subject to equations (3) and (4), which can then be combined into a single constraint:

(5) $x = y - \left(\dfrac{pg}{t}\right) y.$

The first-order condition is

(6) $U'(g) = V'(x)\dfrac{py}{t}.$

In figure 4.1 the budget constraint is represented by the straight line from the origin, whereas the preferences are represented by indifference curves whose level increases as they move southeast (the two arguments have an opposite effect on utility). The slope is

(7) $R(y, a, g) = \dfrac{da}{dg}\bigg|_U = U = \dfrac{u'(g)}{v'(x)}.$

The slope of the budget constraint is

(8) $\dfrac{da}{dg} = \dfrac{p}{t}.$

At the optimum, the slopes of the two curves are equal.

Now let us observe in figure 4.1 the preference-matching issue. Region A is richer than region B. Conventional wisdom, derived from experience, says that rich regions have a higher demand for public goods than poor regions, but this view is not granted by economic analysis. In fact, in the case of a publicly provided good, even if this good were a normal one, there would be no guarantee that the optimal quantity demanded would increase with income because the price—which is each individual's share of the total cost—will increase with the quantity. We thus face the usual problem regarding prevalence of the income versus the substitution effect. To have the demand for g increasing with income, however, we need to make an explicit, although reasonable, specific assumption.[9] In graphic terms, this assumption implies that the indifference curve of a rich in-

---

9. See Borck (1998) on this issue.

Figure 4.1
Preference Matching and Production Efficiency

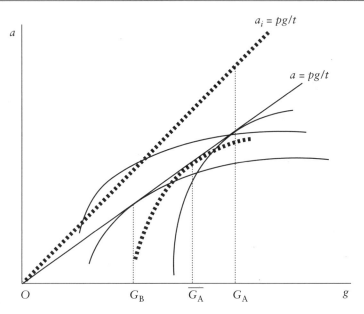

dividual (region) crosses that of a poor one only once and from below, as figure 4.1 shows.

Thus, curves like U_A are those of the rich voters of A region, whereas curves like U_B represent the preferences of the poor, region B, voters. If g is provided by the central government according to the traditional hypothesis of uniformity across all regions, then the median voter will be a resident of region A and the quantity G_A is produced.

The optimal quantity for region B is G_B, which is smaller than G_A. The distance between the two types of U_B indifference curves in figure 4.1 measures the welfare loss, which is the traditional result found in the literature of fiscal federalism: Centralization brings a welfare loss for those areas that have different preferences than those of the national median voter.

The central government may have wrong perceptions of local preferences—in figure 4.1 the dotted indifference curve shows its wrong perception of preferences of region A—and be able to only approximate the quantity preferred by the median voter, such as in the case of $\overline{G_A}$. In this case, both regions would suffer from a welfare loss. With decentralization, preference matching would be solved, with a gain in utility for both regions.

The second issue, production efficiency, may also be illustrated with the help of figure 4.1. Here, P is the minimum cost, so G_A would ensure the optimum for region A because its preferred quantity is produced at the minimum cost, that is, with the minimum tax rate. The central government could be inefficient, however, by using the wrong combination or excessive quantities of productive factors. In that case, the price of the publicly provided good would increase, and the slope of the budget line (the implied tax rate) would be higher. This possibility is shown in figure 4.1 by the dotted budget line $a_i = pg/t$, whose slope is now steeper because of the higher cost p.

In conclusion, decentralization could reduce cost if regions are able to select the appropriate combination of production factors or use only the minimum required quantity. Thus, technical inefficiency would be eliminated.

REFERENCES

Ahlin, H., and E. Mörk. 2007. Effects of decentralization on school resources: Sweden 1989–2002. Working Paper 9. Department of Economics, Uppsala University.

Ahmad, E., M. Albino-War, and R. Singh. 2006. Subnational public financial management: Institutions and macroeconomic considerations. In *Handbook of fiscal federalism*, E. Ahmad and G. Brosio, eds., 405–427. Cheltenham, UK: Edward Elgar.

Ahmad, E., and G. Brosio, eds. 2006. *Handbook of fiscal federalism*. Cheltenham, UK: Edward Elgar.

Akai, N., and M. Sakata. 2005. Fiscal decentralization, fiscal commitment, and regional inequality: Evidence from state-level cross-sectional data for the United States. Cirje F Series Faculty of Economics, University of Tokyo.

Ambrosiano, F., and M. Bordignon. 2006. Normative versus positive theories of revenue assignments in federations. In *Handbook of fiscal federalism*, E. Ahmad and G. Brosio, eds., 306–338. Cheltenham, UK: Edward Elgar.

Arze del Granado, J., J. Martinez-Vazquez, and R. McNab. 2005. Fiscal decentralization and the functional composition of public expenditure. Working Paper 05-01. Andrew Young School of Policy Studies, Georgia State University, Atlanta.

Balaguer-Coll, T., D. Prior, and E. Tortosa-Ausina. 2006. Decentralization and efficiency in Spanish local government. Working Paper 206-02. Department of Economics, University Jaume I, Castelló de la Plana, Spain.

Barankay, I., and B. Lockwood. 2007. Decentralization and the productive efficiency of government: Evidence from Swiss cantons. *Journal of Public Economics* 91(5–6): 1197–1218.

Behnisch, A. B., and T. D. Stegarescu. 2003. Public sector centralization and productivity growth: Reviewing the German experience. ZEW Discussion Paper 02-03.

Borck, R. 1998. Centralization of public good supply with majority voting. *Finanzarchiv* 55:21–40.

Bradford, D., R. Malt, and W. Oates. 1969. The rising cost of local public services: Some evidence and reflections. *National Tax Journal* 22:185–202.

Breton, A. 2002. An introduction to decentralization failures. In *Managing fiscal decentralization*, E. Ahmad and V. Tanzi, eds., 31–45. London: Routledge.

Breuss, F., and M. Eller. 2004. Fiscal decentralization and economic growth: Is there really a link? *Journal for Institutional Comparisons* 2:3–9.

Brosio, G., A. Cassone, and R. Ricciuti. 2002. Tax evasion across Italy: Tarioba non-compliance or inadequate civic concern? *Public Choice* 112:259–273.

Cantarero, P. D., and M. P. Sanchez. 2006. Decentralization and health care outcomes: An empirical analysis within the European Union. Working Paper. University of Cantabria, Spain.

Cao, Y., Y. Qian, and B. Weingast. 1997. From federalism, Chinese style, to privatization, Chinese style. Mimeo.

Crivelli, L., M. Filippini, and I. Mosca. 2007. Federalism and regional health care expenditures: An empirical analysis for the Swiss cantons. MECOO, Quaderno 04-07, Università della Svizzera Italiana.

Documentation Française. 2007. La réforme de la décentralisation: la révision constitutionnelle. http://ladocumentationfrancaise.fr/dossiere/reforme-decentralisation.

Ebel, R. D., and S. Yilmaz. 2002. On the measurement and impact of fiscal decentralization. Policy Research Working Paper 2809. Washington, DC: World Bank.

Faguet, J. P. 2004. Does decentralization increase government responsiveness to local needs? *Journal of Public Economics* 88(March):667–693.

Feld, L. P., G. Kirchgässner, and C. A. Schaltegger. 2004. Fiscal federalism and economic performance: Evidence from Swiss cantons. Mimeo.

Hayek, F. 1945. The use of knowledge in society. *American Economic Review* 35:519–530.

Garcia-Milà, T., and T. J. McGuire. 2002. Fiscal decentralization in Spain: Asymmetric transition to democracy. Mimeo.

Jakubowski, M., and I. Topińska. 2006. Impact of decentralization on public service delivery and equity. Education and health sectors in Poland, 1998–2003. Mimeo.

Jiménez, D., and P. C. Smith. 2005. Decentralisation of health care and its impact on health outcomes. Discussion Papers in Economics 2005/10. University of York.

Jin, J., and H. Zou. 2002. How does fiscal decentralization affect aggregate, national, and subnational government size? *Journal of Urban Economics* 52(2):270–293.

Lin, J. Y., R. Tao, and M. Liu. 2003. Decentralization, deregulation, and economic transition in China. Mimeo.

Lockwood, B. 2006. The political economy of decentralization. In *Handbook of fiscal federalism*, E. Ahmad and G. Brosio, eds., 33–60. Cheltenham, UK: Edward Elgar.

Montero-Granados, R., and J. M. de Dios Jiménez. 2007. Decentralisation and convergence in health among the provinces of Spain (1980–2001). *Social Science and Medicine* 64:1253–1264.

Moreno, L. 2002. Decentralization in Spain. *Regional Studies* 36:300–408.

Oates, W. E. 1993. Fiscal decentralization and economic development. *National Tax Journal* 46:237–243.

OECD. *See* Organisation for Economic Co-operation and Development.

Organisation for Economic Co-operation and Development. 2002. Fiscal decentralization in EU applicant states and selected EU member states. Paris: Centre for Tax Policy and Administration.

Rico, A., and S. Léon. 2005. *Health care devolution in Europe: Trends and prospects.* Working Paper 2005-1. Oslo: Health Care Organization Norway.

Robalino, D. A., O. F. Picazo, and A. Voetberg. 2001. Does fiscal decentralization improve health outcomes? Evidence from a cross-country analysis. World Bank Country Economic Department Series 2565. Washington, DC: World Bank.

Rodriguez-Pose, A., and A. Bwire. 2003. The economic (in)efficiency of devolution. Department of Geography and Environment, London School of Economics.

Salinas Peña, P. 2007. Evaluation of the effects of decentralization on educational outcomes in Spain. XIV Encuentro de Economía Pública, Universidad de Santander, Spain.

Seabright, P. 1996. Accountability and decentralization in government: An incomplete contracts model. *European Economic Review* 40:61–89.

Solé-Ollé, A., and A. Esteller-Moré. 2005. Decentralization provision of public inputs, government responsiveness to local needs, and regional growth: Evidence from Spain. Working Paper. Barcelona: Institut d'Economia de Barcelona.

Strumpf, K., and F. Oberholzer-Gee. 2002. Endogenous policy decentralization: Testing the central tenet of economic federalism. *Journal of Political Economy* 110:1–36.

Tanzi, V. 2002. Pitfalls of decentralization. In *Managing fiscal decentralization*, E. Ahmad and V. Tanzi, eds., 17–30. London: Routledge.

Thiessen, U. 2000. Fiscal federalism in Western European and selected other countries: Centralization or decentralization? What is better for economic growth? Discussion Paper 224. Berlin: Deutsches Institut für Wirtschaftsforschung.

———. 2003. Fiscal decentralization and economic growth in high-income OECD countries. *Fiscal Studies* 24:237–274.

Weingast, B. 1995. The economic role of political institutions: Market preserving federalism and economic development. *Journal of Law, Economics, and Organization* 11:1–31.

Yagi, K. 2004. Decentralization in Japan. Working Paper 30. Keio University Policy and Governance, Japan.

COMMENTARY
Paul Bernd Spahn

In their study on local service provision in countries belonging to the Organisation for Economic Co-operation and Development (OECD), Etisham Ahmad, Giorgio Brosio, and Vito Tanzi pose this question: Does decentralization "improve" local service provision? They survey decentralization policies, distinguishing political, fiscal, and regulatory aspects and calling attention to the intricacies of a multifaceted concept of local self-government. This concept may be affected by national regulation, interference by trading partners, strings attached to intergovernmental transfers, lack of own resources and unfunded mandates, or outright submission where local governments act as agents of the central government. It also emphasizes that decentralization is often the result of political developments rather than a quest for efficiency in public service delivery. This consequence is illustrated by reference to a general tendency toward decentralization in OECD countries, although some recentralizing drifts were also observed, notably in Scandinavian countries (e.g., higher education in Denmark).

Despite this meticulous discussion, including the need for adequate data on outcomes for proper analysis, the authors start with a numerical snapshot from an OECD publication that exhibits "classical" decentralization coefficients such as the share of subnational spending of general government spending (together with some qualitative characteristics). This snapshot is noteworthy because most, if not all, empirical studies examined in the second part of the chapter rely on similar statistics despite their recognized inadequacy to measure decentralization. My faith in such indicators vanished when I learned that Uzbekistan, a country with dual submission of provinces and municipalities to central power, had a decentralization coefficient of 53 percent in 2005, much higher than for the United States and roughly equivalent to that of Canada and Scandinavian countries (Spahn 2006). I strongly believe that decentralization has more to do with governance and incentives than with accounting.

What can be said about the outcome of these developments in OECD countries? Ahmad, Brosio, and Tanzi distinguish three strands of effects: production efficiency, preference matching, and growth.

Production Efficiency

In theory, say Ahmad, Brosio, and Tanzi in chapter 4 (this volume, p. 80), "decentralization is posited to operate through the production function by reducing waste and corruption, and by searching for innovative techniques." In practice, realizing these benefits may be impaired by the imposition of national standards or constraints on the use of input, including bans on privatization or outsourcing of service delivery. I believe that the overwhelming part of the literature still dwells excessively on the public sector as an efficient provider of services, such as in health, education, or housing. The private sector is often overlooked.

There are, however, massive efficiency gains to be reaped by the private provision of these services. Some OECD countries have given the private sector a role in these areas for a long time (e.g., for housing and health in Germany or education in Belgium and The Netherlands). Even in tax administration, where the authors identify production "indivisibilities," supposedly an argument for the central provision of service, there is a conspicuous change through information technology that allows the state to shift more and more administrative functions onto taxpayers while focusing on tax collection and tax audits. This division of functions proves that there are no natural indivisibilities in tax administration.[1] I share the concern expressed by the authors that local tax administrators may have difficulties learning to deal with taxpayers "at arm's length," yet that is only a quest for strengthening external audit functions.

As to the empirical studies presented, I hope that the methodology is sound and uses appropriate "control variables" in addition to the decentralization indicators. For instance, if Barankay and Lockwood (2007) examine the relationship between educational outcomes and decentralization in Switzerland via the share of students with a high school exam who enter universities, one would hope that the effect of urban versus rural regions, the socioeconomic situation of parents, the share of students with migratory background, and—not the least—the education systems have been properly taken into account. At least the empirical results of the study, and of a similar study for Spain, are comforting: The outcome of secondary education is positively related to decentralization and the quality of decentralization.

The result is of little comfort to Germany or Austria, both federal countries, that rank low in the so-called Pisa study by the OECD. This study is indeed much more specific on outcomes: in mathematics and natural sciences, only unitary countries are among the top five. Benignly, in reading there are two federal countries among the winners: Australia and Canada. At least reading appears to be positively related to decentralization.[2]

As to health, a cross-country study by Robalino, Picazo, and Voetberg (2001) regresses infant mortality on a decentralization indicator, which also shows a positive relationship between outcomes and decentralization. Again, this finding is comforting. I would not overrate their conclusion, though, that the marginal effects of decentralization diminish as GDP increases. After all, the

---

1. When I started my studies in the early 1960s, the classical example for production indivisibilities was the telephone. This paradigm is now uncommon nearly everywhere today.

2. Germany and Austria, both federal countries, have cartelized their education systems through interstate contracts aimed at generating "homogeneity." In fact, they act like a unitary state but with limited flexibility because multilateral contracts are difficult to amend, which could be one cause of the bad performance of Germany's educational systems compared with other OECD countries.

reduction of infant mortality has a lower bound, which is not true for the gross domestic product.

At least the multitude of empirical studies on this topic has proven beyond doubt that decentralization can be a major cause of statistics.

Preference Matching

In theory, lower-level governments can be expected to better respond to the preferences for public services of their citizens. These advantages, however, are disputed "on the grounds that higher-level governments are quite capable of matching services to preferences, whereas lower levels may lack incentives and capabilities of doing so effectively" (this volume, p. 80). I share the authors' concern about a lack of incentives and capabilities of local governments, but I decline the proposition that central governments are more capable of matching services to preferences. Let me illustrate by reference to India.

In 2005 the government of India, realizing that local infrastructure is an important impediment to economic development and growth, initiated a massive investment program for urban renewal in 2005.[3] The $30 billion program focuses on 63 Indian cities and megacities, some of which are larger in population than many nation-states. Could one reasonably expect the Indian government to be "capable of matching services to preferences" for urban renewal? Ask the minister for urban development himself! It would give him sleepless nights if you expected him to do so. Of course, he is worried about a lack of local administrative capacity, a weak institutional framework for local governance, ill-prepared city development plans, and difficulties to incorporate private-sector efficiencies. He is concerned about the financial feasibility of investment projects, including operating and maintenance costs needed to ensure the sustainability of development projects. All are reasons for him to insist on a number of reforms to be initiated by the Indian states and municipalities. The minister would never claim to be in a position to match local services with preferences himself, however. When implementing programs, lower-level authorities tend to have a comparative advantage in terms of both production efficiency and preference matching. The empirical studies consulted on preference matching are few and basically inconclusive.

Growth

I believe that any connection between decentralization and economic growth—positive or negative—is purely coincidental. If decentralization reforms in Italy had been accompanied by lower growth during the 1990s, couldn't that have

---

3. The Jawaharlal Nehru National Urban Renewal Mission of the Government of India is administered by the Ministry of Urban Development.

something to do with globalization or exchange rate policies preparing the country for the European Monetary Union? If economic growth had been high in Ireland or Norway despite recentralization, couldn't that have something to do with taxation or buoyancy of the oil market? And what about low growth in Japan with bad policies and macroeconomic constraints? Even where so-called control variables are used to eliminate such effects, the short-run effect of structural variables on the economy is hard to measure, especially where decentralization is approximated by the "classical" indicators. What is a "control variable" for one person is a key variable for others. There are clear methodological limits to regression analysis.

REFERENCES

Ahmad, E., G. Brosio, and V. Tanzi. 2008. Local service provision in selected OECD countries: Do decentralized operations work better? In *Fiscal decentralization and land policies*, G. K. Ingram and Y-H. Hong, eds., 73–104. Cambridge, MA: Lincoln Institute of Land Policy.

Barankay, I., and B. Lockwood. 2007. Decentralization and the productive efficiency of government: Evidence from Swiss cantons. *Journal of Public Economics* 91(5–6): 1197–1218.

Robalino, D. A., O. F. Picazo, and A. Voetberg. 2001. Does fiscal decentralization improve health outcomes?: Evidence from a cross-country analysis. World Bank Country Economic Department Series 2565. Washington, DC: World Bank.

Spahn, P. B. 2006. *Local government and intergovernmental relations in Uzbekistan*, Aide-Mémoire (first draft, preliminary). Washington, DC: World Bank.

DECENTRALIZATION, LOCAL GOVERNANCE, AND LAND POLICY

5

Political Structure and Exclusionary Zoning: Are Small Suburbs the Big Problem?

William A. Fischel

T he inquiry "Are small suburbs the big problem?" arose from a casual statement I made at a Lincoln Institute conference to the Institute's president, Greg Ingram. I said that smaller local governments were more likely to adopt antigrowth regulations than larger jurisdictions. Ingram, who had formerly lived in a large jurisdiction that is notable for its zoning innovations (Montgomery County, Maryland), asked me if I knew of any systematic evidence for that claim. I certainly know lots of stories. The most embarrassing is from my hometown, Hanover, New Hampshire (population 11,000), which recently rezoned most of the developable land in town from its former 3-acre minimum lot size to 10-acre minima. It was done by voter initiative in response to a large development that would have utilized the 3-acre minimum, which had been in the ordinance for more than 30 years. In my experience, and based on my reading of a wide range of literature (Rolleston 1987; Rudel 1989), small-town democracy is the hotbed of zoning excesses.

Ingram, though, might point out that Montgomery County, Maryland, has for many years had 25-acre minimum lot sizes in large parts of the county. The county is not small; the 2000 population was 873,341 on a land area of 496 square miles. Moreover, the supersize acreage requirement was imposed by the county legislature, not a plebiscite of any kind. Montgomery County stands as at least a partial rebuke to the conventional wisdom (I have had a part in making

---

I thank without implicating Lee Anne Fennell for her insightful comments on an earlier draft.

it conventional, if not wisdom) that the excesses of land use regulation are the product of local democracy.

I should add, by the way, that Montgomery County's 25-acre minima are somewhat misleading. Landowners subject to them can use them as currency for transferable development rights (TDRs). Developers who own vacant parcels closer to the Washington, DC, area, can increase the allowable density if they purchase the TDRs that were assigned to the 25-acre-minimum lots when the program was created (Walls and McConnell 2007). So, although the 25-acre standard looks two-and-a-half times worse than Hanover's 10-acre minimum size, the Maryland program's net effect may not really be so exclusionary, although it does seem to raise housing prices there (Pollakowski and Wachter 1990).

Exclusionary Zoning: Selective and General Controls

An early expression of the importance of small suburbs as engines of antigrowth is Robert Ellickson's "Suburban Growth Controls: An Economic and Legal Analysis" (1977). The trend that Ellickson spotted was the change in orientation of new zoning. Instead of being a municipal expression of the good housekeeping maxim—a place for everything, but everything in its place—or even a device for *selective* exclusion of the poor, as Charles Haar (1953) had pointed out many years ago, the new zoning standards sought to limit all growth. This trend was first called the "growth control" movement, and it has continued to the present under the aliases of "growth management" and "smart growth." It is primarily a suburban phenomenon. Michael Danielson (1976) offered a still-useful book explaining the political grounds for its virulence in the suburbs, and in many and ongoing works on the subject, Anthony Downs (1973, 1994) has identified suburban jurisdictions as the primary source of exclusion.

The title of this chapter invokes the term *exclusionary zoning*, and not everyone agrees what exclusionary means. All zoning excludes something from somewhere. One modern connotation of the term focuses on low-income housing. An ordinance is said to be exclusionary if it makes insufficient provision for low-income housing. The focus of this chapter, however, is land use policy that discourages *all* housing development, not only new units for the poor. A policy that reduces total expected housing starts by 50 percent but reserves 10 percent of those that are allowed for a certain income-segment is still exclusionary. Because housing units are durable and hence over time liable to be sold to lower-income buyers, fewer units for the rich will ultimately mean fewer units for the poor. "Inclusionary" zoning, which requires that housing developers also build and subsidize special units for low-income buyers or renters, would benefit the metropolitan area's poor only if the inclusionary policy is not accompanied by a reduction in the overall rate of housing development (Pendall 2000; Weicher and Thibodeau 1988). It appears that most "inclusionary" zoning programs are in affluent suburbs that are otherwise quite antigrowth. Their "inclusionary zoning" may be a way of either heading off hostile legal action or helping the city or town save tax money on salaries for public employees for whom the "affordable" housing is earmarked.

Regardless of the merits of my criticism of some aspects of "inclusionary" zoning, however, the reader should understand that in this chapter, "exclusionary" zoning means attempts to reduce the overall rate and ultimate density of housing development. The benchmark for "reduce" is the rate of development and density that would have maximized aggregate local land values in the context of a competitive market for communities. The first part of this criterion, maximizing *aggregate* land value, assumes that there is some level of land use control that is necessary to internalize localized spillover effects (Mills 1979). I am not comparing regulation to no regulation. Optimal regulation maximizes the aggregate value of land, not the value of each parcel taken by itself, since one parcel's most valuable use may cause a net loss to neighboring parcels. The second part of the criterion attempts to discount the monopoly zoning effects, to be discussed presently.

My general thesis is that small suburbs do indeed present a big problem for efficient development of metropolitan areas. I will develop the political economy argument for that hypothesis presently, but first I will present the new evidence I have in support of it, which is contained in figure 5.1. The reader will note

Figure 5.1
Elasticity of Supply and Local Government Structure in 42 MSAs

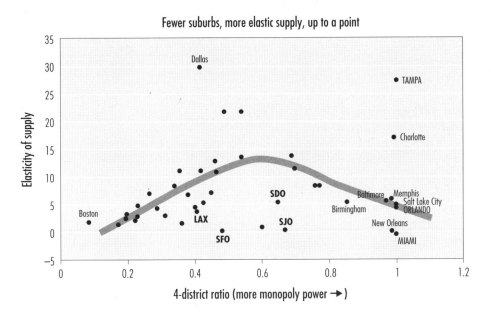

Source: See data appendix.

that this order inverts the usual rhetoric of an economics paper, in which theory comes first and evidence testing the hypothesis comes afterward. The usual sequence makes it appear that the theory was not developed as an ad hoc rationalization for the evidence that has been assembled. I can sidestep that anxiety (which we usually hold anyway, despite the sequence of presentation) by pointing out that the theory that I will advance is one I expressed years ago in *The Economics of Zoning Laws* (Fischel 1985), especially the chapter "The Political Geography of Zoning."

Empirical Evidence: Fragmented Metropolitan Statistical Areas and Housing Supply Elasticity

The vertical axis in figure 5.1 is the elasticity of the supply of housing units in selected Metropolitan Statistical Areas (MSAs) as measured by Green, Malpezzi, and Mayo (2005, 336) for the period 1979 to 1996. (The cities and data are in the appendix.) I regard this elasticity as an index of the degree of regulatory restriction that prevails in the MSA. Green, Malpezzi, and Mayo estimated these elasticities to test whether the index of metropolitan land use regulations developed by Malpezzi (1996) could explain variations in supply elasticity. They found that they could, but not with a great deal of confidence because the regulatory index was the only significant variable in their regression besides density. I submit that their measure of elasticity of supply is actually a better measure of regulatory restrictiveness than the index that Malpezzi employed, which was the product of a survey of developer opinions. (My opinion follows Glaeser, Gyourko, and Saks 2006.) The estimated elasticities in Green, Malpezzi, and Mayo already control for population growth, density, net cost of capital, commuting time, and preexisting density and prices (Mayer and Somerville 2000). Thus, the only intrametropolitan differences left to be explained are natural and contrived restrictions on supply.

In defense of my focus on raw elasticity measures, I would point out that the "natural" constraints on supply such as wetlands and steep slopes are seldom by themselves enough to deter a developer. As the son of a former excavating contractor, I am perhaps overly informed about what a bulldozer can do, but earthmoving is not all that difficult. Most of the large cities of the world have filled in bays and lopped off hills even before earthmoving became mechanized. The supposedly physical or topographic constraints on development are simply natural land forms that are comparatively easy to regulate.

The horizontal axis in figure 5.1 is the four-school-district concentration ratio for the Urbanized Area (UA) of the MSA in 2000 as developed by Battersby and Fischel (2007). The concentration ratio is the aggregate *land area* of the four largest school districts within the UA divided by the land area of the UA. If the UA land area were 100 square miles and the largest district had 20 square miles of its territory within the UA, the next largest had 15 square miles, the third largest 10, and the fourth largest 5, the concentration ratio would be 50 percent (20 + 15 + 10 + 5 = 50; 50/100 = 50%). Any one of these districts might have more land outside the UA, but only the land area of the district within the UA is counted.

The four-district ratio was developed in conscious imitation of the four-firm concentration ratio from industrial organization. Battersby and Fischel sought to develop a consistent, geographically based measure of the extent of Tiebout (1956) competition among school districts. Tiebout competition is spatial—you have to live in the jurisdiction to attend school there—so our measure of potential choices is by land area, not population. We used the UA as our base because on average 90 percent of MSA land area is essentially rural. The rural parts of most MSA counties are not realistic choices for most home buyers, and the counties that make up most MSAs (all except those of New England) vary considerably in size. Thus, MSA-based measures of school district competition are problematical for comparative purposes. The UA consists of the developed part of the central city plus the contiguous, built-up suburban area of the city. "Suburban" in this case does not refer to municipal or school district boundaries; its extent is determined mainly by housing density. The UA thus offers a nationally consistent, boundary-free basis for comparing how many local governments are available in the part of the MSA where most people live.

The four-district ratio is a measure of relative competitiveness. Because UA area varies (roughly in proportion to population), a large UA with a 40 percent concentration ratio will have larger units of governments than a small UA with a 40 percent ratio. I will nonetheless speak of "competitive" UAs—those with low concentration ratios—as having generally "small" governments. The simple correlation between average district size (measured by number of pupils) and the concentration ratio is 0.47 in the Battersby and Fischel group. This figure is not impressively large, but it does suggest that the more competitive UAs also have smaller units of government.

School districts are limited-purpose municipal corporations, and one of their limits is that they do not do zoning. That would be fine if the school district and the municipality that does the zoning have overlapping boundaries. Only about a third of cities correspond exactly to their school districts, but I have found that most other cities have some correspondence with a single district (Fischel 2007). For present purposes, I submit that the geographic structure of school districts is a reasonable proxy for the geographic structure of the governments that do zoning. A more precise measure would require a state-by-state inventory of which local governments have final say about zoning. My hypothesis gets some support from the left side of figure 5.1. The farthest left observation is the Boston area. It has hundreds of relatively small school districts, and they actually do correspond to zoning units because school districts usually overlap town boundaries in New England. The four largest districts in Boston occupy only 8.5 percent of the UA land area. (If arrayed by population, the concentration ratios would be slightly higher, but not by much. UA boundaries are truncated to include only densely built-up areas, so within-UA density does not vary much except in the largest cities.) At the same time, the estimated supply elasticity for Boston is quite low.

As the four-district ratio increases along the horizontal axis of figure 5.1, the elasticity of supply generally increases. The UAs in uppercase bold type (LAX, SFO, SJO, and SDO) are in California, where development restrictions are especially stringent, so they have low elasticity of supply for their level of concentration. The main exceptions are the very highly concentrated areas (four-district ratios greater than 0.90), which are mainly in areas in which the school district and the county are the same. These areas are mainly in the South (the Florida UAs are in uppercase) and the arid parts of the West (Salt Lake City is in this group). In these areas, the county is also the major, if not the exclusive, player in regulating the supply of greenfield development. In these areas, the monopoly effect of exclusionary zoning prevails over the political influence of developers. These behavioral propositions are now ripe for more careful explanation.

Local Government Politics: Median Voter or Interest Group?

Land use regulation in the United States has long been the prerogative of local government. Next to the quality of schools, zoning is the local function that residents care most about. Zoning is not the province of experts in the United States; it is a highly political activity. To understand zoning, one must have a political model of local government and a grasp of the institutional setting in which local governments operate.

The competing political models of local government are the median voter model and the interest-group model. The median voter model holds that to determine the demand for any local public service, look at the characteristics of the voters that might determine personal demand for that service and pick the voter with the median characteristic. Thus, if the demand for school spending is thought to be responsive to income, the voter with the median income in the district is a good proxy for the district's demand for education.

The median voter model assumes that local political leaders are faithful conduits for voters' opinions. Thus, the city councils that formulate zoning and changes in zoning ask themselves what they think the majority of voters within their jurisdiction would want them to do. In many jurisdictions, and for zoning issues in particular, the city council does not even have to ask itself. The voters will tell them directly. Voter referenda and voter initiatives are two straightforward checks on the actions of public officials in zoning.

Econometric studies of local public goods in a variety of contexts suggest that the median voter model can be regarded as the political analog of perfect competition (Holcombe 1989). Like the competitive model, the median voter model is used by economists in a wide variety of circumstances, and almost all empirical studies of local government invoke it, but the issue I am examining is whether the accuracy of the median voter model varies by the size of the government unit being examined. On this topic there are fewer studies, but those that have addressed the question have found that the median voter model is less reliable for larger jurisdictions.

The study most directly on point is Turnbull and Mitias (1999), who compared the median voter model's predictions with an open set of alternative explanations for government tax and expenditure patterns. They found that the median voter model dominated others in a sample of municipalities, but when applied to counties and state governments in the same region as the municipalities (the upper Midwest), no particular model consistently explained spending variations. Their study was confirmed for French cities by Josselin, Rocaboy, and Tavéra (2005). Bigger cities give results that diverge from that predicted by the median voter model.

Other studies indirectly support this claim. Bloom and Ladd (1982) found that public officials in smaller Massachusetts towns were more responsive to voter concerns by lowering rates after a property revaluation, whereas officials in larger cities took revaluation as an excuse to raise taxes and spending. Romer, Rosenthal, and Munley (1992) found that smaller New York school districts conformed to the predictions of the median voter model, but not the largest city districts. Political scientists generally have regarded smaller governments as more responsive to voters rather than to business groups (Burns et al. 1993; Dahl and Tufte 1973). Eric Oliver (2000) documents the greater political participation by residents in smaller cities, in contrast to voter indifference in larger cities. Hanke and Carbonell (1978) noted that developer interests were able to forestall California's coastal zone legislation by their influence over state legislators; it passed only after a voter initiative bypassed the legislative gridlock. John Matsusaka's extensive studies (1995, 2000) found that the 23 states that have voter initiatives had smaller and more decentralized public sectors, which suggests that in normal, representative state politics (that is, politics in states that lack statewide initiatives), the will of the majority does not always prevail.

The interest-group theory of local government takes its cue from theories of national politics, in which the ability of voters to monitor their elected officials is attenuated (Stigler 1971). In these models, the key assumption is that the majority of voters cannot easily determine which candidates will work for their interests. Candidates for public office will require funds to persuade voters to elect them. Raising funds for political candidates is more easily done by groups organized around sources of income. Thus, dairy farmers are more likely contributors to candidates for state office; the more numerous consumers of milk will usually be unorganized. A one-cent increase in milk prices does the large number of consumers a few cents' worth of harm per family, but it does the small number of dairy farmers thousands of dollars in benefit. Hence, dairy farmers are easy to organize and more likely to contribute to political figures.

Applying the interest-group model to local land use regulation seems straightforward to some observers (Benson 1981; Denzau and Weingast 1982). Owners of developable land, developers, building trades, and their suppliers and others whose income would rise with development would seem likely to form the classic interest group. Relaxing the zoning laws would usually increase their incomes. Most such interests have their own trade organizations, so the costs of raising funds to help influence elections and decision making would be low. Plenty of city folklore as well as some influential sociology (Molotch 1976) has it that local officials are beholden to prodevelopment interests.

But the interest-group model requires some modification with respect to land use decisions. Homeowners at the local level are a powerful offset to development interests. Homeowners seldom have a common source of income to unite them (most do not even work in the same jurisdiction), but they do have a common source of wealth: their homes. For most homeowners, the property on which they live in the jurisdiction in which they vote is the most valuable asset they have. Indeed, surveys indicate that most homeowners do not own much else (Tracy, Schneider, and Chan 1999). Nor can they easily diversify or insure their investment against adverse neighborhood change. They are an interest group united by a common type of asset as opposed to a common source of income.

Homeowners also have an organizational advantage that other groups do not. They live in close contiguity to one another, and their children usually attend school together. Local public schools are the most important source of local contacts for adults (Fischel 2006). Because local schools usually overlap with the local government that does the zoning, homeowners can easily form a group to jawbone city officials about the evils of some threatening development. It is worth emphasizing how the median voter and interest group models differ. In the median voter model, it is assumed that everyone has the same interest; it is only a matter of ranking choices about it from lesser to greater amounts. So, school spending and growth restrictions are both positive goods for most homeowners. The median voter selects the amount, not whether to have them. The political process—voting—merely determines how much will be obtained collectively. Interest-group theory arrays people over conflicting interests: Higher milk prices are always bad for consumers and are usually good for producers ("usually" because of the threat of consumer substitution at higher prices). With respect to zoning, more restrictions are usually desired by homeowners and usually opposed by developers. The "usually" here is to rule out extreme cases in which a paucity of regulations would harm developers' ability to market their homes because of spillover effects and in which homeowners might prefer more development to achieve economies of scale in local services. Neither extreme is likely to prevail within the usual range of entitlement battles in metropolitan areas.

Loudoun County as a Synecdoche for Large-Jurisdiction Zoning —

The key empirical question is where the median voter model (the unopposed homeowners) is likely to prevail and where the mixed interest group (homeowners versus developers) model will prevail. The interest group model is more likely to produce a more elastic supply of housing since developer interests will at least partially counter the interests of homeowners. To illustrate this with a real example, I summarize a news story that ran in the *Washington Post* on January 21, 2007, about the politics of zoning in Loudoun County, Virginia.

Loudoun County is in what was once the "exurban" part of the Washington, DC, metropolitan area. The three close-in suburban counties of Washington are Fairfax County, Virginia, and Montgomery County and Prince Georges County in Maryland. Loudoun is a long step outward, west of Washington Dulles Airport, which straddles the Fairfax-Loudoun border about 25 miles from downtown Washington. As development pushed out (or was pushed out) from Fairfax County, Loudoun County has been transformed into a suburban county since about 1980, growing to about 170,000 population in 2000. As is typical of much American suburban development, the initial suburbanites are quite affluent and, of course, are almost all homeowners. Loudoun County is responsible for all the land use decisions within its territory except for a few incorporated towns that appear to take up a very small fraction of the county's 520 square miles.

With a headline that pretty much tells the whole story ("The Loudoun Network: Political Backers Gain from Growth; Influence of Developers, Allies Runs Deep"), the *Post* reporters detailed how the development lobby worked. In 1999 Loudoun's prodevelopment majority on the County Board of Supervisors, which makes and alters the zoning laws, was replaced by an antidevelopment majority. One of the supervisors who was defeated back in 1999 was active in the development industry and is herself a longtime landowner. She organized a campaign to enable a prodevelopment group to regain control of the Board, recruiting candidates and helping them raise funds for their campaigns. As the *Post* summarized her handiwork, "Overall, companies and individuals tied to the development industry poured more than $490,000 into supervisor campaigns in Loudoun, more than seven times the figure four years earlier, according to data from the nonprofit Virginia Public Access Project."

The campaign succeeded in electing a six-member (of nine) majority on the board, and they went right to work reversing the antidevelopment policies of the previous board. In the process, the development interests that financed their election apparently prospered. A later article in the *Post* reported that a county and federal investigation is now under way to determine whether the benefits received were the result of anything more than the quotidian give and take of Virginia politics.

Large county and big city governments in other metropolitan areas have usually been regarded as being more favorably disposed toward developers than the average homeowner. Political scientists generally have regarded big cities as probusiness (Banfield 1965; Frieden and Sagalyn 1989). It is widely agreed that the main motive for the huge spate of suburban incorporations in Southern California in the 1950s and 1960s was to escape the prodevelopment land use policies of the county and larger city governments, especially those of both the city and county of Los Angeles (Cion 1966; Miller 1981). I found that the primary force leading to suburban municipal incorporations in the Seattle area in the 1990s was what homeowners regarded as the overly prodevelopment policies of King County and anxiety that annexation to larger cities would leave them similarly unprotected (Fischel 2001, chapter 10). Historian Jon Teaford (1997) documented the many instances in which twentieth-century suburban incorporations were undertaken so that existing homeowners could take over the land use controls. Teaford also describes how metropolitan governance plans foundered on the question of which government would do the zoning. Paul Lewis (2001) reviewed political science literature and presented original survey evidence from California that indicates that larger units of local government tend to be more inclined to support job growth, whereas smaller units are more protective of neighborhood housing amenities. Lewis found that jurisdiction size rather than location (central city versus suburb) was the critical factor.

Stories like that of Loudoun County, Virginia, are extremely rare in smaller suburban communities. In a small town, the number of issues is likely to be fewer. Voters will have some indication, from various informal contacts as well as public records, of where candidates stand. In this situation, the amount of money spent by a candidate has less influence on the outcome. Indeed, in many small towns, changes in zoning laws, even sometimes changes in the zoning classification of a single parcel, are subject to voter referenda.

Typology of Local Governments

The political process is not the only factor that inclines smaller governments toward a no-growth syndrome. The fragmentation of the metropolitan land area into numerous governing units causes the median voter in each unit to adopt a narrower view of her interests. Figure 5.2 is a schematic to assist in seeing the problem. Each lettered shape is a municipality that controls land use within its borders. Economic activity is assumed to occur only within the "metropolitan area," which includes all the contiguous municipalities. Because the topic at this point is geographic structure, not politics, I assume now that only homeowners vote in each municipality and that the median voter model applies. That is, there is no special development interest that can influence politics à la Loudoun County. The question now is, in which type of community would the developer of a substantial number of homes get a better reception from authorities, who are always mindful of the interests of existing homeowners. To improve the motivation of the example, let us suppose that the developer who proposes the new homes and needs a rezoning is doing so in response to increased demand caused by growing employment opportunities in the metropolitan area.

The home-owning residents most likely to be responsive to the home builder are those in Q, the isolated city in figure 5.2. Additional employment in Q-burg confers economic benefits on many existing residents. Aside from own employment prospects being improved, the additional jobs will improve the chances that children, other family members, and friends will stay in the city and not move to another. I am assuming that voters can see the connection between

Figure 5.2
Archetypes of Urban Governance

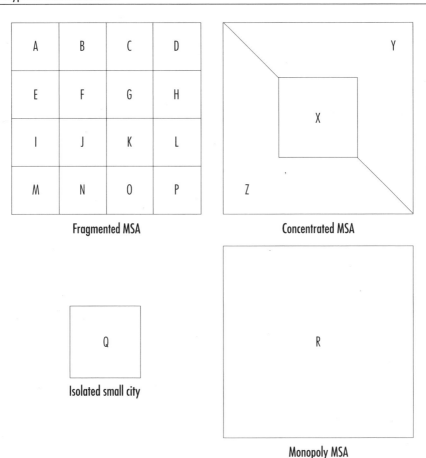

building the new homes and the additional jobs, but if they do not see it immediately, the employers themselves will let it be known that high housing costs would be a deterrent to their relocation plans. Of course, immediate neighbors to the development may object, but their objections will be met by the observation that the larger community's economic health depends on the homes being built somewhere. My claim here is not that the Q-burg city council will prostrate themselves before developers. It is only that they will have more reason to try to overcome neighborhood opposition to development.

Now consider the same situation in any one of the municipalities in the fragmented metropolitan area, say community J in Fragmented MSA in figure 5.2.

To keep the comparison fair, I assume that employment opportunities are rising by the same percentage in the larger metropolitan area as they were in the smaller, isolated city that was just considered. The additional employment, however, is not necessarily located in the municipality in J-ville, where the housing developer wishes to build. Job growth could as likely be in any of the towns A through P, and therein lies the problem for a housing developer who is responding to the increased metropolitan employment. The developer's proposal to build on a parcel in J-ville will inconvenience some neighbors. Community authorities in J will *not* hear much from other residents of J about the need for housing to accommodate the increased employment, even if they are well aware of the benefits to themselves and their families. The J-ville NIMBYs could correctly point out that the proposed housing could just as easily go in another town nearby. If it did, residents of J-ville would still get the same employment benefit but not have to put up with the additional housing. Because every town would face the same situation, the housing developer in the fragmented metropolitan area would have a more difficult time getting regulatory permissions in any locale.

An intermediate situation arises in the Concentrated MSA in figure 5.2, which has the same population and area as the Fragmented MSA, but which is divided into only three large local governments, X, Y, and Z. A housing developer in X will have a somewhat easier time with the regulators, but not because developers in a jurisdiction like X, Y, or Z are likely to be able to form an interest group; we are still maintaining that the home-owning median voters are in charge. Rather, any one of these jurisdictions will be able to internalize some benefit from the developments that give rise to the demand for new housing. Some of the suppliers to the housing industry may live in X, and some workers who would be employed in the new businesses or in the housing development will be voters in X. Thus, opponents to the new housing development will find that some members of their community will actively favor the new development. One can hardly predict any particular political outcome, but it seems safe to say that the housing developer will be treated more charitably in one of the communities X, Y, or Z in the Concentrated MSA than in A or B or C or . . . or P in the Fragmented MSA. It will not be as smooth a ride for the developer as in Isolated City Q, but I am assuming now that the developer does not have the option of taking his business to Q or to any other MSA.

Intermetropolitan migration of business might temper the decisions of any of the areas considered here, but I have proposed that the only jurisdiction that can effectively respond to that threat is the isolated small city, Q in figure 5.2. (The special case of the Monopoly MSA is discussed below.) Lonesome Q-burg does not require the cooperation of other jurisdictions to respond, as the other cities would. It also has more reason to be responsive. Small cities are numerous and less specialized in their economic activities and are thus more vulnerable to migration of footloose firms.

Side Payments to Mitigate Growth Restrictions

The preceding discussion assumed that development interests and homeowner interests are battling over initial entitlements to develop land. These entitlements are the on-the-books regulations that cannot quickly be changed in the face of unwanted development. The focus has not been on *exchange* between those parties or their representatives. There has been some implicit exchange, as when a homeowner thinks in her own mind that she might be willing to give up some neighborhood amenity—that nice open field across the street—to improve the chances that her son will get a job in the area. Economics, though, is mostly concerned with interpersonal exchange, as when Jonetta agrees to maintain Kevin's garden for a monetary fee or some goods in kind, say Kevin's shoveling her sidewalk in the winter. It is these exchanges that mitigate all the antidevelopment positions.

Consider the following hypothetical, which uses the story of Loudoun County as a fanciful example. During the period of 2000 to 2004, an antidevelopment coalition of elected supervisors made it difficult to develop. The supervisors downzoned (made more restrictive) much of the open space, they declared moratoriums on water and sewer lines that would make development possible, and they expanded the definition of wetlands to make much land undevelopable. But what the county supervisors can do, they can also undo. If developers were so inclined, they could pay to get the lots rezoned, build the water and sewer mains themselves, and create wetland reserves to offset their filling-in those on which they sought to build. The land use regulations on the books just represent the beginning point of a bargaining process.

Such deals do not have to be illegal or even shady. The money for the rezoning can go into the county treasury and used to lower taxes or for spending on whatever the county wants. If such deals can easily be made, the rate of development in Loudoun County should not have been much lower during the 2000 to 2004 reign of the antidevelopment party than it was before or after. One might suspect that the money that the development industry spent to buy (in this utterly fanciful scenario) the 2004 election was simply a smaller amount than it was costing to buy back the development rights when the antidevelopment board was in charge. The developers, of course, would rather have development entitlements for free, but we usually do not assume that a developer who has inherited money builds more than one who has to borrow.

The preceding analysis is also fanciful because such exchanges as I describe are actually quite costly to make. It is not the entitlements themselves that are at issue; it is the cost of making the transactions that is the barrier we are concerned with. I have in several previous works (Fischel 1985, 1995, 2001) described the costs that retard transactions in land use permits: lack of knowledge about reservation prices; the endowment effect, which makes people reluctant to trade what they already possess; risk aversion by homeowners; legal impediments on contract zoning; the inefficiencies of barter exchange; rent-seeking by otherwise unaffected parties; moral indignation; and just plain spite. The issue that is relevant to this inquiry is why these transaction costs might be larger in the Fragmented MSA than in the Concentrated MSA.

One answer might be the greater degree of specialization in government in larger cities. The democratic virtues of the small town can be a drawback in bargaining with that small town for development permissions. Citizen planning has its virtues, but the involvement of numerous parties in negotiations surely adds to the cost of getting to an agreement. A larger unit of government usually channels the process through more predictable and professional lines of review. The conditions might be as rigorous as they are in a small town, but the number of occasions that the developer has to agree to them is apt to be fewer. It is also probable that developers themselves can specialize in larger jurisdictions, with apartment developers knowing how to respond to different regulatory hurdles than might be faced by a developer of industrial property.

The more likely reason for larger cities' attraction to development is the aforementioned political and geographic considerations. Developers in large cities can organize and influence elections and decisions more easily than those in smaller venues, so they start in a better bargaining position. They do not have to go so far in negotiations to get to a viable position. In smaller communities where the developers start from less advantageous positions, the road to a viable development is longer and deters more travelers. The extreme entitlements that some communities obtain (e.g., 25-acre minimum lot size) are especially problematic in land use because the first stage of development is apt to be the last stage of development. Intensifying land use after an area has become even lightly populated is much more difficult to do since the buyers of homes on multiacre lots are apt to be especially vociferous NIMBYs. It is for this reason, by the way, that private developers of multistage projects always hold a majority of votes in the homeowner associations that they set up until almost all the lots have been sold (Reichman 1976). They worry that an early handoff to residents would allow the newcomers to alter subsequent development. Developers subject to public zoning cannot do so because of the one-person, one-vote rule (Nelson 1999).

Monopoly Power's Ambiguous Effect on Zoning Politics

Another effect of jurisdiction size is its potential to confer monopoly benefits on the community. Such a community is represented by the Monopoly MSA in figure 5.2, where R is the sole unit of government in charge of land use regulation. Unlike the isolated small city represented by Q in figure 5.2, New R City does not have close substitutes to which developers and residents could locate. Demand for location in R is somewhat inelastic, which gives the opportunity for those who control the gates to extract some monopoly benefits. The main issue is who will get those benefits.

Entry into the development business is sufficiently easy that developers themselves could not take advantage of a public monopoly. To put it bluntly, if one developer can buy a city council's approval, others can, too. Existing homeowners are more likely candidates for monopoly benefits. The gain from monopoly control of development arises from making competition for existing homes more scarce in their market. The scarcity has nothing to do with the benefits of open space preservation or lesser road traffic; it is simply that there are fewer sites available. Another potential source of monopoly rents to homeowners is larger side payments, such as jacked-up exactions and other side payments from developers, which can be substituted for local taxes. The aforementioned transaction costs plus some judicial restraints on the scope of exactions tend to limit this source of monopoly rents, however (Fischel 1995, 347).

Communities in the Fragmented MSA cannot take advantage of monopoly rents because developers and home buyers can go to alternative communities in the same market. Monopoly in the isolated city (Q in figure 5.2) is limited by the large numbers of other small cities that employers can choose from. Therefore, it is the Concentrated MSA in which monopoly inclinations might arise. Jurisdictions X, Y, and Z might each have some monopoly power, and their mutual agreements to limit development are more easily entered into, which would make them more like the R government in the Monopoly MSA of figure 5.2. Such agreements would not be illegal, as they would be in the private sector under the Sherman Antitrust Act. The judicial application of antitrust law to local zoning decisions was deflated by the U.S. Congress in the early 1980s and was entirely discarded by the U.S. Supreme Court a few years later (Kinkade 1992).

It seems to me that monopoly gains are the most plausible reason for the empirical observations on the far right side of figure 5.1, which contradict my basic hypothesis that fragmentation produces exclusion. These urban areas (Baltimore, Memphis, Salt Lake City, Orlando, New Orleans, and Miami) have a high concentration ratio but also have very low elasticity of supply, which I take to be the result of stringent regulations. The reason is that concentration is so great that a single unit of government controls most of the developable land.

For a single jurisdiction that controls a large amount of a growing MSA's territory, the gains to existing homeowners from stringent development restrictions are not just the creation of amenities. The added scarcity value for the home they own goes on top of that. This prospective monopoly value helps overcome the greater organization problems that homeowners have in larger jurisdictions. More is at stake for homeowners than just the quality of their neighborhood. Someone seeking office in a large county can appeal to homeowners not only by promising to protect their neighborhoods from inroads, but by promising to make sure that housing developments that would not affect their neighborhoods directly will not be built and thus maintain the scarcity of their homes.

Econometric studies of monopoly zoning started with Bruce Hamilton (1978), whose evidence suggested the widespread existence of monopoly power.

I found Hamilton's data to be flawed and presented evidence that the monopoly effect was limited to a few highly concentrated metropolitan areas (Fischel 1980). This view is generally consistent with my interpretation of figure 5.1 here. My results are generally supported by subsequent studies by Louis Rose (1989) and James Thorson (1996). Monopoly zoning seems to exert an independent effect only in a few highly concentrated metropolitan areas.

I had at one time been skeptical of the monopoly-zoning explanation because I have never heard an elected official utter anything that seemed consistent with it. Candidates do not usually run for city council or county supervisor on the platform of "let's make housing more expensive so we insiders will profit more." They talk instead about the environment and quality of life and small-town character and even, at the end of a long list of goals, "affordable housing." But I have since noticed that almost no industrial cartel sees its goals as simply restricting supply to raise price and profits. The organizers want the market to be "orderly." They want to preserve "product quality." They want to ensure that "high cost" producers can "stay in business." Consumers, they say, will ultimately be better off for their farsighted activities that forestall "destructive competition." International cartels for diamonds and petroleum, as well as many domestic seekers of government protection, offer these and many other rationales for monopoly behavior.

Nor are nonprofit organizations immune from self-delusion on this matter. I was in the 1970s a faculty-committee observer of the erstwhile cartel that coordinated financial aid awards to students among Ivy League and other selective colleges and universities. The "overlap group," as it was called, sought to ensure that no institution offered more financial aid (i.e., a lower price) to prospective applicants than another. My first reaction as a naive assistant professor was, Isn't this an illegal price-fixing scheme? It was carefully explained to me that this system was for the good of the students and that the universities were hardly profit-making monopolists. Years later the antitrust lawyers at the U.S. Justice Department took notice and induced the overlap group to desist from sharing information about financial aid. (For details and a partial defense of the process, see Hoxby 2001.)

Returning to zoning, it should be noted that local political candidates invoke the benign-sounding goals that monopolists might use even in competitive markets like those in the Fragmented MSA in figure 5.2. What makes cities in a highly concentrated MSA different is that the voters who own homes have better reason to pay attention to such claims. If housing prices have ticked upward in a monopoly community, homeowners, including especially those who most recently purchased homes, have a strong reason to pay attention to overall growth controls. Residents of communities in the Fragmented MSA also gain from higher metropolitan housing prices, but there is not much that any single community can do to shore them up. Each jurisdiction has only a small fraction of the land area, and so additional restrictions whose sole purpose is to prop up housing prices will not work. (The cynical might suggest that support for metropolitan-wide growth legislation is the product of homeowners in fragmented MSAs who realize that only such concerted regulation can offer them the monopoly gains.

One difficulty with this theory is that this same monopoly price helps development interests overcome their free rider problems, too. As prices for home sites rise, developers are willing to pay more to pry more of them loose from regulatory restrictions. Both forces (homeowner restrictions and developer expansion) cannot simultaneously prevail. Thus, the scenario of highly concentrated MSAs is likely to be characterized by wide swings in regulatory regimes. Sometimes the homeowners will dominate; at other times developers will call the shots. Such swings seem to have characterized Loudoun County and some other counties in the Washington, DC, MSA. When the homeowners get control of land use governance, the restrictions are likely to have even greater effects than they would in a fragmented MSA. A slow-growth policy in a large suburban county promotes especially high housing prices because developers have fewer alternative jurisdictions with which to deal. Fragmented MSAs have many communities. Each of them will be difficult for developers to dominate, but they can at least make deals, and some communities are more willing to deal than others.

This "pillar to post" regulatory regime of monopolistic suburbs may explain the wide variation in elasticity of supply of MSAs on the far right side of figure 5.1. Consider the three Florida MSAs represented there. All are highly concentrated, mainly because county governments control most exurban zoning decisions. Miami, which is mainly Dade County, had the lowest elasticity of supply of the entire group presented by Green, Malpezzi, and Mayo (2005), whose estimates I used. Miami's supply elasticity was actually negative over the period they examined. One contributor to this low elasticity was the urban growth boundary that the county established during this period. Many cities have urban growth boundaries, but for most of them, the boundary's only effect is to create "leapfrog" development patterns, in which developers who would have located in the rural parts of city G (to refer to figure 5.2's Fragmented MSA) simply move out to city D or some other jurisdiction. But an urban growth boundary in Monopoly MSA, such as one that might be established in jurisdiction R in figure 5.2, leaves developers with fewer options.

By the same token, when developers get the upper hand in a jurisdiction with a large amount of developable space, the effect on metropolitan housing supply will be much more expansive, which may account for the extreme variation in housing supply elasticity among the Florida MSAs in figure 5.1. Miami-Dade may have been in the grip of an antidevelopment crowd, while the developers may have been in control in the Tampa MSA (mainly Hillsborough County) during the period.

State and Judicial Protection of Development Interests

This chapter so far has dealt solely with the structure of local government as if local government were completely autonomous. Local governments are everywhere "creatures of the state," and local (and state) land use decisions are reviewable by state courts. The federal government has only one city, Washington, DC, and federal courts have been loath to intervene in local land use matters, so supervision of zoning has been the province of state legislatures and state courts. Federal environmental regulations affect urban land use, of course, and in general they have tended to retard rather than promote development. But because their application is uniform across the country, federal regulation is not a good candidate to explain national variations in metropolitan housing supply.

State governments have done little to encourage local governments to increase housing supply by relaxing regulations. This is because state governments are historically more creatures of local governments than vice versa (Burns and Gamm 1997). If a state court invokes the hoary principle called Dillon's rule (named after Judge John Dillon [1871], whose treatise on municipal law predated zoning) and strikes down some local zoning innovation because it was not explicitly authorized in state legislation, the locality's delegation to the state legislature will usually remedy that deficiency (Libonati 1993, 18). Legal scholars observe the first step (the judge's decision) but not the second (the legislative correction), and so debate about the jurisprudential merits of Dillon's rule is kept alive even though its practical effects on municipal autonomy have been negligible since zoning became widespread in the 1920s.

Very few states have attempted to override local zoning decisions about housing. The most notable exception is Oregon, whose metropolitan land use boards can strong-arm local governments into rezoning for higher densities (Knaap and Nelson 1992). Oregon's problem is that the same boards also stringently limit outward growth of suburban development, so its net effect on housing prices is not clear (Mildner, Dueker, and Rufolo 1996). Almost all the other statewide zoning interventions retard housing supply rather than promote it. The state-promoted interventions have simply added another layer of review at which the developer can get tripped up (Popper 1988). A developer can go from "yes" (at the local level) to "no" at the state or regional level, but cannot go up the same ladder from "no" to "yes." A possible exception was the spate of state legislation in the 1990s whose intent was to improve developers' positions in regulatory takings controversies. Steven Eagle (2005) keeps tabs on the legal aspects of this movement, but I have seen no persuasive examination of their economic effects.

Two other attempts by state governments to override local decisions have focused on low-income ("affordable") housing rather than overall supply. Massachusetts has an "antisnob" zoning law that requires communities to have a certain mix of housing units, and New Jersey, in response to the *Mt. Laurel* exclusionary-zoning decisions, has a similar requirement (Fischel 2001, 272). The drawback of these otherwise admirable thrusts is that both let the community off the hook once it has certified a minimum *fraction* of its existing housing stock as affordable. The incentive for such communities thereafter is to do their best to retard *all* housing development so that they will not be out of compliance and thus subject to another round of costly obligations. New Jersey and Massachusetts have both had their programs in effect since the 1980s, and there is no evidence that housing prices have become more affordable as a result (Mitchell 2004). Both states also share the distinction of having more farmland preservation programs than any other states (Kotchen and Powers 2006).

The more traditional resort for developers who are aggrieved by local zoning decisions is to go to the courts. A great deal has been written about the regulatory takings doctrine, which would seem to be a considerable aid to developers. Under this doctrine, a community that downzones a parcel just as it becomes ripe for development is thought of as taking at least part of the property without the just compensation that is required by the Fifth Amendment of the U.S. Constitution as well as all state constitutions. Although this doctrine was hailed as a great boon to development-minded landowners and a bane to open-space preservationists, little has come of it. The U.S. Supreme Court's pronouncements about this have generated much commentary, but it seems clear that the Court is not willing to push aside its traditional deference to state laws about property and articulate clear rules for when a regulation verges into a taking. No state court has taken up this challenge, either.

That is not to say that state courts never help aggrieved developers. Pennsylvania and Illinois are two states whose courts have for some time been willing to assist aggrieved developers (Coyle 1993; Mitchell 2004). The real outlier among the state courts, though, is California. Since about 1970, the California Supreme Court has been regarded by both developers and environmentalists as the most antidevelopment of all major courts. Prior to 1970, California's rules were similar to those of most other states except perhaps Pennsylvania and Illinois. The rule was that "the municipality never loses." This rule sounds antidevelopment, but one must consider that there are municipalities that are prodevelopment, and even many that are antidevelopment can be persuaded by various side payments to allow some development. After 1970, however, the California Supreme Court altered many doctrines that had worked to a developer's advantage or facilitated the deals between developers and communities. The rule that emerged can be summarized as "the developer always loses," regardless of whether local authorities favor or oppose the deal.

The main evidence for the California court's change is an extraordinarily detailed project carried out by a group of UCLA law professors, DiMento et al. (1980), whose work I reviewed and supplemented in Fischel (1995). An alternative explanation for California's antidevelopment stance could be the voter initiative. Gerber and Philips (2005) demonstrate that urban growth boundaries adopted by local voter initiatives in California are more stringent and more difficult to modify than ordinary legislative regulation. But there are reasons to be skeptical about the importance of initiatives in this regard. Local initiatives are widely available in other states, even in states in which statewide initiatives are not used, so California local governments are not especially unusual. California's initiative began early in the twentieth century, well before the state became known for its hostility to development. (A U.S. Bureau of the Census study [1969, 143] found that West

Coast housing values were about the same as the national average in the 1960s.) Nor is it clear that the initiative always works against development. Prodevelopment forces can use the initiative to their advantage when faced with a NIMBY-influenced local legislature. I would not dismiss the role of "ballot-box zoning," as it is decried in the legal literature (Callies, Neuffer, and Calibosco 1991), but one needs to examine the larger political situation before assuming that it is more important than jurisdiction size in determining land use decisions.

My reason for this diversion into the politics of state judicial systems is to explain the special role of California MSAs in figure 5.1. Four of them are represented: San Francisco, San Jose, Los Angeles, and San Diego. All are on the low side of the supply elasticity estimate for the (moderate) degree of fragmentation of their school districts. (School districts in California usually do not correspond to municipal boundaries, but the size and spatial distribution of school districts do seem to be similar to those of the municipal and county territory that they share.) The especial low elasticity of supply in the California MSAs is the result of the extraordinary antidevelopment stance of the California courts. Rather than being the defenders of property rights or even neutral arbiters, most observers of the California courts regard them as committed adversaries to almost any intensive land use development.

Conclusions and Policy Implications

The picture in figure 5.1 broadly confirms the chief hypothesis of this chapter: Metropolitan areas with more fragmented government structures—many small suburbs—are more likely to have stringent development restrictions, which reduce the elasticity of supply of housing, than are other metropolitan areas. MSAs whose local government structure is characterized by fewer and larger local governments respond to increased demand for housing with larger amounts of housing, not just increased prices. The chief reason is that in larger jurisdictions developers can bring more political clout and homeowners have a more difficult time organizing.

MSAs whose land use is controlled by very few jurisdictions, however, appear to be subject to the monopoly zoning effect. Even if antidevelopment forces do not consciously think that they are promoting a monopoly, the extra boost to the value of already-established homes makes it more likely that homeowners will overcome the free rider problems of political participation in large jurisdictions. The other qualification to this account is that the courts can make a difference, as can be suggested here by a negative example. Prior to 1970, California was not an expensive place to live. During the 1970s, California's housing prices shot up to a permanently high plateau, higher than almost anywhere else in the country (Quigley 2007). How much of that can be attributed to the judicial downgrading of developers' rights cannot easily be estimated, but it is difficult to ignore the role of the courts in making California a much more costly place to live.

I have been writing about land use regulation and local government since the early 1970s, and one lesson from experience is that there are no quick fixes to the problems of regulatory excess. Indeed, most policy debate has been fixated on how to increase regulation, not decrease it. For this reason, my own policy recommendations would focus on mitigating opposition rather than simply running over it with new laws and legal doctrines.

An important reason that homeowners are so concerned about development in almost any jurisdiction is that they have no way to insure against adverse outcomes to their property values. Homeowners can insure against fires that destroy their building, but they cannot insure against the adverse effects of neighborhood decline. Opposition to even benign development thus often spirals out of control. I have suggested that homeowners' anxieties might be controlled by offering home-value insurance (Fischel 2001, 268). There are a few instances of that being done, but a better-organized market is necessary for the idea to have much effect on development. The reason for the lack of an organized insurance market is not entirely clear. It should not be assumed, however, that just because there is no market, it is inefficient to develop one. As Robert Shiller (1993) has pointed out, markets for many risks have been developed in recent years.

A home-value insurance market could go some distance to assuaging the forces that line up against development interests. It would also make it easier for developers to acquire entitlements by lowering the transaction costs of bargaining. Instead of having to perform specific, often unnecessary, mitigation programs, developers could simply purchase home-value insurance for nearby community residents. Home-value insurance does have its downside in the form of adverse selection and moral hazard (Shiller and Weiss 1994). It would probably take some public funds to create a viable market, but it might be worth it. The tendency of suburban land use regulations to repel new development has large costs that require creative approaches to deal with.

APPENDIX: DATA FOR FIGURE 5.1

The four-district concentration ratios in table 5.1 below are from Battersby and Fischel (2007), for Urbanized Areas in 2000. The housing supply elasticities in table 5.1 are from Green, Malpezzi, and Mayo (2005) for the period of 1979 to 1996. The mismatch between dates is not important because school districts in urban areas are quite stable, and 2000 UA boundaries are always within the borders of earlier MSA borders. Three of the Green, Malpezzi, and Mayo MSAs were excluded because Battersby and Fischel did not have concentration ratios for them. Those omitted are Fort Lauderdale, Honolulu, and Syracuse. Note that Green, Malpezzi, and Mayo omitted New York and several other large MSAs (e.g., Cleveland, Seattle, and Sacramento) for lack of data about land use regulation, which were assembled by Malpezzi (1996).

Table 5.1
Sample Cities for Figure 5.1

MSA	Four-District Ratio (percent)	Supply Elasticity
Akron	38.0	6.64
Albany	36.2	1.55
Atlanta	54.0	21.60
Baltimore	96.9	5.52
Birmingham	85.3	5.33
Boston	8.5	1.77
Buffalo	31.1	2.84
Charlotte	99.4	17.00
Chicago	19.4	2.48
Cincinnati	33.9	8.25
Columbus	54.0	13.50
Dallas	41.3	29.90
Denver	69.8	11.40
Detroit	23.0	4.74
Grand Rapids	46.5	10.80
Hartford	22.7	2.85
Houston	46.1	12.80
Indianapolis	35.4	11.00
Kansas City	41.9	11.00
Los Angeles	40.4	3.73
Memphis	98.4	5.63
Miami	100.0	−0.30
Milwaukee	40.2	4.45
Minneapolis	28.8	4.21
New Orleans	98.6	0.06
Oklahoma City	68.8	13.70
Orlando	100.0	4.50
Philadelphia	19.7	3.09
Phoenix	48.8	21.70
Pittsburgh	17.1	1.43
Portland, Oregon	44.8	7.14
Providence	22.3	2.10
Rochester	42.5	5.25
Salt Lake City	100.0	4.69
San Antonio	76.0	8.23
San Diego	64.9	5.33
San Francisco	48.2	0.14

Table 5.1
(*continued*)

MSA	Four-District Ratio (percent)	Supply Elasticity
San Jose	66.8	0.33
St. Louis	26.5	6.89
Tampa	100.0	27.40
Toledo	60.2	0.83
Tulsa	77.1	8.25

Sources: Battersby and Fischel (2007); Green, Malpezzi, and Mayo (2005).

REFERENCES

Banfield, E. C. 1965. *Big city politics*. New York: Random House.
Battersby, S., and W. A. Fischel. 2007. The competitive structure of urban school districts in the United States. Working Paper. Department of Economics, Dartmouth College, Hanover, NH.
Benson, B. L. 1981. Land use regulation: A supply and demand analysis of changing property rights. *Journal of Libertarian Studies* 5:435–451.
Bloom, H. S., and H. F. Ladd. 1982. Property tax revaluation and tax levy growth. *Journal of Urban Economics* 11:73–84.
Burns, J. M., J. W. Peltason, T. E. Cronin, and D. B. Magleby. 1993. *State and local politics: Government by the people*. 7th ed. Englewood Cliffs, NJ: Prentice Hall.
Burns, N. E., and G. Gamm. 1997. Creatures of the state: State politics and local government, 1871–1921. *Urban Affairs Review* 33:59–96.
Callies, D. L., N. C. Neuffer, and C. P. Calibosco. 1991. Ballot box zoning: Initiative, referendum and the law. *Washington University Journal of Urban and Contemporary Law* 39:53–98.
Cion, R. M. 1966. Accommodation par excellence: The Lakewood plan. In *Metropolitan politics: A reader*, M. N. Danielson, ed., 43–53. Boston: Little, Brown.
Coyle, D. J. 1993. *Property rights and the Constitution: Shaping society through land use regulation*. Albany: State University of New York Press.
Dahl, R., and E. R. Tufte. 1973. *Size and democracy*. Stanford, CA: Stanford University Press.
Danielson, M. N. 1976. *The politics of exclusion*. New York: Columbia University Press.
Denzau, A. T., and B. R. Weingast. 1982. Foreword: The political economy of land use regulation. *Urban Law Annual* 23:385–405.
Dillon, J. F. 1871. *Commentaries on the law of municipal corporations*. Boston: Little, Brown.
DiMento, J. F., M. D. Dozier, S. L. Emmons, D. G. Hagman, C. Kim, K. Greenfield-Sanders, P. F. Waldau, and J. A. Woollacott. 1980. Land development and environmental control in the California Supreme Court: The deferential, the preservationist, and the preservationist-erratic eras. *UCLA Law Review* 27:859–1066.

Downs, A. 1973. *Opening up the suburbs: An urban strategy for America.* New Haven, CT: Yale University Press.

———. 1994. *New visions for metropolitan America.* Washington, DC: Brookings Institution.

Eagle, S. J. 2005. *Regulatory takings.* 3rd ed. Charlottesville, VA: Lexis Publishing.

Ellickson, R. C. 1977. Suburban growth controls: An economic and legal analysis. *Yale Law Journal* 86:385–511.

Fischel, W. A. 1980. Zoning and the exercise of monopoly power: A reevaluation. *Journal of Urban Economics* 8:283–293.

———. 1985. *The economics of zoning laws.* Baltimore: Johns Hopkins University Press.

———. 1995. *Regulatory takings: Law, economics, and politics.* Cambridge, MA: Harvard University Press.

———. 2001. *The homevoter hypothesis.* Cambridge, MA: Harvard University Press.

———. 2006. Why voters veto vouchers: Public schools and community-specific social capital. *Economics of Governance* 7:109–132.

———. 2007. The congruence of American school districts with other local government boundaries: A Google-Earth exploration. Working Paper. Department of Economics, Dartmouth College, Hanover, NH.

Frieden, B. J., and L. B. Sagalyn. 1989. *Downtown, Inc.: How America rebuilds cities.* Cambridge, MA: MIT Press.

Gerber, E. R., and J. H. Philips. 2005. Evaluating the effects of direct democracy on public policy: California's urban growth boundaries. *American Politics Research* 33:310–330.

Glaeser, E., J. Gyourko, and R. Saks. 2006. Urban growth and housing supply. *Journal of Economic Geography* 6:71–89.

Green, R. K., S. Malpezzi, and S. K. Mayo. 2005. Metropolitan-specific estimates of the price elasticity of supply of housing and their sources. *American Economic Review* 95:334–339.

Haar, C. M. 1953. Zoning for minimum standards: The Wayne Township case. *Harvard Law Review* 66:1051–1063.

Hamilton, B. W. 1978. Zoning and the exercise of monopoly power. *Journal of Urban Economics* 5:116–130.

Hanke, S. H., and A. J. Carbonell. 1978. Democratic methods of defining property rights: A study of California's coastal zone. *Water Supply and Management* 2:483–487.

Holcombe, R. G. 1989. The median voter model in public choice theory. *Public Choice* 61:115–125.

Hoxby, C. M. 2001. Benevolent colluders? The effects of antitrust action on college financial aid and tuition. NBER Working Paper 7754. Cambridge, MA: National Bureau of Economic Research.

Josselin, J-M., Y. Rocaboy, and C. Tavéra. 2005. Local public expenditure behaviour: The influence of municipality size on the relevance of demand or supply models. Working Paper. Faculté des sciences économiques, University of Rennes.

Kinkade, B. S. 1992. Municipal antitrust immunity after *City of Columbia v. Omni Outdoor Advertising. Washington Law Review* 67:479–500.

Knaap, G., and A. C. Nelson. 1992. *The regulated landscape: Lessons on state land use planning from Oregon.* Cambridge, MA: Lincoln Institute of Land Policy.

Kotchen, M. J., and S. M. Powers. 2006. Explaining the appearance and success of voter referenda for open-space conservation. *Journal of Environmental Economics and Management* 52:373–390.

Lewis, P. G. 2001. Looking outward or turning inward? Motivations for development decisions in California central cities and suburbs. *Urban Affairs Review* 36:696–720.

Libonati, M. E. 1993. *Local government autonomy.* Washington, DC: U.S. Advisory Commission on Intergovernmental Relations.

Malpezzi, S. 1996. Housing prices, externalities, and regulation in U.S. metropolitan areas. *Journal of Housing Research* 7:209–241.

Matsusaka, J. G. 1995. Fiscal effects of the voter initiative: Evidence from the last thirty years. *Journal of Political Economy* 103:587–623.

———. 2000. Fiscal effects of the voter initiative in the first half of the twentieth century. *Journal of Law and Economics* 43:619–644.

Mayer, C. J., and C. T. Somerville. 2000. Land use regulation and new construction. *Regional Science and Urban Economics* 30:639–662.

Mildner, G. C., K. J. Dueker, and A. M. Rufolo. 1996. *Impact of the urban growth boundary on metropolitan housing markets.* Portland, OR: Center for Urban Studies, Portland State University.

Miller, G. J. 1981. *Cities by contract: The politics of municipal incorporation.* Cambridge, MA: MIT Press.

Mills, D. E. 1979. Segregation, rationing, and zoning. *Southern Economic Journal* 45:1195–1207.

Mitchell, J. L. 2004. Will empowering developers to challenge exclusionary zoning increase suburban housing choice? *Journal of Policy Analysis and Management* 23:119–134.

Molotch, H. 1976. The city as a growth machine: Toward a political economy of place. *American Journal of Sociology* 82:309–332.

Nelson, R. H. 1999. Privatizing the neighborhood: A proposal to replace zoning with private collective property rights to existing neighborhoods. *George Mason Law Review* 7:827–880.

Oliver, J. E. 2000. City size and civic involvement in metropolitan America. *American Political Science Review* 94:361–373.

Pendall, R. 2000. Local land use regulation and the chain of exclusion. *Journal of the American Planning Association* 66:125–142.

Pollakowski, H., and S. M. Wachter. 1990. The effects of land use constraints on housing prices. *Land Economics* 66:315–324.

Popper, F. 1988. Understanding American land use regulation since 1970. *Journal of the American Planning Association* 54:291–301.

Quigley, J. M. 2007. Regulation and property values in the United States: The high cost of monopoly. In *Land policies and their outcomes*, G. K. Ingram and Y-H. Hong, eds., 46–65. Cambridge, MA: Lincoln Institute of Land Policy.

Reichman, U. 1976. Residential private governments: An introductory survey. *University of Chicago Law Review* 43:253–306.

Rolleston, B. S. 1987. Determinants of restrictive suburban zoning: An empirical analysis. *Journal of Urban Economics* 21:1–21.

Romer, T., H. Rosenthal, and V. G. Munley. 1992. Economic incentives and political institutions: Spending and voting in school budget referenda. *Journal of Public Economics* 49:1–33.

Rose, L. A. 1989. Urban land supply: Natural and contrived restrictions. *Journal of Urban Economics* 25:325–345.

Rudel, T. K. 1989. *Situations and strategies in American land-use planning.* Cambridge: Cambridge University Press.

Shiller, R. J. 1993. *Macro markets: Creating institutions for managing society's largest economic risks.* Oxford: Clarendon Press.

Shiller, R. J., and A. N. Weiss. 1994. Home equity insurance. NBER Working Paper 4830. Cambridge, MA: National Bureau of Economic Research.

Stigler, George J. 1971. The theory of economic regulation. *Bell Journal of Economics* 2:3–21.

Teaford, J. C. 1997. *Post-suburbia: Government and politics in the edge cities.* Baltimore: Johns Hopkins University Press.

Thorson, J. A. 1996. An examination of the monopoly zoning hypothesis. *Land Economics* 72:43–55.

Tiebout, C. M. 1956. A pure theory of local expenditures. *Journal of Political Economy* 64:416–424.

Tracy, J., H. Schneider, and S. Chan. 1999. Are stocks overtaking real estate in household portfolios? *Current Issues in Economics and Finance* (Federal Reserve Bank of New York) 5:1–6.

Turnbull, G. K., and P. M. Mitias. 1999. The median voter model across levels of government. *Public Choice* 99:119–138.

U.S. Bureau of the Census. 1969. *New one-family homes sold and for sale: 1963–1967.* Washington, DC: U.S. Department of Commerce.

Walls, M., and V. McConnell. 2007. *Transfer of development rights in U.S. communities.* Washington, DC: Resources for the Future.

Weicher, J. C., and T. G. Thibodeau. 1988. Filtering and housing markets: An empirical analysis. *Journal of Urban Economics* 23:21–40.

COMMENTARY
Lee Anne Fennell

Bill Fischel's contribution to this volume addresses an intriguing question: whether smaller local governments tend to impose more restrictive land use policies than do their larger counterparts. This comment will explore some questions of methodology, theory, and policy that flow from Fischel's important study.

Methodology

First, it is helpful to consider the degree of fit between the proxy measures Fischel employs and the variables in which he is most interested: jurisdiction size and exclusionary local policies.

The four-district concentration index Fischel uses (Battersby and Fischel 2007) seems well-designed to differentiate fragmented metropolitan areas from ones with concentrated governance structures. Fischel also presents evidence that the jurisdictions within more fragmented metropolitan areas tend to be smaller in population size. It is not clear from the data, however, that size as such—as opposed to metropolitan fragmentation—is doing any of the work in producing the results that Fischel observes. Nor does Fischel's approach show whether the larger or the smaller jurisdictions within a given metropolitan area are responsible for the restrictions on that area's overall housing supply. Further work examining the effects of fragmentation while controlling for jurisdiction size would be useful in breaking out the relative effects of these two factors.

Fischel uses the housing supply elasticities of metropolitan statistical areas (MSAs) developed by Green, Malpezzi, and Mayo (2005) as a measure of local regulatory restrictiveness. Not all inelasticities of supply are products of the local political process, however. For land to be developed into housing units, it must already be (or must be made, at some price) both physically suitable and legally available. As effective as bulldozers and the like may be in transforming the landscape, employing them is not costless. Supply may also be limited by state or federal restrictions on the development of certain kinds of lands, such as those in environmentally sensitive areas, that could apply heterogeneously in different urban areas. In addition, as Green, Malpezzi, and Mayo (2005) note, housing supply inelasticity may be observed in falling markets simply because housing is durable; when prices fall, supply cannot quickly contract in response. Thus, areas with falling home prices may show inelasticity that is an artifact of housing's durability rather than the product of local land use restrictions. Controlling for these effects would help to pinpoint the degree to which variation in elasticity among MSAs can be attributed to the effects of local political activity.

Theory

Fischel's results, illustrated in figure 5.1, show that metropolitan fragmentation and housing supply inelasticity go together, "up to a point" (Fischel, this volume, figure 5.1). Fischel also finds a good deal of inelasticity among the most highly concentrated metropolitan areas—those in which the four largest jurisdictions make up all or nearly all of the populated urban area. Fischel's theoretical account contains more than one line of argument and leaves open some questions about which way the causal arrow points.

Fischel explains the correlation between inelasticity and fragmentation as follows: Fragmented metropolitan areas conform politically to a median voter model dominated by homeowners, who typically wish to exclude new development, whereas jurisdictions within more concentrated urban governance structures are more likely to be dominated by interest-group politics and hence friendlier to developers. On this account, fragmentation facilitates exclusion by giving homeowners the upper hand politically. As Fischel recognizes, though, the structure of metropolitan areas can be changed by the people living within them. Indeed, Fischel observes (this volume, p. 119) that "it is widely agreed that the main motive for the huge spate of suburban incorporations in Southern California in the 1950s and 1960s was to escape the prodevelopment land use policies of the county and larger city governments." Hence, it is possible that exclusion-minded homeowners are influencing both governance structures and substantive land use policies. It is also possible that exclusionary homeowners disproportionately select into particular governance structures.

Interestingly, Fischel's homeowners also seem capable of controlling outcomes within highly concentrated governance structures (see this volume, figure 5.1). Fischel argues that because current homeowners in such areas have a large degree of monopoly power and an accordingly large stake in exclusionary policies, they manage to solve their own collective action problems to overcome the otherwise considerable special interest clout of developers. This account raises an interesting question, however. Do differently structured metropolitan areas yield different political outcomes because of the effect of structure on the relative political power of homeowners and developers, or do these structural differences do their work by influencing the substantive desires of homeowners?

That many relatively concentrated urban areas have relatively elastic housing supplies does not show that developers have gained the upper hand in those areas, of course. Fischel's analysis of "archetypes of urban governance" (see this volume, figure 5.2) makes this point clear. For example, he posits that the inhabitants of "isolated city Q" might be more warmly disposed toward development because they desire agglomeration benefits that (by assumption) they can only obtain by allowing more development within Q. As Fischel recognizes, that explanation flows directly from a homeowner-dominated model; the homeowners simply happen to have interests that are more closely aligned with those of developers than is the case in the more fragmented urban structures. Thus, variations in regulatory restrictiveness that are produced by motivational differences among homeowners would be observationally equivalent to variations produced by differences in the relative political power of homeowners and developers.

Policy

If differences in land use policies stem from differences in homeowner motivation rather than from differences in jurisdiction size or urban structure as such, the introduction of mechanisms that help align the interests of homeowners and developers might be more effective than structural reform. To simplify a bit, we can understand developer-homeowner conflicts as disconnects between the interests of current and prospective residents. Newcomers and incumbents might have identical consumption preferences for regulation, but the incumbents are in a position to impose land use restrictions on newcomers that do not apply to themselves, whether for monopolistic reasons or to put the "fiscal squeeze" on newcomers (White 1975). Conversely, newcomers might put a squeeze on incumbents by consuming more services or contributing fewer tax dollars (Hamilton 1975).

Bargains or other arrangements could enable current and future homeowners to take each other's interests into account. For example, a condominium developer in Los Angeles recently offered a coalition of homeowners an equity share in the proposed development (Miller 2006). Alternatively, as Fischel suggests, insurance against falling home values might address homeowner risk aversion that manifests itself in socially costly land use policies (see, e.g., Fischel 2001, 268; Shiller and Weiss 1999). Given the high costs of exclusion, creative engagement with such possibilities is in order.

REFERENCES

Battersby, S., and W. A. Fischel. 2007. The competitive structure of urban school districts in the United States. Working Paper. Hanover, NH: Dartmouth College Economics Department.

Fischel, W. A. 2001. *The homevoter hypothesis*. Cambridge, MA: Harvard University Press.

———. 2008. Political structure and exclusionary zoning: Are small suburbs the big problem? In *Fiscal decentralization and land policies*, G. K. Ingram and Y-H. Hong, eds., 111–136. Cambridge, MA: Lincoln Institute of Land Policy.

Green, R. K., S. Malpezzi, and S. K. Mayo. 2005. Metropolitan-specific estimates of the price elasticity of supply of housing and their sources. *American Economic Review* 95:334–339.

Hamilton, B. W. 1975. Zoning and property taxation in a system of local governments. *Urban Studies* 12:205–211.

Miller, D. 2006. Homeowners may get share of future project. *Los Angeles Business Journal*, October 16.

Shiller, R. J., and A. N. Weiss. 1999. Home equity insurance. *Journal of Real Estate Finance and Economics* 19(1):21–47.

White, M. J. 1975. Fiscal zoning in fragmented metropolitan areas. In *Fiscal zoning and land use controls*, E. S. Mills and W. E. Oates, eds., 31–100. Lexington, MA: Lexington Books.

6

School Finance Reforms and Property Tax Limitation Measures

Daniel P. McMillen and Larry D. Singell Jr.

T he U.S. federalist system has historically placed responsibility for educational funding on local governments that have used property tax revenues as a primary source of support for both elementary and secondary education (de Bartolome 1997; Shapiro, Puryear, and Ross 1979). The property tax revolts that began in California in the 1970s, however, have rippled through the contiguous United States such that 43 of these 48 states had placed explicit limits on property taxation by 2005 (Anderson 2006). These property tax limitation measures have worked in concert with legal challenges to educational finance systems and legislative school finance reform that have occurred in more than two-thirds of the states over this same time period in an attempt to limit, centralize, and equalize funding across districts (Figlio, Husted, and Kenny 2004). There is now growing evidence that this triumvirate of school finance limitations has adversely affected educational outcomes including school expenditures, class sizes, student test scores, and teacher quality and that these effects differ across school districts (Downes, Dye, and McGuire 1998; Figlio 1998; Matsusaka 1995; Murray, Evans, and Schwab 1998; Silva and Sonstelie 1995).

This chapter extends this literature by using the Common Core of Data (CCD) for school districts and a kernel density approach to examine the effects of tax limits and educational finance reform across the entire distribution of educational outcomes in 1990 and 2000. In particular, the analysis exploits the differences in the timing and type of state limitations on educational spending to compare the per-pupil expenditure and class-size distributions before and after the adoption of tax limitations or educational finance reforms and relative to states that did not initiate such changes. The results show that these joint tax and reform measures yield systematic distributional effects that differ from separately adopting either a tax limitation or finance reform measure and relative to states that adopt neither. These results provide unique insights into apparent differences across states in the extent to which tax limits, litigation, and school finance reform have affected district-level school outcomes (Sokolow 1998).

Studies using voter survey data consistently indicate that tax limitation initiatives passed as a result of a consensus view that imposing fiscal constraints on governments would not result in a reduction in services (Citrin 1979; O'Sullivan, Sexton, and Sheffrin 1995; Shapiro, Puryear, and Ross 1979). Early studies of tax limitation measures during the 1970s and 1980s found mixed evidence regarding their adverse effects on student outcomes. For example, Downes (1992) compared performance on the California Assessment Program test before and after Proposition 13 was instituted and found no long-run reduction in student performance at any point on the performance distribution. On the other hand, Downes and Figlio (1998) used the National Longitudinal Data of 1972 (NLS72) and the National Educational Longitudinal Data (NELS) and found that, on a statewide basis, the imposition of tax or expenditure limits on local government reduced student performance on standardized tests in mathematics and that this deterioration was relatively greater in economically disadvantaged areas.

The difficulty of isolating the effect of tax limitation measures is partly because more recent measures differ from their earlier predecessors. Specifically, Figlio (1998) shows that the 1990s-era tax revolts differed from those of the 1970s and early 1980s in that they were less likely to offer significant state replacement of lost funds to local school districts and tended to combine tax rate limits with limits on tax assessments as opposed to placing general limits on expenditures or revenues. Moreover, Evans, Murray, and Schwab (1997) and Downes and Figlio (1999) show that states have implemented major school finance reforms close in time to the passage of tax limits such that the effect of tax limits can only be isolated by looking across the states or by examining the long-run experience in a state in which a limit was passed and no major changes in the school finance system had occurred.

Manwaring and Sheffrin (1997) document that 32 states experienced legal challenges to their educational finance systems between 1971 and 1995 and that these challenges, even when unsuccessful, initiated legislative education finance reforms in the state to preempt further future legal remedies. The general tenet of these reform movements was to transfer funding responsibility from the local to the state level in an attempt to equalize educational spending across districts. Nonetheless, they found significant heterogeneity in the effects of these equalization measures across states. For example, Washington's move to a centralized system in the 1980s was found to significantly reduce per-pupil expenditures, whereas Wisconsin's reforms—which initiated reforms directed at spending more on lower-income districts but not restricting upper-end districts—led to greater overall spending on education.

Overall, education finance reform studies suggest that school finance equalization programs often imposed different tax prices across districts and states for spending an additional dollar on local school spending. For example, Hoxby (1998), using Census of Government and Census of Population and Housing school-district summary files for 1972, 1982, and 1992, shows that poor districts typically enjoy relatively higher spending under most equalization schemes but can actually lose spending under the most restrictive schemes in states such as California and New Mexico. Similarly, Figlio and Rueben (2001) exploit detailed individual level data in the NLS72, the High School and Beyond, and the NELS to show that United States Supreme Court rulings in a state reduce significantly per-pupil school revenue inequality. Alternatively, Card and Payne (2002) use data from the 1977 and 1992 Census of Government merged with district characteristics from the 1980 and 1990 Census of Population and Housing to estimate how the relationship between median family income and state aid per student (total spending per student) in a school district changes in response to school finance reform. Their results indicate that, in the aftermath of negative court decisions, states tended to increase the relative funding available to lower-income districts, but with only modest effects regarding equalization on SAT scores across income categories.

Overall, prior work suggests that property tax limitation measures, particularly post-1990 initiatives, tended to lower average educational outcomes, but also affected the distribution of expenditures; whereas legal and legislative educational finance reforms frequently raised the relative spending of poorer districts, but yielded ambiguous effects on the absolute level of spending. Thus, tax limitation measures and school reform both tended to centralize school funding either by implicitly preventing locally high-demand districts from spending at desired levels in the case of statewide tax limits or by explicitly ceding funding responsibility from local to state government in the case of legal reform. On the other hand, these findings also suggest that the tax limitation or spending equalization measures occurring in close succession may well yield different effects than either occurring in isolation and that there may well be both level and distributional effects on school outcomes.

A kernel density of per-pupil expenditures and class size is used here to examine how this distribution varies before versus after a state experiences a property tax limitation, a legal or legislative reform, or both and relative to a similar comparison made for states that did not experience either a property tax limitation or an educational finance reform. These distributional comparisons mimic the difference-in-difference approach adopted in prior regression analyses that exploit the natural experiment arising from the adoption of property tax limitations and educational reforms (Figlio 1998).

In the subsequent section, we define the school finance regimes and provide descriptive evidence regarding how school service levels differ across regimes in the CCD that are used to calculate the various kernel densities. The empirical approach and the kernel density results for the population of school districts in the continental United States in 1990 and 2000 are described, followed by discussions of the difference in the density differences by school finance regime for expenditures per student and class size.

The Data

The data source for the empirical analysis is the CCD, the Department of Education's primary database on public elementary and secondary education in the United States. The CCD, first published in 1987, is a comprehensive, annual, national database that includes both administrative and financial data for every U.S. school district. Our analysis uses school-district data for 1990 and 2000 that, respectively, follow the first wave of tax revolts and educational finance reforms that largely occurred in the decade prior to 1990 or that follow a second wave that largely occurred in the early to mid-1990s. Specifically, in comparison with a base group of school districts that reside in states that never passed a substantive tax limitation measure and did not enforce a court-mandated or legislative educational finance reform, there are four distinct local finance regimes faced by school districts that operate in states that (1) passed tax limits prior to 1990; (2) passed tax limits and adopted educational finance reform prior to 1990; (3) passed tax limits prior to 2000; and (4) passed tax limits and adopted educational finance reform prior to 2000. In other words, in each of the four categories, we compare the district-level resource distributions for a period when there is a change in the local educational finance regime to (1) a prior period when there is no change; and (2) a base group of districts that made no explicit or substantial change in local financing in either period.

These four local finance regimes offer a natural division of states into groupings with potentially different and changing educational service-level distributions. Specifically, Figlio and Rueben (2001) note that reform frequently follows closely with the passage of tax limitation measures such that there are no states that enacted a binding tax limit without adopting a legislative or legal reform over the same period, either prior to 1990, or between 1990 and 2000. On the other hand, we distinguish between states that jointly pass tax limitations and educational finance reforms and those that simply enacted reforms because prior work shows that this distinction is essential in isolating the effect of such fiscal restrictions on average educational service levels (e.g., Downes and Figlio 1999; Evans, Murray, and Schwab 1997). At the same time, we distinguish between the 1980-era versus 1990-era tax limitation measures because prior work indicates that the latter reform measures are generally more fiscally restrictive than their earlier counterparts (e.g., Figlio 1998).[1]

---

1. Findings of previous work are used to help determine the placement of the states into the various school finance regimes, which inevitably involves some value judgments. For example, Indiana is included in our base category because, although it adopted a tax limit in 1974, Sokolow (1998) indicates that this limit was effectively nonbinding. Alternatively, Manwaring and Sheffrin (1997) identify many states that adopted only weak legislative finance reforms to head off further litigation after a failed court case. For example, Idaho is included in the control states because it adopted a weak legislative reform in 1978 after an unsuccessful court case in 1975 that was later repealed in 1992. The broad conclusions are not sensitive to the necessary judgment calls regarding the school finance regimes.

The principal variables used to measure school service levels in the analysis are district-level measures of average class size and per-pupil expenditures, which have previously been used as measures of school-district resources (e.g., Figlio 1998). Although the evidence linking measures of school quality and student outcomes, such as test scores or post-school earnings, are mixed, parents, business leaders, and policy analysts have focused explicitly on class size and per-pupil expenditures as key metrics in the evaluation of the public provision of education (e.g., Betts 1995). Thus, because public perception of the quality of local schools is so closely linked to both class size and per-pupil expenditures, these measures capture the tradeoff (real or perceived) between school performance and tax limitation measures or legal reform.

As seen in table 6.1, the expenditure values suggest that tax limits and finance reforms typically occurred in states that have relatively high per-student expenditures.[2] In particular, the base group of districts that were not subject to tax limits or reform had lower per-student expenditures in 1990 than those that experience either a tax limit or a reform over the period of study. This pattern continued in 2000, with the base category having lower per-student expenditures in all regimes with the exception of districts that reside in states that enacted reform and tax limits in the 1990s. On the other hand, average class size yields a far less consistent pattern across the local expenditure regime categories, suggesting that tax limits and finance reforms relate more to controlling non-instructional expenditures.[3]

To focus on distributional change comparisons in service levels that are independent of initial service-level differences, the empirical analysis will focus on the average class size and per-pupil expenditures normalized by their 1990 levels. Normalization is necessary because states differ systematically in their levels of expenditures and class sizes. For example, as can be seen in table 6.1, Tennessee's school districts had the lowest average expenditure per pupil in 1990 at $3,356. Although the average increased to $5,032 in 2000, Tennessee's average expenditure per pupil remained well below the national average of $6,712. Similarly, although California's average class size fell from 22.5 in 1990 to 20.2, it

2. The U.S. city average consumer price index (all items) was used to express all expenditures in terms of 1990 dollars.

3. Table 6.1 also indicates heterogeneity in the number (and thus size) of the districts across the control and four treatment groups. Although heterogeneity in size does not necessarily create direct empirical problems, that control states, on average, have fewer districts than the treatment states may suggest that tax revolts and legal reform may more naturally arise when there are many districts in a state such that there is the possibility of greater heterogeneity in school financing. Unlike standard regression procedures, a single large district (such as New York City) has little effect on kernel density estimates, which are designed to characterize the entire distribution of outcomes; it also means, however, that New York City is given no more weight than small districts when estimating the densities. Each district is given equal weight in estimation regardless of size.

Table 6.1
Average Service Level by Tax and Reform Regime

State	Tax and Reform Regime	Number of Districts	Revenue 1990 ($)	Revenue 2000 ($)	Avg. Class Size 1990	Avg. Class Size 2000
Alabama	No reform or tax limits	127	3,807.43	5,489.40	19.05	15.11
Delaware	No reform or tax limits	16	5,637.67	7,685.76	17.18	15.70
Idaho	No reform or tax limits	102	4,005.19	5,542.55	18.03	16.04
Indiana	No reform or tax limits	291	4,897.93	6,615.82	17.96	17.25
Mississippi	No reform or tax limits	148	3,403.95	5,001.14	18.09	16.11
Nevada	No reform or tax limits	16	6,710.15	6,947.12	17.66	15.62
North Carolina	No reform or tax limits	117	4,859.22	6,107.27	16.01	15.12
North Dakota	No reform or tax limits	157	5,151.11	6,072.86	14.83	12.36
Pennsylvania	No reform or tax limits	498	6,209.94	7,238.35	16.38	16.40
Rhode Island	No reform or tax limits	31	6,399.85	7,554.93	14.58	13.66
Mean		**150**	**5,108.24**	**6,425.52**	**16.98**	**15.34**
Arkansas	Reform and no tax limits before 1990	307	3,540.32	4,819.79	14.11	12.99
Connecticut	Reform and no tax limits before 1990	123	8,507.07	8,275.58	14.08	13.93
Georgia	Reform and no tax limits before 1990	172	4,415.31	5,879.20	16.35	15.58
Illinois	Reform and no tax limits before 1990	488	4,399.77	6,315.00	16.71	15.06
Kentucky	Reform and no tax limits before 1990	171	3,360.18	5,659.29	17.32	14.82
Louisiana	Reform and no tax limits before 1990	66	4,196.72	5,143.66	16.38	14.77
Maine	Reform and no tax limits before 1990	116	5,869.10	7,275.61	14.88	12.39
Maryland	Reform and no tax limits before 1990	24	6,088.38	6,707.54	17.41	16.40
Missouri	Reform and no tax limits before 1990	448	4,341.05	5,593.65	14.90	13.19
New Jersey	Reform and no tax limits before 1990	255	8,112.40	9,604.83	14.41	13.57
Oklahoma	Reform and no tax limits before 1990	416	4,030.19	5,028.87	14.20	13.93
South Carolina	Reform and no tax limits before 1990	84	4,667.73	6,205.46	16.90	14.77
South Dakota	Reform and no tax limits before 1990	158	4,723.72	6,092.16	12.73	12.36

Table 6.1
(*continued*)

State	Tax and Reform Regime	Number of Districts	Revenue 1990 ($)	Revenue 2000 ($)	Avg. Class Size 1990	Avg. Class Size 2000
Texas	Reform and no tax limits before 1990	962	5,186.47	7,018.52	14.28	12.69
Utah	Reform and no tax limits before 1990	40	4,000.43	5,075.85	21.85	19.58
Virginia	Reform and no tax limits before 1990	131	5,312.69	6,424.65	15.36	13.52
Washington	Reform and no tax limits before 1990	246	6,258.35	6,696.69	18.63	18.27
West Virginia	Reform and no tax limits before 1990	55	4,039.81	6,279.23	15.31	13.84
Wisconsin	Reform and no tax limits before 1990	377	5,913.41	7,734.94	15.29	14.26
Wyoming	Reform and no tax limits before 1990	46	7,385.05	7,734.58	12.62	12.19
Mean		**234**	**5,217.41**	**6,478.25**	**15.68**	**14.41**
Arizona	Reform and tax limits before 1990	99	5,695.56	6,108.99	17.65	16.99
California	Reform and tax limits before 1990	377	5,330.72	6,172.30	22.50	20.21
Colorado	Reform and tax limits before 1990	171	5,986.47	7,043.22	14.16	13.86
Iowa	Reform and tax limits before 1990	341	4,740.24	6,318.77	14.53	14.13
Massachusetts	Reform and tax limits before 1990	224	6,341.29	7,604.11	16.94	13.08
Minnesota	Reform and tax limits before 1990	288	5,667.58	6,950.24	16.70	14.78
New Mexico	Reform and tax limits before 1990	88	5,722.27	7,213.84	16.60	14.74
Ohio	Reform and tax limits before 1990	610	4,504.18	5,983.23	19.40	17.18
Mean		**275**	**5,498.54**	**6,674.34**	**17.31**	**15.62**
Kansas	Reform and no tax limits after 1990	297	5,577.06	6,262.14	13.44	13.13
New Hampshire	Reform and no tax limits after 1990	71	6,299.34	6,723.52	15.28	14.12

(*continued*)

Table 6.1
(*continued*)

State	Tax and Reform Regime	Number of Districts	Revenue 1990 ($)	Revenue 2000 ($)	Avg. Class Size 1990	Avg. Class Size 2000
New York	Reform and no tax limits after 1990	623	8,866.38	10,002.03	13.82	13.16
Tennessee	Reform and no tax limits after 1990	118	3,356.55	5,032.17	19.01	15.67
Vermont	Reform and no tax limits after 1990	61	7,088.43	8,454.86	16.78	12.49
Mean		**234**	**6,237.55**	**7,294.94**	**15.67**	**13.71**
Florida	Reform and tax limits after 1990	67	5,952.06	6,089.71	16.86	17.83
Michigan	Reform and tax limits after 1990	524	5,112.89	6,955.22	15.18	17.63
Montana	Reform and tax limits after 1990	165	6,583.02	6,871.40	12.31	12.38
Nebraska	Reform and tax limits after 1990	234	5,663.63	6,349.54	12.49	12.43
Oregon	Reform and tax limits after 1990	165	5,842.19	6,630.55	16.50	17.03
Mean		**231**	**5,830.76**	**6,579.28**	**14.67**	**15.46**

Sources: Common Core of Data and authors' calculations.

had the highest average class size among the 48 contiguous states in both years.[4] It follows that if the data are not normalized, these changes would be observed only as a slight change at the extremes of the national distribution.

Table 6.2 shows that, by normalizing, average class size and real expenditures per pupil always have an average for 1990 of 1.00 across each state's jurisdictions. The 1990 data thus measure how a jurisdiction's average class size or expenditure differs from the statewide average. The 2000 data are also normalized by the 1990 statewide mean. Thus, if a jurisdiction's value for the (normalized) average class size rose from 1.00 to 1.20 between 1990 and 2000, then its average class size began the decade at the state average but rose to a level 20 percent higher than the 1990 average. The normalization allows us to pool

---

4. These figures are calculated as the simple average of the values from each jurisdiction in the state.

Table 6.2
Normalized Service Levels by Local Expenditure Regime

Variables	Base Group: No Reform or Tax Limits	Reform, but No Tax Limits, Before 1990	Reform and Tax Limits, Before 1990	Reform, but No Tax Limits, in 1990s	Reform and Tax Limits in 1990s
Normalized expenditures in 1990 by 1990	1.00 (0.22)	1.00 (0.28)	1.00 (0.20)	1.00 (0.27)	1.00 (0.24)
Normalized expenditures in 2000 by 1990	1.26 (0.28)	1.31 (0.37)	1.23 (0.34)	1.22 (0.39)	1.25 (0.36)
Normalized class size in 1990 by 1990	1.00 (0.15)	1.00 (0.15)	1.00 (0.17)	1.00 (0.14)	1.00 (0.20)
Normalized class size in 2000 by 1990	0.93 (0.14)	0.92 (0.14)	0.93 (0.15)	0.90 (0.15)	1.05 (0.20)
Number of observations	1,722	4,120	1,177	2,230	1,462

Note: Standard errors are in parentheses.
Sources: Common Core of Data and authors' calculations.

data across states while maintaining the ability to determine whether the overall distributions have shifted to the right or left over time.

Although the normalization yields a mean level of service of one in each of the five categories for 1990 in table 6.2, the mean values of the real per-student expenditures in 2000 are larger than 1.00 for each regime, indicating a general rise in real expenditures between 1990 and 2000. Alternatively, the normalized value of class size is less than 1.00 in 2000 for all categories except those districts that reside in states that passed tax limits and adopted reform during the 1990s, suggesting that the general trend of smaller classes did not occur in the later period when school districts faced the most comprehensive state-level restrictions on the local finance of education. Interestingly, the standard errors of both normalized expenditures and class size tend to be larger in reform states than in the base category, suggesting that legal and political pressure may be driven by relative district-level inequality in the state. The empirical analysis compares the 1990 and 2000 revenue and class-size distributions for each of the four school finance regimes relative to the same comparison made for the base category of states that imposed no property tax limits or school finance reforms on their local school districts.

Empirical Approach and Results for the Population of School Districts

The objectives here are to analyze changes in the distributions of per-student expenditures and average class sizes between 1990 and 2000 and to determine whether the changes in the distributions differ for states with tax reforms and property tax limitation measures. The basic tool for this descriptive analysis is a nonparametric estimator of the underlying density function. Using x_{90} to represent either the normalized average class size or expenditure per capita in 1990, the kernel density function estimate at a target value x is

$$(1) \qquad \hat{f}_{90}(x) = \frac{1}{nh} \sum_{i=1}^{n} K\left(\frac{x_{90i} - x}{h}\right).$$

where n is the number of observations and h is a parameter (the "bandwidth") that controls the degree of smoothing. Similarly, the density at the target value x for 2000 is

$$(2) \qquad \hat{f}_{00}(x) = \frac{1}{nh} \sum_{i=1}^{n} K\left(\frac{x_{00i} - x}{h}\right).$$

The change in the density between 1990 and 2000 is simply

$$(3) \qquad \Delta(x) = \hat{f}_{00}(x) - \hat{f}_{90}(x).$$

We use an Epanechnikov kernel for all calculations: $K(u) = .75(1 - u^2)$ if $|u| \leq 1$ and $K(u) = 0$ otherwise. For both average class size and expenditure per student, we calculate the density functions at 400 equally spaced alternative values of x and then use graphs to summarize the results.

The kernel density function is the same conceptually as a smoothed histogram. The degree of smoothing is controlled by the bandwidth, h. Following Silverman (1986), we use a simple rule of thumb to determine the bandwidths: $h_{90} = 1.06 \, \text{var}(x_{90}) n^{-.20}$ and $h_{00} = 1.06 \, \text{var}(x_{00}) n^{-.20}$. Experimentation with alternative bandwidths produced only minor variation in the appearance of the estimated density functions, with wider bandwidths tending to yield a higher degree of monotonicity and smoother distributions.

Figure 6.1a presents the estimated density functions for real expenditure per student for 1990 and 2000 for the full sample of school districts in the 48 contiguous states. Our normalization procedure produces a 1990 density function that is centered on a value close to 1.0. The 1990 function is skewed to the right: although expenditures are clustered near the state average for most school districts, many districts have quite high levels of expenditures per student. Although expenditures are in real rather than nominal terms, the density function shifts markedly to the right in 2000 as districts increased their spending levels.

Figure 6.1
Estimated Density Functions for Real Expenditure per Student: All School Districts

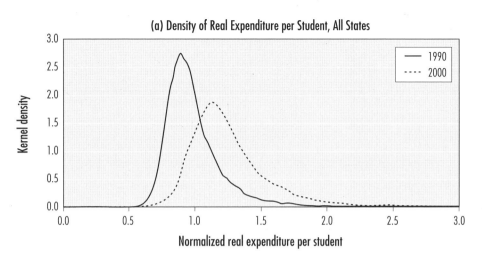

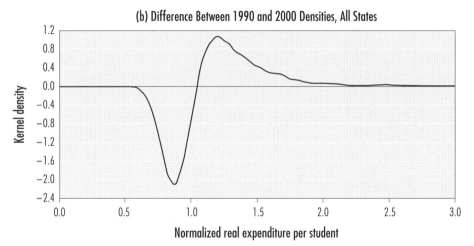

The 1990 function also exhibits a higher variance. Figure 6.1b presents the same information in a different light by showing the *change* in the estimated density functions from 1990 to 2000. The estimated densities decline at low levels of expenditures per student, with a corresponding increase at high levels. Both figures imply that expenditures per student increased over time for the full sample of school districts. Figure 6.2 presents the estimated density functions and the change in densities for average class sizes for the full sample of school districts.

Figure 6.2
Estimated Density Functions for Average Class Size: All School Districts

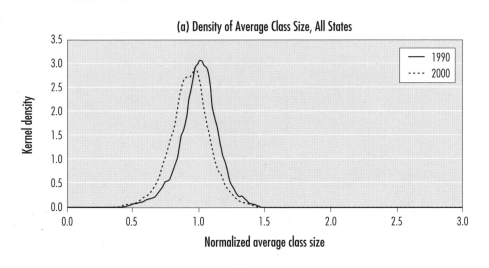

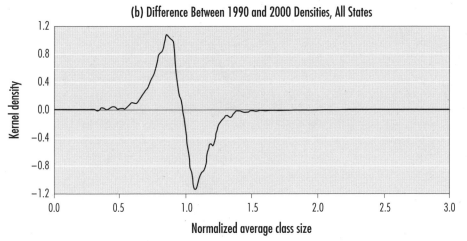

The distribution shifted to the left between 1990 and 2000 as the number of school districts with high average class sizes declines.

Difference in Density Differences by Regime: Expenditure per Student

For the full sample of school districts, expenditure per student increased and average class size fell between 1990 and 2000. In this section, we use a difference-in-differences approach to determining whether the change in the densities differs across five state groupings by school finance regime: (1) a base group with no binding finance reforms or tax limits; (2) states that adopted binding reforms prior to 1990; (3) states that adopted binding reforms and tax limits prior to 1990; (4) states that adopted binding reforms in the 1990s; and (5) states that adopted reforms and tax limits in the 1990s.

Figure 6.3 shows the estimated density functions for real expenditure per student in 1990 and 2000 for the base group of states (figure 6.3a), along with the change in the estimated densities (figure 6.3b). The graphs, which look very similar to their comparable graphs in figure 6.1 for the full sample of districts, again show that real expenditure per student increased substantially over time. Indeed, the estimated densities look sufficiently similar across the five groups that we save space by omitting these base density-function estimates and their differences for the other groups of states.

Interesting results emerge when we compare the change in densities between 1990 and 2000 across groups. Figure 6.4 shows changes relative to the base group, that is, $\Delta_1(x) - \Delta_0(x)$, where the function $\Delta(x)$ is given in equation (3), the base group is denoted by 0, and 1 denotes any of the four alternative groups. Figure 6.4a shows that compared with the base group, the number of school districts with expenditures per pupil in the middle of the distribution increased markedly for states that adopted reforms prior to the 1990s. This push toward the middle of the distribution can be interpreted as a form of egalitarianism: compared with the base group, states adopting reforms prior to 1990 closed the 1990s with fewer districts with low per-student expenditures, but also fewer districts with high levels of expenditure per student. Together, the results in parts (a) and (b) of figure 6.4 suggest that policies adopted before 1990 reduced the variance of per-student expenditures relative to the base group. The variance was reduced both by reducing the number of low-expenditure districts and by reducing the number of districts with high levels of per-student expenditures.

Parts (c) and (d) of figure 6.4 show comparable density differences for districts in states that adopted reforms in the 1990s and states that adopted tax limits in the 1990s. In both cases, the effect of the policy changes was to increase (relative to the base states) the number of districts in the middle of the per-student distribution and to decrease the number of districts in either tail. Thus, 1990s-era reforms and tax limits followed the same trend as earlier policies in leading to greater equality. Again, this apparent egalitarianism was achieved by increasing the number of low-expenditure districts and by reducing the number of high-expenditure districts.

Figure 6.5 alters the comparison group to consider differences in policies that were adopted around the same time. Figure 6.5a shows that, when compared with states that had only reforms prior to 1990, districts in states that also adopted tax limits were much less likely to have high levels of per-student expenditures. In contrast, figure 6.5b shows that 1990s-era limits led to a higher number of districts in both tails of the distribution. The reforms of the 1990s

Figure 6.3
Base Group: No Reforms or Tax Limits

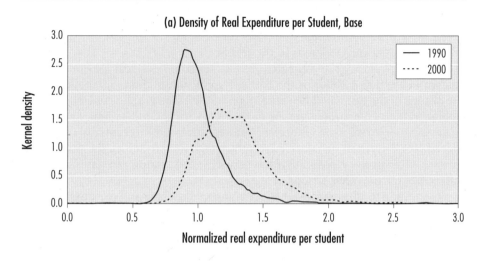

(a) Density of Real Expenditure per Student, Base

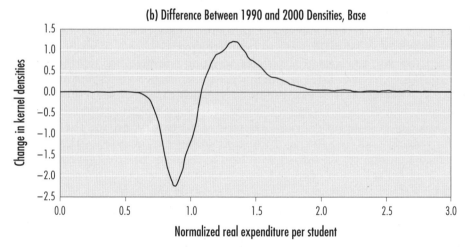

(b) Difference Between 1990 and 2000 Densities, Base

appear to have been motivated by a greater degree of egalitarianism than tax limits from the same era. Pre-1990s tax limits continued to hold down per-student expenditure levels in the 1990s.

Figure 6.6 shows the results for additional combinations of comparison groups. Figure 6.6a provides further evidence that 1990s-era reforms reduced the number of high- and low-expenditure districts: relative to states adopting reforms prior to 1990, the number of districts in the middle of the distribution is much higher for states that adopted reforms in the 1990s. Figure 6.6b suggests that 1990s-era tax limits reduced the number of districts with high levels of per-student

Figure 6.4

Difference Between Estimated Densities for Expenditure per Student: Various Categories Versus Base Group

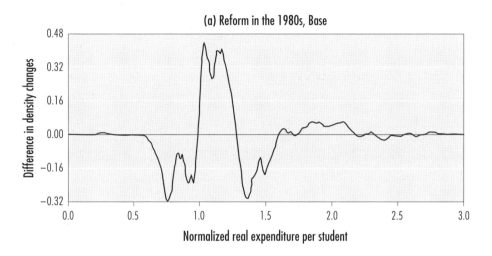

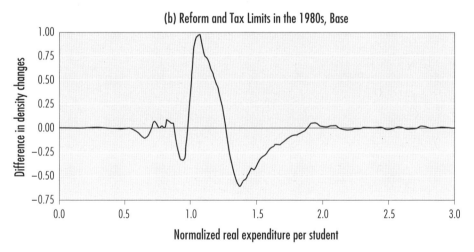

(continued)

expenditure compared with districts that adopted reforms earlier. Figure 6.6c suggests that 1990s-era reforms led to a higher degree of egalitarianism than the combination of reforms and tax limits prior to 1990. Similarly, figure 6.6d suggests that 1990s-era tax limits produced a more equal distribution of per-student expenditures than the combination of reforms and tax limits from before 1990.

Overall, figures 6.4, 6.5, and 6.6 suggest that both reforms and tax limits do indeed influence the distribution of per-student expenditures. Whether adopted

Figure 6.4
(*continued*)

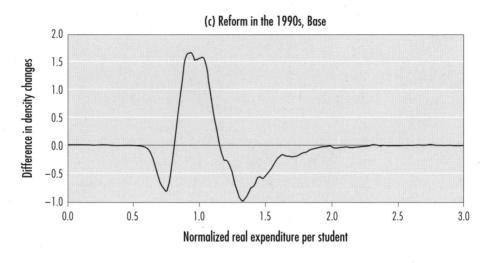

(c) Reform in the 1990s, Base

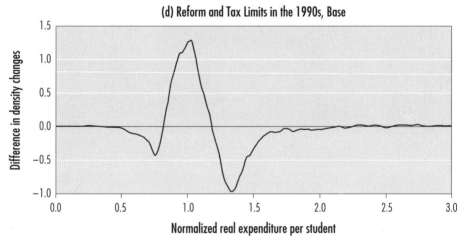

(d) Reform and Tax Limits in the 1990s, Base

during the 1990s or before, both reforms and tax limits tended to produce a more equal distribution of per-student expenditure over the 1990s by reducing the number of districts with unusually high and unusually low expenditures, as compared with the base group of states. Tax limitation measures tended to increase the number of districts with low levels of per-student expenditures. Whether they were adopted before 1990 or after, reforms tended to lead to a more equal distribution of per-student expenditures over the 1990s by reducing the number of districts in the tails of the distribution. The 1990s-era reforms appear to have been particularly effective at narrowing the distribution of per-student expenditures.

Figure 6.5

Expenditures: Comparison of Density Changes by Policy Within Decade of Enactment

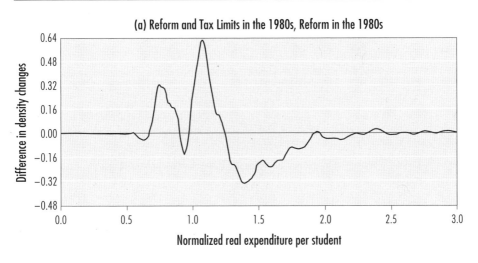

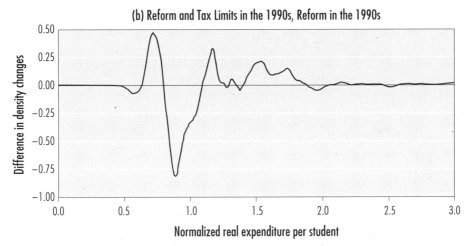

Difference in Density Differences by Regime: Average Class Size

A series of graphs can show the difference-in-difference density function estimates for average class size. As was the case for per-student expenditures, the base density function estimates for 1990 and 2000 look similar across the five state groupings by school finance regime. The distribution of average class sizes shifted to the left between 1990 and 2000 for all five categories; that is, average

Figure 6.6
Expenditures: Comparison of Density Changes Across Decades

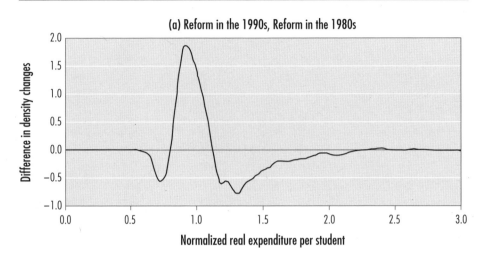

(a) Reform in the 1990s, Reform in the 1980s

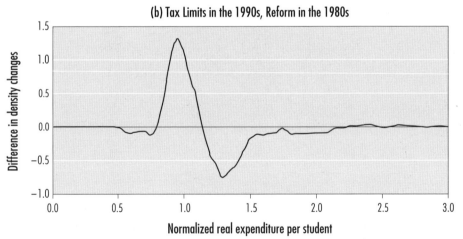

(b) Tax Limits in the 1990s, Reform in the 1980s

class sizes decreased. Because the national data shown in figure 6.2 are representative of each category, we do not present the density functions for each category. Instead, we concentrate on the differences across regimes in the density function changes.

Figure 6.7 shows the difference in the density function differences relative to the base group of states. Although the results are noisy for states adopting reforms prior to 1990, the overall pattern in both parts (a) and (b) suggests that both reforms and tax limits adopted before 1990 lead to fewer districts with high average class sizes and more districts with low class sizes. Parts (c) and (d)

Figure 6.6
(*continued*)

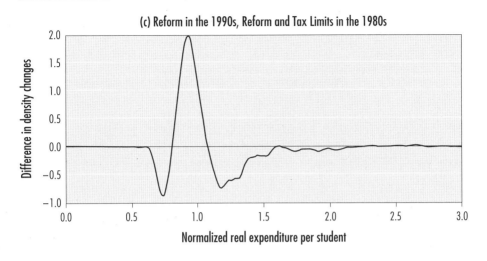

(c) Reform in the 1990s, Reform and Tax Limits in the 1980s

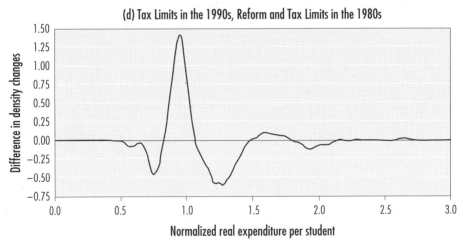

(d) Tax Limits in the 1990s, Reform and Tax Limits in the 1980s

suggest that 1990s-era policies led to much different results. Compared with the base group, 1990s-era reforms led to a greater clustering of districts at average class sizes slightly higher than their 1990s-era mean values. In contrast, 1990s-era tax limits led to a large increase in the number of districts with high average class sizes.

Figure 6.8 shows differences in policies that were adopted around the same time. Figure 6.8a implies that by the end of the 1990s states with pre-1990s-era reforms had many more districts with average class sizes slightly higher than the 1990 mean when compared with states with both reforms and tax limits. In

Figure 6.7
Difference Between Estimated Densities for Average Class Size: Various Categories Versus Base Group

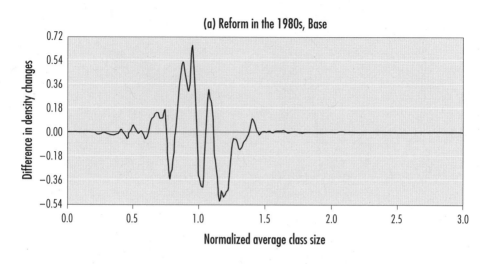

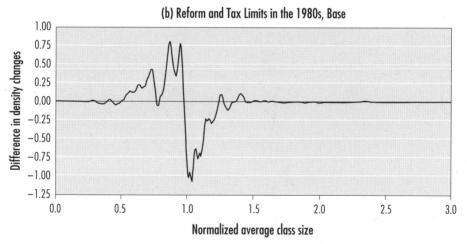

other words, reforms led to a more equal distribution of average class sizes than reforms combined with tax limits. Figure 6.8b shows that tax limits adopted in the 1990s produced a higher number of districts with average class sizes during the 1990s than was the case for states that adopted reforms in the 1990s. Figure 6.9 shows the results for additional combinations of comparison groups. The results are consistent across all four panels: 1990s-era policy led to more districts with high average class sizes as compared with either pre-1990s policy.

Figure 6.7
(*continued*)

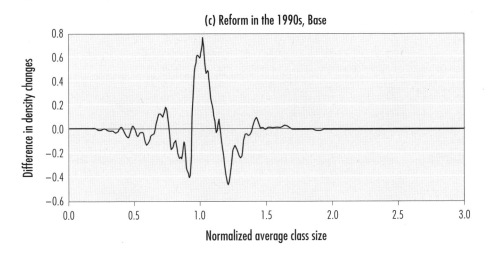

(c) Reform in the 1990s, Base

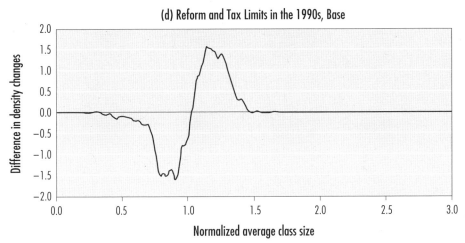

(d) Reform and Tax Limits in the 1990s, Base

Conclusions

Prior work has found that property tax limits and school finance reforms, on average, tend to reduce school service levels and student-level performance, but that such initiatives can also lessen the inequality across school districts and yield improvements in relative resources of economically disadvantaged districts (e.g., Card and Payne 2002). This analysis builds on prior work by using the CCD and nonparametric kernel density techniques to compare how changes in

Figure 6.8
Average Class Size: Comparison of Density Changes by Policy Within Decade of Enactment

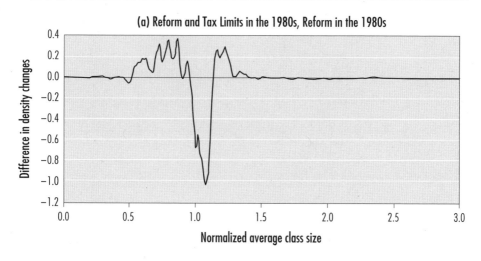

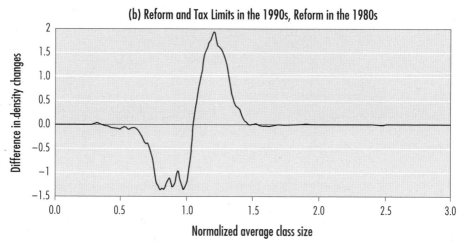

school finance regimes (i.e., tax limits and school finance reforms) affect school-district level real expenditures per student and class sizes across the whole distribution and in comparison to districts that did not adopt tax limits or school finance reforms. The results provide compelling evidence that both tax limitation measures and school finance reforms affect the full distribution of school service levels relative to districts that do not adopt such initiatives. On the other hand, the results also show that the joint effect of tax limits and school finance reforms is different than that of reform on its own and that, whereas earlier era

Figure 6.9
Average Class Size: Comparison of Density Changes Across Decades

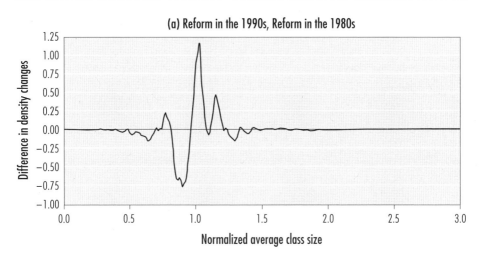

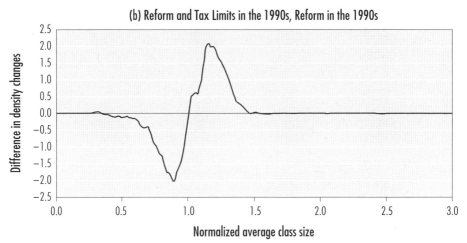

(continued)

reforms in the 1970s and 1980s yield effects over several decades, 1990s-era policies generally had more pronounced distributional effects.

For real expenditures per student, the results suggest that whether adopted during the 1990s or before, both reforms and tax limits tended to yield greater equality of expenditures by reducing the number of districts in the tails of the distribution. Tax limitation measures, however, tended to yield a greater number of low-expenditure districts, whereas expenditure reform measures lead to more

Figure 6.9
(*continued*)

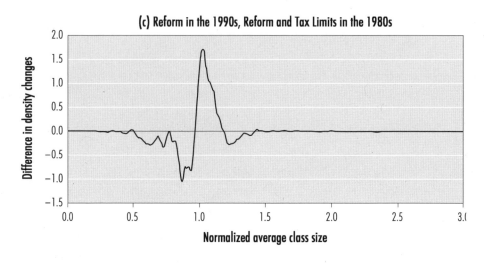

(c) Reform in the 1990s, Reform and Tax Limits in the 1980s

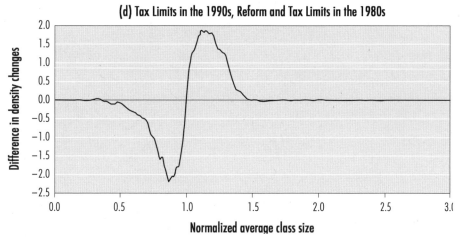

(d) Tax Limits in the 1990s, Reform and Tax Limits in the 1980s

equalization around the mean. These findings are similar for pre- and post-1990s-era school finance regimes, but are particularly pronounced in the later era.

At the same time, although class sizes uniformly declined between 1990 and 2000 across all school finance regimes, the results suggested that pre-1990s-era tax and reform policies tend to lead to fewer districts with high average class sizes and more districts with low class sizes such that there was a general movement toward greater equality across school districts. In contrast, the 1990s-era tax limits led to large increases in the number of districts with high average class sizes, whereas the 1990s-era reforms led to greater clustering of districts around the average. The difference in the differenced density functions for class size yield a far more noisy set of diagrams than for expenditures, however, suggesting that tax limits and school finance reforms can regulate the general level of expenditures at the local level but that school districts exercise greater control on whether the funds are spent on instruction versus alternative school services.

Overall, the results provide strong evidence that the fiscal federalism movement that began in California with Proposition 13, although reducing the overall level of school services, did not cause a general race to the bottom; rather, it tended to equalize resources across districts. The general narrowing of the school service distribution does not necessarily imply an overall improvement in social welfare because the differences in the distribution are likely to reflect genuine differences in preferences regarding the value placed on school resources. Moreover, this equalization in public spending with regard to education may yield private responses to educational spending that may undo this public policy. Thus, further work needs to be done to understand the general equilibrium effects of tax limitation and educational reform policies.

REFERENCES

Anderson, N. B. 2006. Property tax limitations: An interpretative review. *National Tax Journal* 59(3):685–694.

Betts, J. R. 1995. Does school quality matter? Evidence from the National Longitudinal Survey of Youth. *Review of Economics and Statistics* 77(2):232–250.

Card, D., and A. A. Payne. 2002. School finance reform, the distribution of school spending, and the distribution of student test scores. *Journal of Public Economics* 83(1):49–82.

Citrin, J. 1979. Do people want something for nothing: Public opinion on taxes and spending. *National Tax Journal* 32(2):113–129.

de Bartolome, C. A. M. 1997. Positive model of foundation aid as redistribution. *Journal of Policy Analysis and Management* 16(1):32–47.

Downes, T. A. 1992. Evaluating the impact of school finance reform on the provision of public education: The California case. *National Tax Journal* 45(4):405–419.

Downes, T. A., R. F. Dye, and T. J. McGuire. 1998. Do limits matter? Evidence on the effects of tax limitations on student performance. *Journal of Urban Economics* 43(3):401–417.

Downes, T. A., and D. N. Figlio. 1998. School finance reforms, tax limits, and student performance: Do reforms level-up or dumb down? Memo, Tufts University, Cambridge, MA.

———. 1999. Do tax and expenditure limits provide a free lunch? Evidence on the link between limits and public sector service quality. *National Tax Journal* 52(1):113–128.

Evans, W. M., S. E. Murray, and R. M. Schwab. 1997. Schoolhouses, courthouses, and statehouses after Serrano. *Journal of Policy Analysis and Management* 16(1):10–31.

Figlio, D. N. 1998. Short-term effects of a 1990s-era property tax limit: Panel evidence on Oregon's Measure 5. *National Tax Journal* 51(1):55–70.

Figlio, D. N., T. A. Husted, and L. W. Kenny. 2004. Political economy of the inequality in school spending. *Journal of Urban Economics* 55(2):338–349.

Figlio, D. N., and D. S. Rueben. 2001. Tax limits and the qualifications of new teachers. *Journal of Public Economics* 80(1):49–71.

Hoxby, C. M. 1998. All school finance equalizations are not created equal. NBER Working Paper 6792. Cambridge, MA: National Bureau of Economic Research.

Manwaring, R. L., and S. M. Sheffrin. 1997. Litigation, school finance reform, and aggregate educational spending. *International Tax and Public Finance* 4(2): 107–127.

Matsusaka, J. G. 1995. Fiscal effects of the voter initiative: Evidence from the last 30 years. *Journal of Political Economy* 103(3):587–623.

Murray, S. E., W. M. Evans, and R. M. Schwab. 1998. Education finance reform and the distribution of educational resources. *American Economic Review* 88(4): 789–812.

O'Sullivan, A., T. Sexton, and S. Sheffrin. 1995. *Property taxes and tax revolts.* Cambridge: Cambridge University Press.

Shapiro, P., D. Puryear, and J. Ross. 1979. Tax and expenditure limitation in retrospect and in prospect. *National Tax Journal* 32(2):1–10.

Silva, F., and J. Sonstelie. 1995. Did Serrano cause a decline in school spending? *National Tax Journal* 48(2):199–215.

Silverman, B. W. 1986. *Density estimation for statistics and data analysis.* New York: Chapman and Hall.

Sokolow, A. D. 1998. The changing property tax and state-local relations. *Publius: The Journal of Fiscal Federalism* 28(1):165–187.

COMMENTARY
Dennis Epple

As this study by Daniel McMillen and Larry Singell documents in table 6.1, all but 10 states have undertaken educational reform over the last several decades. In addition, many states have adopted tax limitation measures. They classify states into five groups based on whether and when they adopted tax limits or expenditure reforms. The reference group of 10 states has, since 1970, adopted neither tax limits nor education expenditure reforms. Two groups are made up of states that had expenditure reforms before 1990. One of these groups, comprising eight states, adopted both tax limits and expenditure reforms before 1990. The other of these groups, made up of 20 states, adopted expenditure reforms before 1990 but did not adopt tax limits. The two remaining groups adopted expenditure reforms after 1990. One of these groups, comprised of five states, did not adopt tax limits, whereas the other group, also comprised of five states, did adopt tax limits.

The objective is to provide a graphical portrayal of how the distributions of class size and expenditure vary across these five groups of states, in 1990 and in 2000. The unit of analysis is the school district. Because the focus is on distributional effects, differences in levels are removed by dividing per-student expenditure in each district in a state by the 1990 state average expenditure per student. Similarly, class size within each district is divided by 1990 average class size in the state in which the district is located. This normalization is done for all districts using 1990 data. A similar normalization is undertaken for the year 2000. Thus, for example, year 2000 expenditure per student in each district in a state is divided by average expenditure per student in that state in 1990. This creative strategy permits graphical portrayal of differences in distributions while removing effects of differences across states in levels of expenditures per pupil and class size.

The comparisons suggest that states adopting reforms before 1990 moved toward a more equal distribution of expenditures relative to the reference group of states. Similarly, states adopting reforms during the 1990s moved toward more equal expenditure across districts relative to the reference group of states. Extensive comparisons are presented to characterize the relative effect of reforms and tax limits within each time period. These comparisons are provided for both expenditures per student and class sizes.

The graphical approach in the chapter proves to be informative about distributional patterns for different combinations of tax limits and expenditure reforms. The salient changes that are found are presumed to be causally related to the reforms. As with any difference-in-difference analysis, however, one cannot rule out the possibility that the differences that are found are due to factors other than the reforms. In econometric analysis employing difference-in-difference estimation, one can potentially control for changes in economic and demographic factors that influence changes in expenditures. The graphical approach does not permit such controls. Hence, to lend a causal interpretation to the graphical findings, one must assume that there are not systematic differences across the groups of states in such factors that may be driving differences in expenditures or class sizes.

An important limitation of the graphical analysis is that it weights all districts equally. If districts were of approximately equal size, this limitation would not be a great concern. In reality, however, the distribution of school district sizes is skewed. For example, the largest 24 districts in the United States serve more than 12 percent of the students in the nation. The 8,700 smallest districts serve fewer than 12 percent of the nation's student population.[1] There is no ready graphical adjustment to reflect this difference in district sizes, but this heterogeneity in district sizes needs to be kept in mind in interpreting the graphical results.

The graphical analysis may also provide a different interpretation of the evidence than conventional summary statistics. For example, consider table 6.2. The table indicates that the base group of states had an increase of 1.26 in normalized expenditure between 1990 and 2000 with a standard deviation of 0.28. Farther over in the same row, we see that states with a reform but no tax limits in the 1990s had an increase in normalized expenditure of 1.22 with a standard deviation of 0.39. This comparison of standard errors suggests that reform in the 1990s increased the inequality in relative expenditures relative to the reference states. By contrast, figure 6.4c suggests that expenditures in the reform states became more equal. The comparison of distributions in figure 6.4c gives a richer portrayal of effects throughout the distribution, but it is not clear how to reconcile the seemingly different conclusions arising from the two approaches. It would be valuable in future research to attempt to reconcile these different measures of distributional effects.

McMillen and Singell's analysis provides an innovative and interesting approach to studying changes in education spending and class size. Nonparametric analysis is an attractive approach for providing insights about changes over the entire distribution. Because the analysis does not control for difference in district sizes or changing economic and demographic factors, the results are perhaps best viewed as descriptive. Such graphical analysis could be useful in future efforts as a supplement to econometric analyses of changes in the distribution of educational expenditures and class sizes.

---

1. See table 7 of http://nces.ed.gov/programs/quarterly/vol_4/4_3/3_4.asp#H4.

7

Decentralization and Environmental Decision Making

Shelby Gerking

A large share of responsibility for environmental policy in the United States rests with the federal government, due largely to two long-standing and widely held reservations about the ability of state and local governments to effectively carry out this function. The first reservation is that state and local officials may be too lax in setting environmental regulations if pollution generated in their jurisdiction is exported to another. The second is that even if exportation of pollution does not occur, local officials still may pay too little attention to environmental quality if they compete with one another in a "race to the bottom" to attract capital (Break 1967; Cumberland 1980). Revesz (2001), however, persuasively debunks general environmental policy prescriptions in favor of federal intervention. In addition, Oates (2002, 8) contends that more empirical work is needed to estimate the magnitude of distortions that would arise if state and local governments exercised more authority over environmental policy.

Oates and Schwab (1988) present a benchmark case against which to assess possible distortions that might arise if responsibility for environmental policy is shifted from the federal government to state and local governments. They demonstrate that a "race to the bottom" will not occur if several conditions are met, including that local jurisdictions have access to a full range of tax and regulatory

I thank Arik Levinson for numerous constructive comments and for providing a portion of the hazardous waste tax data used in this study, and I thank Randy Moffett for research assistance. The Lincoln Institute of Land Policy and the Galloway Endowment at University of Central Florida provided partial financial support.

instruments and that the economy is competitive, with no externalities (for further discussion, see Levinson [1997]). Because these conditions will not always hold, a vast theoretical literature has developed to explore implications of departures from this pure case (for surveys, see Wellisch [2000] and Wilson [1996, 1999]). The magnitude of distortions identified in these papers rests on two interrelated issues: (1) the extent to which state and local governments would set environmental stringency at a different level than would the federal government; and (2) the extent to which firms respond to changes in stringency of environmental regulation. If federal responsibility for the environment is decentralized to state and local governments and those governments set the same level of stringency as the federal government (e.g., the Oates and Schwab pure case), distortions do not arise. Correspondingly, if federal responsibilities for the environment are reassigned to state and local governments and firms do not alter their behavior in the face of changes in environmental regulations, no distortions arise.

Empirical studies of these issues differ greatly both in approach and in their findings. One branch of the literature attempts to treat both issues at once. For example, Bulte, List, and Strazicich (2007), Fredriksson and Millimet (2002), Goklany (1999), and List and Gerking (2000) consider specific situations in which states had an opportunity to play a leadership role in establishing environmental policy and find little evidence that environmental quality suffered. Another set of studies looks at how firms respond to changes in environmental policy. Recent studies of federal clean air regulations that divide the United States into attainment and nonattainment areas (e.g., Becker and Henderson 2000; Greenstone 2002) find that firms either relocate or shift production and pollution to areas where regulations are less strict, whereas earlier studies, surveyed by Jaffe et al. (1995), suggest little evidence of these effects.

The aim in this chapter is to analyze implications of further decentralizing environmental policy in a situation in which exportation of pollution to other jurisdictions is of possible importance. The focus is on the particular case previously considered by Sigman (1996) of generation and disposal of chlorinated solvent waste, a group of toxic chemicals that can be shipped across state boundaries. This case is worth a further look for three reasons. First, generation of toxic waste is likely to be relatively more sensitive to changes in regulatory policy than plant relocation decisions, so firm responses may be easier to identify. Second, Sigman's study as well as studies of toxic waste imports by Levinson (1999a, 1999b) found that firms are quite sensitive to changes in disposal taxes imposed by state governments. Consequently, these studies suggest that distortions may arise if further decentralization of toxic waste regulation from the federal government to state and local governments would result in less stringent controls. Third, the Sigman and Levinson studies covered only the early years of the Toxic Release Inventory (TRI) program. (For a description of this program, see Hamilton [2005].) Thus, it will be of interest to determine if these results hold after updating the analysis to the most recent years for which data are available.

In the remainder of this chapter, estimation of firms' responses to hazardous waste taxes is motivated by a simple model proposed by Levinson (1999a) to compare the marginal social cost of toxic waste disposal with the marginal private cost of disposing of this waste, inclusive of state taxes. The disparity between these costs is determined by the interaction of (1) the fraction of the waste shipped out of state; and (2) the elasticity of waste generation (or waste disposal) with respect to disposal costs. This elasticity is estimated using data assembled for the period from 1988 to 2004 on plant-level generation and disposal of chlorinated solvent waste and state taxes on hazardous waste disposal.

Two main results emerge from the empirical analysis. First, when analyzing the data over the entire 1988 to 2004 time period, generation and disposal of chlorinated solvent wastes do not respond to changes in disposal costs occasioned by changes in state tax rates. By 2004, however, disposal of these chemicals had decreased dramatically due to technical changes that permitted increased use of aqueous metal cleaners and greater reuse and recycling of chemical cleaners. These technical changes may well have reduced firms' responsiveness to waste disposal taxes, thus making it difficult to conclude that distortions arising from decentralization of environmental policy are likely to be small. Second, during the early years of the TRI program (1988 to 1990) and prior to the time these technical changes occurred, generation and disposal of chlorinated solvent waste did not respond to changes in disposal tax rates. This outcome reverses Sigman's (1996) findings and strengthens the conclusion that no efficiency consequences arise from assigning greater responsibility for regulating chlorinated solvent waste to the states.

Model

Levinson (1999a) developed a model to show how distortions can arise in toxic waste disposal because of the interaction between waste exportation and the elasticity of firms' waste disposal practices with respect to disposal costs. The model envisions M jurisdictions. Each jurisdiction has a fixed amount of industrial activity that produces hazardous waste. Waste is unsightly or poses a health hazard to the identical residents of each jurisdiction; thus, it is a public bad.

Each jurisdiction has two available options to reduce residents' exposure to waste. First, although it is costly to transport waste, waste can be shipped to another jurisdiction, where it becomes somebody else's problem. Second, jurisdiction officials can tax disposal of waste in their own jurisdiction. The disposal tax rate is differentiated according to whether the waste is locally generated or is shipped from another jurisdiction. In several court cases, discriminatory taxation of waste disposed of in one state but generated in another has been found to violate the commerce clause of the United States Constitution (see Urie 1995). Nonetheless, states can (and do) to some extent follow the "not-in-my-back-yard" (NIMBY) principle by less direct means, such as taxing the disposal of waste on the generating plant's site at one rate and taxing off-site disposal at another (higher) rate.

Residents of each jurisdiction get utility from consuming the composite good y and get disutility from disposal of waste in their jurisdiction (W). Thus, the utility of each resident in each jurisdiction is

(1) $U = U(y, W)$.

In equation (1), $W = W_D + W_I$, where W_D and W_I denote, respectively, local or domestic waste disposed of locally and waste imports generated outside the jurisdiction but disposed of locally. Each resident of each jurisdiction receives a pro rata share of profits from local industrial production (π) and tax revenue generated by waste disposal. Thus, the budget constraint is

(2) $y = \frac{1}{n}(\pi - qW) + \frac{1}{n}(\tau_D W_D + \tau_I W_I)$,

where the price of y is normalized to unity, n is the number of residents in the jurisdiction, q is private waste disposal costs (assumed to be the same for the two types of waste), and $\tau_j, j = D, I$ is the sum of per unit private waste disposal costs plus the tax rates on disposal for the two types of waste. Costs of transportation on imported waste from other jurisdictions are ignored, and private waste disposal costs are treated as exogenous.

Local firms produce the consumption good (y), purchase competitively supplied inputs, generate waste (g), and maximize profits. Firms take as exogenous waste disposal taxes in other jurisdictions as well as prices and quantities of inputs other than waste. Let f denote the production function. Local profits are then given by

(3) $\pi = f(g) - \tau_j g$,

where $\tau_j, j = D, E$ is the per unit cost of disposing of local waste locally and the per unit cost of exporting local waste to another jurisdiction for disposal and other variables are as defined in equation (2). To maximize profits, each firm disposes of waste at least cost. Therefore, if all waste is homogeneous, if jurisdictions are treated as points in space, and if the cost of transporting waste is a constant multiple of distance, firms either will dispose of all waste locally ($g = W_D$) or will ship all waste for disposal in another jurisdiction. On the other hand, as discussed more fully by Levinson (1999a), if waste produced by different firms is heterogeneous and possibly subject to different transportation charges, a fraction of it may be disposed of locally (W_D / g) and the remainder would be shipped to another jurisdiction.

Jurisdiction officials choose τ_D and τ_I by setting tax rates so as to maximize their constituents' utility subject to the budget constraint in equation (2) while accounting for profit maximization by firms as in equation (3). The optimal choice of disposal costs for imported waste from other jurisdictions can be found by solving

(4) $-n\left[\dfrac{\partial U/\partial W}{\partial U/\partial y}\right]\dfrac{\partial W_I}{\partial \tau_I} = W_I + \tau_I\dfrac{\partial W_I}{\partial \tau_I}.$

Thus,

(5) $\tau_I^* = K\left[\dfrac{\eta_I - 1}{\eta_I}\right]^{-1},$

where K is the population of the jurisdiction multiplied by the negative of the marginal disutility of waste divided by the marginal utility of income and η_I is the absolute value of the elasticity of waste imports to the jurisdiction with respect to a change in disposal costs τ_I. In addition, $K = -n(\partial U / \partial W) / (\partial U / \partial y)]$ is interpreted as the marginal social cost of waste disposal. Equation (5) shows that local officials will behave as a single-price monopolist, operating on the elastic part of the demand curve for waste disposal by waste generators in other jurisdictions. Thus, the disposal price per unit of waste paid by nonresidents will exceed the marginal social cost of waste disposal; that is, $\tau_I^* / K > 1$. Also, the ratio τ_I^* / K is inversely related to η_I, so if η_I increases, more waste is deterred from entering the jurisdiction by a given increase in τ_I, and as η_I grows without bound, the value of τ_I^* / K will tend toward unity.

Correspondingly, the optimal tax inclusive cost to dispose of locally generated waste can be found by solving for τ_D from

(6) $\dfrac{\partial f}{\partial g}\dfrac{\partial g}{\partial \tau_D} = K\dfrac{\partial W_D}{\partial \tau_D},$

where $\partial f / \partial g = \tau_D$. Thus, denoting the absolute value of the elasticity of local waste disposal with respect to the local tax rate as η_D, the optimal cost to dispose of locally generated waste is

(7) $\tau_D^* = K\left[1 - \dfrac{1 - (g/W_D)}{\eta_D}\right]^{-1}.$

In the case in which all local waste is disposed of locally ($g = W_D$), the cost of local disposal of local waste is set equal to marginal social cost ($\tau_D^* = K$). Thus, in this model, if pollution is not exported, no distortions arise and $K / \tau_D^* = 1$ regardless of the value of η_D. In the case in which waste is heterogeneous (i.e., $W_D < g$), the jurisdiction will inefficiently set the cost of local disposal below marginal social cost. Therefore, $\tau_D^* < K$ and $\tau_D^* \le K \le \tau_I^*$.

To better appreciate the relationship between the private cost of disposing of local waste locally and the marginal social cost of waste disposal, consider how the magnitude of the ratio K / τ_D^* varies with g / W_D and η_D. A useful starting point is the case in which $\eta_D = 1$. In this situation, equation (7) can be rewritten as $K / \tau_D^* = g / W_D$, indicating that the ratio of the marginal social cost of disposal to the optimal local private disposal equates to the reciprocal of the fraction of waste that is exported. If a jurisdiction can export more of its own pollution, it will have a lower incentive to control it. In addition, if the waste is entirely exported ($W_D = 0$), then K / τ_D^* becomes arbitrarily large regardless of the value of η_D and waste might be better controlled by a higher level of government.

Furthermore, for a given value of g / W_D, the magnitude of K / τ_D^* is inversely related to the value of η_D: the value of K / τ_D^* is smaller if $\eta_D > 1$ than if $\eta_D < 1$. In the extreme case in which the elasticity of waste disposal with respect to cost approaches infinity, K / τ_D^* approaches unity, but a small deviation of τ_D^* from K has a comparatively large effect on production of waste. In the other extreme case in which $\eta_D = 0$, firms do not alter the amount of waste generated in the face of tax changes and the ratio K / τ_D^* is arbitrarily large. In that situation, a marginal increase in the jurisdiction's tax rate not only does not distort choices made by firms as to the amount of waste to generate, but it also has no effect on income of the jurisdiction's residents. Increased tax revenue redistributed to residents would be exactly offset by reduced distributions of profits. Waste reduction would instead have to be achieved using policy instruments not directly considered in the model, such as a sufficiently large tax increase, so that firms would earn less than normal profits at all possible output levels.

Prior Estimates

Several studies present evidence on the behavior of firms and environmental policy makers when transboundary pollution is at issue. Results of selected studies are briefly summarized here. Alberini and Bartholomew (1999) and Alberini and Frost (2007), for example, find that firms generating spent chlorinated solvent waste are sensitive to potential future liability costs that can arise if the disposal facility used becomes a Superfund site. Other studies (reviewed below) identify evidence, in both U.S. and international contexts, that pollution control is less stringent when a portion of the pollution is exported to other jurisdictions. Three studies, described in greater detail at the end of this section, develop estimates that can be used to compute values of τ_I^* / K and K / τ_D^*.

Seven studies, summarized in table 7.1, consider the possibility that regulators are too lax in setting environmental policy for pollutants that are likely to cross jurisdictional boundaries in the United States. Four of these studies (Gray and Shadbegian 2004; Helland and Whitford 2003; Novello 1992; Sigman 1996) deal with pollution within the United States; the remaining three studies (Levinson 1999a, 1999b; Sigman 1996) are discussed in more detail later on. Novello (1992) finds that regulatory stringency weakens when local emissions of volatile organic compounds and nitrogen oxides affect ozone levels in downwind states. Sigman (2005) looks at how states set water quality standards for rivers if they are authorized to assume responsibility for implementation and

Table 7.1

Studies of Pollution Exportation in the United States

Author and Date	Nature of Study	Results
Novello (1992)	Interstate transmission of air emissions	Regulatory stringency weakens when air emissions are exported to downwind states.
Sigman (2005)	Effects of state involvement in setting water quality standards for rivers	Some states allowed water quality to degrade by about 4%, with environmental costs to downstream states of about $17 million.
Gray and Shadbegian (2004)	Environmental regulation of pulp and paper mills	Plants whose pollution affects residents of other states generally have higher emissions.
Helland and Whitford (2003)	Econometric analysis of Toxic Release Inventory data	Facilities' emissions were found to be systematically higher when located in counties that border other states.
Levinson (1999a, 1999b)	Estimates of response to hazardous waste imports to hazardous waste import taxes	Interstate hazardous waste shipments were found to be negatively related to the tax rate on hazardous waste.
Sigman (1996)	Estimates of responsiveness of chlorinated solvent waste generation to hazardous waste disposal taxes	Generation of chlorinated solvent waste is strongly negatively related to waste disposal taxes.

enforcement of U.S. Clean Water Act regulations and if a portion of discharges will end up in downstream states. Sigman's analysis indicates that states in this situation allow water quality to degrade by about 4 percent, with a comparatively small environmental cost to downstream states of $17 million. Gray and Shadbegian (2004), in their study of environmental regulation of pulp and paper mills, find that plants whose pollution affects residents of other states generally have higher emissions than plants whose pollution affects only their home state. Helland and Whitford (2003) cite court cases in which the plaintiff alleges more lenient treatment of polluters when the incidence of pollution falls outside the jurisdiction and then present econometric evidence based on data from the TRI demonstrating that facilities' emissions are systematically higher in counties that border other states than in counties that are within the home state.

Among studies conducted in an international context (see summary in table 7.2), Sigman (2002) shows that countries protect less vigorously against effluent discharges into rivers that transport perhaps one-third of them to other countries downstream, a finding that is consistent with her work on the Clean Water Act

Table 7.2
Studies of Pollution Exportation in an International Context

Author and Date	Nature of Study	Results
Sigman (2002)	Analysis of effluent discharges into rivers that cross international boundaries	Countries protect less vigorously against such discharges.
Murdoch and Sandler (1997a, 1997b)	Inefficiently low taxes on chlorofluorocarbon emissions providing an incentive for international cooperation	Incentives to cut back on emissions rise with national income, as implied by the theory.
Murdoch, Sandler, and Sargent (1997)	Incentives for international cooperation to control air emissions of sulfur and nitrogen oxides among European countries	Theoretical model developed leads to an empirical representation that yields reasonable results for sulfur but less satisfying results for nitrogen oxides.
Davies and Naughton (2006)	Gains from international cooperation arising from cross-border pollution spillovers	Support for this idea was found by analyzing data on treaty participation.

cited above. Murdoch and Sandler (1997a, 1997b) consider the idea that inefficiently low taxes and regulations on pollution (chlorofluorocarbon emissions in this case) provide an incentive for international cooperation. Murdoch, Sandler, and Sargent (1997) also look into this issue in their study of European sulfur and nitrogen oxide air emissions. Davies and Naughton (2006) extend the model developed in the previous section by permitting firms subject to environmental taxes to relocate in other countries with weaker environmental regulations. They show that greater cross-border spillovers increase gains from cooperation and find support for this hypothesis using data on treaty participation.

Levinson (1999a, 1999b) (for a summary, see table 7.1) estimates the responsiveness of waste imports to waste import taxes (η_I) by focusing on interstate shipments of hazardous waste from 1989 to 1995. In 1991, for example, approximately 10 percent of all hazardous waste generated in the United States was shipped across state boundaries. Data on hazardous waste shipments are taken from the TRI, and data on tax rates that states apply to hazardous waste imports are compiled from *Tax Day*, a Commerce Clearinghouse publication. Also considered is that during the late 1980s and early 1990s, many states levied higher taxes on waste imports than on locally generated waste, despite a series of Supreme Court rulings that discriminatory tax treatment of interstate waste imports represents an unconstitutional violation of the Commerce Clause. A key finding from the empirical analysis is that interstate hazardous waste shipments for disposal is negatively related to the tax rate applied to imported waste. This outcome suggests that higher taxes deter interstate shipments of hazardous waste.

Estimates of the elasticity of waste imports with respect to waste import taxes are between 0.09 and 0.13. As Levinson (1999a) argues, these tax elasticities are considerable, given that taxes are only a part (less than 10 percent) of overall disposal costs, and suggest that waste disposal taxes in different states are close substitutes. Estimates of η_I can be obtained from these tax elasticities by redefining the tax base as the sum of private disposal costs (estimated to be approximately $156 per ton in 1993) plus applicable taxes on imported waste (which averaged about $15 per ton across the 48 contiguous states, including those with a zero tax rate). These estimates, which range from 1.06 to 1.45, are consistent with the notion that states behave as single-price monopolists in setting local disposal costs and imply that local officials set charges to dispose of imported waste at between 3 and 12 times marginal social cost; see equation (5).

Estimates of η_I would be larger and estimates of τ_i^* / K would be correspondingly smaller, however, had transportation costs (ignored in the model) been factored into the calculations. Assuming that transportation costs were $0.25 per ton-mile in the early 1990s and that the average length of an interstate trip was 300 miles (Deyle and Bretschneider 1995), private disposal costs per ton would increase by 48 percent, to $231 (= $156 + $75). After accounting for these additional costs, estimates of η_I corresponding to those presented by Levinson (1999a) would range from 1.47 to 2.13. Values of τ_i^* / K would decline to a range of 1.88 to 3.13.

Instead of looking at how interstate shipments of waste respond to discriminatory taxation, Sigman (1996) considers the response of local waste generation to local disposal costs for the case of spent chlorinated solvents used in metal parts cleaning (for a summary, see table 7.1). Her work builds on earlier studies (Deyle and Bretschneider 1995; USEPA 1984; Wolf and Camm 1987) that differed considerably in their findings on the sensitivity of waste generation to waste management costs. Sigman regressed plant-level data on chlorinated solvent waste generation from the TRI on tax-inclusive costs of disposing of these chemicals and other variables for the period 1987 to 1990. To focus on metal cleaning applications, data were drawn from 31 states that imposed either land disposal or incineration taxes on waste generation and from facilities in six manufacturing sectors. Disposal of chlorinated solvents was achieved mainly by incineration, so cost data were developed by adding U.S. government estimates of incineration costs to state taxes on incineration of in-state wastes.

This cost variable, however, exhibits little variation over time for a given state, so use of fixed-effects estimation (see table IV in Sigman [1996, 209]), which uses only within-plant information, is likely to lead to fragile estimates of η_D. Because the estimate of private incineration costs is assumed to be the same for all states, the tax rate represents the only source of variation in the cost variable used in the regression model. In addition, 20 of the 31 states did not change their incineration tax rate over the 1987 to 1990 period, and 7 of the remaining 11 states changed this tax rate only once. The extent to which lack of variation in the cost variable might result in fragile estimates of η_D is investigated in the next section.

In any case, a key finding is that chlorinated solvent waste generation is quite sensitive to tax-inclusive costs of disposal; for example, Sigman's table IV and accompanying discussion (Sigman 1996, 210) show that when out-of-state tax rates, plant effects, and time effects are controlled, η_D is estimated to be 7.83. This value is at the low end of corresponding elasticities estimated in several equations using other methods (at the high end is $\eta_D = 22$). In addition, Sigman states (p. 207) that "49% of the [chlorinated solvent] waste was managed in the state where it was generated." Thus, $g / W_D = 2.04$, and the estimate of $\eta_D = 7.83$ implies that $K / \tau_D^* = 1.133$. This calculation illustrates that the relatively high estimated sensitivity of chlorinated solvent disposal to changes in disposal costs combined with the relatively large percentage of these wastes shipped out of state means that the marginal social cost of this activity is more than 13 percent higher than the price paid by waste generators.

State taxes represent only about 2 percent of total disposal costs. In 1987 state taxes on incineration (a relatively expensive disposal option) averaged $12 per ton, whereas spent chlorinated solvent disposal costs were estimated to be $659 per ton. Thus, Sigman (1996) estimates that elimination of state taxes would stimulate production of chlorinated solvent waste by only 5 percent to 12 percent. Nonetheless, because of a relatively low ratio of state taxes to total disposal costs, average incineration taxes would have to be increased by about $86 per ton, or by a factor of 7.17 (= 86/12), to bring K into equality with τ_D. Although such a large percentage increase in disposal taxes is perhaps politically infeasible, the estimate $\eta_D = 7.83$ suggests the implausible result that a 13 percent increase in total disposal costs would roughly eliminate the generation of chlorinated solvent waste.

New Estimates

There are new estimates of the response of spent chlorinated solvent waste generation to state taxation of this activity. Waste of this type arises from cleaning metal parts using tetrachloroethylene (perchloroethylene), trichloroethylene, 1,1,1-trichloroethane, or dichloromethane (methylene chloride). With the exception of trichloroethane, these chemicals are regarded as either possible or probable human carcinogens (USEPA 2005). Data on industrial disposal of these chemicals are taken from the TRI for the period 1988 to 2004. Thus, they extend the time period considered in the earlier study (1987 to 1990) by 14 years, which, in turn, allows for more possible changes in disposal tax rates levied by each state.

Table 7.3 shows that between 1988 and 2004, industrial disposal of all four chemicals declined sharply, from 421.11 million pounds in 1988 to 289.55 million pounds in 1991 to 16.75 million pounds in 2004. Thus, the quantity of these chemicals disposed of in 2004 represents only 4 percent of the quantity disposed of in 1988. Introduction of effective aqueous cleaners has resulted in a substitution away from use of chlorinated solvents in many applications; in applications in which they are still used, increased recycling and reuse has further lowered

Table 7.3
Trends in Industrial Disposal of Chlorinated Solvents (in millions of pounds)

Chemical	1988		1991		2004	
	Off-Site	Total	Off-Site	Total	Off-Site	Total
Tetrachlororethylene	1.39	37.72	0.12	17.65	0.14	2.47
Trichloroethylene	1.47	57.45	0.12	36.55	0.07	6.34
1,1,1-Trichloroethane	5.95	187.02	1.01	149.15	0.01	0.08
Dichloromethane	7.81	138.92	0.50	86.20	0.23	7.86
Total	16.62	421.11	1.75	289.55	0.45	16.75

Source: Data taken from the U.S. Environmental Protection Agency Toxic Release Inventory Explorer, http://www.usepa.gov/triexplorer.

quantities disposed. Table 7.3 also indicates that all four chemicals are mainly disposed of on the site where they were generated; the fraction of spent chlorinated solvents disposed of off-site was 3.9 percent (16.62/421.11) in 1988 and 2.6 percent (0.45/16.75) in 2004. These estimates, computed directly from TRI data, show that out-of-state disposal of chlorinated solvent waste is a much less frequent occurrence than assumed by Sigman.

The next step is to analyze data on disposal of the four chemicals listed in table 7.3 by plant and over time. All plants are involved in manufacturing and are classified in six specific manufacturing sectors to maintain consistency with Sigman (1996) and to focus on sectors in which the four chemicals would be used for cleaning metal parts. These data form an unbalanced panel because plants do not appear in the inventory in years when releases are below minimum reporting thresholds. In any case, 37,397 observations are available from 8,030 different plants, representing 46 of the contiguous 48 states. Plants from Arkansas and Maryland do not appear in the data set because of difficulties determining their waste disposal tax rates. The average is 4.66 observations available per plant.

For each plant in each year, the main data elements consist of total production-related chlorinated solvent waste generated and total quantity of this type of waste that was disposed of either on-site or off-site. The former measure is referred to as "waste generated," and the latter measure is referred to as "waste disposal." Waste disposal figures generally are lower than figures for waste generated because spent chlorinated solvents can be recycled or used as fuel. The plant-level data do not break down quantities of waste disposed of on-site versus off-site; thus, it is not possible to distinguish intrastate from interstate waste shipments.

Table 7.4 presents means of chlorinated solvent waste generated and waste disposed for all plants in the data set for selected years. These tabulations indicate that after 1991, the number of chlorinated solvent waste generators declined over time, whereas waste generation per plant increased. Apparently, many plants that in the early 1990s generated relatively small quantities of this type of waste

Table 7.4
Chlorinated Solvent Waste Generated and Disposed: Means of Sample Plants for Selected Years

Year	Chlorinated Solvent Waste Generated (in tons)	Chlorinated Solvent Waste Disposed (in tons)	Number of Plants
1988	37.84	35.46	3,288
1991	87.69	24.98	5,006
1995	110.01	7.89	2,210
2000	229.80	18.28	1,080
2004	270.99	9.09	718

now fall below the reporting threshold. In addition, the ratio of waste disposed to waste generated has fallen over time, indicating the increased importance of reuse, recycling, and use of these chemicals as fuels.

Data on tax rates applicable to the disposal of spent chlorinated solvent waste were assembled in two stages. First, Levinson's data on on-site and off-site disposal tax rates per ton of waste by state and year were obtained for the period 1988 to 1995. These data, obtained from *Tax Day*, are fully described in his two previously referenced papers (Levinson 1999a, 1999b). Second, these tax data were brought forward to the year 2004 by a LexisNexis search of each state's statutes. This search was conducted by first verifying the Levinson data for the years 1991 to 1995 and then extending these data forward to 2004. The year 1991 was the earliest year for which a LexisNexis search of state statutes could be performed. Disposal tax rate data obtained in the search for the period 1991 to 1995 are virtually identical with those used by Levinson, but the Levinson data for 1988 to 1990 lack complete agreement with the incineration tax data reported by Sigman (1996).

The LexisNexis search underscored a number of differences between states in the tax treatment of the production and disposal of toxic waste. In some states (e.g., Alabama), several separate waste disposal taxes are levied on a common base to earmark the resulting revenue streams for different purposes. Thus, it was necessary to identify and then add each of these individual taxes together to obtain the total tax rate that would be seen by waste generators. In other states (e.g., Georgia), taxes are levied not only on toxic waste disposal, but also on recycling of waste and use of waste as a fuel. Illinois and Kentucky tax disposal of waste by volume, rather than by weight; tax rates for these states were converted from cents per gallon to dollars per ton using the number of gallons in a ton of water. New York and Maine impose graduated waste disposal tax rates, and a weighted average of these rates was computed to obtain a single tax rate faced by the "average" waste generator.

Table 7.5
Average On-Site and Off-Site Disposal Tax Rates, Selected Years

Year	On-Site Disposal Tax Rate (per ton)	Number of States Levying This Tax	Off-Site Disposal Tax Rate (per ton)	Number of States Levying This Tax
1988	$13.18	18	$18.50	21
1991	$17.82	23	$26.58	26
1995	$18.59	26	$23.24	31
2000	$22.70	29	$47.02	33
2004	$22.78	29	$47.14	33

Table 7.5 shows trends in on-site and off-site disposal tax rates for selected years. Figures presented are unweighted averages of state tax rates for all states that levy these taxes. As indicated, more states levy taxes on off-site disposal than on on-site disposal, and, as predicted by the model, off-site disposal tends to be taxed at higher rates than on-site disposal. Also, the number of states imposing these types of taxes increased over the years; tax rates on both types of disposal have risen as well. As indicated above, tax rates from 1988 to 1995 were compiled by Levinson. Off-site tax rates for these years include any discriminatory taxes applied to interstate shipments of waste. The decline in average off-site tax rates between 1991 and 1995 is probably due to the decline in the importance of discriminatory taxation of these interstate shipments following unfavorable Supreme Court rulings. The increase in average off-site disposal tax rates between 1995 and 2000 is due to comparatively large increases in these rates by two states, Kansas and Oregon.

Further analysis of the tax rate data indicates that over the period 1988 to 2004, on-site disposal tax rates (used in the analysis below) changed an average of 1.71 times in each state. California changed its on-site disposal tax rate eight times over this period, Utah and Louisiana changed their on-site disposal tax rates six times; and most other states changed their tax rates one to three times. Several states, including Massachusetts and New Jersey, did not levy an on-site disposal tax at any time between 1988 and 2004. In all, 14 states left their tax rates unchanged for the entire period, including those that did not levy such a tax. Most of the on-site disposal tax rate changes occurred before 1995; lengthening the time period examined beyond 1990 is nonetheless useful in contributing additional within-state and thus within-plant variation to the disposal cost variable.

Effects of changes in tax rates on chlorinated solvent waste disposal and generation are presented in table 7.6. In each regression, the unit of observation is a plant in a given year. Waste disposal tax rates are matched to plants according to the state in which they are located and the year in which they were observed.

Table 7.6
Estimates of Elasticity of Chlorinated Solvent Waste Generation and Disposal with Respect to
On-Site Disposal Costs, 1988–2004

Dependent Variable	Disposal	Disposal	Disposal	Generation
Explanatory variable	(1)	(2)	(3)	(4)
Natural logarithm of	−1.811[a]	−0.301	0.956	−0.604
on-site disposal costs	(0.040)	(0.648)	(0.625)	(0.593)
Constant	21.247	[b]	3.219	14.048
	(2.618)		(4.069)	(3.862)
N	34,717	34,717	34,717	35,675
R^2	0.0006	0.811	0.831	0.819
Plant effects	No	Yes	Yes	Yes
Time effects	No	No	Yes	Yes

Note: Standard errors are given in parentheses beneath the coefficient estimates.
[a]Denotes significance at the 1% level.
[b]Denotes omitted variable.

Plants are assumed to take waste disposal tax rates as exogenous. Levinson (1999a, 1999b) bases his analysis on the possible endogeneity of state tax rates (the idea that states that receive a lot of waste respond by enacting high taxes); his analysis, however, was at the state level rather than at the plant level. Waste disposal is the dependent variable of primary interest because it is the quantity of waste produced that is subject to taxation. Sigman (1996) used waste generation as the dependent variable in her study, so this variable is analyzed here as well. Values of waste generation and waste disposal might be used interchangeably for many plants in the early years of the sample, but, as indicated in table 7.4, the ratio of waste disposal to waste generation declines substantially with the passage of time. Both waste disposal and waste generation are measured in natural logarithms after eliminating the plant and year observations for which these variables are zero (2,680 observations in the case of waste disposal and 1,722 observations in the case of waste generation).

Because inclusion of plant effects and year effects (see below) control for many other factors, including plant-specific factors, that might be expected to affect waste disposal, the only explanatory variable in all regressions is the natural logarithm of the on-site cost of disposing of chlorinated solvent waste. As in Sigman (1996), the cost measure was computed as private disposal cost ($659) plus the on-site disposal tax rate for states that levy such a tax. The on-site tax rate rather than the off-site tax rate is used here because, as indicated above, the overwhelming percentage of chlorinated solvent waste is disposed of on-site.

The tax rate is the only source of variation in the disposal cost measure; thus, this variable does not change for plants located in states that did not levy an on-site disposal tax or did not change the disposal tax over the sample period. A distance-weighted average of other states' disposal tax rates is not included because it appears that out-of-state shipments often go to states with specialized disposal facilities rather than to neighboring states.

In the table 7.6 column (1) regression, in which the dependent variable is chlorinated solvent waste disposal, estimation is by ordinary least squares. The column (2) regression adds plant fixed effects to control unobserved heterogeneity across plants. Plant effects fully account for differences in plant size, plant location, plant output, management compliance with TRI reporting, and other factors that vary across plants, but not over time. The column (3) regression adds time effects to the regression of waste disposal on disposal costs. Time effects control factors that affect all plants but that change over time, such as changes in federal regulatory policy toward production and disposal of toxic chemicals and innovations that promote alternative and less hazardous cleaning methods. Hausman tests reject random-effects estimates in favor of fixed-effects estimates in the specifications shown in columns (2) through (4).

In the table 7.6 column (1) regression, based on 34,717 observations, the estimate of the elasticity of waste disposal with respect to disposal costs is –1.811. This estimate is significantly different from zero at the 1 percent level, although $R^2 = 0.0006$ for this regression. As indicated in column (2), $R^2 = 0.811$ once the 7,661 plant effects are added. The column (2) estimate of the elasticity remains negative, but it is not significantly different from zero at conventional levels. Controlling for unobserved heterogeneity among plants reduces both the magnitude and significance of the elasticity of waste generation with respect to cost. When time effects are added in column (3), this elasticity estimate turns positive and is not significantly different from zero at conventional levels.

In column (4), the dependent variable is the natural logarithm of chlorinated solvent waste generation. This regression, based on 35,675 observations, has $R^2 = 0.819$. Estimates indicate that the elasticity of waste generation with respect to cost is negative, but not significantly different from zero at conventional levels after controlling for both plant and time effects. This estimate implies much less sensitivity of waste generation to disposal taxes than do the results of Sigman (1996), but is nonetheless consistent with estimates presented in columns (2) and (3) that control for plant effects and time effects.

The column (1) estimate of the elasticity of waste disposal with respect to cost, although it was not conditioned on plant effects and time effects, can be used to obtain an illustrative estimate of K / τ_D^* by assuming that all waste shipped off-site is shipped out of state. From table 7.6, using $\eta_D = 1.81$ from column (1) together with an estimate of $g / W_D = 1.027$ for 2004, yields $K / \tau_D^* = 1.015$. This estimate suggests that an on-site disposal tax rate increase of $10.23 would be needed in the "average" state to bring marginal social cost and marginal private disposal costs into equality. In 2004 this dollar amount represented a 45 percent increase in the tax (see table 7.5), a 1.5 percent increase in disposal costs, and a 2.67 percent reduction in chlorinated solvent disposal. Because of the comparatively larger estimates of both the extent of out-of-state shipments and of $\eta_D = 7.83$, Sigman's 1996 results, described previously, show a much larger reduction in disposal for a smaller conjectured tax increase.

Estimates in table 7.7, columns (2) through (4), on the other hand, suggest that both generation and disposal of chlorinated solvent waste do not change in the face of changes in state tax rates, at least over the range of tax rates observed for the 1988 to 2004 period. This outcome implies that although taxes on waste disposal raise revenue, they do not distort choices of the quantity of waste disposed. Thus, the value of K / τ_D^* is arbitrarily large. Based on these estimates, state tax policies based on a desire to export pollution have been ineffective.

As mentioned earlier, an important qualification regarding these results is that the number of plants included in the data set becomes smaller with the passage of time partly because of technical changes in the disposal of chlorinated solvent waste. Over time, an increasing number of plants generate amounts of chlorinated solvent waste that fall below threshold values that trigger a re-

Table 7.7
Estimates of the Elasticity of Chlorinated Solvent Waste Generation and Disposal with Respect to Disposal Costs, 1988–1990

Dependent Variable	Disposal	Generation	Disposal	Generation	Disposal	Generation
Explanatory variable	(1)	(2)	(3)	(4)	(5)	(6)
Natural logarithm of on-site disposal costs	1.594 (1.841)	1.406 (1.731)	b	b	b	b
Natural logarithm of disposal costs using incineration tax rate	b	b	−7.530[a] (3.132)	−9.699[a] (2.971)	−1.131 (3.318)	−2.198 (3.141)
Constant	−0.376 (11.988)	0.982 (11.275)	b	b	17.388 (21.563)	24.442 (20.411)
R^2	0.869	0.868	0.869	0.869	0.870	0.870
N	9,785	9,785	7,792	7,792	7,792	7,792
States	46	46	31	31	31	31
Plant effects	Yes	Yes	Yes	Yes	Yes	Yes
Time effects	Yes	Yes	No	No	Yes	Yes

Note: Standard errors are given in parentheses beneath the coefficient estimates.
[a]Denotes significance at the 1% level.
[b]Denotes omitted variable.

porting requirement. Since 1989 these threshold values have been set at 25,000 pounds per year for a chemical manufactured or processed at a facility and 10,000 pounds per year for a chemical used at a facility (*Code of Federal Regulations* 2007). It would therefore be of interest not only to model the response of the larger generators to changes in tax treatment, but also to model attrition from the sample as many generators reduce their reliance on chlorinated solvents. Modeling attrition, however, may turn out to be challenging because some plants leave the data, only to return in subsequent years (see Greene 2003).

Nonetheless, conclusions drawn from the table 7.6 regressions are robust to a number of alterations in the specifications given in table 7.7. First, column (1) shows that when the waste disposal equation with plant and time effects is re-estimated using data from 1988 to 1990 to roughly coincide with the time period used in previous studies (Alberini and Frost 2007; Sigman 1996), the cost elasticity estimate does not differ significantly from zero. If the natural logarithm of waste generation is used as the dependent variable in the column (2) regression, the cost elasticity estimate also does not differ significantly from zero. In both of these regressions, this outcome is the same if the cost elasticity estimate is conditioned only on plant effects. In addition, the column (1) and column (2) results are not sensitive to whether the sample is restricted to plants on which a time series of six or more observations are available.

Second, columns (3) and (4) of table 7.7 show estimates of the cost elasticity of waste disposal and waste generation for the period 1988 to 1990 when (1) the cost variable is computed using the incineration tax rates taken from Sigman (1996, 201); (2) the sample is restricted to the 31 states for which incineration tax rates are available; and (3) cost elasticity estimates are conditioned only on plant effects. Outcomes of these regressions, similar to those reported by Sigman, show that cost elasticity estimates are large, negative, and significantly different from zero. As shown in columns (5) and (6), however, these one-way fixed-effects estimates are fragile, confirming the conjecture in the previous section. When time effects are added to both of these regressions, the cost elasticity estimate is no longer significantly different from zero at conventional levels. Therefore, when both plant effects and time effects are included in the regression, the elasticity of both waste disposal and waste generation with respect to costs is no different from zero, no matter which tax variable is used.

Thus, it appears that Sigman obtained different results from those presented in columns (1) and (2) of table 7.7 because (1) as noted earlier, her estimates of state waste disposal tax rates differed from those used here and in the Levinson studies; and (2) her findings are based on a one-way fixed-effects analysis in which only plant effects were included, rather than on the two-way fixed-effects analysis including both plant effects and time effects as described in her narrative (Sigman 1996, 210). Importantly, adding time effects—see columns (5) and (6)—to the regressions containing only plant effects—columns (3) and (4)—destroys the significance of the coefficient of the waste disposal tax variable.

Third, cost elasticity estimates, re-estimated for the entire 1988 to 2004 data set using a log-linear functional form rather than a log-log functional form, did not differ significantly from zero (results not shown). This outcome holds no matter whether the dependent variable measures waste generation or waste disposal. A linear specification was not tried because it implausibly suggests that a $1 tax change has the same absolute effect on waste generation and disposal for a small firm as for a large firm.

Conclusions

Many distortions appear when subnational governments have authority over aspects of environmental policy. Efficiency losses can arise when policies undertaken by these governments distort the behavior of firms by encouraging relocation or by encouraging emission of more than the optimal amount of pollution. Thus, in deciding whether to decentralize environmental decision making, it is helpful to have an idea of how large these distortions may be. After analyzing the response of firms that generate and dispose of chlorinated solvent waste to changes in state taxation, two main results emerge. First, generation and disposal of chlorinated solvent wastes do not respond to changes in disposal costs occasioned by changes in state tax rates between 1988 and 2004. Disposal of these chemicals decreased dramatically over this period, however, due to technical changes that permitted increased use of aqueous metal cleaners as well as greater reuse and recycling of chemical cleaners. These technical changes may well have reduced firms' responsiveness to waste disposal taxes, thus making it difficult to conclude that distortions arising from decentralization of environmental policy are likely to be small. Second, during the early years of the TRI program (1988 to 1990) and prior to these technical changes, generation and disposal of chlorinated solvent waste did not respond to changes in disposal tax rates. This outcome reverses Sigman's (1996) findings and serves to strengthen the conclusion that no efficiency consequences arise from assigning states greater responsibility for regulating chlorinated solvent waste.

The results presented here differ from those presented by Sigman for at least two reasons. First, Sigman used different data on state waste disposal tax rates than those used in the present study. This study used state waste disposal tax rates obtained through a LexisNexis search of state statutes from 1991 forward. Tax rates obtained in this way are virtually identical to those used by Levinson (1999a, 1999b) for the period 1991 to 1995. Levinson's tax data do not correspond to those used by Sigman for the years 1988 to 1990 that predated the availability of information from the LexisNexis search. Second, further analysis for the early years of the TRI program uncovered a possible problem with Sigman's results. She indicates that her finding of a strong negative association between waste disposal taxes and waste generation was based on a two-way fixed-effects analysis, whereas the analysis presented here finds essentially the same result when only plant effects are included. When time effects are added, the strong association between waste disposal taxes and waste generation is destroyed. In any case, models of interjurisdictional competition frequently demonstrate that such competition is inefficient. The empirical results presented here, however, suggest that because taxes on the disposal of this waste do not affect firm behavior, at least in the case of chlorinated solvent waste, this inefficiency does not arise.

REFERENCES

Alberini, A., and J. Bartholomew. 1999. The determinants of hazardous waste disposal choice: An empirical analysis of halogenated solvent waste shipments. *Contemporary Economic Policy* 17:309–320.

Alberini, A., and S. Frost. 2007. Forcing firms to think about the future: Economic incentives and the fate of hazardous waste. *Environmental and Resource Economics* 36:451–474.

Becker, R., and J. V. Henderson. 2000. Effects of air quality regulation on polluting industries. *Journal of Political Economy* 108:379–421.

Break, G. 1967. *Intergovernmental fiscal relations in the United States*. Washington, DC: Brookings Institution.

Bulte, E., J. A. List, and M. C. Strazicich. 2007. Regulatory federalism and the distribution of air pollution emissions. *Journal of Regional Science* 47:155–178.

Code of Federal Regulations. 2007. Thresholds for Reporting. Title 40, part 372.25.

Cumberland, J. H. 1980. Efficiency and equity in interregional environmental management. *Review of Regional Studies* 10:1–9.

Davies, R. B., and H. T. Naughton. 2006. Cooperation in environmental policy: A spatial approach. Working Paper. Department of Economics, University of Oregon, Eugene.

Deyle, R. E., and S. I. Bretschneider. 1995. Spillovers of state policy innovations: New York's hazardous waste regulatory initiatives. *Journal of Policy Analysis and Management* 14:79–106.

Fredriksson, P. G., and D. L. Millimet. 2002. Strategic interaction and determination of environmental policy across the United States. *Journal of Urban Economics* 51:101–122.

Goklany, I. M. 1999. *Clearing the air: The real story of the war on air pollution*. Washington, DC: Cato Institute.

Gray, W. B., and R. J. Shadbegian. 2004. "Optimal" pollution abatement—whose benefits matter, and how much? *Journal of Environmental Economics and Management* 47:510–534.

Greene, W. H. 2003. *Econometric analysis*. Upper Saddle River, NJ: Prentice Hall.

Greenstone, M. 2002. The impacts of environmental regulation on industrial activity: Evidence from the 1970 and 1977 Clean Air Act Amendments and the Census of Manufacturers. *Journal of Political Economy* 110:1175–1219.

Hamilton, J. T. 2005. *Regulation through revelation*. Cambridge: Cambridge University Press.

Helland, E., and A. B. Whitford. 2003. Pollution incidence and political jurisdiction: Evidence from the TRI. *Journal of Environmental Economics and Management* 46:403–424.

Jaffe, A. B., S. Peterson, P. Portney, and R. Stavins. 1995. Environmental regulation and the competitiveness of U.S. manufacturing: What does the evidence tell us? *Journal of Economic Literature* 33:132–163.

Levinson, A. 1997. A note on environmental federalism: Interpreting some contradictory results. *Journal of Environmental Economics and Management* 33: 359–366.

———. 1999a. NIMBY taxes matter: The case of state hazardous waste disposal taxes. *Journal of Public Economics* 74:31–51.

———. 1999b. State taxes and interstate hazardous waste shipments. *American Economic Review* 89:666–677.

List, J. A., and S. Gerking. 2000. Regulatory federalism and environmental protection in the United States. *Journal of Regional Science* 40:453–472.

Murdoch, J. C., and T. Sandler. 1997a. The voluntary provision of a pure public good: The case of reduced CFC emissions and the Montreal protocol. *Journal of Public Economics* 63:331–349.

———. 1997b. Voluntary cutbacks and pre-treaty behavior: The Helsinki protocol and sulfur emissions. *Public Finance Review* 25:139–162.

Murdoch, J. C., T. Sandler, and K. Sargent. 1997. A tale of two collectives: Sulphur versus nitrogen oxides emission reduction in Europe. *Economica* 64:281–301.

Novello, D. 1992. The OTC challenge: Adding VOC controls in the Northeast. *Journal of the Air Waste Management Association* 42:1053–1056.

Oates, W. E. 2002. A reconsideration of environmental federalism. In *Recent advances in environmental economics*, J. A. List and A. J. de Zeeuw, eds., 1–32. Cheltenham, UK: Edward Elgar.

Oates, W. E., and R. M. Schwab. 1988. Economic competition among jurisdictions: Efficiency enhancing or distortion inducing? *Journal of Public Economics* 35: 333–354.

Revesz, R. L. 2001. Federalism and environmental regulation: A public choice analysis. *Harvard Law Review* 115:553–641.

Sigman, H. 1996. The effects of hazardous waste on waste generation and disposal. *Journal of Environmental Economics and Management* 30:199–217.

———. 2002. International spillovers and water quality in rivers: Do countries free ride? *American Economic Review* 92:1152–1159.

———. 2005. Transboundary spillovers and decentralization of environmental policies. *Journal of Environmental Economics and Management* 50:82–101.

Urie, M. C. 1995. Share and share alike? Natural resources and hazardous waste under the commerce clause. *Natural Resources Journal* 35:309–380.

U.S. Environmental Protection Agency. 1984. The feasibility and desirability of alternative tax systems for Superfund: CERCLA Section 301(a)(1)(G) Study. Washington, DC: USEPA.

———. 2005. Toxic Release Inventory (TRI) basis of OSHA carcinogens. http://usepa.gov/tri/chemical/oshacarc/htm.

USEPA. *See* U.S. Environmental Protection Agency.

Wellisch, D. 2000. *Theory of public finance in a federal state.* Cambridge: Cambridge University Press.

Wilson, J. D. 1996. Capital mobility and environmental standards: Is there a theoretical basis for a "race to the bottom"? In *Harmonization and fair trade*, vol. 1, J. Bhagwati and R. Hudec, eds., 393–427. Cambridge, MA: MIT Press.

———. 1999. Theories of tax competition. *National Tax Journal* 52:269–304.

Wolf, K., and F. Camm. 1987. *Policies for chlorinated solvent waste—an exploratory application of a model of chemical life cycles and interactions.* Santa Monica, CA: Rand Corporation.

COMMENTARY
Lawrence Susskind

Shelby Gerking raises two important questions about the capacity of state and local governments to formulate and implement effective environmental policy. Both have to do with whether or not state and local officials are likely to set appropriate standards. His first concern is that public policy makers might not be able or willing to deal effectively with cross-border pollution. Second, he is worried that they might engage in what has been dubbed "a race to the bottom" by setting inappropriately low standards in an effort to compete with their neighbors for new investment. Gerking quotes Wallace Oates (2002, 8), who contends that "additional empirical estimates of distortions associated with transboundary pollution are needed prior to judging how state and local governments might perform if they are given more authority over environmental policy."

This statement is unsettling. After all, state and local government officials already regulate most land use in the United States (although the U.S. federal government certainly owns a lot of land in the western part of the country). State and local governments currently regulate the siting of most industrial production and waste disposal facilities. State and local governments also intervene to ensure that water supplies are maintained and that nonpoint sources of pollution are regulated. It is through local regulatory enforcement that we deal with most public health threats in the United States, including the building and regulation of most sewage systems and efforts to guarantee building safety. I am not sure that another study of a single effort to regulate the generation and disposal of one kind of hazardous waste (chlorinated solvents) will tell us more than we already know about state and local efforts to formulate and implement effective environmental policy. Most already do a good job of protecting human health and safety and managing natural resources. One reason state and local governments are much more responsive to environmental concerns than the federal government is that a great many constituents press them all the time to be sure that they are doing everything possible to tend to such matters.

Gerking argues, however, that the generation of this particular kind of toxic waste is likely to be sensitive to changes in regulatory policy. His overriding question is whether the volume of chlorinated solvent waste shipped from one jurisdiction to another is responsive to state disposal taxes, especially over time. His main finding is that generation and disposal of chlorinated solvent wastes have not responded to changes in disposal costs occasioned by changes in state tax rates (over the range of tax rates actually levied). Subject to a number of qualifications, Gerking (this volume, p. 171) finds that "no efficiency consequences arise from assigning greater responsibility for regulating chlorinated solvent waste to the states."

This conclusion is not surprising given the very small portion of total industrial production costs represented by disposal of this kind of waste, but it is troubling. Isn't it more important to find out whether taking environmental management responsibility away from state and local governments and giving it to the federal government will minimize adverse environmental and health effects and not just provide efficiency gains? Isn't it necessary to look at the whole intergovernmental system to understand how the parts work together? Typically, the federal government sets legal and institutional standards within which states and localities must choose different ways of managing the environmental challenges that each faces. In my view, the way each jurisdiction deals with the specific challenges it faces is far more important than the way the average state or locality behaves. That states and localities differ markedly in the environmental management strategies they adopt makes sense given the wide range of situations they face. There are more than 150 cities with populations of more than 100,000 in the United States. Our goal should be to empower them to respond to the unique social, economic, and environmental circumstances (and trade-offs) they face in ways that the public thinks is fair.

A significant point is that disposal of chlorinated solvents is achieved mainly by incineration. The United States' real goal, as a nation, ought to be to reduce the total volume of such waste being incinerated because the health and environmental effects of such disposal, as has been clearly demonstrated for quite some time, can be quite serious, especially for the most susceptible segments of the population. More care should be given to finding strategies that bring about an overall reduction in the volume of waste generated. As it turns out, that's exactly what's been happening, although we do not find out from Gerking's chapter why that has occurred.

Because state taxes represent only 2 percent of total disposal costs, decisions about whether to store, ship, recycle, or incinerate waste tend to be more a function of considerations other than tax policy. Gerking reports that in 1987 state taxes on incineration averaged $12 per ton, while spent chlorinated solvent disposal costs were estimated to be $659 per ton. Corporate decision makers should focus primarily on finding cost-effective ways to reduce the waste byproducts of their production processes rather than on figuring out how to manipulate federal, state, or local regulatory policy.

The most important fact mentioned in Gerking's chapter is that the quantity of several specific chemicals regarded as either possible or probable human carcinogens disposed of in 2004 represented only 4 percent of the quantity disposed of in 1988. Substitution of new aqueous cleaners has resulted in a move away from chlorinated solvents. Where they are still used, increased recycling and reuse has further lowered the quantities disposed. All these chemicals turn out to be disposed of primarily where they are generated: the fraction disposed of off-site was 39 percent in 1988 and 2.6 percent in 2004. It is crucial to figure out why. One good way is to talk to the public, private, and civil society actors involved. Ask them directly, How and why did the volume of waste you produced go down so dramatically? What changes did you make? What can we learn from your experience about further reducing the levels of waste and contamination of all kinds?

Where did the pressure for substitution or innovation come from? Where did the investment in recycling options originate? A series of studies completed by the Environmental Technology and Public Policy Program at the Massachusetts Institute of Technology, entitled Public Entrepreneurship Networks (Laws et al. 2001), highlights five key roles that various public, private, and civil society actors play when this kind of substitution occurs:

1. *Pioneers* who recognize opportunity, seize initiative, and catalyze action by making commitments
2. *Public venture capitalists* who understand and embrace risk and who package financial, social, and human capital to meet project-driven needs
3. *Superintendents* who provide an environment in which innovation can flourish by fostering the development of relationships that are sustained through formal and informal networks
4. *Mediators* who build consensus on goals and directions and who bring directed problem solving to bear on conflicts that threaten to stall or derail the development of ventures
5. *Stewards* who focus attention on the common good, maintain standards for responsible behavior, and facilitate the coalescence of democratic community around programs of action

Given what is at stake, it is neither practical nor desirable to rely entirely on private or nongovernmental actors to consistently fill these roles. Government action must not threaten the web of relationships that generates the attention and energy needed to make these networks effective. These networks pose a challenge for government agencies. Their participation is essential, yet efforts to "legislate" change may disrupt the very patterns of innovation they seek to promote. Identifying public entrepreneurship networks and understanding how they work is only the first step.

The usual discussion about which level of government ought to be in charge of environmental regulation actually misses the point. There would not be a race to the bottom if civil society is significantly involved in policy making and enforcement. There is no need to worry about a race to the bottom if we focus on innovation and technology sharing rather than regulation. Substitution and recycling will occur as companies compete for a larger share of the market and as civil society continues to reward investors and stockholders for greening their companies.

Gerking points out that some states maintain specialized disposal facilities. Shouldn't wastes be shipped responsibly to places that have invested in building the most advanced facilities, even if that involves out-of-state shipment? Of course. It would always be preferable for groups of states to form partnerships to handle the disposal of different wastes so that each state in the partnership can take responsibility for one or two specialized facilities that benefit the larger region. It does not make sense for each locality or state to build all the necessary facilities. If there is sufficient substitution and recycling nationally, the volume that will remain to be processed can be treated in the most environmentally sensitive way in a small number of locations. Such thinking would suggest moving away from transboundary shipment of waste. Instead, we should look more closely at what kinds of agreements might be generated among states, localities, private investors, and civil society to produce the most environmentally and economically sustainable results.

Gerking finds that "an on-site disposal tax rate increase of $10.23 would be needed in the 'average' state to bring marginal social cost and marginal private disposal costs into equality. In 2004 this dollar amount represented a 45 percent increase in the tax . . . , a 1.5 percent increase in disposal costs, and a 2.67 percent reduction in chlorinated solvent disposal" (this volume, p. 184). Is it really necessary, however, to ensure that all the states were operating in exactly the same way, given the substantial differences in the level of waste produced in each state (which is natural given the variation in patterns of industrial development)? Gerking also concludes that "state tax policies based on a desire to export pollution have been ineffective" (this volume, p. 184). This statement comes as no surprise. States are working together on a wide variety of tasks. Governors in western states, in particular, know that any direct or indirect effort to shift pollution to another state would raise the threat of retaliatory measures on any number of other issues. So, they prefer to collaborate as much as possible.

Gerking's study, like many other environmental economic analyses, takes one particular question out of context: out of the larger intergovernmental context, out of the regional setting in which policy actually gets made and implemented, and out of the complicated context represented by the political deals that have been made over the years. He seems to agree with the notion that there is an optimal amount of pollution and an optimal allocation of pollution among jurisdictions that can be calculated by considering average levels across jurisdictions at a particular point in time. The optimal amount of pollution, however, is very much a function of the level of investment in, and sharing of, technological innovation (including both high- and low-tech options). In addition, it no longer makes sense to think about firms making business decisions solely in terms of the costs and benefits of particular choices they face. Instead, they have to be concerned about how "green" they are perceived to be if they want to maintain their market share. They need to build and maintain partnerships with the state and local governments within which they operate. They have to be more innovative in reducing the total volume of pollution if they want to reduce their operating costs. They have to be sensitive to the pressures that civil society, particularly in areas near where they operate, can impose on share value.

Finally, I do not think the analogy between companies and countries or localities and countries operating internationally holds. International law provides a very different context within which countries and multinationals have to think about investments in pollution reduction, innovation, and recycling.

REFERENCES

Gerking, S. 2008. Decentralization and environmental decision making. In *Fiscal decentralization and land policies*, G. K. Ingram and Y-H. Hong, eds., 169–189. Cambridge, MA: Lincoln Institute of Land Policy.

Laws, D., L. Susskind, J. Abrams, J. Anderson, G. Chapman, E. Rubenstein, and J. Vadagama. 2001. Public entrepreneurship networks. Cambridge, MA: MIT Environmental Technology and Public Policy Program. web.mit.edu/dusp/etpp.

Oates, W. E. 2002. A reconsideration of environmental federalism. In *Recent advances in environmental economics*, J. A. List and A. J. de Zeeuw, eds. Cheltenham, UK: Edward Elgar.

8

A Cross-Country Comparison of Decentralization and Environmental Protection

Hilary Sigman

The division of responsibility for environmental policy between national governments and lower-level governments has changed over time. Historically, environmental policy was largely conducted through provision of local services, such as waste disposal and water supply. In the United States, movement toward centralization began in the 1960s and early 1970s. President Richard M. Nixon created the U.S. Environmental Protection Agency in 1970 to manage burgeoning federal environmental policy.

For a variety of reasons, however, recent trends in the United States have been toward decentralization. First, U.S. environmental policies have always been a hybrid of centralized standard setting and decentralized enforcement; as activity has progressed from establishing standards toward enforcing them, states (and sometimes counties) make a greater share of decisions. Second, many states now wish to surpass federal standards; for example, some states are developing clean-up programs for sites not covered by the federal Superfund program or are even addressing global public goods, such as climate. Finally, political support for decentralization seems to have gained strength. Recent United States Supreme Court decisions—for example, limiting federal control over wetlands in cases involving the Clean Water Act—tend to restrict the federal government's role (Wroth 2007).

I am grateful to Maureen L. Cropper, Yu-Hung Hong, Gregory K. Ingram, and participants at the Lincoln Institute of Land Policy's International Conference symposium for their comments.

In other countries, trends may differ; for example, the European Union has been "harmonizing" environmental laws, effectively reducing decentralization. Thus, it is important to understand the implications of decentralization for environmental outcomes.

An extensive theoretical literature addresses the effects of decentralization on supply of local public goods. This literature concludes that decentralization can improve welfare, but only under certain conditions. Environmental policy fits easily into this framework, with the environment differing from other public goods mostly in that environmental protection is sometimes funded through implicit taxes—costs of compliance with command-and-control regulations—rather than direct fiscal measures.

Several hypotheses in the decentralization debate imply that it affects levels of environmental protection. First, some authors are concerned about the prospect of destructive competition, usually in the form of a "race to the bottom"; such competition would likely result in lower environmental protection when policies are decentralized. Studies support the conclusion that regulatory competition occurs in federal systems, but find it difficult to ascertain whether such competition is destructive (Fredriksson and Millimet 2002; Levinson 2003). Second, with interjurisdictional environmental spillovers, jurisdictions may free ride, giving rise to higher levels of transboundary pollutants with greater decentralization. Previous studies have found evidence of free riding by jurisdictions within the U.S. federal system (Gray and Shadbegian 2004; Helland and Whitford 2003; Sigman 2005). Third, distributive politics within the central government may give rise to more environmental protection than local decision making would (Besley and Coate 2003; Lockwood 2002). Finally, some authors have posited that local governments are either more or less susceptible to environmental or industrial pressure groups (Esty 1996; Revesz 2001).

To test the net effects of these factors, this chapter examines the relationship between decentralization and environmental protection across countries. Four different measures of environmental protection or realized environmental quality are examined: (1) air pollution; (2) treatment to improve water pollution; (3) sanitation access; and (4) land conservation. As measures of decentralization, the equations use, alternately, a standard qualitative measure of federalism and a measure of decentralization of environmental expenditures. Other country characteristics, such as gross domestic product (GDP) and the quality of government, are included. The results do not suggest a strong association between decentralization and environmental protection, which is consistent with the traditional model of decentralization in public goods provision and inconsistent with concerns about a race to the bottom.

Hypotheses

Many normative claims about the effects of decentralization on public goods provision have positive implications for the association between these variables.

Table 8.1
Summary of Hypotheses About Effects of Decentralization

Hypothesis	Effect of Decentralization on Environmental Protection
Uniform central policies (Oates 1972)	?
Destructive competition:	
Race to the bottom	−
Race to the top (NIMBY)	+
Interjurisdictional environmental free riding:	
For regional pollutants	−
For local pollutants	0
Redistribution in central legislature	−
Scale economies in interest-group influence	+/−

At the risk of oversimplification, table 8.1 summarizes the implications of several hypotheses for the effects of decentralization on environmental protection.[1]

A first hypothesis about decentralization is that it allows greater variability in environmental protection according to local costs and benefits, as under Oates's decentralization theorem (1972). The central government may be unable to vary stringency either because it has less information about local conditions than local governments or because it finds variation costly for political reasons. Under these conditions, the implications of decentralization for the level of environmental protection are unclear and depend on the model of government decision making and on the distribution of preferences. For example, if all states have the same costs for environmental protection but voters with greener preferences are concentrated in a few states, these few states will choose less pollution than the remaining states. A national median voter might choose the same average pollution, resulting in no effect of decentralization. A national government elected by the states (along the lines of the U.S. Senate), however, could choose less pollution control because the few green states' preferences are less influential. Because all outcomes seem possible, table 8.1 simply reports uncertainty for this effect.

Destructive regulatory competition would also give rise to differences in pollution levels between decentralized and centralized regimes. Destructive competition models typically assume that each level of government maximizes welfare within its borders. Without market imperfections or redistributive public poli-

---

1. In this discussion, I assume that decentralization is chosen through forces exogenous to environmental policy, such as historical constitutional choices in the case of federalism. If the level of decentralization is endogenously chosen, it is harder to make predictions about cross-sectional patterns.

cies, welfare-maximizing state governments will make efficient choices for local pollutants (Oates and Schwab 1988; Wilson 1996). Both market failures and redistributive policies are common, however, so destructive competition seems a practical possibility (Kunce and Shogren 2005; Oates 2002). The competition may take the form of a race to the bottom, in which counties lower environmental standards to compete for scarce capital, or a race to the top, in which they raise environmental standards so as to shift to other jurisdictions the costs of polluting activities, such as waste disposal. Empirical evidence supports the view that environmental competition arises within the U.S. federal system (Fredriksson and Millimet 2002; Levinson 2003).

Interjurisdictional environmental spillovers are a third possible source of differences in environmental protection. Failing to consider the welfare of neighbors, subnational governments will provide less environmental protection than the national government for pollutants that cross internal borders. Several studies find empirical evidence that U.S. states free ride on one another (Gray and Shadbegian 2004; Helland and Whitford 2003; Sigman 2005). Thus, as represented in table 8.1, free riding would reduce environmental protection with decentralization for regional problems, but would have no effects for local environmental problems.

The central government decision-making process can yield a fourth set of effects. Besley and Coate (2003) conclude that the central government may provide too high a level of local public goods when regional spillovers arise.[2] The overprovision comes from strategic voting for representatives to the central legislature. Thus, Besley and Coate would predict that environmental protection would fall with decentralization. In contrast to the destructive competition and spillover hypotheses, however, the resulting reduction in environmental protection is welfare improving.

Finally, a few authors have advanced hypotheses about the role of scale economies in interest groups' influence at different levels of government. The argument does not seem to have been formalized, and proponents even disagree about the nature of the economy. Some argue that environmental groups cannot wield influence as effectively at the state level as the federal level (Esty 1996); better-funded industry groups may overcome high fixed costs to maintain an office and informed staff in each state capital and thus be better represented at lower levels. For example, Morriss (2000) argues that the U.S. Clean Air Act's delegation to the states creates complexity that favors regulated industries. Others have argued that the scale economy is a spending threshold that must be met to be heard above the din at the national level. This argument would mean that

---

2. Lockwood (2002) also finds inefficient provision of local public goods under a variety of rules governing the decisions of the central legislature. He does not report results about the level of public good provision, however, so the implications for the current analysis are unclear.

centralization favors industry, whereas grassroots environmental organizations would have a comparative advantage in state capitals (Revesz 2001).

A few recent studies look at the empirical effects of changes in decentralization. List and Gerking (2000) and Millimet (2003) examine the changes before and after 1980, when they argue that the Reagan administration scaled back the central government's role in U.S. environmental policy. List and Gerking conclude that no change in environmental spending or air pollution (nitrogen oxide and sulfur dioxide emissions) arose after 1980, whereas Millimet argues that a race to the top in spending (but not air pollution) arose by the mid-1980s. Although both papers interpret their results in terms of regulatory competition, the broader set of hypotheses discussed above may also be relevant to interpreting their results.

In a similar vein, Goklany (1999) looks at an earlier reduction in decentralization. Goklany argues that states had aggressive air pollution regulation before federal policy was strengthened in 1970 and thus did not participate in a race to the bottom. Most federal environmental policies are minimum standards, which states' standards may exceed. Some states do set higher standards, for example, extending regulations to hazardous wastes not covered by federal policy. Oates (2002) points out that this behavior is also evidence against a race to the bottom.

In Sigman (2007), I explore the effects of decentralization on water pollution in rivers around the world; that study uses a panel of countries over time and focuses on both a local and a regional pollutant. The evidence suggests an increase in pollution with decentralization only when country fixed effects are included and perhaps only for the regional pollutant, where interjurisdictional free riding may be to blame. In addition, the water pollution data provide observations at multiple sites within a country. Under Oates's decentralization theorem, decentralization would likely be associated with greater spatial variability.[3] The empirical results in Sigman (2007) support the hypothesis that spatial variability in environmental quality is higher in federal countries. The analysis presented here complements that study by addressing a broader set of environmental protection activities and by focusing specifically on environmental expenditure decentralization, a measure that is available only recently and thus not feasible as an explanatory variable for the water pollution panel.

Data

To test the hypotheses in table 8.1 empirically requires data on environmental protection and decentralization across countries, as well as some other country characteristics.

---

3. For example, Strumpf and Oberholzer-Gee (2002) find empirical evidence that more heterogeneous preferences encourage decentralization of policies for regulation of alcohol in the United States.

ENVIRONMENTAL PROTECTION

The analysis focuses on several measures of environmental protection, broadly defined. The measures concern not only traditional pollution, but also environmental health and land preservation.

Several criteria helped select environmental protection measures. The measures must be available from a source with a consistent definition for as large a number of countries as possible. The environmental goods should be ones for which government activities may account for a substantial share of the variance; measures dominated by variation in natural conditions, such as water availability, are less appropriate. As a result, several measures are closer to inputs than outputs of the environmental quality production function. The government influences most of the chosen measures by its expenditures, rather than by regulating private behavior. One decentralization measure used in the equations focuses on decentralization in spending specifically; spending-related environmental outcomes may therefore be more likely to show an effect of measured decentralization than other environmental outcomes.

The final restriction is the most limiting. This analysis requires data based on observed environmental protection. A number of cross-country emissions measures are available (WRI 2007). Although temptingly complete in coverage, these emissions data are calculated by applying industry-level pollution intensities to industrial output from national accounts. Because they assume homogeneity in pollution intensities, these measures may miss the effects of enforcement or selective implementation of national standards.

With these restrictions, four environmental measures were chosen. Two measures are inputs to water pollution: access to improved sanitation and the level of treatment provided by public sewage treatment works (the latter is available only for Organisation for Economic Co-operation and Development, or OECD, countries). A third measure is ambient air pollution—specifically, sulfur dioxide (SO_2) in large cities—which measures environmental quality and only implicitly government environmental protection. A final measure is the share of land set aside for parks and conservation purposes.

MEASURES OF DECENTRALIZATION

Measuring environmental decentralization across countries presents a challenge. Given the complexity of environmental policy, it is difficult to conceive of an ideal measure, let alone implement it in practice. The conceptual challenge is that countries use very different regulatory structures, so statutory rules may be a poor guide to true power. For example, in the United States, most environmental standards are established by the federal government, but implementation and enforcement are devolved to the states (Sigman 2003). The flexibility that states gain from power over implementation and enforcement appears to be substantial (Helland 1998). For example, the U.S. General Accounting Office (USGAO 1996) reports that water pollution permits issued by the states under federal technology standards varied by several orders of magnitude in the allowable pollution, although they were written for similar facilities. In addition, only some of the decision making responsible for water pollution may come through environmental regulations; decisions about land use and municipal spending on sewers will also be important, but may not be in the portfolio of an environmental agency or ministry.

This chapter takes two different approaches to measuring decentralization. The first is to use a general characterization of countries as federal and nonfederal.[4] An established political science literature has agreed on a list of federal countries and found that this characterization correlates with other measures of decentralization (Treisman 2002). The federalism characterization has a few advantages relative to other potential decentralization measures. First, it is exhaustive in coverage across countries, allowing the largest possible sample sizes for the regressions. Second, it characterizes the broadest range of government functions. It includes not only explicit environmental policies, but also other functions with environmental implications, such as land use regulations. Unlike fiscal decentralization measures, federalism may reflect decentralization of authority that has little fiscal effect, such as decentralization of regulations that require firms to spend on pollution control.

The second approach is to use decentralization of environmental expenditures. This approach sacrifices the advantages above for a measure of decentralization that is specific to the environment. A long tradition of empirical work uses fiscal or expenditure decentralization, which is defined as the ratio of subnational (state, provincial, and local) government spending to total governmental spending, with intergovernmental transfers netted out. The environmental measure used is the analogous measure of environmental spending only: the ratio of subnational environmental expenditures to total environmental expenditures. Data on expenditures are from the International Monetary Fund's Government Finance Statistics (GFS) (IMF 2007). Beginning in 1998, a few countries report environmental expenditures, allowing the measure to be calculated, but the data are very limited, especially for lower levels of government. To include as many countries as possible, the estimated equations use average environmental expenditure decentralization for any year (from 1998 through 2004) in which GFS contains sufficient data.[5]

---

4. The federal countries represented in the data are Argentina, Australia, Austria, Belgium, Bosnia and Herzegovina, Brazil, Canada, Comoros, Ethiopia, Germany, India, Malaysia, Mexico, Micronesia, Nepal, Nigeria, Pakistan, Russia, St. Kitts and Nevis, Sudan, Switzerland, United Arab Emirates, United States, Venezuela, and Yugoslavia (still in existence in the air pollution data).

5. In place of these country averages, it is possible to use country fixed effects for environmental decentralization from a regression of this variable on year dummies, which would adjust for any global time trends in environmental decentralization. When this approach was taken, the time effects were negligible and the country fixed effects virtually identical to the de-meaned country averages, so country averages are used for simplicity.

Thirty-five countries have at least one year's data on environmental expenditure decentralization. Figure 8.1 presents a map of these data. In the concluding section to this chapter, table 8.6 contains the expenditure decentralization measure for all countries for which it is available, ranked by this measure, and also reports the values of all left-hand-side variables for this subset of countries.

The share of environmental expenditure at the subnational level is fairly high, with a median across countries of 66 percent. The values range from 1 percent in Moldova and 3 percent in Uganda to 95 percent in Belgium and 98 percent in China.[6] The correlation between environmental expenditure decentralization and total expenditure decentralization across countries is only 0.2. Environmental decentralization, however, does seem to be greater in federal countries; median environmental decentralization is 83 percent in federal countries, compared with 60 percent in nonfederal countries.

OTHER COUNTRY CHARACTERISTICS

The analyses include a few other country characteristics to distinguish the effect of decentralization from other heterogeneity with which it may be correlated. Given the small number of observations, the equations must include only a parsimonious selection of other variables. To avoid known areas of potential omitted variable bias, the focus is on variables that earlier literature associates with decentralization.

First, income is likely to be a major factor in environmental quality. The Penn World Table (Heston, Summers, and Aten 2006) provides annual per capita income levels standardized for cross-country comparisons. For a few countries, the current data extend only to 2003 and for some equations have been linearly extrapolated to 2004. Some previous studies have found that pollution rises and then falls with income, a pattern sometimes called the "environmental Kuznets curve" (e.g., Grossman and Krueger 1995; Selden and Song 1994). The estimated equations include a cubic in income to adjust flexibly for these effects.

Second, the political structure of a country may be associated with both federalism and environmental quality. Earlier research has suggested that more responsive governments choose lower pollution than do autocratic regimes (Barrett and Graddy 2000; Congleton 1992). Because more repressive governments may also tend to be more centralized, it is important to consider political freedom in these equations. Freedom House (2007) annually evaluates countries' "political rights" on a scale from 1 (most extensive rights) to 7 (fewest rights).

In a similar manner, government corruption may also need to be included in the equations. Studies have found that corruption plays an important role in

---

6. The highest value is actually New Zealand, which reports negative central environmental expenditures in the only year it has data (2004), implying a decentralization value of more than 100 percent. GFS documentation seems to suggest that negative expenditures reflect asset sales. This value has been set to missing in the equations; the results were not sensitive to including it.

Figure 8.1 Environmental Expenditure Decentralization by Country

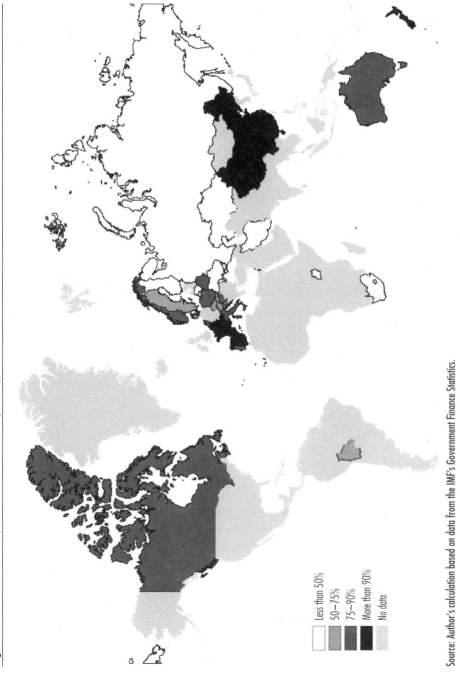

Less than 50%
50–75%
75–90%
More than 90%
No data

Source: Author's calculation based on data from the IMF's Government Finance Statistics.

environmental outcomes (Damania, Fredriksson, and List 2003; Welsch 2004) and that decentralization or federalism is a source of corruption (Fisman and Gatti 2002; Treisman 2000). Thus, a link between decentralization and environmental protection may come through this pathway, unless the equations explicitly account for corruption. The equations use annual measures of corruption (based on surveys) from the International Country Risk Guide (Political Risk Services 2007). The values range from 0 (most corrupt) to 6 (least corrupt); the index has been rescaled from 1 to 7 to allow it to be converted to logarithms.

Finally, the equations include one or two measures of population density. These measures are the population per square kilometer and the share of the population that is urban. The effects of these variables depend on the measures of environmental protection. A dense country may have higher costs for setting aside protected lands, whereas a dense and urban country may have lower per capita costs for sanitation networks.[7] The benefits of land conservation and pollution control may also be greater in a denser country because more people can enjoy these public goods.

Empirical Analysis

Estimated equations have the form

(1) $\ln(EP_i) = f(D_i, GDP_i, POLRT_i, CORRUPT_i, DENSITY_i) + \varepsilon_i,$

where EP_i is the environmental protection measure, D_i is the measure of decentralization, GDP_i is GDP per capita, $POLRT_i$ is the index of lack of political rights, $CORRUPT_i$ is the index of lack of corruption, and $DENSITY_i$ is the country population density and urbanization. The equations use a log-log functional form, except for the GDP variables which are in a cubic to follow earlier literature.

One potential concern in the interpretation of the results is the possibility of colinearity between the decentralization variables of interest and other country characteristics. Such colinearity could make it hard to identify the effect of decentralization. In practice, the correlation coefficients between decentralization and the other variables are all below 0.5.[8]

---

7. The equations were also estimated with population density separated into the log of the country's population and the log of the country's area to allow a more flexible relationship. The coefficients of interest were unaffected by replacing these two variables with population density, so the reported equations use this simpler specification.

8. The correlation coefficients between the log of environmental expenditure decentralization and the variables used in the equations are 0.46 with GDP, −0.41 with the log of lack of political rights, and 0.40 with the log of lack of corruption. Much higher correlations prevail among these other country characteristics.

ACCESS TO IMPROVED SANITATION

The variable access to improved sanitation is the share of households that have access to improved sanitation in 2004 from a World Health Organization/ UNICEF survey.[9] It includes not only connection to public sewers and septic systems, but also some forms of pit latrines that are considered relatively sanitary. The shares of population with improved sanitation range from 9 percent (in Eritrea and Chad) to 100 percent in the most developed countries. Countries with 100 percent access account for about 20 percent of all countries and half the countries with environmental decentralization data. For this reason, the equations are estimated using a top-censored Tobit model.

The results are presented in table 8.2. The estimates provide some evidence of a relationship between decentralization and sanitation access. The point estimate on federal countries is negative, but not statistically significant. In the much smaller sample with data available for both sanitation access and environmental expenditure decentralization, the coefficient on the latter is negative and statistically significant at 5 percent. Because they suggest lower environmental protection with greater decentralization, these coefficients would be consistent with the bulk of the hypotheses concerning decentralization, such as the race to the bottom.[10] Interjurisdictional environmental spillovers probably do not account for the negative effect because sanitation is fairly local in its benefits.

Not surprisingly, the other coefficients in this equation suggest that GDP per capita has a statistically significant effect on sanitation access. The coefficients on the GDP terms are jointly statistically significant at 1 percent. The predicted values increase in GDP over the entire range of the GDP distribution, although at lower rates with higher GDP.[11]

The two measures of the quality of government, political rights and control of corruption, do not enter with statistically significant coefficients. Population density and urban share of population both have statistically significant positive coefficients in column (1). These variables probably represent lower cost per household for sewer systems.

PUBLIC WASTEWATER TREATMENT LEVELS

The next measure focuses on the quality of the treatment provided in countries with high sanitation access. Three levels—primary, secondary, and tertiary—are

---

9. These data and the protected lands data are from the World Resource Institute's Earth-Trends database (WRI 2007).

10. These coefficients would also be consistent with inefficient central government decision making, such as that proposed by Besley and Coate (2003). This inference, however, implies that some developing countries have excessively good sanitation (conditional on their income). Although such overprovision is a theoretical possibility, it seems more likely that these models do not represent conditions in lower-income countries.

11. For convenience in reporting the coefficients, GDP values in this and subsequent estimated equations are in units of 10,000 constant 2000 U.S. dollars.

Table 8.2
Tobit Estimates: Share of Population with Access to Improved Sanitation, 2004

	Dependent Variable: Log(Pop. share with improved sanitation)	
	(1)	(2)
Federal country	−0.161	
	(0.104)	
Log(Envir. expend. decentralization)		−0.112**
		(0.048)
GDP per capita	.804***	1.684*
	(0.260)	(1.068)
GDP^2	−0.149	−0.985
	(0.163)	(1.004)
GDP^3	0.005	0.225
	(0.033)	(0.403)
Log(Lack of political rights)	−0.014	−0.033
	(0.069)	(0.067)
Log(Lack of corruption)	0.125	−0.032
	(0.109)	(0.202)
Log(Country population density)	0.117***	0.059
	(0.028)	(0.040)
Log(Share of population urban)	0.428***	0.250
	(0.101)	(0.153)
Observations	111	25

* $= p < .10$
** $= p < .05$
*** $= p < .01$

Note: Standard errors are in parentheses. Constant is included but not shown.

used to describe the extent of treatment in public treatment works, each level providing an improvement in the quality of water discharged to the environment. These treatment processes are sequential, so plants with secondary treatment provide primary treatment as well.[12]

OECD provides data on the share of public treatment that is secondary and tertiary. The data are reported at five-year intervals from 1980 through 1995 and

---

12. Primary treatment involves separating solids from water. Secondary treatment is biological. Tertiary treatment is designed to raise discharged water back to the level in the environment and may include several chemical or physical processes.

in 2002. Coverage is spotty, with many countries appearing for only a year or two, and data are very incomplete in any given year. Most countries with multiple years of data increase the share of treatment in the higher treatment categories. To adjust for time trends without limiting the sample by focusing on a single year, a first-stage equation regresses secondary or tertiary treatment shares on year and country dummies. The coefficient on the country dummy is the measure of EP_i, environmental protection for country i. Time-varying right-hand-side variables (except decentralization) are averages for the years the country provides treatment data. The sample size is small because it includes only OECD countries, but most observations have environmental decentralization data, so the number of observations falls only slightly between the two columns.

Table 8.3 presents results from an equation for the share of treatment that is secondary or better. Similar results (on a slightly smaller sample) were estimated for the share of treatment that is tertiary and are not presented. The results do not suggest any effect of either federalism or environmental expenditure decentralization

Table 8.3
Ordinary Least Squares Estimates: Share of Public Wastewater Treatment That Is Secondary or Better

	Dependent Variable: Log(Secondary treatment share)	
	(1)	(2)
Federal country	0.216 (0.170)	
Log(Envir. expend. decentralization)		−0.415 (0.247)
GDP per capita	2.383 (2.211)	−2.206 (1.524)
GDP²	−1.148 (1.167)	1.358 (0.892)
GDP³	0.170 (0.192)	−0.241 (0.151)
Log(Lack of political rights)	0.122 (0.293)	0.064 (0.141)
Log(Lack of corruption)	0.654 (0.658)	−0.232 (0.380)
Log(Country population density)	0.062 (0.038)	0.021 (0.039)
Observations	23	14
R^2	0.45	0.50

Note: Robust standard errors are in parentheses. Constant is included but not shown.

on this measure of inputs into environmental protection. Indeed, the equations do not produce any statistically significant coefficients (or even joint significance for GDP variables), perhaps because the sample size is simply too small to estimate any effect with much precision.[13]

AIR POLLUTION

The best worldwide monitoring data on conventional air pollutants are the United Nations' Global Environmental Monitoring System (GEMS) Air data set.[14] GEMS/Air reports annual means and sometimes short-period maxima for a few air pollutants, mostly in large cities from 1972 through 2001. Coverage for most pollutants is fairly limited. The focus here is on SO_2, which has about 2,200 city-year observations, about twice as many observations as the next most widely measured pollutant. At least one observation is available for 44 countries.

The GEMS/Air data provide information at a more disaggregated level than the country, making possible some additional controls. In particular, the data provide the name of the city in which the monitor is located, whether it is in an urban, suburban, or rural setting, and whether the local land use is residential or industrial. The GEMS/Air cities were manually matched by name to urban population.[15]

A two-stage estimation procedure is used to control for these local characteristics and the long time period over which the data are available. The first-stage equation is

$$(2) \qquad \ln SO2_{ijt} = h(Citypop_{ij}, Landuse_{ijt}, Loctype_{ijt}) + \alpha_t + \alpha_i + \varepsilon_{ijt},$$

where the dependent variable is the annual mean SO_2 levels at monitoring site j in country i in year t. The right-hand-side variables include the city population (and a dummy variable for missing city population, mostly for smaller cities or rural areas) and a vector of dummy variables each for land use and location type. Year effects, α_t, and country effects, α_i, are estimated. The estimated country effect, α_i, is then used as environmental protection from equation (1); specifically, $\alpha_i = \ln(EP_i)$. The results of this first stage are not shown, but they do suggest a strong effect of population and a downward time trend in pollution levels.

Table 8.4 contains the estimates of the second stage in which the country effects are regressed on country characteristics, as in equation (1) above. The second-stage equations are weighted by the number of observations for country

---

13. The equation is shown without the urbanization variable, which was also not statistically significant. It seems less likely that these values are important in this OECD-only data set than in the other data sets.

14. The data are no longer maintained, but an archived version can be downloaded from USEPA (2002).

15. Population is a one-time snapshot. Disappointingly, GEMS/Air does not provide the geographic coordinates of the stations, which would have made it possible to use Geographic Information System, or GIS, software to construct better local population measures.

Table 8.4

Weighted Least Squares Estimates: Country-Level Determinants of SO_2 Concentrations

	Dependent Variable: Country SO_2 Fixed Effect	
	(1)	(2)
Federal country	0.210	
	(0.190)	
Log(Envir. expend. decentralization)		−0.359
		(0.262)
GDP per capita	0.688	−4.087*
	(1.185)	(1.892)
GDP²	−0.482	3.278
	(0.987)	(3.39)
GDP³	0.117	−0.841
	(0.219)	(0.925)
Log(Lack of political rights)	0.561***	−0.474
	(0.194)	(0.963)
Log(Lack of corruption)	0.421	−2.160
	(0.511)	(2.705)
Log(Country population density)	0.200***	0.109
	(0.052)	(0.091)
Observations	44	17
R^2	0.40	0.76

$^* = p < .10$
$^{**} = p < .05$
$^{***} = p < .01$

Note: Robust standard errors are in parentheses. Constant is included but not shown. The dependent variable is α_i from equation (2) in the text and is implicitly in logs. The equations are weighted by the total number of observations for the country.

i in the first stage to reflect differences in the variance of the measurement error of α_i between countries with many monitoring stations for many years and those with few observations.

The results in table 8.4 do not point to a strong effect of decentralization on air pollution levels. The point estimate suggests 20 percent higher air pollution in federal countries, but this estimate is not statistically significant. In addition, the direction of the effect reverses when environmental expenditure decentralization is used. Environmental expenditure decentralization may be a less relevant measure of decentralization in public policies for air quality than for the other measures of environmental quality studied here because air pollution policies typically rely on regulation of private parties rather than on direct expenditures. This difference could explain why these equations are the only ones in which the two measures of decentralization have inconsistent signs.

A few other covariates have the expected effects in table 8.4. An *F*-test (not reported in table 8.4) rejects the hypothesis that all the coefficients on GDP terms jointly equal zero at 10 percent for the equation in column (1). Pollution appears to rise with GDP over most of the range, although the curve has almost flattened out by the 75th percentile. In column (1), countries with poorer political rights (a higher value of the Freedom House index) have higher pollution, consistent with earlier results in the literature. Country population density also increases pollution; this effect is statistically significant only in column (1), but a similar point estimate emerges from column (2).[16] The dependent variable has already been adjusted for the population of the city in which the monitor is located, so the effect of country density may represent longer-range transport of SO_2.

LAND CONSERVATION

The final environmental protection measure is the share of land in the country that is designated as protected by the World Conservation Union. Protected areas include wilderness areas, national parks, and areas managed for habitat protection. The variable does not include areas managed primarily for resource extraction, even if they are subject to sustainable use and in natural states. The data represent 2004 and derive from a United Nations source (WRI 2007). These data are available for the most comprehensive set of countries in this study, with 119 countries present in the federal equation and 33 in the expenditure decentralization equation. Median protected land area is 7 percent of the country (and the mean is 9.5 percent); the range is from 1.4 percent in Moldova and 2.5 percent in the Czech Republic to 28 percent in Switzerland and 29 percent in Mauritius.

In table 8.5, the dummy variable for federalism and the variable for environmental expenditure decentralization both have positive point estimates; the point estimate on the latter is statistically significant. These results would be consistent with higher levels of environmental protection in decentralized countries. This effect is counter to several prominent hypotheses, including the race to the bottom, interjurisdictional environmental spillovers, and some of the models of inefficient central governmental decision making. It might be consistent with an interest-group model in which environmental groups fare comparatively better at the local level (as proposed by Revesz 2001) or with the standard Oates (1972) view with certain population distributions and voting systems.

---

16. Urbanization is not included in the second stage because the first stage already adjusts for city size.

Table 8.5
Ordinary Least Squares Estimates: Share of Country Area That Is Protected Land, 2004

	Dependent Variable: Log(Share of land area protected)	
	(1)	(2)
Federal country	0.226	
	(0.275)	
Log(Envir. expend. decentralization)		0.390*
		(0.140)
GDP per capita	−0.546	−1.101
	(0.708)	(1.031)
GDP²	0.239	0.348
	(0.351)	(0.491)
GDP³	−0.023	−0.030
	(0.046)	(0.062)
Log(Lack of political rights)	−0.475*	0.112
	(0.234)	(0.158)
Log(Lack of corruption)	0.425	0.785
	(0.377)	(0.535)
Log(Country population density)	0.015	0.111
	(0.071)	(0.102)
Log(Share of population urban)	−0.358	−0.424
	(0.319)	(0.477)
Observations	119	33
R^2	0.16	0.33

* = $p < .10$
** = $p < .05$
*** = $p < .01$

Note: Robust standard errors are in parentheses. Constant is included but not shown.

The GDP coefficients are not jointly statistically significant at conventional levels.[17] Lack of political rights reduces protected areas in the first equation. Somewhat surprisingly, a country's population density does not have a statistically significant effect on protected area. Although this variable would seem to indicate higher costs from protecting land, the point estimates of the coefficient are positive.

---

17. The point estimates suggest an inverted-U shape: protected land falls with per capita GDP until somewhere above the 75th percentile, when it begins to rise again.

Conclusions

The empirical results present little evidence of a consistent effect of decentralization on environmental protection. Although environmental protection is sometimes lower with greater decentralization, it also appears that it may sometimes be higher, as in the equations for land conservation. The results support earlier research that is skeptical of a dramatic race to the bottom. Although most of the environmental protection measures considered here give rise to regional public goods, the results also do not suggest interjurisdictional environmental free riding, contrary to prior research (including my own) that finds evidence of such free riding. The only evidence of a negative effect of decentralization is on sanitation access, the most local of the goods considered.

In addition to these direct findings, this study underscores the need for better international data on environmental quality. Studying the effects of decentralization (and many other questions of government effectiveness) requires data that reflect the net effects of government policies, including the effects of potentially differential local enforcement of central government rules. Data on local environmental conditions may disclose these effects, whereas calculated emissions data cannot. Unfortunately, few international efforts currently collect data on local conditions; even the GEMS/Air program used here seems to have effectively ended several years ago. Without renewed efforts in this direction, the true effects of environmental policies, whether of central or local governments, may never be fully understood.

Table 8.6
Environmental Expenditure Decentralization and Environmental Protection Measures by Country

Country	Federal	Environmental Expenditure Decentralization	Land Area Protected (%)	Sanitation Access (%)	SO$_2$ Index	Secondary Treatment Index
Moldova	0	1.0	1.4	68		
Uganda	0	1.6	7.3	43		
Mauritius	0	13.9	29.8	94		
Lithuania	0	23.0	9.2			
Iran	0	25.5	6.4		0.945	
Ukraine	0	40.3	3.3	96		
Russian Federation	1	41.6	5.4	87		
South Africa	0	44.1	5.3	65		
Finland	0	44.2	3.1	100	−0.393	0.272
Kazakhstan	0	48.2	2.9	72		
Denmark	0	51.0	21.8	100	−0.300	0.134
Croatia	0	51.1	6.0	100		
Slovenia	0	54.1	14.4			

Table 8.6

(*continued*)

Country	Federal	Environmental Expenditure Decentralization	Land Area Protected (%)	Sanitation Access (%)	SO$_2$ Index	Secondary Treatment Index
Luxembourg	0	55.7	14.4	100		0.080
Czech Republic	0	59.3	2.5	98		0.180
Slovakia	0	60.2	7.3	99		
Bolivia	0	65.0	11.1	46		
Austria	1	65.7	28.0	100	0.972	0.166
Sweden	0	72.7	9.8	100	−0.224	0.276
Belarus	0	75.8	6.3	84		
Portugal	0	77.7	4.4		−0.260	−0.231
Hungary	0	77.8	8.8	95		−0.002
Netherlands	0	79.7	4.9	100	−0.220	0.237
Norway	0	79.8	6.1	100		0.012
Canada	1	81.3	5.3	100	−0.697	0.025
Poland	0	81.6	11.0		0.116	0.075
Italy	0	84.3	7.2		1.154	0.225
Australia	1	85.5	6.7	100	−0.401	
Israel	0	86.9	18.4		−0.880	
Spain	0	92.1	8.0	100	0.218	−0.166
Switzerland	1	93.5	28.7	100	0.539	
France	0	93.8	3.0		0.005	
Belgium	1	95.4	2.7	100	0.598	
China	0	97.9	11.3	44	0.850	

Note: Only countries with environmental and decentralization data are ranked by this measure. The SO$_2$ index and secondary treatment index are the country fixed effects from the first-stage regressions reported in the text.

REFERENCES

Barrett, S., and K. Graddy. 2000. Freedom, growth, and the environment. *Environment and Development Economics* 5(October):433–456.

Besley, T., and S. Coate. 2003. Centralized versus decentralized provision of local public goods: A political economy approach. *Journal of Public Economics* 87:2611–2637.

Congleton, R. D. 1992. Political institutions and pollution control. *Review of Economics and Statistics* 74(3)(August):412–421.

Damania, R., P. G. Fredriksson, and J. A. List. 2003. Trade liberalization, corruption, and environmental policy formation: Theory and evidence. *Journal of Environmental Economics and Management* 46:490–512.

Esty, D. C. 1996. Revitalizing environmental federalism. *Michigan Law Review* 95:570–653.

Fisman, R., and R. Gatti. 2002. Decentralization and corruption: Evidence across countries. *Journal of Public Economics* 83:325–345.

Fredriksson, P. G., and D. L. Millimet. 2002. Strategic interaction and the determination of environmental policy across U.S. states. *Journal of Urban Economics* 51:101–122.

Freedom House. 2007. Freedom in the World. http://www.freedomhouse.org.

Goklany, I. M. 1999. *Clearing the air: The real story of the war on air pollution.* Washington, DC: Cato Institute.

Gray, W., and R. J. Shadbegian. 2004. "Optimal" pollution abatement: Whose benefits matter, and how much? *Journal of Environmental Economics and Management* 47:510–534.

Grossman, G. M., and A. B. Krueger. 1995. Economic growth and the environment. *Quarterly Journal of Economics* 110:353–377.

Helland, E. 1998. The revealed preferences of state EPAs: Stringency, enforcement, and substitution. *Journal of Environmental Economics and Management* 35(3)(May):242–261.

Helland, E., and A. B. Whitford. 2003. Pollution incidence and political jurisdiction: Evidence from the TRI. *Journal of Environmental Economics and Management* 46:403–424.

Heston, A., R. Summers, and B. Aten. 2006. Penn World Table Version 6.2. Center for International Comparisons, University of Pennsylvania, Philadelphia. http://pwt.econ.upenn.edu.

IMF. *See* International Monetary Fund.

International Monetary Fund. 2007. Government finance statistics CD. Washington, DC: International Monetary Fund.

Kunce, M., and J. F. Shogren. 2005. On interjurisdictional competition and environmental federalism. *Journal of Environmental Economics and Management* 50:212–224.

Levinson, A. 2003. Environmental regulatory competition: A status report and some new evidence. *National Tax Journal* 56:91–106.

List, J. A., and S. Gerking. 2000. Regulatory federalism and environmental protection in the United States. *Journal of Regional Science* 40:453–471.

Lockwood, B. 2002. Distributive politics and the costs of centralization. *Review of Economic Studies* 69:313–337.

Millimet, D. L. 2003. Assessing the empirical impact of environmental federalism. *Journal of Regional Science* 43:711–733.

Morriss, A. P. 2000. The politics of the Clean Air Act. In *Political environmentalism*, T. Anderson, ed., 263–318. Stanford, CA: Hoover Institution.

Oates, W. E. 1972. *Fiscal federalism.* New York: Harcourt.

———. 2002. A reconsideration of environmental federalism. In *Recent advances in environmental economics*, J. A. List and A. de Zeeuw, eds., 1–32. Cheltenham, UK: Edward Elgar.

Oates, W. E., and R. M. Schwab. 1988. Economic competition among jurisdictions: Efficiency enhancing or distortion inducing? *Journal of Public Economics* 35:333–354.

Political Risk Services. 2007. International Country Risk Guide Researchers Dataset (electronic). East Syracuse, NY: PRS Group Inc.

Revesz, R. 2001. Federalism and environmental regulation: A public choice analysis. *Harvard Law Review* 115:5536–5541.

Selden, T. M., and D. Song. 1994. Environmental quality and development: Is there a Kuznets curve for air pollution? *Journal of Environmental Economics and Management* 27:147–162.

Sigman, H. 2003. Letting states do the dirty work: State responsibility for federal environmental regulation. *National Tax Journal* 56:107–122.

———. 2005. Transboundary spillovers and decentralization of environmental policies. *Journal of Environmental Economics and Management* 50:82–101.

———. 2007. Decentralization and environmental quality: An international analysis of water pollution. NBER Working Paper 13098. Cambridge, MA: National Bureau of Economic Research.

Strumpf, K. S., and F. Oberholzer-Gee. 2002. Endogenous policy decentralization: Testing the central tenet of economic federalism. *Journal of Political Economy* 110:1–36.

Treisman, D. 2000. The causes of corruption: A cross-national study. *Journal of Public Economics* 76:399–457.

———. 2002. Defining and measuring federalism: A global perspective. Working Paper. Department of Political Science, UCLA.

U.S. Environmental Protection Agency. 2002. AIRS Executive. http://www.epa.gov/airs/aewin/.

USEPA. *See* U.S. Environmental Protection Agency.

USGAO. *See* U.S. General Accounting Office.

U.S. General Accounting Office. 1996. Water pollution: Differences in issuing permits limiting the discharge of pollutants. Washington, DC: GAO.

Welsch, H. 2004. Corruption, growth, and the environment: A cross-country analysis. *Environment and Development Economics* 9:663–693.

Wilson, J. D. 1996. Capital mobility and environmental standards: Is there a race to the bottom? In *Harmonization and fair trade*, J. Bhagwati and R. Hudec, eds., 395–427. Cambridge, MA: MIT Press.

World Resource Institute. 2007. EarthTrends environmental information. http://earthtrends.wri.org.

WRI. *See* World Resource Institute.

Wroth, L. K., ed. 2007. *The Supreme Court and the Clean Water Act: Five essays.* http://www.vjel.org/books/pdf/PUBS10004.pdf.

COMMENTARY
Maureen L. Cropper

Hilary Sigman asks an interesting and important question: Other things being equal, do countries with decentralized environmental policies have better or worse environmental quality than countries with centralized environmental policies? Because the effects of decentralization on environmental policy should vary with the nature of the environmental good, she asks the question for four environmental indicators: (1) access to improved sanitation; (2) wastewater treatment; (3) ambient sulfur dioxide (SO_2); and (4) the size of protected areas.

When should decentralization in the provision of environmental goods work, and when should it not? Some centralized coordination is likely to be needed in at least two cases. The first case is when there are physical spillovers in pollution, such as when residents of Washington, DC, breathe the pollution emitted by a power plant in Ohio or when people living along the Rio Grande in New Mexico suffer water pollution produced in Colorado. In this case, environmental regulations set at the state level will not provide sufficient incentives to internalize all the pollution externalities unless states coordinate their actions. A second case, much discussed in the "race to the bottom" literature, is when there are no physical spillovers but, rather, pollution is produced by mobile firms. If, in this instance, firms that produce long-lived hazardous waste can locate anywhere, city managers may introduce lax environmental regulations to attract such industries.

In some cases, however, decentralization should work well. Sewage collection, garbage collection, and drinking water treatment are all examples of environmental goods that are successfully provided at the local level. Their provision entails few spillovers, and they are financed by the households and firms that immediately benefit from their provision.

Based on this discussion, we would expect decentralization of environmental policy to lead to greater provision of access to improved sanitation, but not necessarily to optimal levels of wastewater treatment or SO_2 because water pollution and air pollution can be exported. Because some of the benefits of protected areas may accrue to persons outside local jurisdictions, these areas might also be underprovided. The results of Sigman's study in the two cases in which indicators of decentralization are significantly related to environmental quality— that decentralization reduces access to improved sanitation and increases the amount of land allocated to protected areas—are therefore surprising.

What accounts for these counterintuitive results? First, it is difficult to control for factors besides decentralization of environmental policy that affect the level of environmental quality. Second, it is difficult to measure the degree of decentralization of environmental policy. Environmental quality should increase with factors that measure people's willingness to pay for a better environment and decrease with factors that increase the costs of environmental protection. We expect the demand for environmental protection to vary with income and the cost of providing certain environmental services (water treatment) to decline with population density, but geographic factors that affect environmental quality— for example, topographic and meteorological factors that predispose cities to higher levels of particulate air pollution—are more difficult to measure.

The degree of decentralization of environmental policy is especially difficult to assess. The measure that is available for the largest group of countries— whether the country has a federal system of government—is clearly a very crude gauge of decentralization. By this definition, the United States is classified as having a decentralized environmental policy, which is true for some aspects of environmental policy, but not for others. In the case of air pollution control, for example, states possess the authority to set emissions standards for air pollution sources in existence as of 1970; these emission standards, however, must meet national ambient air quality standards. In the 1980s it became clear that many power plants had met national ambient air quality standards in the state in which they were located by building tall stacks that exported air pollution to other states. The reaction was a federal statute (Title IV of the 1990 Clean Air Act Amendments) that drastically cut the SO_2 emissions of power plants nationwide.

The second measure of decentralization—the proportion of government expenditures on environmental protection made by local governments—also has limitations. The chief limitation is that for many forms of environmental protection, such as expenditures to control air or water pollution, it is the polluter who pays. The cost of providing environmental protection is not paid out of the government's budget. This measure of fiscal decentralization may work well for wastewater treatment or even for protected areas, but would not be expected to work well for access to sanitation (much of which is privately provided) or air quality.

What, then, are other approaches to measuring the effects of decentralized environmental policy on environmental quality? The key policy issue, in my opinion, is whether decentralization leads to environmental degradation when there are physical spillovers in pollution. Transboundary spillovers are the rule for most of the criteria air pollutants (fine particles, SO_2, nitrogen oxides, ground-level ozone) and also for water pollutants such as biochemical oxygen demand. One approach to measuring the effects of environmental policy decentralization, which Sigman has used to good effect (Sigman 2005), is to obtain microlevel panel data on environmental quality that spans a period during which the degree of decentralization in environmental policy changed. In the case of water pollution in the United States, states received the right to control water pollution from the federal government at different times. Using panel data on water quality at 500 monitoring stations, Sigman examines whether water quality at a monitoring station worsened when an upstream state gained control over water quality from the federal government. The use of fixed effects allows one to control for difficult-to-measure geographic factors that may affect water quality, and the measure of decentralization—whether the state has authority to set and enforce standards—is well defined.

REFERENCE

Sigman, H. 2005. Transboundary spillovers and decentralization of environmental policies. *Journal of Environmental Economics and Management* 50:82–101.

9

Interjurisdictional Competition Under U.S. Fiscal Federalism

Sally Wallace

There is little debate about the United States being a decentralized country. In terms of governance, there are 50 state governments plus the District of Columbia and 87,525 local governments.[1] Various fiscal measures of decentralization, including expenditure and revenue shares of subnational government, also support the claim. For instance, in 2005 the federal government collected 58.5 percent of all federal, state, and local tax revenue (excluding off-budget funds); states collected 24.5 percent; and local governments collected 17 percent.[2] On the expenditure side, the federal government made 47 percent of all government expenditures in 2005, whereas states made 28 percent of all expenditures and local governments made 25 percent. Although it is somewhat difficult to compare measures of decentralization among countries, the U.S. subnational revenue and expenditure shares put decentralization in the United States at a higher level than that of the Organisation for Economic Co-operation and Development (OECD) averages of 32 percent for expenditures and 19 percent for taxes (Bahl and Martinez-Vazquez 2008).

The system of fiscal federalism in the United States allows state governments to structure their tax and expenditure policies and to define the fiscal powers

---

1. According to the U.S. Bureau of the Census, in 2002 local governments included 3,034 counties, 19,429 municipalities, 16,504 townships, 35,052 special districts, and 13,506 independent school districts (U.S. Bureau of the Census 2002).

2. Including the "off-budget" social insurance receipts, the federal government collects 66 percent of tax revenue, the state collects 20 percent, and local governments collect 14 percent.

and responsibilities of their local governments. The result is that state and local governments in the United States possess significant latitude to make expenditure and taxing decisions for their constituents or "constituents in waiting," those whom they would like to attract to their jurisdictions. The subnational government share of expenditures and revenues in the United States has increased since the 1980s, which may reflect an increase in the ability to engage in competition for economic development.[3] In 1980 the state and local share of all government expenditures was 42.3 percent, and the state and local share of tax revenue (including payroll taxes) was 30.1 percent. By 1990 those shares had increased to 43.7 percent and 32.7 percent, respectively. In addition, as noted above, by 2005 the shares of state and local expenditures and revenues had increased yet again. With state and local governments playing an important role in U.S. public finances, there is good reason to expect those governments to be players in the bid for economic development. This situation can be contrasted with other federal systems such as France, Belgium, New Zealand, and Greece, where provincial and local governments have less autonomy with respect to tax and expenditure policy.

The United States Constitution gives state governments plenty of room to determine their tax structure, explicitly disallowing only duties on imports or exports. Among states in the United States, some local governments are more free to choose their fiscal instruments than others. One way to measure how much fiscal latitude local governments have been given is an index of the extent of "home rule" versus "Dillon's rule." Home rule refers to the ability of local governments to undertake activities unless specifically disallowed by the state (similar to the federal/state relationship); Dillon's rule refers to the situations in which local governments are allowed to undertake activities explicitly allowed by the state (Geon and Turnbull 2004). Geon and Turnbull developed an index of the extent of home rule, or Dillon's rule, for counties in the United States using information on the constitutional, legislative, and institutional characteristics reported in Krane, Rigos, and Hill (2001). For the 38 states for which they have data, 12 (32 percent) are classified as strong home rule states and 9 (24 percent) are classified as strong non–home rule states. The remainder are somewhere in between. Their analysis suggests that the playing field among local governments in the United States may not be level in terms of local governments' ability to set fiscal policies to attract new business, an interesting caveat discussed below.

---

3. There are at least two sides to this argument. First, one reason for the increased presence of state and local governments in the U.S. fiscal arena is due to increased responsibilities of the subnational governments for expenditures such as Medicaid and education. In this case, the increased size of the state and local sectors may not reflect additional leverage in attracting business, but, in fact, may suggest less ability to attract businesses through tax reductions. At the same time, state and local governments have become a bigger player in terms of taxation and expenditure and, as such, may have more leverage to engage in economic development competition and more tools to use.

The ways to promote economic development in the United States include a host of state and local tax strategies (property tax abatements and corporate income tax reductions, for example), cost-reduction strategies (job training, land price reductions), and other inducements aimed at improving general business climate (ease of incorporation, providing quality public services). Some of these strategies are targeted to particular business opportunities, and others are more general strategies offered to any business or individual. This study focuses on interjurisdictional competition among local governments. This competition is comprised of general incentives ("good business climate") and specific or targeted tax (property tax abatements) and expenditure strategies (infrastructure development).[4] On the expenditure side, both traditional public goods expenditures (better schools, roads, etc.) as well as the use of public funds for targeted expenditures such as training facilities and programs specific to attracting companies, land deals, and the like are considered. This study asks whether there is evidence that interjurisdictional competition in the United States has been "good" in terms of increasing welfare.

In this chapter, actual strategies of interjurisdictional competition in Alabama, North Carolina, Georgia, and Texas are used to shed light on the effects of those specific strategies on improving welfare, measured indirectly as improvements in employment and personal income. First, the theoretical and empirical literature on interjurisdictional fiscal competition is surveyed. This survey demonstrates a lack of consensus regarding the welfare and distributional implications of such competition in the United States. After presenting a set of illustrative cases of specific incentive packages in the Southeast, possible directions are considered for future research that could help the policy world better understand and develop fiscal incentives as the competition matures.

The following section highlights the findings of the theoretical literature regarding competition and efficiency. It is followed by a brief survey of selected empirical studies that deal with interjurisdictional competition. Then, case studies are described, and the effects of the tax and expenditure incentives on local economic development are considered. Finally, policy implications of competition from the perspective of findings in the literature and the need for additional research are examined.

Does Interjurisdictional Competition Promote Efficiency?

As many contributors to this volume have noted, fiscal decentralization can lead to a more efficient provision of local public goods, but only under a well-known

---

4. This definition of tax competition is close to the definition presented in Wilson and Wildasin (2004), where they also provide alternative definitions of tax competition. Fiscal competition refers to the expenditure and revenue side of the budget, and, as such, fiscal packages may include a combination of tax breaks and specific expenditures.

set of conditions. There are many caveats to the decentralization-efficiency conclusion, including issues related to the mobility of capital and labor, the existence of externalities, and economies of scale in public goods production and provision.

Interjurisdictional competition—competing for mobile bases—is a natural outcome in a U.S.-type system of fiscal federalism. If subnational governments (state and local) are given significant expenditure assignments and allowed substantial taxing power, they can respond to individuals and businesses in a manner that may enhance economic efficiency in a Tiebout world. Jurisdictions that do not respond to their citizens' demands risk losing population and businesses, and this sorting is efficient under certain conditions. Jurisdictions can use these same instruments to attract new and expanding businesses. The greater the ability of local governments to set tax and expenditure policy, the greater leverage they can exercise in doing business with individuals and companies.

This study looks at horizontal fiscal competition for mobile tax bases (between governments at the same level). Theory regarding the implications of interjurisdictional competition on efficiency is well developed (Fischel 1975; Oates 1972; Tiebout 1956). Individuals and businesses vote with their feet to push governments to more closely match their demands with the package of taxes and expenditures that is offered. In the case of competition for local economic development, the incentive package (usually a targeted type of tax and expenditure package) is a motivator for movement of factors (capital and labor) among jurisdictions.[5] Competition comes in the form of specific tax and expenditure package bids to attract mobile factors. With mobile factors (particularly capital), competition pushes the net tax rate on capital down and the proverbial "race to the bottom" is on.

The questions that have arisen are whether this type of competition, which is quite expected in a decentralized system, is efficient and whether there truly is a race to the bottom. Irrespective of the answer to the theoretical question is the more real-world issue: Why would state and local governments in the United States engage in these policies if they were not welfare enhancing, and how much competition is sustainable?[6]

The argued inefficiency of interjurisdictional competition is a departure from the basic Tiebout model, which would predict that competition increases welfare. In fact, Oates (1972), Wilson (1986), and Zodrow and Mieszkowski (1986)

---

5. A number of other types of interactions among governments are discussed in the general competition literature. For example, copycat behaviors associated with yardstick or other competition may influence local economic development tools. Here the spatial models of competition that analyze copycat and yardstick competition models are only briefly discussed, although they are all related and are important parts of the general literature on competition.

6. A closely related theoretical question is why jurisdictions engage in specific competition at all. Glaeser (2001) presents five alternative reasons for this competition, four of which are grounded in welfare or revenue maximization and one of which is corruption and influence.

conclude that tax competition can *reduce* welfare. More recently, a literature has developed that finds that interjurisdictional competition can be welfare *enhancing* (see Wilson 1999; Wilson and Wildasin 2004). Can these competing theories help us understand the effect of tax and expenditure incentives?

Returning to the Tiebout model, competition is viewed as a means to efficiently sort factors of production among jurisdictions. In one case of tax competition, the taxes imposed are equal to the marginal cost of any expansion in public goods associated with attracting new business (investment). Brennan and Buchanan's Leviathan model (1980) uses the Tiebout view to show that competition keeps Leviathan at bay and is welfare enhancing.

Oates (1999, 1134) notes that "in their eagerness to promote economic development with the creation of new jobs, . . . state and local officials tend to hold down tax rates, and consequently, outputs of public services so as to reduce the costs for exiting and prospective business enterprise." The inefficiency "sticks" because many of the assumptions of the Tiebout model do not hold: mobility is not costless, voting for the "right" tax and expenditure package is not easy due to packaging of referenda and lumpiness of tax rate adjustments, and there are barriers to information on costs and benefits. A Leviathan view is quite different; the differences in the tax rates may, in fact, be more in line with constituent preferences, but precompetition, bureaucracy, and political influences pushed taxes and expenditures above their optimal levels.

In Zodrow and Mieszkowski's model, differentials in the tax rates on capital, as a form of interjurisdictional competition, yield fiscal externalities as capital migrates from high-taxed to relatively low-taxed jurisdictions, thus expanding the tax base of other jurisdictions. The failure of jurisdictions to account for these externalities leads to inefficiently low levels of taxation. This literature has been extended to include the interaction of competition and environmental externalities. In an attempt to pull in new firms, localities also may reduce their environmental standards (Cumberland 1981).

Wilson (2001) and Wilson and Wildasin (2004) present models in which interjurisdictional competition could be welfare enhancing and potentially lead to larger government. In Wilson (2001), if the revenue associated with capital expansion is used to finance a public input (versus a public good) and self-motivated government officials are in play, (tax) competition that attracts capital can lead to more efficient government production. The result is that, given a tax structure, officials choose a level of public input. Increased public input increases the productivity of capital, thereby attracting capital. Wages rise, and the net tax base expands. In another interesting case, summarized by Wilson and Wildasin (2004), tax competition could reduce the rents associated with tax exporting. In their example, if property is owned by nonresidents, some of the property tax burden may be exported. In this case, a lack of representation could lead to inefficiently high property tax rates. Competition for mobile capital could dampen the tendency to set these exportable taxes at an inefficiently high level (return of Leviathan).

Each theoretical model of interjurisdictional competition is developed with a series of assumptions regarding the mobility of factors, the total supply of factors of production, the general openness of the economy, the production of public goods, the use of tax revenue, pre-existing distortions, benevolence of the leaders, tax structure, expenditure benefits, information asymmetries, and so forth. Most theoretical models of competition start from similar points regarding the objective function of governments: either maximize utility of their constituents or maximize revenue. If we look to these models to yield policy advice regarding the effects of various tax and expenditure incentives schemes, the notion that the "devil is in the details" resounds loudly. The assumptions required to make the models "work" are restrictive.

To create a model that can guide our thinking about how to use local fiscal incentives, it is necessary to check how closely the underlying assumptions approximate the local setting. In fact, each case becomes unique as far as applicable assumptions regarding pre-existing distortions (e.g., the existing mix of distortionary taxes), the relative size of the local economy (small cities versus large counties), capacity utilization in the public sector, supply of labor (consider areas with high levels of domestic or international migration or tight labor markets), mobility of factors, quality of information about the costs of attracting business, and even the instruments made available to local governments (e.g., caps on property taxes, availability of local income taxes). Including all the particular nuances that pertain to a *specific* incentive scheme would create an intractable model.[7] The theoretical models, then, may not lead us toward good policy advice. Instead, it could be useful to turn to the empirical evidence to examine what has been learned thus far about the effects of interjurisdictional competition on welfare and government.

Empirical Studies

A substantial empirical literature is directly or closely related to the issue of competition. Unfortunately, it does not help policy makers identify the "best" strategy for fiscal incentives. As noted above and by other authors (in particular, Wilson and Wildasin 2004), various theoretical models can be supported by the same empirical finding. For instance, the finding that states mimic the tax policy of neighbors may mean that competition for mobile tax bases leads to a race to the bottom in terms of tax rates, or it may be used to support the notion of yardstick competition, where citizens view relative tax and expenditure policies as a way to evaluate the performance of their officials.

The empirical literature considered here attempts to measure the effects of competition on welfare. Translating the theoretical effect of competition on wel-

---

7. Specific or targeted tax incentives will also induce additional distortions between new and pre-existing capital and labor mobility due to exacerbated price differentials.

fare to an empirical model is difficult, so the approach tends to be indirect. Economic growth is the typical proxy used to measure welfare, and it is usually operationalized by measuring the change in the level of gross state product, change in the level of employment, or change in the level of personal income. These factors seem to be accepted as empirical measures. Interjurisdictional competition has been modeled in various ways, including differences in tax rates, expenditures by type, and general business climate. If taxes or expenditures matter in business location decisions or, more generally, in economic growth (gross state product, employment), changes in the relative level of taxes and expenditures (competition) will have an effect on those same measures.

Before focusing on interjurisdictional competition in the form of taxes, expenditures, and economic development, it is worthwhile to mention other related work in this area. First, do tax differentials have an impact on welfare? Without entering into the debate regarding magnitudes, many studies find that tax differentials do matter (Auerbach 1997; Harberger 1962). The implicit assumption in the theoretical models underlying the empirical work is that tax differentials (which could result from incentive packages) encourage mobile factors to migrate toward the lowest tax jurisdiction given a level of expenditures. The result is a change in prices of factors and outputs, which, depending on price elasticities (among other parameters), could lead to welfare loss. The more targeted and local the incentive, the more prices are distorted. In addition, greater mobility of capital and labor occurs at the local level, however, which tends to lessen the welfare loss.

Several studies have been made of the *determinants* of the use of specific incentive and other economic development tools in the competition literature (Anderson and Wassmer 1995; Edmiston and Turnbull 2003). Using Georgia data on incentives, Edmiston and Turnbull find that the use of incentives (a dichotomous choice variable) is significantly affected by the use of such incentives in surrounding states, which is evidence of competition as a motivator in determining the use of incentives. Also, a large literature exists on copycat behavior of governments, including yardstick competition models, which might be considered a type of competition. Some of the pioneering empirical work here includes Besley and Rosen (1998), Case (1992), Case, Hines, and Rosen (1989), and Ladd (1992).

Turning to the empirical literature that focuses on taxes and economic development, Mark, McGuire, and Papke (1997), Tannewald (1996), Wasylenko (1997), and others conclude that taxes do matter in business location decisions, but the magnitude of the impact varies substantially among these studies. Still, the results suggest that taxes have a relatively small impact on economic development in the United States. Papke (1996) notes that nontargeted general tax incentives create a small effect on the after-tax rate of return to capital and so have a limited effect on business location decisions. Tannewald finds that in choosing expansion sites, businesses pay as much attention to the level of public services as they do to the after-tax rate of return. Bartik (1991) reports similar findings. Mark, McGuire, and Papke (1997) survey economic development and fiscal policy research up to 1997 and conclude that the literature regarding the effect of taxes on economic development is inconclusive. The authors summarize the literature that addresses the impact of enterprise zones on economic activity. They conclude that the results are mixed and likely to be influenced by the nuances of a particular enterprise zone package of incentives. Like the theoretical literature, these studies suggest that many other conditions matter in explaining economic growth and job creation, including public expenditures, labor costs, location, and transportation costs.

The literature on the cost benefit of particular types of tax and expenditure incentives is specific to targeted tax and expenditure programs.[8] These studies often use multiplier effects to gauge the local impact of interjurisdictional competition in the form of targeted tax and expenditure incentives. Those incentives produced by local governments are often done ex ante, and ex-post follow-ups are rare. Connaughton and Madsen (2001), however, conducted one ex-post study that was done for the incentive packages offered in South Carolina (for BMW) and in Alabama (for Mercedes-Benz). They conclude that in the case of BMW, the job growth associated with the firm location was much smaller than that estimated by the state. LeRoy, Lack, and Walter (2007) analyzed about 4,000 economic development incentives in Michigan from 2001 to 2004 and conclude that these incentives have led to "inefficient and unsustainable land use patterns by reducing the number of jobs in the state's largest metro area" (p. 101). They argue that targeted incentives can lead to net fiscal loss for local governments.

This brief review of the theory and empirical evidence of tax competition demonstrates that, under various conditions, interjurisdictional competition may or may not be welfare enhancing. At the same time, empirical studies suggest that taxes, at least, seem to matter in business location decisions and to some extent in the migration behavior of individuals. There is little consensus on the magnitude of impact of tax differentials on job creation and economic development, however.

So, has interjurisdictional competition led to an increase in welfare? Are we on a race to the bottom? Because targeted fiscal incentives and other benefit incentive schemes are likely to be small relative to the U.S. economy, it would be difficult to isolate an empirical impact of specific incentives on the entire economy. Earlier work does demonstrate that tax-induced distortions can lead to significant welfare losses in the economy. If the costs of specific incentive packages were estimated for the entire country, it might be possible to estimate the effects of the competition on welfare nationally; the likelihood of calculating the total cost of these incentives, however, is low (as is the ability to control for other factors).

In this debate, it might be helpful to analyze the impact of specific targeted incentives on the local economy. This kind of approach obviously neglects the

---

8. Koven and Lyons (2003) provide a good set of case studies.

welfare impacts of fiscal externalities, which may, over time, be large. It also fails to specifically estimate the welfare cost of the incentive-induced price differentials. This type of analysis does, however, offer a practical look at the impact of these incentives on the economy.[9] If targeted incentives are not generating significant net economic benefits locally and the public sector shrinks in relative terms, there may be a "bad" type of competition. That, of course, is not a definitive statement regarding welfare effects because the presence of the Leviathan mechanism may be in play.[10]

Competition in the United States

State and local governments offer a variety of actual incentive packages to lure business. The "drop in the bucket" relationship between targeted packages of taxes, expenditures, and general business support, and trends in the macro economy and public finances, stacks the deck against finding evidence of an impact of specific types of competition at a national level. It might be useful, however, to ask where evidence can be found of a national race to the bottom in terms of local taxes. As reported by Wilson and Wildasin (2004), Slemrod (2001) found evidence of convergence in taxes among countries (1985–1995), but Alm, Chen, and Wallace (2003) did not (in the case of U.S. state and local taxes). Looking at published census data on state and local government finances, several interesting trends may be observed. First, between 1980 and 2004, state and local taxes more than tripled (in nominal terms), income taxes more than quadrupled, sales taxes grew by 3.5 times and property tax by 3.6 times, and intergovernmental revenue more than quadrupled.

As a share of personal income, state and local tax revenue rebounded after 1982 and, since 1982, has increased from 9.6 percent of personal income to 10.41 percent in 2004 (figure 9.1). State and local expenditures as a share of personal income also increased over this time period, from 15.7 percent of personal income in 1982 to 19.6 percent in 2004.

At the local level, considering all general revenue, property taxes as a share of local government general revenue have declined (from 33.7 percent in 1977 to 28.1 percent in 2004), while sales tax revenues at the local level have increased as a share of total general revenue (from 4.6 percent in 1977 to 6.1 percent in 2004). The pattern of change in these shares is demonstrated in figure 9.2. It is difficult to conclude from these data alone that a marked shift has occurred in the level or composition of taxes. A similar conclusion is reached in Alm, Chen, and Wallace

---

9. It also omits the distinction between new firms and expanding firms, or tax incentives to keep firms.

10. For example, Zax (1989) finds evidence that competition does help contain government expenditures.

Figure 9.1
State-Local Revenue as a Share of Personal Income

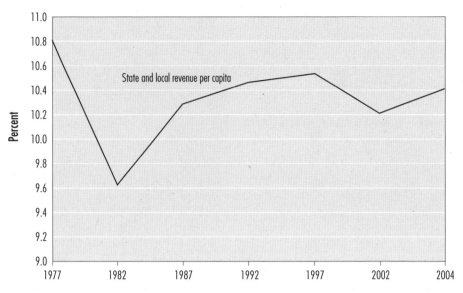

Source: Tax Policy Center, State and Local Government Finance Data Query System.

(2003). At best, it could be argued that a small shift away from the property tax (in relative terms) toward income tax at the state and local levels has taken place. It could also be argued, however, that these taxes would have been higher absent the various incentive programs proliferating during this period.

Turning to case studies of specific incentive packages in the South, the data in table 9.1 summarize a few of the many relatively large incentive packages offered to companies since 1993. In this region, Alabama has been one of the most active states in attracting large businesses. The auto industry has led the way in the region in terms of incentive-related investment. The Center for Automotive Research (2003) studied automotive capital investment in North America between 1993 and 2003. It found that although the average investment between 1998 and 2003 was similar for the North and South, the *growth* in automotive investment was greater in southern states. The study also found a significant difference between the North and South in the mix of incentive packages offered. In relative terms, northern states offered more incentives in the form of tax abatement, whereas southern states offered a package more evenly balanced between abatements and infrastructure development. Southern states also offered more in terms of employee recruitment and training, and larger overall incentive packages. On an absolute

Figure 9.2
Taxes as a Percent of General Revenue of Local Government

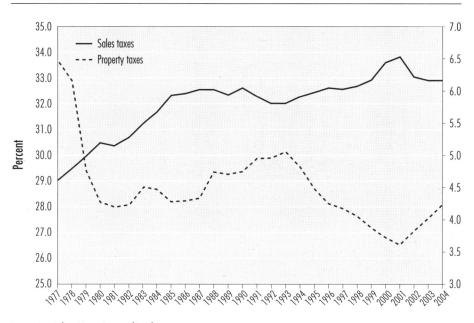

Source: Tax Policy Center, State and Local Government Finance Data Query System.

level, northern states offered, on average per incentive package, $69.7 million in abatements, $10.9 million in infrastructure, and $2.5 million in training and employee recruitment, whereas southern states offered $54.3 million, $62.9 million, and $25.7 million, respectively. These findings (particularly the package of incentives in southern states) support the conclusions of previous studies that suggested that taxes may be important in business location decisions but that public goods, infrastructure, and general quality of life are also important.

Table 9.1 includes the cost of the incentive package per job from direct employment effects. This calculation does not include any induced or indirect employment effects, which would make the per job cost substantially lower. The table also includes employment effects taken from a variety of economic impact studies. Additional studies of the same business locations may exist, but those cited provide ample room for discussion here.

As shown in table 9.1, state and local governments have employed a variety of tax and expenditure programs to attract industry. All the cases reviewed included the following incentives: state and local property and sales tax abatements, financing of land acquisition and site development, and some type of training. Other incentives include job tax credits, specific road development, and,

Table 9.1
Illustrative Examples of Targeted Tax Incentives in the South

State (year of agreement)	Business Courted	State Cost of Tax Incentives	Sample of Incentives and Intergovernmental Partnerships	Initial Employment Impact (no. of employees)	Evidence of Economic Impact (total jobs: direct, induced, and indirect)	Cost per Job (direct jobs) in Nominal Terms and in 2006 Dollars (in parentheses)
South Carolina (1992)	BMW	$150 million	Payment in lieu of taxes (property tax), state technical education, state job creation tax credit, state–port authority–county lease purchase of land, state and county revenue bonds	1,900; expansion to 4,327	South Carolina State Development Board: 10,137 (based on direct jobs of 1,900). Connaughton and Madsen: 4,845 (based on direct jobs of 1,900). University of South Carolina: 16,691 (based on direct jobs of 4,327).	$78,947 ($113,441)
Alabama (1993)	Mercedes-Benz	$258 million	State and local sales tax abatements, site and infrastructure development, state education subsidies (classes at the University of Alabama), local government low-interest loans	1,500	Holmes and McCallum: 9,575	$172,000 ($239,967)
Alabama (1999)	Honda	$158 million	State and local tax abatements (corporate, property tax), site preparation and purchase, state training	1,500	None available	$105,333 ($127,462)

State (year)	Company	Investment	Incentives	Jobs	Jobs estimate	Cost per job
Alabama (2002)	Hyundai	$252 million	State and local property and sales tax abatements, site development, state training facility	2,200	Auburn University of Montgomery, reported in *FDI Magazine*: 11,000	$114,545 ($128,362)
Mississippi (2000)	Nissan	$295 million; expansion to $363 million	State jobs tax credit, local property tax abatements, site and road preparation and development, state training facilities	5,800	University of Southern Mississippi: 16,215	$62,586 ($73,271)
Texas (2003)	Toyota truck plant	$133 million	Facilities development, infrastructure development, property tax abatements	2,000	Texas comptroller's office estimate: 16,000	$66,500 ($72,861)
Georgia (2006)	Kia plant	State: $248.05 million (at minimum employment of 2,500) Local: $147 million	State jobs tax credits, city/county property tax abatements, state/local sales tax exemptions, state technical education (building and education), state land purchase, state grading and infrastructure development (potential federal transportation fund use)	2,500 (contractual minimum)	Reported in Georgia General Assembly legislation: 14,000	$158,200 ($158,200)

Sources: Texas: Federal Reserve Bank of Dallas (2004); South Carolina: Connaughton and Madsen (2001), University of South Carolina (2002); Alabama: Holmes and McCallum (1993), Linn (2002); Georgia, Alabama, South Carolina, and Mississippi: Hill and Brahmst (2003), McCandless (2006).

231

in the case of Alabama and Mercedes-Benz, a "Saturday school" for children of foreign employees to help them excel in studies, particularly math.

The direct cost per job in nominal terms varies widely. In real terms, the largest cost per job was the package given for Mercedes-Benz in Alabama, at $239,967 per job in 2006 dollars. That is more than three times the per unit cost for the Toyota incentives in Texas. In Alabama, the state felt the high cost of the deal very early. Public school officials did not release funds needed to pay out part of the incentive package, and the state had to raid its pension system to make the payment and repay the pension account with a loan at 9 percent interest. Governor Jim Folsom Jr. lost his reelection bid in the midst of the postincentive controversy. Still, two economic impact studies of the Alabama Mercedes-Benz deal find the deal to be very positive for the state. Holmes and McCallum (1993) estimated total employment effects of 9,575. A direct employment impact of 1,500 jobs yields an implicit employment multiplier of 6.3. Kebede and Ngandu (1999) estimate that the multiplier effects of the Alabama case would lead to cost recovery of the incentives in four to seven years.

How reliable are economic impact studies of incentive packages? Are they reasonable empirical approaches, providing answers regarding the potential welfare benefits of this competition? The short answer is probably not, at least not in their current stage. The economic impact studies found were ex-ante studies. The ex-post analysis was typically done on an ad hoc basis and simply looked at employment trends without controlling for the multitude of other factors that affect regional employment, factors that make it difficult to isolate the effect of an incentive package.

Economic impact studies use input-output models to analyze the impact of direct employment and expenditures on induced impacts ("ripple effects" due to expenditures in other industries) and on indirect impacts (impacts of increased spending by employees in the supply chain). As is well known, because expenditures in any one sector will require expenditures in other sectors (induced effects) and newly employed individuals will spend part of their earnings, expansionary investment will increase the overall level of economic activity. These complicated interactions are often summarized in a multiplier, which is the result of an underlying production and consumption model of the economy. The larger the multiplier, the larger the total effect (direct, indirect, and induced) on the economy.

The size of the multiplier is a function of the production process as well as the propensity of employees to consume locally. The closer the supply chain is to the actual production in question, the larger the potential multiplier because more of the productive activity stays within physical proximity of the main production activity (in this case, automobile manufacturing). In general, national multipliers can be expected to be larger than regional multipliers when estimating the effects of business investment in a local area, which is the case with most of the literature on the economic effects of the investments in the automotive sector. The published economic impact studies should give some pause regarding the conclusions. The University of South Carolina (2002) reports a jobs multiplier of 3.9 in its analysis of BMW, Hill and Brahmst (2003) report a job multiplier of 7.5 for the industry, the implicit jobs multiplier used by Holmes and McCallum (1993) is 6.3, and Bivens (2003) reports general employment multipliers in the manufacturing industry of 2.91 and, for auto parts, of 4.6.

The difference in employment multipliers demonstrates the debate regarding the impact of the automotive industry. Understanding those impacts, however, is an important step to determining the net benefits of these incentive programs. Connaughton and Madsen (2001) present a case against the size of multipliers used to justify the public investment for the Alabama Mercedes-Benz and South Carolina BMW incentive packages. They focus on the supply-chain relationships and the assumptions regarding the expansion of the supply chain in these two cases. Recall that the more local the supply chain, the larger the multiplier effect. Connaughton and Madsen demonstrate that, in the case of the original South Carolina and Alabama impact studies, estimates were made of the increased supply chain, and that increased supply chain was included as a direct employment effect. This double counts the employment effect because the multiplier of the U.S. Census RIMS II model used in both cases includes an indirect effect of the supply chain.

Connaughton and Madsen (2001) estimate a time-series model of the growth in supply-chain firms (defining 34 Standard Industrial Classification industries as suppliers of the automobile manufacturing industry) before and after operations began in South Carolina's BMW plant. They use a straightforward model of the general form for the period 1982 to 1997:

$$Firms_t = \alpha_0 + \alpha_1 Firms_{t-1} + \alpha_2 Dummy_t + \alpha_3 Trend_t^* Dummy_t + e_t.$$

In this regression, the variable *Firms* is the number of supply-chain firms, *Dummy* is a dummy variable for the post-BMW operations period (1995–1997), and *Trend* is a year dummy variable. The dummy variable, and, in alternative specification, the interaction of the dummy and trend variable, are insignificant. Connaughton and Madsen conclude that there is little reason to believe the expanded supply-chain argument used in supporting the tax incentive package in South Carolina. In addition, they provide data on the domestic versus imported content of BMW production, making South Carolina content only 13.9 percent of total value of the final output (Connaughton and Madsen 2001, 301). This analysis demonstrates the type of scrutiny that is warranted in the case of economic impact studies used to justify the benefits relative to the costs of tax incentives. The authors convincingly question an important underlying assumption regarding the magnitude of the multiplier, which, in turn, will have large effects on the bottom-line calculations of the benefits of such investments.

Other issues seem to be missing from the economic impact analyses of the industry. Three are listed here. First, the studies appear to assume that employment is not displaced from other areas. Although a displacement effect could be captured in a lower multiplier, that does not appear to be the case in the analyses reviewed for this analysis. Relatively high unemployment in the Southeast was one reason given for the early incentive packages, so the job displacement effect may not have been much of a worry. In the late 1990s, however, trends in employment were quite different, but still did not seem to be taken into account in the analysis of the economic impacts.

Second, the interpretation of the incentive package itself should be carefully modeled, and again, it is not obvious how it should be done. If the investment of the automotive industry includes the monies paid out through incentives (not future tax liabilities reduced, but the cost of infrastructure and so on), the loss of government expenditures in other areas should be used to offset the net new spending.

Finally, to the extent that taxes on residents are increased to offset the cost of incentive packages, changes in consumption or income of residents should also enter into the analysis. For example, if governments have to raise income taxes to offset the cost of incentive programs, a person's work behavior or purchases of various goods and products may change. In the long run, these secondary outcomes could, in fact, affect the level of revenue from local sales or income taxes.

Where Are We Now?

This review of the theoretical, empirical, and existing economic impact literature on the effects of interjurisdictional competition on welfare has not brought us very far in being able to advise state and local governments about the most effective types of incentives as governments engage in competition. The theoretical and empirical literatures are constrained by assumptions that may not be relevant to actual cases. The empirical literature is hampered by the question, What are we measuring? Welfare changes? A proxy for welfare? Effects on revenue? The economic impact literature is all over the map regarding the multiplier effects of investment, is often not forthcoming about labor market assumptions, and looks at local benefits seemingly without including potential costs (and benefits) in the state, region, and country. This review suggests that the theoretical or empirical evidence at this point on the effect of interjurisdictional competition on welfare is inconclusive.

To return to the central question—is interjurisdictional competition good or bad in its effects on welfare?—the literature needs to more closely measure changes in welfare. I could not find one study of these incentives that asked the question that if $200 million is spent on attracting an automobile plant, is that better than investing $200 million in schools? Or, does the type of automobile manufacturer matter? Are all jobs created equal? Would the incentives have yielded more benefits in one area versus another, including across state borders? If we give up x amount of dollars in land deals, infrastructure development, and so forth to attract a business, who pays for that expenditure? What is the resulting distribution of tax burdens?

Competition for jobs continues, perhaps increasingly as the global economy becomes more interconnected. From the perspective of state and local governments, it is not clear that this race to the bottom has yielded overall declines in tax rates. There has been some increased use in relative terms of personal income taxes, however. Corporate income tax shares have fallen (although the period 2004 to 2006 saw a slight increase in those tax revenues), and property taxes have come under fire from local citizens responding to large increases in assessments during the housing boom. So, although incentive packages may reflect a potential race to the bottom due to interjurisdictional competition, at some point taxes are changed to supplement the incentive packages. Is the growth in taxes and expenditures lower than it otherwise would be in the absence of targeted incentives?

Although the literature reviewed here is inconclusive, it is difficult to believe that the uncoordinated, mixed packages of incentives among state and local governments are made in a welfare-maximizing way. A Tiebout framework would, for example, suggest that tax incentives could increase welfare, but the types of incentive packages that can be seen today provide a complicated series of price distortions and change the tax burdens of residents in sometimes unpredictable ways (due to the volatile nature of the actual costs of these packages). It could very well be that simpler strategies, such as having government provide better information for firms to make location decisions, would increase the efficiency of competition. At this point, the policy implications of alternative strategies are unknown.

To provide research that is useful to the policy debate on tax incentives, it is necessary to be practical and to employ economic theory and applied empirical work to answer these important questions. In an intergovernmental system like the United States, the notion of cooperation may be out of reach at this time, but research can shed some light on overall welfare implications. Given the specificity of many fiscal incentive programs, a case study approach—similar to that begun here—may be the best way forward toward understanding the actual economic cost of incentive packages in the U.S. system. Advocates, politicians, and bureaucrats engaged in economic development are unlikely to champion such research.

REFERENCES

Alm, J., S. Chen, and S. Wallace. 2003. State and local governments' susceptibility to globalization. *State Tax Notes* (January 6):43–51.

Anderson, J., and R. Wassmer. 1995. The decision to bid for business: Municipal behavior in granting property tax abatements. *Regional Science and Urban Economics* 25(6):739–757.

Auerbach, A. 1997. The future of fundamental tax reform. *American Economic Review* 91(3):574–595.

Bahl, R., and J. Martinez-Vazquez. 2008. The determinants of revenue performance. In *Making the property tax work: Experiences in developing and transitional countries*, R. Bahl, J. Martinez-Vazquez, and J. Youngman, eds., 35–57. Cambridge, MA: Lincoln Institute of Land Policy.

Bartik, T. 1991. *Who benefits from state and local economic development policies?* Kalamazoo, MI: W. E. Upjohn Institute for Employment Research.

Besley, T. J., and H. S. Rosen. 1998. Vertical externalities in tax setting: Evidence from gasoline and cigarettes. *Journal of Public Economics* 70(3):383–398.

Bivens, J. 2003. Updated employment multipliers for the U.S. economy. Economic Policy Institute Working Paper 268. Washington, DC: Economic Policy Institute.

Brennan, G., and J. Buchanan. 1980. *The power to tax: Analytical foundations of a fiscal constitution.* New York: Cambridge University Press.

Case, A. 1992. Neighborhood influence and technological change. *Regional Science and Urban Economics* 22(3):492–508.

Case, A., J. R. Hines Jr., and H. S. Rosen. 1989. Copycatting: Fiscal policies of states and their neighbors. NBER Working Paper 3032. Cambridge, MA: National Bureau of Economic Research.

Center for Automotive Research. 2003. *The book of deals.* Washington, DC: Center for Automotive Research.

Connaughton, J. E., and R. A. Madsen. 2001. Assessment of economic impact studies: The cases of BMW and Mercedes-Benz. *Review of Regional Studies* 31(Winter):293–303.

Cumberland, J. H. 1981. Efficiency and equity in interregional environmental management. *Review of Regional Studies* 2:1–9.

Edmiston, K., and G. Turnbull. 2003. Local government competition for economic development. Fiscal Research Center Working Paper 83. Andrew Young School of Policy Studies, Georgia State University, Atlanta.

Fischel, W. A. 1975. Fiscal and environmental considerations in the location of firms in suburban communities. In *Fiscal zoning and land use controls*, E. Mills and W. Oates, eds., 119–173. Lexington, MA: D. C. Heath.

Geon, G., and G. Turnbull. 2004. The effect of home rule on local government behavior: Is there no rule like home rule? Urban and Regional Analysis Group Working Paper 04–05. Andrew Young School of Policy Studies, Georgia State University, Atlanta.

Glaeser, E. 2001. The economics of location-based tax incentives. Harvard Institute of Economic Research Discussion Paper 1932. Cambridge, MA: Harvard Institute of Economic Research.

Harberger, A. 1962. The incidence of the corporate income tax. *Journal of Political Economy* 70:215–240.

Hill, K., and E. Brahmst. 2003. *The auto industry moving south: An examination of trends.* Washington, DC: Center for Automotive Research.

Holmes, M. R., and E. McCallum. 1993. *Economic impact analysis of the Mercedes-Benz AG multipurpose vehicles production facility for the state of Alabama.* Troy, AL: Troy State University and Flours Siting and Consulting Services.

Kebede, E., and M. Ngandu. 1999. The economic impact of the Mercedes-Benz investment on the state of Alabama. *Journal of Agricultural and Applied Economics* 2:371–382.

Koven, S. G., and T. S. Lyons. 2003. *Economic development: Strategies for state and local practice.* Washington, DC: International City / County Management Association.

Krane, D., N. Rigos, and B. Hill Jr. 2001. *Home rule in America: A fifty-state handbook.* Washington, DC: Congressional Quarterly Press.

Ladd, H. 1992. Mimicking of local tax burdens among neighboring countries. *Public Finance Quarterly* 20(4):450–467.

LeRoy, G., A. Lack, and K. Walter. 2007. The geography of incentives: Economic development and land use in Michigan. *State Tax Notes* (January 15):101–127.

Linn, J. 2002. Car wars: Honda's $450 million Alabama expansion will create 2,000 new jobs. *Site Selection.* http://www.siteselection.com/ssinsider/bbdeal/bd020715 .htm.

Mark, S. T., T. McGuire, and L. Papke. 1997. What do we know about the effects of taxes on economic development? Washington, DC: DC Tax Revision Commission.

McCandless, M. E. 2006. Kia building a $1.2 billion assembly plant in Georgia. *Business Facilities* (May). http://www.businessfacilities.com/bf_06_11_news1.php.

Oates, W. E. 1972. *Fiscal federalism.* New York: Harcourt.

———. 1999. An essay on fiscal federalism. *Journal of Economic Literature* 37: 1120–1149.

Papke, J. 1996. The convergence of state-local business tax costs: Evidence of de facto collaboration. In *Proceedings of the Eighty-eighth Annual Conference on Taxation*, 195–206. Columbus, OH: National Tax Association.

Slemrod, J. 2001. Are corporate tax rates, or countries, converging? Mimeo.

Tannewald, R. 1996. State business climate: How should it be measured and how important is it? *New England Economic Review* (January/February):23–38.

Tax Policy Center. Various years. State and Local Finance Data Query System. Washington, DC: Urban Institute / Brookings Institution. http://www.taxpolicycenter .org/slf-dqs/pages.cfm.

Tiebout, C. M. 1956. A pure theory of local expenditures. *Journal of Political Economy* 64:416–424.

University of South Carolina. 2002. The economic impact of BMW on South Carolina. Moore School of Business, University of South Carolina, Columbia.

U.S. Bureau of the Census. 2002. 2002 Census of governments, Government Organization 1(1). Washington, DC: U.S. Government Printing Office.

Wasylenko, M. 1997. Taxation and economic development. *New England Economic Review* (March/April):37–52.

Wilson, J. D. 1986. A theory of interregional tax competition. *Journal of Urban Economics* 19:296–315.

———. 1999. Theories of tax competition. *National Tax Journal* 52:269–304.

———. 2001. Welfare-improving competition for mobile capital. Department of Economics, Michigan State University, East Lansing. Mimeo.

Wilson, J. D., and D. E. Wildasin. 2004. Capital tax competition: Bane or boon? *Journal of Public Economics* 88:1065–1091.

Zax, J. 1989. Is there a leviathan in your neighborhood? *American Economic Review* 79:560–567.

Zodrow, G., and P. Mieszkowski. 1986. Pigou, Tiebout, property taxation and the underprovision of local public goods. *Journal of Urban Economics* 19:356–370.

COMMENTARY
Jeffrey S. Zax

Sally Wallace asks whether there is evidence that tax competition in the United States has been effective in potentially increasing welfare. Her answer is convincing: the existing literature is inconclusive.

Ex-ante predictions of the effects of subsidies for employer relocations are contaminated by self-interest and implausible mercantilist models of export-driven multiplier effects. The relatively few ex-post evaluations struggle to control adequately for characteristics, apart from subsidies, that might affect industrial location. They have not paid nearly enough attention to the deeper questions of econometric identification in what are, essentially, models of peer effects (Manski 1995).

In addition, empirical work, at least, has focused entirely on estimating the effects of new employers on local economic activity. If these employers are relocating, there are presumably also effects on the location from which they originate, effects that will almost certainly be in opposite directions. Therefore, empirical work has an unambiguous bias toward overestimating the net welfare effect of any employer relocation.

At the same time, the existing literature has not taken full advantage of the insights that might be available from economic theory. These insights suggest that subsidies for relocating employers are almost certainly not Pareto-improving. The effects of such subsidies, and hence their probable motivation, are, with equal certainty, distributional.

Can These Subsidies Ever Be Pareto-Improving?

For subsidies to relocating employers to be Pareto-improving, they must remedy some market failure. For example, if the quality of local workers was not well known, there might be justification for government action to introduce the workers to new employers, but this scenario seems unlikely. There are ample private incentives for employers and employees to share this information. Moreover, the credibility of a home jurisdiction regarding the quality of its resident workers must be suspect. Consequently, information failures are unlikely to provide adequate justification for employer relocation subsidies.

Similarly, employers typically do not provide conventional local public goods or remedy conventional local externalities. It may be argued that jobs are an antidote to any externalities created by unemployment or underemployment, but, once again, those who suffer from these conditions have plenty of incentive to seek remedies through private action. Moreover, as discussed below, there is no guarantee, either theoretically or in practice, that the labor demands of new employers will be fulfilled by residents, whether or not they were previously unemployed.

Consequently, there is nothing to suggest that market failures justify subsidies to employers. To the contrary, these subsidies are more likely to distort markets than remedy existing distortions.

What Must Be the Distributional Effects?

Of course, the redistributional nature of employer subsidies is widely acknowledged, at least superficially. This naive distributional theory is simply that the advent of a new employer will provide more employment for residents, thereby improving their welfare.

The truth is surely more complicated and less hopeful. These subsidies clearly increase the welfare of the recipient employer, but that employer is, by definition, not an ex-ante constituent of the sponsoring jurisdiction. Therefore, this transfer, of itself, cannot be in the jurisdiction's interest.

The introduction of a new employer to the local labor market will shift the local demand curve for labor, which will, initially, increase equilibrium employment and wages. The supply of labor to most local labor markets, however, includes many workers who are not local residents. Once again, they are not ex-ante constituents of the jurisdiction providing the subsidy. Any transfers that they receive are mistargeted from the perspective of that jurisdiction's citizens.

Moreover, labor is mobile. Temporarily increased returns to labor will encourage migration. Migration will continue until wages are equal across all locations. In the long run, at least as a first approximation, employer relocations cannot benefit workers, whether or not they are the intended beneficiaries.

A new employer will also affect local real estate markets. If increased commercial or industrial activity generates negative externalities—in the form of pollution or congestion, as examples—aggregate demand for real estate may fall. This reduced demand cannot be the intended effect of employer subsidies.

Of course, the new employer will itself increase demand for real estate. If the net effect of its relocation is an increase in demand for real estate, local owners of real property will clearly benefit from the subsidy to a new employer. Renters will, just as clearly, suffer. Moreover, because land is immobile, these effects will be permanent.

Two issues are therefore raised here. First, there does not appear to be a compelling welfare argument for costly local government policies that redistribute in favor of property owners. Second, there is a surprising downward-stickiness to property tax rates. Consequently, increases in property values often seem to entail increases in property tax liabilities. The paradoxical effect may be that, even if incumbent property owners are appropriate subsidy beneficiaries, the only way for them to "cash in" would be to "cash out" by selling their property and leaving the jurisdiction.

In sum, basic economic principles indicate that subsidies to relocating employers are certainly good for the employers and probably good for owners of real estate. They probably have no effect on workers, however, even though workers are usually the intended beneficiaries. If this intent is genuine, surely other forms of transfers would be better targeted and more effective.

Why Do These Subsidies Occur?

Two motivations may sustain the use of subsidies to relocating employers, despite their disturbing distributional properties. First, it is possible that these properties are not appreciated. In this case, jurisdictions participate sincerely in a competition for a relatively fixed set of employers. This competition must be essentially a zero-sum game. Its continuation is therefore indicative of a coordination failure.

Second, it is possible that the distributional consequences of these subsidies are actually intentional. Self-aggrandizing bureaucrats with agenda control may use these subsidies, in effect, to obtain what they may think of as a "better class of citizenry." All else being equal, increases in real estate prices will drive renters and owners with modest cash flows out of the jurisdiction. They will typically be replaced by the higher-skilled, higher-income workers required by the types of employers toward whom these subsidies are usually directed.

These compositional shifts may be all that a self-interested bureaucrat requires to declare victory. They are clearly the true objectives underlying the eminent domain excesses that have become so common. Moreover, with these objectives, reliance on the implausible ex-ante justifications usually offered in support of employer subsidies becomes understandable. Despite their absurdity, they are more likely to rally public support than would disclosure of the true purposes.

What Should We Do?

The natural way to verify the true effects of employer relocation subsidies would be to conduct the following experiment. Identify two matched counties. In the first, choose 1,500 blue-collar workers at random and assign them to jobs in a Mercedes-Benz plant. In the second, choose 1,500 blue-collar workers at random and give them the per worker subsidy of $239,967 reported by Wallace (table 9.1). The contrast between the subsequent evolution of economic activity in these two counties should be very revealing.

While waiting for the outcome of this experiment, local governments can best use their resources by resisting the temptation to gamble on the long-term commercial viability of large-scale industrial projects. This policy is an exercise with regard to which they have no skill.

Instead, local governments should concentrate on the tasks for which they were designed: providing bundles of local public goods and taxes that are appropriate for their constituents. If they can ensure that schools are good, public spaces appealing, streets paved and plowed, garbage collected, and crime controlled, the market will surely take care of the rest.

REFERENCE

Manski, C. F. 1995. *Identification problems in the social sciences.* Cambridge, MA: Harvard University Press.

EMERGING CHALLENGES AND OPPORTUNITIES

10

Local Government Finances: The Link Between Intergovernmental Transfers and Net Worth

Luiz de Mello

A large literature shows how the sharing of revenue between different levels of government and the design of intergovernmental transfer schemes affect subnational finances (see de Mello 2000 for a review of the literature). Depending on how shared funds are raised (from a common pool of revenue, for instance) and transfer arrangements are designed (unconditional or special purpose, open- or closed-ended, matched or unmatched, discretionary or formula based, etc.), an increase in transfer receipts may lead to a reduction in subnational government net worth. The basic idea is that transfers reduce the marginal cost of provision to be borne by local taxpayers, especially when financed by a common pool of resources mobilized elsewhere in the economy. This cost shifting discourages local revenue mobilization or induces fiscal profligacy, leading to a buildup of debt in the recipient jurisdiction. Causality, however, may also run in the opposite direction: a fall in net worth may trigger an increase in transfers from higher levels of government. Such is the case when grants are of the ex-post gap-filling type, as with outright bailouts of subnational jurisdictions in financial distress by higher levels of government.

I thank Andrew Dean, Ronald C. Fisher, Yu-Hung Hong, Gregory K. Ingram, Peter Jarrett, Val Koromzay, Diego Moccero, and the conference participants at the Lincoln Institute International Conference for comments and discussions. The views expressed in this chapter are my own and do not necessarily reflect those of the Organisation for Economic Co-operation and Development.

Against this background, using a panel of Organisation for Economic Co-operation and Development (OECD) countries from 1980 through 2005, this study tests for (1) the presence of a stable, long-run statistical association between changes in transfer receipts and subnational net worth; and (2) the direction of causality between changes in transfer receipts and net worth. If a stable long-run association is found to exist and changes in transfer receipts temporally cause changes in net worth, the empirical findings would lend credence to the cost-shifting hypothesis. If causality is found to run in the opposite direction, the results would favor the ex-post soft-budget-constraint hypothesis. In particular, panel-based unit roots and cointegration techniques can be used to test for the existence of a stable relationship between transfer receipts and net worth and, should this relationship exist, to estimate the relevant long-term parameter.

This chapter's main contribution is twofold. First, it fills a gap in the empirical literature by testing for temporal causality in the association between intergovernmental transfers and subnational net worth, with an emphasis on local governments. Although there is a large literature on how intergovernmental transfer arrangements affect subnational finances (reviewed below), the analysis of temporal causality between transfer receipts and subnational net worth is a novelty. Second, attention is shifted away from the use of country-specific budgetary data, which is common in the empirical literature, toward cross-country national accounts data. In doing so, this study aims to highlight statistical regularities that go beyond country-specific institutional arrangements, while dealing with the effect that these arrangements can have on subnational public finances by exploiting heterogeneity in the panel. The main advantage of using national accounts data in the empirical analysis is that they allow for greater cross-country comparability of public finance indicators than do budgetary data, which tend to differ considerably across countries on the basis of differences in coverage and reporting standards.

The following main empirical findings are reported herein:

- There is a stable long-term relationship between transfer receipts and local government net worth for the case of current, but not capital, transfers. The estimated parameter shows that an increase in intergovernmental transfer receipts is associated with a modest reduction in the recipient jurisdiction's net worth over the long term. In addition, a fall in net worth is also associated with an almost one-to-one subsequent increase in transfer receipts.
- The direction of causality is sensitive to the technique used to estimate the long-term parameters. One technique suggests that causality runs from transfers to net worth, which lends support to a large literature on the effect of cost shifting on subnational budget outcomes. Causality also appears to run from net worth to transfer receipts, however, suggesting that transfers may be used as a deficit-financing tool, as when subnational governments are bailed out by higher levels of government.

The Literature

Two main strands of literature suggest a link between intergovernmental transfer receipts and the recipient jurisdiction's indebtedness. One focuses on the association between the design of intergovernmental transfer systems and budget outcomes through cost shifting and predicts that reliance on transfer receipts to finance subnational provision leads to a reduction in subnational indebtedness by weakening incentives for fiscal prudence. Of particular interest in this strand of literature is the "flypaper effect," according to which the "transmission mechanism" between incoming transfers and indebtedness is through expenditure pressures. The other related strand of literature focuses on the effect of soft-budget constraints on subnational finances. Accordingly, higher levels of government may use discretionary grants to bail out lower-level jurisdictions in financial distress. Expectations of financial bailouts reduce the opportunity cost of borrowing, which creates incentives for profligacy. The theoretical underpinning of both strands of literature are therefore that intergovernmental transfers place a wedge between the costs and benefits of local provision, which distorts the incentives faced by local policy makers for fiscal rectitude.

THE DEFICIT-BIAS HYPOTHESIS: TRANSFERS CAUSE INDEBTEDNESS

The basic idea of the deficit-bias literature is that intergovernmental transfer receipts create a wedge between the costs of public provision to be borne by taxpayers in the recipient jurisdiction and the benefits they accrue from public provision, especially when it is financed from a "common pool" of revenue mobilized elsewhere in the economy (Hallerberg and von Hagen 1999; von Hagen and Harden 1995). This wedge allows the recipient jurisdiction to internalize the benefits of expenditure among local residents and to shift provision costs to nonresidents. The upshot is that, due to a range of institutional and political-economy factors, dependence on grants and transfers from higher levels of government creates a deficit bias at the subnational level because it encourages recipient jurisdictions to underutilize their own tax bases at the expense of sharable bases or to spend beyond their means. The incentive to delay fiscal adjustment is another consequence of common-pool financing because individual jurisdictions have limited incentives to act alone and strong incentives to free ride, if the burden of fiscal retrenchment can be shared horizontally across jurisdictional borders and vertically across government levels (Alesina and Drazen 1991; Velasco 1999, 2000).

The deficit-bias hypothesis is conventionally tested in a reduced-form regression setup. The subnational budget balance is regressed on a measure of vertical imbalance, such as the ratio of transfer and grant receipts in revenue, as well as appropriate controls for subnational fiscal stance, such as demographics, terms-of-trade effects, and local income. Despite some variation in the estimating equation, there is plenty of empirical evidence in support of the deficit-bias hypothesis. Cross-country evidence for OECD and non-OECD countries is available from de Mello (1999, 2000) and Rodden (2002), among others. Country-specific evidence is also available: Jones, Sanguinetti, and Tommasi (2000) report evidence of "common pool" incentives for fiscal mismanagement among Argentinean provinces arising not only from intergovernmental revenue-sharing arrangements but also from the political system. Evidence of an association between vertical imbalances and subnational borrowing costs—due to a rising risk premium associated with a subnational deficit bias—is reported by Poterba and Rueben (1997) for U.S. states and de Mello (2001) for OECD and non-OECD countries.

A Special Case: The Flypaper Effect   Of particular interest when examining the "transmission mechanisms" through which revenue sharing affects budget outcomes is the flypaper-effect literature, surveyed by Hines and Thaler (1995), among others. This strand of literature is motivated by the observation that an increase in grants and transfer receipts from higher-level jurisdictions often leads to a rise in subnational spending that is higher than that associated with an equivalent hike in local income. This finding is puzzling because the median voter model of taxpayer behavior predicts that, instead, equally sized changes in unconditional grants and in local income should have an equivalent effect on subnational spending. In other words, although theory predicts that changes in transfer receipts or local income would create an identical income effect that would put upward pressure on local spending, this prediction is not always validated by empirical observation.

The flypaper hypothesis is conventionally tested by running reduced-form regressions of subnational spending on receipts of grants and transfers from higher levels of government, local income, and appropriate controls for other determinants of subnational expenditure, such as demographics. The empirical findings available to date suggest that the flypaper effect is stronger for capital than current transfer receipts (Wyckoff 1988), for matching than unconditional transfers (Gamkhar and Oates 1996), and for government spending on "luxury" goods (i.e., culture and urban amenities) than on normal goods (Deller and Maher 2005a). Another important finding is that the flypaper effect is asymmetric in the sense that spending tends to be very responsive to increases in transfer receipts, especially when the level of future transfers is uncertain, and comparatively insensitive to reductions. This finding is confirmed by the empirical evidence reported by Gramlich (1987) for U.S. states, Benton (1992) for U.S. state and local governments, Melo (1996) for Colombian subnational jurisdictions, Heyndels (2001) for Flemish municipalities, and Deller and Maher (2005b) for Wisconsin local governments, among others.[1]

---

1. There are a number of exceptions. For example, Gamkhar and Oates (1996) use U.S. state and local government data for the period 1953–1991 and show that subnational units respond symmetrically to changes in federal grants, regardless of the type of grant (matching or unconditional). Stine (1994) finds a super-flypaper effect using data for Pennsylvania counties during 1978–1988 in that a reduction in transfers induces the recipient jurisdiction to cut back not only spending but also locally raised revenue.

Although the presence of a flypaper effect is now broadly accepted as a statistical "anomaly" in the public finance literature, empirical evidence has been challenged on several grounds. In particular, the flypaper effect is purported to be due to failure to appropriately deal with the endogeneity of transfer receipts (Knight 2000). The argument is that the level of grants and transfers is affected by the political power of recipient jurisdictions, which, in turn, depends on expenditure pressures at the subnational level. The result is a reverse causality bias in the relationship between transfers and spending; therefore, when transfers are instrumented by variables capturing the political power of receiving jurisdictions (i.e., committee representation, proportion of representatives in the majority party, average tenure of representatives), local income and transfer receipts are found to have similar effects on public spending. Another argument that has been used to challenge the empirical evidence is that the flypaper effect is rather sensitive to the functional form of the estimating equation (Becker 1996). Although there is no a priori reason for sensitivity to functional specifications, empirical evidence is typically stronger for log-linear models than for linear estimating equations.

THE SOFT-BUDGET-CONSTRAINT HYPOTHESIS: INDEBTEDNESS CAUSES TRANSFERS

The basic idea about soft-budget constraints and how they affect local public finances is that expectations of a bailout from higher levels of government reduce the opportunity cost of fiscal profligacy. When subnational jurisdictions are free to borrow, they form expectations about how the central government reacts to their financial stance. Higher-level jurisdictions may be willing to assist local governments financially when the public services they provide benefit the rest of society (Wildasin 1997). Because of these externalities, however, the recipient jurisdiction may face the incentive to spend on items generating benefits that can be internalized among residents, rather than on items with stronger interjurisdictional spillovers. Incentives for bailouts may also be stronger in the case of jurisdictions that are "too big to fail."

If the recipient jurisdiction is deficit-prone and has weak incentives to act responsibly, decentralized fiscal management requires incentives for fiscal prudence; otherwise, local fiscal mismanagement may be detrimental to the system as a whole (Qian and Roland 1998). This macrofinancial spillover effect has been at the core of several subnational financial crises (de Mello 1999, 2000; Prud'homme 1995; Tanzi 1995; Ter-Minassian 1999; among others). Hard-budget constraints, especially in the form of fiscal rules, can be self-imposed, introduced by the central government or complemented by market-based scrutiny. In the absence of these safeguards, subnational financial disarray leads to a buildup of debt, which is often financed through bailouts from higher levels of government. Alternatively, Goodspeed (2002) argues that, although soft-budget constraints reduce the opportunity cost of borrowing, they also increase the cost of future taxes needed to pay off at least part of the incremental debt. Where expectations of higher future taxes mitigate the weak opportunity cost of profligacy, borrowing decisions are efficient, as in the case of hard-budget constraints.

A growing empirical literature looks at the association between intergovernmental transfers and indebtedness. While testing for flypaper-type effects, Levaggi and Zanola (2003) show that recipient jurisdictions respond to a decline in grants and transfers through deficit financing, rather than by hiking locally raised revenue or trimming spending, at least as far as the Italian health care system was concerned during the period from 1989 to 1993. Buettner and Wildasin (2006) focus on a sample of U.S. local governments and show that, especially in the case of large cities, fiscal imbalances are financed essentially by offsetting changes in future expenditures and grants. This evidence suggests that intergovernmental transfers act as a fiscal "cushion" for municipalities, which may, in the case of large cities, indicate a softening of budget constraints. Garcia-Mila, Goodspeed, and McGuire (2001) use data for Spanish regions and find evidence in favor of the soft-budget-constraint hypothesis. Martell and Smith (2004) use U.S. state-level data to test empirically the hypothesis that federal grants affect subnational debt issuance, and whether or not there are asymmetries in this relationship when grants are raised or cut back. The empirical findings suggest a correlation between grants and indebtedness: full-faith and credit debt issuance is reported to be positively correlated with both matching and nonmatching grants, whereas the opposite is true for nonguaranteed debt. The authors nevertheless do not distinguish capital and current transfers when assessing the relationship between transfers and debt.

DISTINGUISHING THE COMPETING HYPOTHESES
The difficulty of distinguishing the deficit-bias hypothesis from the soft-budget-constraint hypothesis is that both are observationally equivalent. A statistically significant coefficient in a reduced-form regression of subnational indebtedness on a measure of vertical imbalances and appropriate controls does not allow the econometrician to distinguish between these hypotheses in the absence of temporal causality testing. The deficit-bias literature assumes that the direction of causality runs from transfer receipts to indebtedness, whereas the opposite is true in the soft-budget-constraint literature. Temporal causality testing has nevertheless not been pursued in the empirical literature.

To shed light on this issue, this study first tests for the presence of a stable, long-term association between transfer receipts and recipient jurisdictions' net worth (discussed below) and then proceeds to test for temporal causality. In particular, the competing hypothesis is tested by the deficit-bias hypothesis.

The Deficit-Bias Hypothesis   The deficit-bias hypothesis can be tested by regressing subnational net worth on intergovernmental transfer receipts:

(1) $D_{it} = \alpha_i^{DB} + \beta^{DB}T_{it} + \nu_{it}^{DB},$

where D_{it} and T_{it} denote, respectively, net worth and transfer receipts in jurisdiction i at time t, α_i^{DB} are fixed effects, and v_{it}^{DB} is an error term.

Equation (1) may include other deterministic elements, such as a time trend. The unit root properties of net worth and transfer receipts will be assessed using conventional panel-based procedures, and cointegration testing will be carried out on the basis of the estimated residuals of equation (1). Two procedures will be used to uncover the long-term parameter (β^{DB}). On the basis of temporal causality testing, the deficit-bias hypothesis will not be rejected if the hypothesis that innovations in transfer receipts affect forecasts of net worth cannot be rejected.

The Soft-Budget-Constraint Hypothesis   The soft-budget-constraint hypothesis will be tested by regressing intergovernmental transfer receipts on subnational net worth:

$$(2) \qquad T_{it} = \alpha_i^{SB} + \beta^{SB} D_{it} + v_{it}^{SB},$$

where T_{it} and D_{it} denote, respectively, transfer receipts and net worth in jurisdiction i at time t, α_i^{SB} are fixed effects, and v_{it}^{SB} is an error term.

As in the case of equation (1), equation (2) may include other deterministic elements, such as a time trend. Conventional procedures will be used to assess the unit root properties of the data, to test for cointegration between transfer receipts and net worth, and to uncover the long-term parameter. On the basis of temporal causality testing, the soft-budget-constraint hypothesis will not be rejected if the hypothesis that innovations in net worth affect forecasts of transfer receipts cannot be rejected.

Data and Unit Root/Cointegration Tests

Data are available from the summary public finances accounts included in the OECD national accounts database. Information is available on intergovernmental transfers paid and received, net worth, and total revenue and expenditure for four levels of government (central, middle tier, local, and social security funds). The use of net worth is preferred to gross indebtedness because it takes into account the accumulation of financial assets by the recipient jurisdiction.[2] For example, investment programs financed by the issuance of government debt would leave net worth unchanged because an increase in indebtedness would be matched by an accumulation of assets. That is not the case of an increase in current spending commitments financed through higher indebtedness. Information is not available on the composition of financial liabilities by debt instrument (e.g., general-purpose

---

2. Net worth is the difference between a jurisdiction's gross financial liabilities, which include debt and other short- and long-term liabilities defined by ESA95/SNA93, and its financial assets, which include cash, bank deposits, loans to the private sector, participation in private-sector companies, holdings in public corporations, and foreign exchange reserves.

or revenue-backed issuances) or on the composition of transfers by type of instrument (e.g., matching or unconditional grants, mandated revenue sharing, discretionary or formula-based transfers). Transfer receipt data can nevertheless be decomposed between current and capital transfers.

For most countries, the public finances time series are relatively short. The central government series are typically longer that those for subnational jurisdictions. At the subnational level, data are more readily available for local governments than for middle-tier jurisdictions. Sample selection was therefore guided primarily by data availability. The largest panel that could be obtained from the database includes 13 countries (or less than one-half of the OECD membership) over the period from 1995 to 2004. The main advantage of using the national accounts database in the empirical analysis is that it allows for greater cross-country comparability of public finances indicators than do budgetary data, which tend to differ considerably across countries because of differences in coverage and reporting standards.

Based on the theoretical argument developed above, the variables of interest are the shares in revenue of transfers received by local governments and their level of indebtedness, measured by the ratio of local government net worth to gross domestic product (GDP). The main descriptive statistics of the variables of interest are reported in table 10.1. For example, current transfers account for 33 percent of local government revenue on average, whereas indebtedness is low, given that net worth is nearly balanced on average. There is considerable variation (as gauged by the standard deviation) in the data in the level of indebtedness and in the share of transfers in revenue, however.

Trends in transfer receipts and local government net worth for all countries in the sample are depicted in figure 10.1. Local government net worth as a proportion of GDP trended upward over the reference period in a number of countries, including Austria, Canada, France, The Netherlands, Spain, and Sweden,

Table 10.1
Descriptive Statistics

	Mean	Standard Deviation	Median	Max.	Min.	Number of Observations
Net worth-to-GDP ratio	−0.01	0.03	−0.02	0.11	−0.07	150
Transfers-to-revenue ratio:						
Total transfers	0.38	0.16	0.37	0.75	0.09	112
Current transfers	0.33	0.14	0.34	0.65	0.05	122
Capital transfers	0.05	0.06	0.04	0.26	0.00	112

Note: The sample spans the period 1995–2004.
Sources: OECD national accounts database and the author's calculations.

Figure 10.1
Indebtedness and Transfers: Local Governments

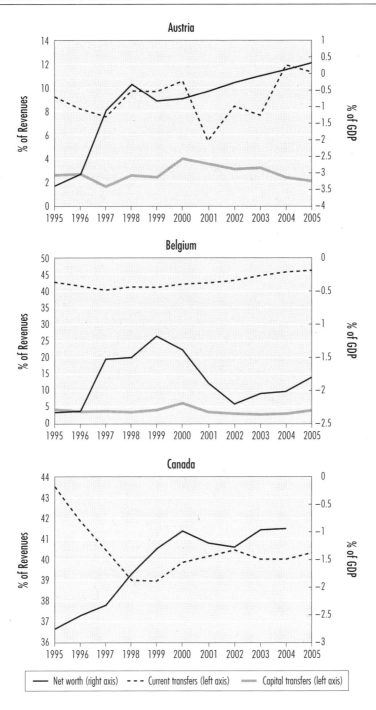

Austria

Belgium

Canada

— Net worth (right axis)   - - - Current transfers (left axis)   Capital transfers (left axis)

Figure 10.1
(*continued*)

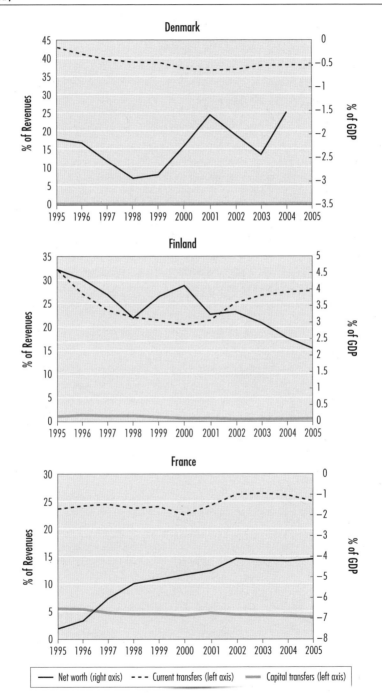

Figure 10.1
(*continued*)

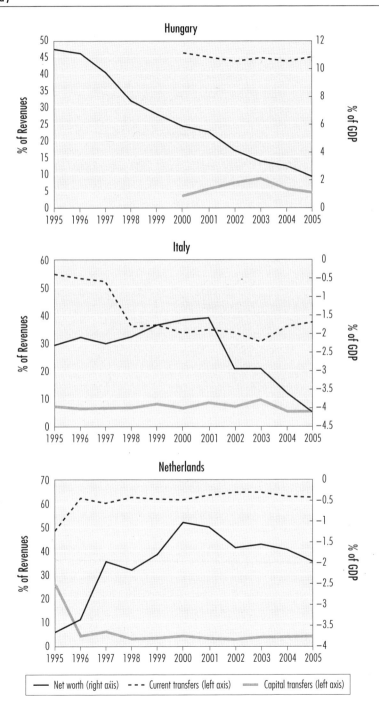

Figure 10.1
(*continued*)

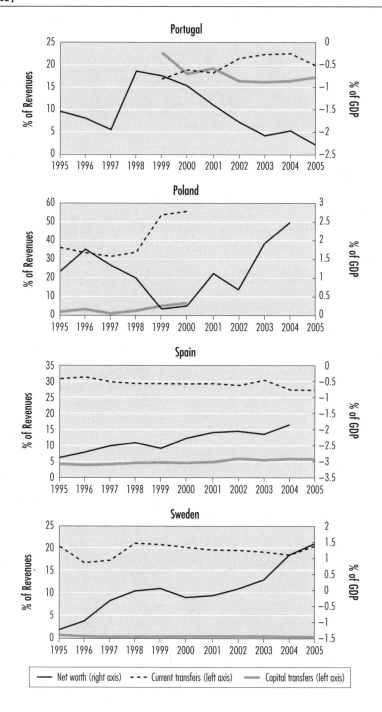

but fell in Finland, Italy, and Portugal. On the other hand, current transfers fell in relation to revenue, albeit often in a gradual manner, in a number of countries, such as Canada, Denmark, Italy, and Spain, while displaying more complex patterns in the remaining countries. The level of capital transfers is typically much lower in relation to revenue in most countries, with the exception of Portugal, and considerably more stable than that of current transfers.

UNIT ROOT TESTS

The unit root properties of the transfer and net worth indicators will be assessed on the basis of four different tests. Three tests are considered for the case in which the cross-sectional units in the panel are independent—Im–Pesaran–Shin (IPS), Maddala–Wu (MW), and Hadri—and one that allows for cross-sectional dependence (CADF).[3] Cross-sectional dependence implies that the time series in the panel are contemporaneously correlated, a phenomenon that may be due to omitted common factors, spatial spillovers, or both. In the case of the variables of interest, the level of subnational indebtedness may be correlated across countries during periods of fiscal retrenchment. An example of such common factor/spatial spillover is the fiscal adjustment effort of the euro-zone countries prior to the common currency's introduction. By the same token, it is important to allow for heterogeneity in the panel when testing for unit roots so that parameter estimates may differ among the different cross-sectional units because the relationship between transfers and indebtedness depends on country-specific institutional settings.

The IPS test is a balanced panel-equivalent of the ADF test with the null hypothesis of a unit root in all cross-sectional units. The alternative hypothesis allows for cross-sectional heterogeneity (i.e., some of the series in the panel are stationary). In other words, rejection of the null hypothesis implies that the variable of interest follows an autoregressive process that contains unit roots in some of the cross-sectional units. The test statistic is a mean-group Lagrange multiplier statistic (t-bar statistic), which converges to a standard normal distribution in large samples (as long as the ratio of N to T tends to a finite nonzero constant as N and T tend to infinity in the case of autocorrelated residuals).

The MW test, proposed by Maddala and Wu (1999), is based on the p-values of individual unit root tests. The null hypothesis is that all series have unit roots, against the alternative that at least one series in the panel is stationary. The MW test differs from the IPS test in the definition of the null hypothesis: it is not based

---

3. There are several methodologies for testing for unit roots in panel data. Typically, they consist of computing panel-analogs of the Dickey–Fuller (DF) or augmented DF tests available for pure time series, but differ on the definition of the null hypotheses (stationarity or non-stationarity), on whether or not the panel is balanced, and on whether or not heterogeneity is permitted among the autoregressive parameters and across the cross-sections (which affects the definition of the alternative hypotheses). Tests also differ as to whether or not the relevant variables are allowed to be correlated contemporaneously across the cross-sectional units. For recent surveys, see Baltagi and Kao (2000) and Breitung and Pesaran (2006), among others.

on the assumption that the autoregressive coefficient is the same across countries, thus allowing for cross-sectional heterogeneity under the null. The test performs similarly or slightly better than the IPS statistic.

The Hadri test is a panel-equivalent of the KPSS Lagrange multiplier test with the null of stationarity (rather than nonstationarity as in the IPS and MW tests) for all individual series. The error terms may be homoscedastic or heteroscedastic across cross-sectional units, and they may be serially correlated, in which case a Newey–West estimator may be used to take account of the long-run variance in the data. The test nevertheless requires independence across the panel's cross-sectional units and performs poorly in small samples when applied to processes with MA(1) errors.

Finally, the cross-section augmented DF (CADF) test proposed by Pesaran (2005) deals with the case in which cross-sectional dependence arises from the presence of a single common factor among the cross-sectional units. The test averages the individual CADF t-statistics for all cross-sectional units in a heterogeneous panel. This test has better size properties than alternative methodologies, such as that proposed by Moon and Perron (2004).

The Results   The results of the unit root tests are reported in tables 10.2 and 10.3. The results of the IPS, MW, and Hadri tests suggest the presence of unit roots in net worth (in levels), regardless of whether the disturbances are homoscedastic or not. The results are robust to the inclusion of a time trend in the regressions, where appropriate, given that net worth appears to have a trend in some countries. As for the intergovernmental transfer indicators, the unit root tests yield mixed results. Whereas the transfer-to-revenue ratio appears to have unit roots in levels on the basis of the IPS (except for capital transfers) and the Hadri tests, regardless of whether the disturbances are homoscedastic or not, the MW test suggests that the transfer variables are stationary in levels (except for capital transfers).

On the basis of the results of the CADF test, which allows for contemporaneous correlation among the series in the panel, both the indebtedness and transfer indicators were found to have unit roots in levels. Again, this finding is important because of the comparatively large number of European Union countries in the sample, which creates considerable scope for spatial spillovers and the presence of common factors affecting trends in public finance indicators during the period of analysis.

In sum, the results are unequivocal as to the presence of unit roots in local government net worth, suggesting that the first-differenced data are stationary. Due to the mixed findings for the transfer-to-revenue ratios and the predominance of evidence pointing to the presence of unit roots in the level variables, the cointegration tests (reported below) will be performed on the premise that the transfer indicators are stationary in first differences. Needless to say, a caveat to consider when interpreting the results of the unit root tests is that the time span for which information is currently available is relatively short. It is well known that unit root tests have stronger predictive power when data are available for

Table 10.2

Panel Unit Root Tests: Cross-Sectional Independence

	Level		First Difference	
	Test Statistics	Number of Observations	Test Statistics	Number of Observations
Im–Pesaran–Shin test [H_0: unit root; t-bar-statistic]				
Net worth-to-GDP ratio	−1.795	120	−2.341***	105
Transfers-to-revenue ratio				
Total transfers[a]	−1.584	120	−2.477***	90
Current transfers	−1.390	136	−1.996**	119
Capital transfers	−3.981***	120	−2.033**	105
Net transfers[a]	−1.411	112	−2.433***	84
Maddala–Wu test [H_0: unit root; Prob > chi sq]				
Debt-to-GDP ratio	0.520	—	0.000***	—
Transfers-to-revenue ratio				
Total transfers[a]	0.000***	—	0.000***	—
Current transfers	0.000***	—	0.000***	—
Capital transfers	0.106	—	0.000***	—
Net transfers[a]	0.000***	—	0.000***	—
Hadri LM test [H_0: no unit root; $Z(tau)$-statistic]				
Net worth-to-GDP ratio				
Homo	7.188***	150	−1.141	135
Hetero	5.886***	150	−0.107	135
Serial correlation	6.231***	150	6.751***	135
Transfers-to-revenue ratio				
Total transfers[a]				
Homo	6.971***	150	−0.432	120
Hetero	5.463***	150	−0.772	120
Serial correlation	5.413***	150	9.197***	120
Current transfers				
Homo	7.056***	170	−1.531	153
Hetero	4.287***	170	−0.029	153
Serial correlation	6.393***	170	7.025***	153
Capital transfers				
Homo	3.436***	150	0.019	135
Hetero	3.139***	150	0.087	135
Serial correlation	6.051***	150	6.817***	135

(continued)

Table 10.2
(*continued*)

	Level		First Difference	
	Test Statistics	Number of Observations	Test Statistics	Number of Observations
Net transfers[a]				
Homo	7.686***	140	−1.261	126
Hetero	5.338***	140	−0.02	126
Serial correlation	5.451***	140	5.359***	126

* = $p < .10$
** = $p < .05$
*** = $p < .01$
Note: The sample spans the period 1995–2004. The regressions for the IPS test include a constant term, and the variables are lagged once. For the Hadri test, "Homo" and "Hetero" refer, respectively, to the statistics under the hypotheses of homoscedastic and heteroscedastic disturbances across cross-sectional units. The statistics under "Serial correlation" were computed by controlling for autocorrelation in the error terms (lag length is truncated at 2).
[a]Twice-differenced.
Sources: OECD national accounts database and the author's estimations.

Table 10.3
Panel Unit Root Tests: Cross-Sectional Dependence

	Level		First Difference	
	Test Statistics	Number of Observations	Test Statistics	Number of Observations
	CADF (H_0: unit root; *t*-bar-statistic)			
Net worth-to-GDP ratio[a]	−2.088	120	2.610***	90
Transfers-to-revenue ratio				
Total transfers[a]	−1.342	120	2.610***	90
Current transfers	−1.627	136	−1.907	119
Capital transfers	−1.883	120	−2.434**	105
Net transfers[a]	−1.423	112	2.610***	84

* = $p < .10$
** = $p < .05$
*** = $p < .01$
Note: The sample spans the period 1995–2004. The regressions include a constant term.
[a]Twice-differenced.
Sources: OECD national accounts database and the author's estimations.

much longer time periods and when the time dimension of the panel is higher than its cross-sectional dimension.

COINTEGRATION TESTS

A number of methodologies are now available for testing for panel cointegration.[4] As with unit root tests, these methodologies are panel counterparts of pure time-series techniques. One method uses residuals-based approaches akin to those of Engle-Granger, such as the Pedroni (1997, 1999) framework, which allows for unbalanced panels and heterogeneity in the slope coefficients as well as fixed effects and trends in the data. The idea of residuals-based tests is that, as in the pure time-series case, if the estimated residuals are stationary, there exists a linear combination among the variables included in the regression.[5]

Again, as in the case of the unit root tests reported above, it is important to allow for cross-sectional heterogeneity to account for the different institutional and country-specific settings that may affect the relationship between intergovernmental transfer receipts and local government net worth. It is not be possible, however, to deal with the presence of common factors and spatial spillovers when testing for cointegration, as was the case of the unit root test analysis reported above. Although recent developments in panel cointegration testing have focused on techniques that allow for cross-sectional dependence arising from common factors, these methodologies require a much larger time dimension than that of the panel considered here.[6]

The Pedroni methodology consists of testing for the presence of unit roots in the residuals of the cointegrating equation. Seven panel statistics are available: four statistics based on the panel's within dimension (panel-ADF statistics) and three based on the panel's between dimension (group-ADF statistics). The null hypothesis is of no cointegration (i.e., unit roots in the residuals) in all cases (Pedroni, 1999, 2001, 2004). The difference between the panel-ADF and group-ADF statistics is related to the specification of the alternative hypothesis: $H_A : \rho_i = \rho < 1$, for all i, for the panel-ADF statistics (where ρ_i is the autoregressive coefficient in a standard ADF equation for the residuals of the cointegrating equation),

---

4. See Baltagi and Kao (2000) and Breitung and Pesaran (2006) for recent surveys.

5. When more than one within-group cointregrating relationship may exist, there are rank-based tests akin to that of Johansen-Juselius for pure time series because, as in the pure time-series case, residuals-based tests do not allow for identifying the number of cointegrating relationships that may exist among the integrated variables of interest. Among these tests is the maximum likelihood test of cointegrating rank in heterogeneous panels proposed by Larsson, Lyhagen, and Lothgren (2001). Of course, that is not the case at hand because there can be at most one cointegrating relationship between two variables.

6. The asymptotic equivalence between estimators based on cross-independence and those based on cross-dependence in nonstationary panel time series has been showed by Groen and Kleibergen (1999), who propose a likelihood-based framework for cointegration in panels with a fixed number of error-correction models.

and $H_A : \rho_i < 1$, for all i, for the group-ADF statistics, so that heterogeneity is allowed under the alternative hypothesis. Although the predictive power of these statistics rises with the panel's time-series dimension, the group-ADF and panel-ADF statistics generally perform well in small samples.

In what follows, cointegration will be tested on the basis of one of Pedroni's residuals-based group-ADF statistics. The test allows for heterogeneity in the panel, which is important, as argued above, on the basis of cross-country differences in institutional settings. It involves the calculation of a t-bar statistic (similar to that computed for the IPS unit root test) on the basis of the autoregressive coefficients of standard ADF equations for the residuals of the cointegrating equations estimated for each cross-sectional unit in the panel. The group-ADF statistic is defined as

$$\Psi_{\bar{t}} = \frac{\sqrt{N}\,(\bar{t}_{N,T} - E[\bar{t}_{N,T}\,(p,\,0)])}{\sqrt{\mathrm{Var}(\bar{t}_{N,T})}} \Rightarrow N(0,\,1),$$

where $\bar{t}_{N,T} = (\sum_{i=1}^{N} t_i)/N$, t_i is the t statistic of each ρ_i in standard ADF equations estimated for the residuals of the cointegration equations estimated for all cross-sectional units in the panel, p is the ADF equation's augmentation order, and $E[\bar{t}_{N,T}(p,\,0)]$ and $\mathrm{Var}(\bar{t}_{N,T})$ are the mean and variance of $\bar{t}_{N,T}(p,\,0)$ under the null hypothesis of no cointegration ($H_0 : \rho_i = 0$), which were tabulated by Pedroni (1999). The group-ADF statistic diverges to minus infinity under the alternative hypothesis. Therefore, the left tail of the normal distribution is used to assess the critical value for rejecting the null: large negative values imply that the null of no cointegration is rejected.

The Results   Because of the need to distinguish between two competing hypotheses (discussed above) and because residuals-based cointegration testing is sensitive to the definition of the cointegrating equation, the group-ADF statistic will be computed for an equation in which net worth is a function of transfer receipts and for another equation in which, conversely, transfer receipts are a function of net worth. The results of the cointegration tests, reported in table 10.4, are not sensitive to the definition of the cointegrating equation. The null of no cointegration was rejected in the case of the current transfer-to-revenue ratio, regardless of the theoretical hypothesis being tested. For the equations including the other transfer indicators, there does not appear to be a common stochastic trend between transfer receipts and local government net worth. On the basis of this test, the long-term coefficients will be estimated for the cointegrating equations defined for local government net worth and current transfer receipts.

ESTIMATING THE COINTEGRATING VECTORS
Having established that a cointegrating relationship exists between the variables of interest, at least for the case of current transfers, the cointegrating vector needs to be estimated under both competing theoretical hypotheses: soft-budget-

Table 10.4

Panel Cointegration Tests: Group-ADF Statistics

Transfer Type	Based on Residuals From:	
	Equation (1)	**Equation (2)**
Total transfers	1.58	1.00
Current transfers	−3.61***	−2.79***
Capital transfers	4.73	−0.51
Net transfers	2.33	0.93

* = $p < .10$
** = $p < .05$
*** = $p < .01$

Note: The sample spans the period 1995–2004. The regressions include an intercept and a time trend.
Sources: OECD national accounts database and the author's estimations.

constraint and deficit bias. Two methodologies will be used in either case: the dynamic OLS (DOLS) and the dynamic fixed-effects (DFE) estimators. Both techniques assume that the cointegrating vectors are identical for all panel units, and neither allows for cross-sectional dependence. The dynamic seemingly unrelated regressions (DSUR) estimator of Mark, Ogaki, and Sul (2005) and Moon and Perron (2004) allow for cross-sectional dependence in the estimation of the cointegration vector. Unlike DOLS, the DSUR estimator exploits the presence of long-run cross-sectional correlation in the equilibrium errors, which makes it more efficient (Westerlund 2005). DSUR, however, is only feasible for panels in which the number of cross-sectional units is significantly smaller than the time-series dimension, and that is not the case for the panel at hand.

The DOLS Estimator   The DOLS estimator, developed by Saikkonen (1991) and Stock and Watson (1993), uses leads and lags of the differenced right-hand-side variable to correct for possible serial correlation and weak exogeneity in a cointegrated regression.[7] Based on equation (1), under the deficit-bias hypothesis, the DOLS equation is defined as

$$(3) \qquad D_{it} = \alpha_i^{DB} + \beta_{DOLS}^{DB} T_{i,t-1} + \sum_{j=1}^{p_1} \xi_j^{DB} \Delta T_{i,t-j} + \sum_{j=1}^{p_2} \psi_j^{DB} \Delta T_{i,t+j} + u_{it}^{DB}.$$

Likewise, based on equation (2), in the case of the soft-budget-constraint hypothesis, the DOLS equation is as follows:

---

7. The DOLS technique, as well as the fully modified estimator of Phillips and Hansen (1990), produces estimators that are asymptotically normally distributed with zero means (Kao and Chiang 1999).

$$(4) \qquad T_{it} = \alpha_i^{SB} + \beta_{DOLS}^{SB} D_{i,t-1} + \sum_{j=1}^{p_1} \xi_j^{SB} \Delta D_{i,t-j} + \sum_{j=1}^{p_2} \psi_j^{SB} \Delta D_{i,t+j} + u_{it}^{SB}.$$

The DFE Estimator   The DFE estimator is based on an autoregressive distributed lag (ADRL) model in the case of pure time series (Pesaran and Shin 1999). Under the deficit-bias hypothesis, the DFE methodology involves the estimation of the following model:

$$(5) \qquad \Delta D_{it} = \sigma_i^{DB} d_i' + \lambda^{DB} D_{i,t-1} + \beta_{DFE}^{DB} T_{i,t-1} + \sum_{j=1}^{p_1} \omega_j^{DB} \Delta D_{i,t-j}$$

$$+ \sum_{j=1}^{p_2} \phi_j^{DB} \Delta T_{i,t-j} + u_{it}^{DB},$$

where d_i' is a vector of time-invariant regressors.

Likewise, in the case of the soft-budget-constraint hypothesis, the DFE equation is as follows:

$$(6) \qquad \Delta T_{it} = \sigma_i^{SB} d_i' + \lambda^{SB} T_{i,t-1} + \beta_{DFE}^{SB} D_{i,t-1} + \sum_{j=1}^{p_1} \omega_j^{SB} \Delta T_{i,t-j}$$

$$+ \sum_{j=1}^{p_2} \phi_j^{SB} \Delta D_{i,t-j} + u_{it}^{SB}.$$

The estimate of the long-run coefficients are given by $\theta_n^{DFE} = -\hat{\beta}_{DFE}^n / \hat{\lambda}^n$, where $\hat{\beta}_{DFE}^n$ and $\hat{\lambda}^n$ are the DFE estimators of β_{DFE}^n and λ^n, for $n = (DB, SB)$ in equations (5) and (6). As mentioned above, the long-term parameter is identical for all cross-sectional units.

Testing for Temporal Causality   Both methodologies used to estimate the cointegrating vector lend themselves to temporal causality analysis. As argued above, temporal causality allows for distinguishing the deficit-bias and soft-budget-constraint hypotheses about an association between intergovernmental transfer arrangements and recipient jurisdiction indebtedness. It can be tested using a conventional F-test. For example, by equation (5), if $H_0 : \beta_{DFE}^{DB} = \phi_j^{DB} = 0$ is rejected for all j, then T_{it} Granger causes D_{it}, which is in support of the deficit-bias hypothesis. Likewise, by equation (6), if $H_0 : \beta_{DFE}^{SB} = \phi_j^{SB} = 0$ is rejected for all j, then D_{it} Granger causes T_{it}, which is in support of the soft-budget-constraint hypothesis.

Temporal causality can be tested in the alternative setting proposed by Hurlin and Venet (2001) for panels with fixed coefficients. For instance, in the case of the deficit-bias hypothesis, temporal causality testing involves the estimation of the following equation:

$$(7) \qquad \Delta D_{it} = \alpha_i^{DB} + \sum_{j=1}^{p_1} \lambda_{(j)}^{DB} \Delta D_{i,t-j} + \sum_{j=0}^{p_2} \xi_{i(j)}^{DB} \Delta T_{i,t-j} + u_{it}^{DB}.$$

Two hypotheses can be considered for the case with homogeneous autoregressive processes:[8] homogeneous noncausality (HNC) and homogeneous causality (HC). The null hypothesis under HNC is $H_0 : \xi_{i(j)}^{DB} = 0$, for all i and j, which is tested against $H_A : \xi_{i(j)}^{DB} \neq 0$, for at least some i and j. Acceptance of the null therefore indicates that transfers do not Granger cause net worth for all cross-sectional units in the panel. Rejection of the null hypothesis indicates instead that for at least one or more units, transfers Granger cause net worth. The HNC statistic is computed by comparing the sum of squared residuals of the unrestricted model in equation (7) (RSS_u) with the sum of squared residuals of a restricted model where the slope coefficients and lags of $\xi_{i(j)}^{DB} \Delta T_{i,t-j}$ are set to zero, leaving only the fixed effects and the lags of the dependent variable to predict current values of ΔD_{it} (RSS_r^{HNC}). The HNC test statistic is computed as

$$(8) \qquad F_{HNC} = \frac{(RSS_r^{HNC} - RSS_u) / Np}{RSS_u / [NT - N(1 + p) - p]},$$

where N, p, and T are, respectively, the cross-sectional dimension of the panel, the number of lags used in equation (7), and the time-series dimension of the panel.

Acceptance of the null on the basis of an F-test distributed $[Np, NT - N(1 + p) - p]$ calls for testing the hypothesis of homogeneous causality (HC). The null hypothesis for HC is $H_0 : \xi_{i(j)}^{DB} = \xi_j^{DB} \neq 0$, for all i and some j, which is tested against $H_A : \xi_{i(j)}^{DB} \neq \xi_i^{DB}$, for at least some i and some j. Acceptance of the null indicates that all cross-sectional units follow the same causal process. The HC test statistic is calculated using the sum of squared residuals from the unrestricted model described above (RSS_u) and the sum of squared residuals of a restricted model in which the slope terms are constrained to equality for all cross-sectional units (RSS_r^{HC}). The HC test statistic is computed as

$$(9) \qquad F_{HNC} = \frac{(RSS_r^{HC} - RSS_u) / p(N - 1)}{RSS_u / [NT - N(1 + p) - p]}.$$

In the case of the soft-budget-constraint hypothesis, the Hurlin–Venet setting involves estimating the following equation:

$$(10) \qquad \Delta T_{it} = \alpha_i^{SB} + \sum_{j=1}^{p_1} \lambda_{(j)}^{SB} \Delta T_{i,t-j} + \sum_{j=0}^{p_2} \beta_{i(j)}^{SB} \Delta D_{i,t-j} + u_{it}^{SB}.$$

The HNC and HC statistics can therefore be computed using equations (8) and (9) to test for temporal causality.

---

8. The same statistics can be calculated for each cross-sectional unit so as to allow for heterogeneity arising from different autoregressive processes, but that case will not be considered here.

The Estimated Vectors and Temporal Causality Tests   The results of the
DOLS and DFE estimations are reported in table 10.5. In the case of the deficit-
bias hypothesis, the magnitude and sign of the coefficients confirm the hypothesis
that an increase in current transfer receipts from higher levels of government is
associated with a decrease in the recipient jurisdiction's net worth over the long
term. The estimated coefficient is small in size and only significant at classical
levels in the DFE regression, however. In the case of the soft-budget-constraint
hypothesis, the cointegrating vector implies that a fall in local government net

Table 10.5
Cointegration Vectors

Hypothesis	Coefficient	N	Number of Lags	R^2 (within)	F
Deficit-bias hypothesis					
DOLS regression	−0.03	120 [14]	1	0.01	0.58
	(0.028)				
H_0: Transfers do not cause net worth (Prob > F)	0.317				
DFE regression	−0.04***	106 [14]	2	0.15	2.64**
	(0.018)				
Implied *LR* coefficient	−0.24				
H_0: Transfers do not cause net worth (Prob > F)	0.063**				
Soft-budget-constraint hypothesis					
DOLS regression	−1.06**	95 [14]	2	0.13	2.32**
	(0.509)				
H_0: Net worth does not cause transfers (Prob > F)	0.311				
DFE regression	−1.12***	106 [14]	2	0.51	15.03***
	(0.314)				
Implied *LR* coefficient	−1.60				
H_0: Net worth does not cause transfers (Prob > F)	0.003***				

$^* = p < .10$
$^{**} = p < .05$
$^{***} = p < .01$

Note: The sample spans the period 1995-2004. The coefficients reported are, respectively, β^n_{DOLS} and β^n_{DFE} for $n = (DB, SB)$, estimated in equations (3) through (6). The *LR* coefficients are computed as $\theta^{DFE}_n = -(\beta^n_{DFE}/\lambda_n)\,\lambda^n$, for λ^n estimated in equations (5) and (6). All models include an intercept and fixed effects (not reported). Standard errors are reported in parentheses. The number of cross-section units is reported in brackets. The number of lags and leads was selected on the basis of the Akaike Information Criterion (AIC).
Sources: OECD national accounts database and the author's estimations.

Table 10.6
Temporal Causality Tests: Hurlin–Venet Methodology

	Hypotheses	
	Transfers Do Not Cause Net Worth	Net Worth Does Not Cause Transfers
F_{HNC}	1.74***	1.12
F_{HC}	1.58***	0.78

* = $p < .10$
** = $p < .05$
*** = $p < .01$
Note: The sample spans the period 1995–2004. The test statistics are described in equations (8) and (9). HNC and HC refer, respectively, to "homogeneous noncausality" and "homogeneous causality." All models include an intercept and fixed effects (not reported). The number of lags and leads was selected on the basis of the Akaike Information Criterion (AIC).
Sources: OECD national accounts database and the author's estimations.

worth is associated with an almost one-to-one increase in current transfer receipts. Evaluated at the sample means, the coefficients estimated by both DOLS and DFE imply that a fall in the ratio of local government net worth from the current level of near balance to about 5 percent of GDP is associated with an increase in transfer receipts from the current level of 33 percent of local government revenue to about 37 percent.

The results of the temporal causality tests, for both the DOLS and DFE equations, are also reported in table 10.5. On the basis of these tests, it appears that transfer receipts do cause net worth in the temporal causality sense in the DFE equation, when the long-term coefficients are estimated by DFE, which supports the deficit-bias hypothesis. Nevertheless, it also appears that net worth causes transfer receipts on the base of the DFE regression, which is in accordance with the soft-budget-constraint hypothesis. The results of the Hurlin–Venet temporal causality tests are reported in table 10.6. On the basis of these tests, there appears to be support for the deficit-bias hypothesis because the null hypothesis that transfers do not Granger cause net worth is rejected comfortably for all cross-sectional units in the panel. There is nevertheless heterogeneity in the panel on the basis of the HC test because the null that all cross-sectional units follow the same causal process is also comfortably rejected.

Summary of the Main Findings and Discussion

This study used OECD national accounts data to shed additional light on the empirical association between intergovernmental transfer arrangements and subnational public finances. In particular, temporal causality analysis was used to distinguish between the deficit-bias and the soft-budget-constraint hypothesis that underscore the empirical association between intergovernmental transfer receipts and recipient jurisdictions' indebtedness (controlling for the accumulation of financial assets). As noted above, the predictions of the deficit-bias and soft-budget-constraint literatures are otherwise observationally equivalent because a statistical association between transfer receipts and net worth is a necessary condition for both predictions. Although the estimation of the long-term parameters by DFE appears to support the deficit-bias hypothesis, there is equally compelling evidence in favor of the soft-budget-constraint hypothesis in the sample of countries under examination. In this latter case, transfer arrangements may act as an alternative financing mechanism for reducing subnational net indebtedness.

The magnitude of the estimated parameters nevertheless suggests that, although an increase in the share of current transfer receipts in local government revenue leads to a modest deterioration in net worth over the long term, a deterioration in local government net worth is associated with a sizable increment in its current transfer receipts (in percent of revenue). To the extent that this finding indicates budget constraints are less hard than possibly desirable, at least as far the OECD countries in the sample are concerned, there is scope for strengthening subnational budget constraints further. One option for doing so is the introduction of fiscal rules, including administrative controls, such as the need for central government approval of subnational borrowing as in Ireland, Japan, Korea, and the United Kingdom.[9] In some countries, including Mexico, local governments are banned from borrowing abroad.

More comprehensive fiscal rules include ceilings on public debt or debt service, expenditure, or budget balances. Golden rules (i.e., budgeted deficits must not exceed investment spending) are in place in some cases (Germany, Switzerland, and the United Kingdom), although other countries (Hungary, Poland, and Portugal) impose ceilings on the public debt or debt service outlays. Outside the OECD area, the experience of Brazil with fiscal rules is instructive because the successful implementation of comprehensive fiscal responsibility legislation has been instrumental in the country's process of fiscal adjustment since the mid-1990s. Also, markets appear to be a poor substitute for fiscal rules, particularly at the subnational level of government, but have complemented fiscal rules in many cases, such as in Canada and the United States. Finally, international experience suggests that, where in place, attention is needed to avoid fiscal gimmickry as a means of bypassing legal restrictions on borrowing. Common mechanisms include channeling expenditures through the tax system, creating off-budgetary funds, and committing government resources through public-private partnerships and loan guarantees, among others.

In addition, a negative association between transfer receipts and net worth may be unrelated to the cost-shifting incentives and their effect on subnational fiscal performance through soft-budget constraints. Such an association may be

9. See OECD (2002, chap. IV; 2003, chap. V) for more information on OECD countries and de Mello (2007) for the case of Brazil.

due instead to different financing mechanisms that are available for subnational governments, such as, for example, securing future revenue from intergovernmental grants. This operation may be an alternative to pay-as-you-go financing of investment projects, for example. In the United States, municipal bonds can be of two types: general obligation (GO), which are backed by general taxation, and revenue bonds, which are financed by receipts of future taxes, fees, lease payments, federal grants, lottery earnings, or tobacco settlement payments. Whereas issuance of GO bonds is often subject to constitutional limits, such is not the case of revenue bonds. An example outside the OECD area is that of the Brazilian states, which resorted to a "revenue anticipation" instrument extensively, including as a deficit-financing tool, until its use was curtailed as a means of reining in subnational indebtedness.[10]

REFERENCES

Afonso, J. R., and L. de Mello. 2002. Brazil: An evolving federation. In *Managing fiscal decentralization*, A. Ehtisham and V. Tanzi, eds., 265–287. London: Routledge.

Alesina, A., and A. Drazen. 1991. Why are stabilizations delayed? *American Economic Review* 81:1170–1188.

Baltagi, B. H., and C. Kao. 2000. Nonstationary panels, cointegration in panels, and dynamic panels: A survey. *Advances in Econometrics* 15:7–52.

Becker, E. 1996. Illusion of fiscal illusion: Unsticking the flypaper effect. *Public Choice* 86:85–102.

Benton, J. E. 1992. The effects of changes in federal aid on state and local government spending. *Publius* 22:71–82.

Breitung, J., and M. H. Pesaran. 2006. Unit roots and cointegration in panels. In *The econometrics of panel data*, L. Matyas and P. Sevestre, eds. Norwell, MA: Kluwer.

Buettner, T., and D. E. Wildasin. 2006. The dynamics of municipal fiscal adjustment. *Journal of Public Economics* 90:1115–1132.

Deller, S. C., and C. S. Maher. 2005a. Categorical municipal expenditure with a focus on the flypaper effect. *Public Budgeting and Finance* 25:73–90.

———. 2005b. A model of asymmetries in the flypaper effect. *Publius* 36:213–229.

de Mello, L. 1999. Intergovernmental fiscal relations: Co-ordination failures and fiscal outcomes. *Public Budgeting and Finance* 19:3–25.

———. 2000. Fiscal decentralization and intergovernmental fiscal relations: A cross-country analysis. *World Development* 28:365–380.

———. 2001. Fiscal decentralization and borrowing costs: The case of local governments. *Public Finance Review* 29:108–138.

———. 2007. Fiscal responsibility legislation and fiscal adjustment: The case of Brazilian local governments. In *Financing cities: Fiscal responsibility and urban infrastructure in Brazil, China, India, Poland and South Africa*, G. E. Peterson and P. C. Annez, eds., 40–73. Washington, DC: World Bank / Sage.

10. See Afonso and de Mello (2002) for more information.

Gamkhar, S., and W. Oates. 1996. Asymmetries in the response to increases and decreases in intergovernmental grants: Some empirical findings. *National Tax Journal* 49:501–512.

Garcia-Mila, T., T. J. Goodspeed, and T. J. McGuire. 2001. Fiscal decentralisation policies and sub-national government debt in evolving federations. Unpublished manuscript.

Goodspeed, T. J. 2002. Bailouts in a federation. *International Tax and Public Finance* 9:409–421.

Gramlich, E. M. 1987. Federalism and federal deficit reduction. *National Tax Journal* 40:299–313.

Groen, J. J. J., and F. Kleibergen. 1999. Likelihood-based cointegration analysis in panels of vector error correction models. Discussion Paper 99-055/4. Tinbergen Institute, Rotterdam.

Hallerberg, M., and J. von Hagen. 1999. Electoral institutions, cabinet negotiations, and budget deficits in the European Union. In *Fiscal institutions and fiscal performance*, J. Poterba and J. von Hagen, eds. Chicago: University of Chicago Press.

Heyndels, B. 2001. Asymmetries in the flypaper effect: Empirical evidence for the Flemish municipalities. *Applied Economics* 33:1329–1334.

Hines, J. R., and R. H. Thaler. 1995. The flypaper effect. *Journal of Economic Perspectives* 9:217–226.

Hurlin, C., and B. Venet. 2001. Granger causality tests in panel data models with fixed coefficients. Unpublished manuscript. University of Paris IX, Paris.

Jones, M. P., P. Sanguinetti, and M. Tommasi. 2000. Politics, institutions, and public sector spending in the Argentine provinces. *Journal of Development Economics* 61:305–333.

Kao, C., and M. H. Chiang. 1999. On the estimation and inference of a cointegrated regression in panel data. Working Paper. Center for Policy Research, Syracuse University, Syracuse, NY.

Knight, B. 2000. The flypaper effect unstuck: Evidence on endogenous grants from the Federal Highway Aid Program. Washington, DC: Board of Governors of the Federal Reserve System.

Larsson, R., J. Lyhagen, and M. Lothgren. 2001. Likelihood-based cointegration tests in heterogenous panels. *Econometrics Journal* 4:109–142.

Levaggi, R., and R. Zanola. 2003. Flypaper effect and sluggishness: Evidence from regional health expenditure in Italy. *International Tax and Public Finance* 10: 535–547.

Maddala, G. S., and S. Wu. 1999. A comparative study of unit root tests for panel data and a new simple test. *Oxford Bulletin of Economics and Statistics* 61:631–652.

Mark, N. C., M. Ogaki, and D. Sul. 2005. Dynamic seemingly unrelated cointegrating regression. *Review of Economic Studies* 72:797–820.

Martell, C. R., and B. M. Smith. 2004. Grant level and debt issuance: Is there a relationship? Is there symmetry? *Public Budgeting and Finance* 24:65–81.

Melo, L. 1996. The flypaper effect under different institutional contexts: The Colombian case. *Public Choice* 111:317–345.

Moon, H. R., and B. Perron. 2004. Efficient estimation of the SUR cointegration regression model and testing for purchasing power parity. *Econometric Reviews* 23:293–323.

OECD. *See* Organisation for Economic Co-operation and Development.

Organisation for Economic Co-operation and Development. 2002. *Economic Outlook* 72. Paris: OECD.

————. 2003. *Economic Outlook* 74. Paris: OECD.

Pedroni, P. 1997. Panel cointegration: Asymptotic and finite sample properties of pooled time series with an application to the PPP hypothesis: New results. Working Paper. Indiana University.

————. 1999. Critical values for cointegration tests in heterogeneous panels with multiple regressors. *Oxford Bulletin of Economics and Statistics* 61(Special Issue):653–670.

————. 2001. Purchasing power parity tests in cointegrated panels. *Review of Economics and Statistics* 83:727–731.

————. 2004. Panel cointegration, asymptotic and finite sample properties of pooled time series tests with an application to the PPP hypothesis. *Econometric Theory* 20:597–625.

Pesaran, M. H. 2005. A simple panel unit root test in the presence of cross-section dependence. Cambridge Working Papers in Economics 0346. University of Cambridge.

Pesaran, M. H., and Y. Shin. 1999. An autoregressive distributed lag modelling approach to cointegration analysis. In *Econometrics and economic theory in the 20th century: The Ragnar Frisch Centennial Symposium*, S. Strom, ed. Cambridge: Cambridge University Press.

Phillips, P. C. B., and B. E. Hansen. 1990. Statistical inference in an instrumental variables regression with I(1) processes. *Review of Economic Studies* 57:99–125.

Poterba, J. M., and K. S. Rueben. 1997. State fiscal institutions and the U.S. municipal bond market. NBER Working Paper 6237. Cambridge, MA: National Bureau of Economic Research.

Prud'homme, R. 1995. On the dangers of decentralization. *World Bank Research Observer* (August):201–210.

Qian, Y., and G. Roland. 1998. Federalism and the soft budget constraint. *American Economic Review* 88:1143–1162.

Rodden, J. 2002. The dilemma of fiscal federalism: Grants and fiscal performance around the world. *American Journal of Political Science* 46:670–687.

Saikkonen, P. 1991. Asymptotically efficient estimation of cointegrating regressions. *Econometric Theory* 58:1–21.

Stine, W. F. 1994. Is local government revenue response to federal aid asymmetrical? Evidence from Pennsylvania county governments in an era of retrenchment. *National Tax Journal* 57:799–816.

Stock, J. H., and M. W. Watson. 1993. A simple estimator of cointegrating vectors in higher-order integrated systems. *Econometrica* 61:783–820.

Tanzi, V. 1995. Fiscal federalism and decentralisation: A review of some efficiency and macroeconomic aspects. *Annual Bank Conference on Development Economics.* Washington, DC: World Bank.

Ter-Minassian, T. 1999. Decentralization and macroeconomic management. In *Fiscal decentralization, intergovernmental fiscal relations and macroeconomic governance*, K. Fukasaku and L. de Mello, eds., 55–66. Paris: OECD Development Centre.

Velasco, A. 1999. A model of endogenous fiscal deficits and delayed fiscal reforms. In *Fiscal institutions and fiscal performance*, J. Poterba and J. von Hagen, eds. Chicago: University of Chicago Press.

———. 2000. Debts and deficits with fragmented fiscal policymaking. *Journal of Public Economics* 76:105–125.

von Hagen, J., and I. Harden. 1995. Budget processes and commitment to fiscal discipline. *European Economic Review* 39:771–779.

Westerlund, J. 2005. Data dependent endogeneity correction in cointegrated panels. *Oxford Bulletin of Economics and Statistics* 67:691–705.

Wildasin, D. E. 1997. Externalities and bailouts: Hard and soft budget constraints in intergovernmental fiscal relations. Policy Research Working Paper 1843. Washington, DC: World Bank.

Wyckoff, P. G. 1988. A bureaucratic theory of flypaper effects. *Journal of Urban Economics* 23:115–129.

COMMENTARY
Ronald C. Fisher

In his interesting and informative chapter, Luiz de Mello explores the causal relationship between intergovernmental revenue received and recipient government net worth. Specifically, the presence of a stable relationship and temporal causality between current grants and recipient government net worth is tested using unit root and cointegration techniques on aggregate local government data from 13 Organisation for Economic Co-operation and Development (OECD) countries for the years 1995 through 2004.

De Mello's results clearly show a small, stable inverse relationship between current grants (for noncapital purposes) and recipient governments' net worth in the long run. The direction of causality is not clear, however, with various test forms giving conflicting results. For instance, de Mello (see this volume, p. 268) notes that "estimation of the long-term parameters . . . appears to support the deficit-bias hypothesis" (grants induce recipient governments to spend more and incur debt), but then also notes that "there is equally compelling evidence in favor of the soft-budget-constraint hypothesis" (fiscal difficulty or higher recipient government debt induces additional grant support). Therefore, support for the "soft-budget constraint" hypothesis from de Mello's analysis in his chapter is not necessarily clear or compelling, although he argues, based on the magnitude of the estimated parameters, that strengthening subnational government budget constraints is appropriate.

At least two issues are raised by de Mello's analysis. First, what is the comparative value of this aggregate, macroeconomic, time-series approach to analyzing grant effects on recipient governments? Second, how should one interpret any results obtained from the aggregate approach?

For purposes of comparison, it may be helpful to review the traditional approach to thinking about and analyzing grant effects. Grants may influence both fiscal choices (i.e., the level and distribution of current expenditures and revenues) as well as the financial condition of recipient governments, including the level and type of debt, capital investment, and cash reserves. Of course, these choices are not independent decisions or amounts, and grants may affect several or all simultaneously. The effects are expected to depend on both the structure of the grants and the legal, political, and fiscal environment in which the recipient governments operate (Fisher 1982). Boadway's (2007) characterization of transfers based on purpose—categorical, revenue-sharing, or equalization grants—seems especially useful and important for hypothesizing about effects and in interpreting evidence. Other important grant characteristics include the allocation factors (especially whether these are predetermined and exogenous to recipient government action) and the matching rate. Environmental factors that are likely to be important include the degree of revenue autonomy for recipient governments, the existence of spending limits or borrowing restrictions, and constraints imposed through mobility of consumers or factors and by the political system.

The aggregate, macroeconomic, time-series approach used by de Mello has several important characteristics. The analysis is cross national, considers all subnational units within each country together, aggregates all types of grants together (except for differentiating grants targeted to current expenditures as opposed to capital goods), and uses national income accounts, rather than budgetary, data. Given this level of aggregation, one might expect that it would be difficult to observe or uncover any fiscal patterns. After all, there is abundant evidence from the microeconomic empirical literature that matching rates, maintenance of effort constraints, and other structural grant features affect the responses (Fisher and Papke 2000). Similarly, different types of subnational governments respond differently to similar grants. From this perspective, that de Mello could find any significant, stable relationships in the aggregate data seems quite a positive accomplishment. It also suggests why the variation in causality results from different cointegration tests is not surprising.

One interpretation of the inverse relationship between intergovernmental transfers and net worth is that recipient governments respond to grants by inefficiently increasing spending and incurring debt, what de Mello calls the deficit-bias hypothesis or transfers cause debt. There are also several other possibilities, as de Mello notes in his final paragraph. It is well known that borrowing costs reflect local fiscal health (Poterba and Rueben 1997). So, it could be that grants, by providing fiscal resources, reduce borrowing costs for the recipient governments, and those governments react appropriately to use debt to a greater degree. It is also possible that grants targeted for capital investment fund only part of the capital cost, requiring localities to incur debt for the remainder. There also is evidence (Temple 1994) that capital goods are normal or even superior for local governments, suggesting that even general-purpose or current expenditure grants may induce recipients to alter the mix of spending toward capital investment. Of course, capital goods are funded disproportionately by debt. Indeed, de Mello does not find any stable long-run relationship between grants for capital purposes and net worth.

Finally, there are issues about how "net worth" is measured and about the relationship to debt. According to de Mello, the measure of net worth used in his study is the difference between financial assets and financial liabilities (which is common for governments). Typically, physical assets are not included in measurement of public-sector net worth. So, debt incurred to construct or acquire physical assets (land, buildings, transportation facilities) may decrease "net worth" as measured, but not net worth in a full accounting sense.

The type of intergovernmental transfer involved would seem to be crucial in interpreting the results that show that "debt causes transfers," that is, that recipient governments are fiscally irresponsible or profligate because they expect higher-level governments to provide a fiscal "bailout." These comments apply as much to the entire "soft-budget-constraint" literature as they do to this specific analysis (Vigneault 2007). The soft-budget-constraint argument, almost by definition, should not apply to either categorical or equalization grants. Increases in recipient government expenditure or debt are intended consequences of categorical grants, likely to offset the inefficiency that results from external benefits of local government services. For categorical grants with matching rates, then, additional local spending *should* generate an increase in grants. Such responses are efficient and necessary for the grant to achieve its intended objective. In the case of equalization grants, allocating grant funds to distressed localities is an explicit objective. Some exogenous source of fiscal stress may very well lead a local government to incur more debt; that economic or fiscal stress also supports increased equalization grant support. Again, that is the intended objective of an equalization program, which should provide disproportionate assistance to distressed jurisdictions (those with high costs or limited resources).

It therefore follows that the area of greatest concern where soft-budget constraints may contribute to inefficiency is in the case of revenue-sharing grants, intended to offset a fiscal imbalance or take advantage of economies of scale in revenue generation. If the allocation approach for the revenue-sharing grants is not predetermined or is subject to change, reflecting a clear commitment on the part of granting governments, there is clearly opportunity for ad hoc, ex-post decisions to assist specific jurisdictions. Such a case would seem to afford the strongest possibility for observing the "soft-budget-constraint" phenomenon.

I am not familiar enough with the grant structure in the 13 OECD nations included in de Mello's study to conclude whether revenue-sharing grants are prominent and these conditions common. In some instances, however, even revenue-sharing grants may have equalization objectives or effects. The United States is the only major industrialized nation without an explicit national equalization grant program. Research by Inman (1988) and others has shown, however, that equalization is often the only explanation consistent with the observed governmental distributional pattern of grants in the United States. If equalization is the ultimate (but perhaps hidden) objective of grants, even where narrow categorical grants dominate, it would not be surprising to observe a pattern of larger relative grants for jurisdictions with low net worth.

In sum, this work by de Mello is valuable on two counts: (1) it illustrates the opportunity to use aggregate, time-series techniques to study responses to grant systems; and (2) it provides preliminary, although inclusive, support for concerns that grants may create incentives for inefficient debt expansion. If true, increased grants in a decentralized system may need to be accompanied by clear and effective fiscal rules. On the other hand, it may just be that grants serve primarily an equalization objective, assisting jurisdictions with low net worth.

REFERENCES

Boadway, R. 2007. Grants in a federal economy: A conceptual perspective. In *Intergovernmental fiscal transfers*, R. Boadway and A. Shah, eds., 55–74. Washington, DC: World Bank.

de Mello, L. 2008. Local government finances: The link between intergovernmental transfers and net worth. In *Fiscal decentralization and land policies*, G. K. Ingram and Y-H. Hong, eds., 245–272. Cambridge, MA: Lincoln Institute of Land Policy.

Fisher, R. 1982. Income and grant effects on local expenditure: The flypaper effect and other difficulties. *Journal of Urban Economics* 12:324–345.

Fisher, R., and L. Papke. 2000. Local government responses to education grants. *National Tax Journal* 1(March):153–168.

Inman, R. 1988. Federal assistance and local services in the United States: The evolution of a new federalist fiscal order. In *Fiscal federalism: Quantitative studies*, H. Rosen, ed., 33–74. Chicago: University of Chicago Press.

Poterba, J., and K. Rueben. 1997. State fiscal institutions and the U.S. municipal bond market. NBER Working Paper W6237. Cambridge, MA: National Bureau of Economic Research.

Temple, J. 1994. The debt/tax choice in the financing of state and local capital expenditures. *Journal of Regional Science* 34:529–547.

Vigneault, M. 2007. Grants and soft budget constraints. In *Intergovernmental fiscal transfers*, R. Boadway and A. Shah, eds., 133–171. Washington, DC: World Bank.

11

Fiscal Decentralization and Income Distribution

Jorge Martinez-Vazquez and Cristian Sepulveda

*E*xtensive academic research and political debate have focused on fiscal decentralization and income distribution. While income distribution historically has been a matter of concern in most countries, an increasing number of countries have recently engaged in some form of decentralization process, and many others are preparing to do so in the near future. The effects of decentralization on income distribution, and on how income distribution issues may affect the decentralization process, have thus far been the subject of very little theoretical or empirical research, however.[1]

Decentralization and the distribution of income, as general concepts, can be analyzed in a variety of ways. This chapter focuses on (1) *fiscal* decentralization, as opposed to administrative and political decentralization, or mere deconcentration;[2] and (2) the income distribution of *households* (or individuals) at the *national* level, as opposed to alternative perspectives such as within-jurisdiction distribution of income among individuals or interregional differences in income distribution.

We thank Gregory K. Ingram, Yu-Hung Hong, and Christine P. W. Wong for very helpful comments on a previous draft. All remaining errors in the paper are ours.

1. An important exception is Beramendi (2003), who develops a political economy model linking political decentralization with income distribution outcomes.

2. See, for example, Rondinelli (1981) for an early discussion of the different concepts of decentralization.

The potential effects of fiscal decentralization on income distribution across individuals in a country must be distinguished from the potential redistributive role played by subnational governments. Whether or not the subnational governments should or, in fact, do actively participate in redistributive policies is not the focus of this chapter.[3] Instead, the central objective is to ascertain *how* fiscal decentralization, measured in a broad sense, might in practice alter a country's distribution of income. The policy relevance of this research question is clear: Governments and most bilateral and multilateral aid organizations are preoccupied with stopping, if not reversing, the deterioration in income distribution experienced by many countries since the 1980s. At the same time, an increasing number of countries around the world have embarked on decentralization reform devolving all kinds of fiscal powers to subnational governments. Therefore, the question is, are these two important policy thrusts actually working against each other, or are the two processes complementary?

Fiscal decentralization can affect the distribution of income via many channels. Some links between decentralization and income distribution can be uncovered in the recent literature on the economic effects of decentralization, such as that on the size and composition of public expenditures, on the size of welfare programs, or on poverty reduction. Other relevant links to be considered include the effect of decentralization on the level and source of government revenues and, more generally, on tax structure in a multilevel context, the interjurisdictional mobility of the population and other factors of production, and the resultant competition among localities.

In our analysis, we review relevant theories and empirical findings in the economic literature that can help explain the potential effects of fiscal decentralization on income distribution, and we discuss the data limitations and main challenges associated with an empirical examination of the problem. We identify several channels through which fiscal decentralization might affect the distribution of income. Later, we consider the limitations associated with the available data and then review the empirical literature to get a sense of the relative effect of decentralization on income distribution.

Theoretical Linkages Between Fiscal Decentralization and Income Distribution

Conventional public finance theory has advised against the active participation of subnational governments in redistributive policies (Brown and Oates 1987; Musgrave 1959; Oates 1968, 1972; Stigler 1957). The reasons behind this ad-

---

3. Regarding the participation of subnational governments in redistributive policies, see, for instance, Bahl, Martinez-Vazquez, and Wallace (2002).

vice are based on efficiency considerations, particularly the potential mobility of population and productive factors. The attempt of one jurisdiction to redistribute welfare benefits from the rich to the poor would, other things being equal, require an increase in the tax burden imposed on nonbeneficiaries, who might eventually move out. At the same time, the poor in neighboring jurisdictions would try to immigrate, leaving the jurisdiction with a smaller tax base.[4] In practice, however, there are few policies where the line between central and local intervention in redistributive policies is clearly drawn. For example, regulatory policies carried out at the local level, like land use and rent controls, almost certainly have the potential to alter the distribution of income (Sewell 1996). In addition, outright redistributive policies are a common practice of subnational governments in decentralized countries.[5]

The involvement of subnational governments in redistributive policies is not, however, the only source of the potential influence of fiscal decentralization on income distribution. By itself, interjurisdictional mobility can have direct and important effects on income distribution. On one hand, mobility may be seen as a response of individuals and households who seek to increase their real income, and so the "pure" self-sorting processes of individuals among jurisdictions offering alternative bundles of public services and tax burdens may well be able to alter income distribution. On the other hand, mobility certainly affects the supply of productive factors and thus also their marginal productivity and return (Wildasin 1994). Fiscally induced migration is considered a source of inefficiencies and thus implies a welfare loss for society.

Interjurisdictional mobility plays an important role in the dynamic effects of fiscal decentralization on allocation efficiency and income distribution. At one extreme, when population and production factors are perfectly immobile, the redistributive policies carried out at the local level might inflict no efficiency costs at all.[6] In such a case, potentially large gains could be obtained by decentralizing some redistributive decisions and bringing them nearer to the poor. Based on the observation that mobility tends to be relatively low in developing countries, some authors have suggested that subnational governments could make a valuable contribution to fighting poverty. Of course, in that context, the concerns would include the accountability of local government officials and

---

4. Clearly, the case against an active redistributive role of subnational governments critically depends on interjurisdictional mobility. When mobility is imperfect or costly, subnational governments may become efficient players. Assuming limited mobility, Pauly (1973) shows not only that under some conditions (majority voting and utility interdependence) the size of redistributive programs increases with decentralization, but also that the performance of local governments is superior to the centralized redistribution.

5. See, for instance, Bahl, Martinez-Vazquez, and Wallace (2002).

6. Some countries (e.g., the former Soviet Union and China) have used internal passports to restrict interjurisdictional mobility.

the potential of local/elite capture as well as the administrative capabilities of subnational governments.

The design of any decentralized fiscal system requires the assignment of expenditure responsibilities, revenue authority, borrowing capacity, and the implementation of a transfer system. Each of these four interdependent elements of government finances may have its own effect on income distribution.

The expenditure and revenue sides of the budget can be distinguished as two separate channels through which income distribution may be altered. Consequently, expenditure decentralization and revenue decentralization can be regarded as alternative, but complementary, sources of changes in income distribution.[7] On the expenditure side, public resources can be transferred directly to the poor, increasing their disposable income, or could also have a pro-poor nature as long as they are intended for or serve their benefit. Important examples of pro-poor expenditures, with an immediate redistributive effect, are primary health and basic education, which per se can also contribute to improve the distribution of income in the short and longer term. Likewise, the progressiveness of the tax system can be used to reduce income inequalities directly; for example, subnational governments might be largely financed by indirect taxes, which tend to be more regressive, or by direct taxes, which generally are more progressive.

Of course, the extent of decentralization—or the degree of autonomy assigned to subnational governments—typically differs for each budgetary component. In practice, either because of the economies of scale associated with the collection of tax revenues or simply because the central government prefers to keep for itself the most buoyant tax bases, the decentralization of expenditure responsibilities is usually not accompanied by comparable tax revenue autonomy. These asymmetric fiscal decentralization arrangements create vertical imbalances and thus require transfers from the center to balance the budget across different levels of government. Equalization transfers are used to address horizontal fiscal imbalances, but, of course, they can have a significant effect on income distribution if, for example, fiscally poorer jurisdictions are also jurisdictions with a higher incidence of the poor. Intergovernmental equalization transfers are also justified on efficiency grounds as a way to reduce spillovers created by autonomous decisions at the local level. Finally, borrowing can alter income distribution by affecting the intergenerational distribution of tax burdens and benefits from services.

The decentralization of expenditure responsibilities may allow local governments to better address the needs and preferences of their constituents, but the independent decision-making processes also create positive and negative exter-

---

7. Although borrowing constitutes a type of revenue for all government units, intergovernmental transfers can be seen as expenditures at the central level or revenues for the local governments. Here, we implicitly follow a local perspective.

nalities. It is well known that uncoordinated tax policy decisions of subnational governments do not take into account interjurisdictional externalities or the mobility of population and production factors. The result is less than optimal provision of public goods and relative unfair distributions of tax burdens.[8] The factors connecting revenue decentralization with income inequality, however, are not yet very well known. One recent attempt to deal with this particular issue is made by Hodler and Schmidheiny (2006), who develop a two-community model where, under heterogeneity of both income and tastes for housing, and the presence of different local tax rates, the progression of the tax schedule leads to a self-sorting process that results in a pattern of household segregation. This process, in turn, is associated with a reduction of the tax schedule's progressiveness. Although the model focuses exclusively on the revenue side of decentralization, it provides a testable hypothesis and a mechanism by which revenue decentralization might reduce the equalizing potential of the tax policy.

In actual practice, subnational taxes can play a redistributive role if they are not markedly regressive and at the same time yield enough funds to help finance redistributive expenditure programs. That may be the reason the theoretical literature addressing the relation between revenue decentralization and distribution of income is rather scarce. In reality, fiscal decentralization would seem to have a greater potential to improve the distribution of income through the expenditure side of subnational budgets. Some expenditure programs may explicitly target individuals or regions with low per capita levels of income or production, whereas others can be oriented to increase the gross regional product (GRP). For example, Arze, Martinez-Vazquez, and McNab (2005) find that the relative share of education and health in overall government expenditures increases with fiscal decentralization. Generally, these services represent an important share of government expenditures, and the services provided represent larger benefits for low-income families; thus, fiscal decentralization might be expected to have a positive effect on the welfare of the poor.[9]

Intergovernmental transfers are a distinctive element of decentralized systems of government. The types of transfers, their magnitude, and the economic justification for them can be significantly different from those found in a centralized system. Many transfers can be considered as a part of redistributive programs at the regional level, but even though regional transfers can plausibly

---

8. See Oates (1972) and Gordon (1983).

9. See, for instance, Martinez-Vazquez (2001). The measurement of these effects is complicated; education and health expenditures do not directly affect personal income because no cash transfers are provided to individuals. Although the effect of transfers in cash on income distribution can be measured via Gini coefficients computed on a disposable income basis, in the case of public expenditures the pro-poor effect must be measured through benefit incidence analysis. Any potentially measurable income effects only show up in future readings of the Gini measures.

be used to address income inequalities among individuals, they are not necessarily meant to have this explicit objective. In particular, equalization transfers (usually constructed to support those subnational governments with lower fiscal capacity or larger expenditure needs) might have, from a benefit incidence point of view, a positive redistributive effect. This effect, however, cannot be taken for granted; it requires that subnational governments receiving larger per capita equalization transfers are also those with poorer populations.

An often forgotten dimension of fiscal decentralization, and one with potential effects on income distribution, is public employment. Alesina, Danninger, and Rostagno (2001) show how public employment is used as a redistributive device in Italy. Given that the cost of living is lower and the private sector is comparatively less attractive in the South, the government implicitly makes the North subsidize the South by offering very similar nominal wages in both places and by allowing for more public employment in the South. The choice of this redistributive mechanism might be related, as proposed by the authors, to the lower visibility and political costs associated with public employment vis-à-vis direct transfers. A similar explanation is suggested by Alesina, Baqir, and Easterly (2000), who, after controlling for economic and demographic factors explaining public employment, observe a positive correlation between income inequalities and public employment in U.S. cities. In this context, fiscal decentralization could not only facilitate the use of public employment for redistributive purposes, but it could also determine the actual focus of the policies. For example, Marqués and Rosselló (2004) find evidence suggesting that the central government in Spain offers more jobs in those regions where ruling authorities come from the same party than in regions where authorities belong to different parties.

The economic literature has also explored the effects of fiscal decentralization on a variety of macroeconomic outcomes, such as economic growth, macroeconomic stability, the size of government, and public expenditure composition. It is clear that these macroeconomic variables can help determine the distribution of income, and we may need to consider them as alternative channels through which fiscal decentralization might alter income distribution.[10]

Oates (1993, 240) has suggested that his decentralization theorem (Oates 1972), which identifies the static benefits arising from tailoring local public services to local preferences, "should also have some validity in a dynamic setting of economic growth." Oates argues that if policies regarding infrastructure and human capital are formulated to take into account regional or local conditions, they "are likely to be more effective in encouraging economic development than centrally determined policies that ignore these geographical differences." If de-

---

10. Martinez-Vazquez and Sepulveda (2007) distinguish between direct and indirect effects of fiscal decentralization on income distribution and classify these alternative channels as indirect.

centralization leads to dynamic gains in *producer* efficiency, there will be an expansion in the production frontier of the economy. In line with this hypothesis, several empirical studies have analyzed the effect of fiscal decentralization on growth,[11] but the results are rather mixed and seem to depend on the stage of development of the countries.[12] In addition, Martinez-Vazquez and McNab (2003) suggest that the causal relationship between fiscal decentralization and growth might not be linear and that there could plausibly be an optimal level of decentralization after which more devolution of fiscal authority has a negative effect on economic development. Overall, the existence of a causal relationship between decentralization and economic growth—and therefore the effect of decentralization on inequality via this channel—has not yet been clearly established. In any case, the potential effect remains significant because it is well known that economic growth can improve income distribution, especially if it is accompanied by a greater demand for unskilled workers and higher relative wages.

The evidence on the effect of fiscal decentralization on macroeconomic stability is even more limited.[13] In a recent study, Martinez-Vazquez and McNab (2006), using a panel data set for developed and developing countries, find that fiscal decentralization is associated with lower rates of inflation for developed countries. On the other hand, Treisman (2000) and Rodden and Wibbels (2002) find no clear relationship between decentralization and the level of inflation.

The size of the government may also affect income distribution. Clearly, public sectors that are relatively small may have less capacity to implement progressive taxation or sizable welfare programs. Public finance theory offers two opposing hypotheses regarding the relationship between fiscal (revenue) decentralization and size of government. On one hand, the Leviathan hypothesis (Brennan and Buchanan 1980) assumes that government officials are self-interested and seek to maximize their own power, represented by the size of the budget under their control. Although their actions would therefore pursue a nonoptimal increase of expenditures, interjurisdictional tax competition arising in the context of fiscal federalism would provide a binding constraint to the

---

11. Two recent surveys are found in Martinez-Vazquez and McNab (2003) and Breuss and Eller (2004).

12. For example, Davoodi and Zou (1998) find a negative relationship in developing countries, whereas a more recent study by Akai and Sakata (2002) finds a significant positive relationship across states in the United States.

13. The classical view (Musgrave 1959) is that macroeconomic policy should be exclusively the responsibility of the central government. Several recent papers, however, have argued that devolving at least some measure of macroeconomic policy to subnational governments can promote, not hinder, macroeconomic stability (Gramlich 1993; Rodden and Wibbels 2002; Shah 1999). Others have argued that fiscal decentralization may aggravate macroeconomic instability (Rodden 2002; Rodden, Eskeland, and Litvack 2003).

inefficient increase in government size. On the other hand, even when policy makers are assumed to be benevolent welfare maximizers, tax competition might impose downward pressure over the revenue collections and the size of government, leading to underprovision of public services. Feld, Kirchgässner, and Schaltegger (2003) reviewed the empirical literature on the effect of decentralization on the size of government and report generally mixed results.[14]

The composition of public expenditures, especially the presence of welfare programs in the government budget and social spending on public education and health, can play a crucial role in determining the distribution of income, whereas other nonredistributive government functions might still induce a change in the available funds for welfare programs. Further, government budgets more oriented to roads and other forms of public infrastructure may have a more equalizing effect on income distribution than budgets more oriented to defense and public-order expenditures.

Another source of potential effects is given by the dynamics in regional inequalities, although we know very little about the effects of decentralization on regional economic disparities. One possible conjecture is that the state of regional development within the country may be less homogeneous under decentralized systems than under centralized systems; beyond some anecdotal evidence, however, it remains a scantly researched question. On the other hand, there has been considerable research on the topic of regional convergence. The relevance of the literature for this analysis is that the distribution of personal income might be expected to improve at the national level if regions tend to converge in terms of per capita GRP. Barro and Sala-i-Martin (1991) have found strong statistical evidence of regional convergence both in the United States and in a group of seven European countries, but they have also found that the rate of convergence is very low, around 2 percent per year. Further, they found that migration explains only a marginal fraction of the convergence rate.[15] Their results are fairly typical of the empirical literature on regional convergence; empirical studies commonly find that some sort of convergence tends to take place, but the rate of convergence is very slow.

The theoretical work in this area identifies several sources of convergence (de la Fuente 2002). First, a necessary condition for convergence is the presence of diminishing returns to scale in the different forms of capital. Second, the rates of technological progress and the reallocation of factors from sectors with low

---

14. In a recent paper, Fiva (2006), using new OECD data based on Stegarescu (2005) classifying subnational taxes according to their degree of autonomy, finds that revenue decentralization reduces the size of the public sector. In addition, Fiva finds that the traditional measures of expenditure decentralization are positively related to government size. We expand the discussion of the OECD data later.

15. The results are referred to as convergence, which accounts for the tendency of poor regions to grow more quickly (or more slowly, if they diverge) than rich regions.

productivity to others with higher productivity determine the existence of con-vergence and its velocity. To our knowledge, there is no study to date on how these sources of convergence may interact, if at all, with fiscal decentralization.

Finally, marked inequalities in the distribution of land are typically asso-ciated with inequality in the distribution of income, especially in the case of developing countries with large rural populations. Land reforms benefiting the poor by the redistribution of property or land use rights have been proposed as a solution to this problem, but a great deal of controversy regarding how to implement them still clouds the debate. Although some international agencies, including the World Bank, advocate for less government intervention in land markets,[16] some notable experiences in state-led land reforms show that some government interventions may be beneficial (Borras and McKinley 2006). Un-fortunately, again there is not much research on how land reform may operate differently, if at all, in decentralized systems of governance. The expected gain in accountability associated with decentralization may not happen; instead, local/elite capture and empowerment of landlords, who would be little interested in redistributing land or income, may take place. In part due to these reasons, Sauer (2006, 179) argues in the context of the Brazilian land reform that "rather than a solution (through greater efficiency and agility), therefore, decentraliza-tion can actually make land reform actions unfeasible." A similar conclusion is reached by Borras (2003), who examines market-led land reforms in Brazil, Colombia, and South Africa and finds no empirical support for the assumption that decentralization could make a contribution to the process via an increase in accountability and transparency.

As a partial conclusion, it seems extremely difficult, and likely incorrect, to allege a priori that fiscal decentralization per se has any predictable effect on income distribution. There are too many dimensions and channels by which fis-cal decentralization may improve or worsen the distribution of income; the net effect is largely an empirical question.

Challenges in Determining the Empirical Effects

We next discuss some of the difficulties associated with estimating the actual effect of fiscal decentralization on income distribution. The definition of the relevant variables and the availability and consistency of the data are the most significant sources of concern, so they will be addressed briefly below. We then review the empirical literature on the determinants of income distribution. If we are interested in detecting what possible role fiscal decentralization may have on income distribution, we need to be aware of and control for all other

---

16. See Deininger and Binswanger (1999) for a review of the World Bank's doctrine on land policy reform.

determinants of income distribution that have been identified in the previous literature. Finally, we explore the relationship between fiscal decentralization and income inequality. In reality, being able to establish a relationship between decentralization and income distribution poses several complex econometric problems that go beyond the scope and the space available here. The econometric estimation of the effect of fiscal decentralization on income distribution is carried out in a separate paper (Martinez-Vazquez and Sepulveda 2007).

VARIABLE DEFINITION AND MEASUREMENT PROBLEMS

The distribution of income can be conceptualized in several ways. A common problem with the available data is the lack of consistency and quality of the indexes. Relevant decisions are whether to use individual or household data and, within those categories, whether to use data on income or on expenditures. If income is chosen, a further choice needs to be made about whether to use gross (or market) income or disposable income.[17] In those cases in which tax policy affects the distribution of income, the disposable measure of inequality should be lower when the overall tax incidence is progressive.

The most popular measure of income inequality is the Gini coefficient.[18] Deininger and Squire (1996) had assembled a large number of Gini coefficients available in the literature. To ensure the quality of the sample, they imposed three main requirements or selection criteria to include a coefficient into their data set: (1) they must be based on surveys of households or individuals (as opposed to national accounts-based estimations); (2) the coverage of the population must be comprehensive; and (3) the measure of income or expenditure must also be comprehensive. The resultant data set included 682 observations for 108 countries and a varied number of periods for each country. This data set was upgraded and corrected by the United Nations University, World Institute for Development Economics Research, leading to the World Income Inequality Database (WIID, version 2.0a), published in 2005, which includes 4,664 observations for 152 countries.

Table 11.1 provides five-year averages of Gini coefficients based on gross income and disposable income for world regions, derived after selecting among

---

17. For a discussion, see, for instance, Chu, Davoodi, and Gupta (2000) and Deininger and Squire (1996). The United Nations University, World Institute for Development Economics Research (2005) defines disposable income in accordance with the concept recommended by the Camberra Group as total income minus employees' social contributions and taxes on income. Note that cash benefits from the government, including social insurance benefits, universal social assistance, and mean-tested social assistance, are included as a part of total income.

18. The Gini coefficient computes the relative size of the area between the Lorenz curve (plotting the share of population against the income share) and the egalitarian distribution (represented by a 45-degree line providing identical shares for income and population).

Table 11.1
Average Gini Coefficient per Region and Period: Gross and Disposable Income Measures

	1971–1975	n	1976–1980	n	1981–1985	n	1986–1990	n	1991–1995	n	1996–2000	n	Avg.	N
Gini (before-tax income)														
Sub-Saharan Africa	n.a.		n.a.		n.a.		63.0	1	53.7	1	53.6	2	56.0	4
South Asia	32.9	2	39.9	2	40.8	2	46.0	1	43.3	1	51.5	1	40.9	9
Europe and Central Asia	n.a.		22.6	2	21.3	2	22.9	6	38.8	13	36.4	14	33.6	37
East Asia and Pacific	45.1	1	51.0	1	45.4	3	47.1	3	46.3	4	46.5	4	46.5	16
Latin America and Caribbean	n.a.		51.0	2	57.2	2	54.2	1	52.7	3	58.0	4	54.1	12
High income: non-OECD	n.a.		n.a.		n.a.		n.a.		45.3	1	n.a.		45.3	1
High income: OECD	36.1	10	33.6	9	36.1	9	37.4	12	38.5	12	37.5	12	36.6	62
Total	36.3	13	36.3	16	37.5	16	38.4	21	42.0	26	40.9	38	39.3	141
Gini (after-tax income)														
Sub-Saharan Africa	n.a.		n.a.		n.a.		52.3	1	48.5	1	n.a.		50.4	2
South Asia	n.a.		n.a.		n.a.		n.a.		n.a.		n.a.		–	
Europe and Central Asia	n.a.		23.6	2	23.1	2	23.0	5	29.9	12	32.0	13	28.9	34
East Asia and Pacific	n.a.		n.a.		n.a.		26.1	1	27.2	1	33.0	1	28.8	3
Latin America and Caribbean	55.7	1	45.4	3	46.2	3	50.4	5	50.2	5	51.6	9	50.0	30
High income: non-OECD	n.a.		36.3	1	n.a.		34.8	1	33.8	1	36.9	1	35.5	4
High income: OECD	33.0	11	30.1	14	28.2	14	29.4	17	31.4	17	31.3	22	30.5	102
Total	34.9	12	32.1	20	30.3	20	32.7	21	35.0	30	35.6	46	33.9	175
Difference														
Sub-Saharan Africa	–		–		–		10.7		5.2		–		5.6	
South Asia	–		–		–		–		–		–		–	
Europe and Central Asia	–		-1.0		-1.7		-0.1		8.9		4.4		4.6	
East Asia and Pacific	–		–		–		21.0		19.1		13.5		17.8	
Latin America and Caribbean	–		5.6		11.1		3.8		2.5		6.3		4.1	
High income: non-OECD	–		–		–		–		11.5		–		9.8	
High income: OECD	3.1		3.5		7.9		7.9		7.1		6.2		6.0	
Total	1.4		4.2		7.2		5.7		7.0		5.3		5.4	

Notes: n: number of observations; N: total; n.a.: not available.
Source: Based on UNU/WIDER, WIID-2.0a.

the available high-quality Gini coefficients.[19] The sample contains 226 observations for 60 countries between 1971 and 2000, from which 48 countries have gross income measures of the Gini coefficients and a different set of 48 countries have disposable income measures of the Gini coefficients. The number of observations (countries) used in the computation of regional averages, displayed under the column labeled *n* in the table, provides an indication of how representative the regional averages are. The difference between the two measures (also in table 11.1) provides an indication of how effective, on average, tax and expenditure policies from the central government are in reducing income inequalities. Unfortunately, there is a small number of observations for which the two measures of the Gini coefficient are available. We would also expect the effect of decentralization policy on income distribution to be more fully captured in Gini coefficients based on disposable income. Some indirect effects of fiscal decentralization through economic growth, macroeconomic stability, and so on, however, should also be present in Gini measures based on gross income.

The regional distribution of Gini coefficients in table 11.1 suggests at least three general observations. First, clear regional patterns can be seen. These regularities are widely recognized in the past empirical literature on cross-country comparisons of income distribution. In particular, econometric analyses usually control for two world regions: (1) sub-Saharan Africa; and (2) Latin America and the Caribbean. Second, significant differences exist between the gross and disposable measures of the Gini coefficient for most of the regions. Third, in terms of both countries and income definitions, the patterns for data availability are quite uneven.

The concept and measurement of fiscal decentralization impose similar challenges to the empirical analysis. The literature about the determinants and effects of decentralization has traditionally used the share of subnational expenditures (or revenues) over consolidated public expenditures as a proxy for the degree of fiscal decentralization. This share is usually computed using Government Finance Statistics (GFS) data from the International Monetary Fund. These data have the serious limitation that they provide no reliable information on the actual level of autonomy truly enjoyed by subnational governments either on the expenditure side or the revenue side of the budget. Unfortunately, case studies

---

19. All the coefficients based on an ambiguous definition of income, and those given a quality rating of 3 and 4 (unreliable) in the data set, were eliminated. Gini coefficients based on expenditures are more common among developing countries and are expected to be lower than those based on income (see Deininger and Squire 1996). Because the final data set includes few expenditure-based observations, we prefer to avoid any possible noise by simply eliminating them. After averaging observations for the same country and year, the remaining data consist of 846 Gini coefficients based on gross income and 1,231 on disposable income. Due to averaging, the time period chosen, eliminating countries with only one Gini coefficient, and eliminating those countries for which no measures of fiscal decentralization are available, the sample was reduced to 141 observations based on gross income and 175 based on disposable income.

clearly indicate that the relationship between subnational expenditure (or revenue) shares in the consolidated budget is not necessarily monotonic with the level of autonomy actually enjoyed by subnational governments. Even though widespread agreement exists about the limitations associated with this proxy, most of the empirical findings currently accepted as valid in the empirical literature are based on these imperfect measures of fiscal decentralization.

Several efforts have been made to overcome these problems. For example, the Organisation for Economic Co-operation and Development (OECD 1999) offered a new classification of subnational tax revenues according to the level of autonomy and computed the values corresponding to each category for 19 countries in 1995.[20] This database has been expanded by Stegarescu (2005). Based on the OECD's classification of subnational tax revenues and using annual data reported by the OECD's Revenue Statistics, Stegarescu extends the database to include 23 OECD countries for the years 1965 to 2000. He also proposes alternative measures of tax autonomy, tax decentralization, and revenue decentralization.[21] This approach to measuring fiscal decentralization can lead to significantly different results. For example, Stegarescu shows that Austria and Germany have very low levels of effective tax autonomy and decentralization, a result that differs considerably from the one obtained by using GFS data on subnational revenue shares.

Unfortunately, the data required to compute the alternative measures of fiscal decentralization for a large number of countries are still not available. The study of the effect of fiscal decentralization on income distribution will have to be based on the imperfect but conventional measure of (expenditure) decentralization (the share of subnational expenditures over total public expenditures); thus, the results may still be subject to important biases. Some recent research shows that these biases can be quite significant. For example, Ebel and Yilmaz

---

20. The tax sources are ranked, decreasingly, from the highest degree of subnational control over revenues to the point where no discretion is allowed. Level (a) considers revenues for which the subnational government can set both the tax rates and the tax bases. In level (b), only the tax rate can be set, whereas in level (c), only the tax base can be set. Level (d) consists of tax-shared revenues. For this last category, four sublevels are considered. In the first two, sublevels (d1) and (d2), the subnational governments can play a part in the definition of the procedures, whereas in the second two, sublevels (d3) and (d4), they have no discretion at all. Finally, level (e) encompasses other taxes where the central government determines both tax rate and tax base. The obvious advantage of this classification is that it allows us to estimate the degree of tax autonomy of subnational governments easily by computing the share of "own" tax revenues on total revenues. Further, the approach is flexible because the degree of autonomy can be manipulated by including or excluding subsequent categories.

21. In each case, the preferred measures consider those tax revenues where the subnational governments have discretion setting both the rate and the base of the tax source (category a) or at least one of them (categories b and c). Although tax autonomy is defined as the share of "own" tax revenues over total subnational tax revenues, tax (or revenue) decentralization is defined as the share of the same "own" tax revenues over consolidated government tax revenues.

(2003) have used the new OECD data on "autonomous" revenues as a proxy for fiscal decentralization to revisit and amend several important findings in the previous empirical literature on fiscal decentralization.[22]

DETERMINANTS OF INCOME DISTRIBUTION

The conventional wisdom regarding the sources of income inequalities identifies the increase in demand for unskilled workers as one of the most important factors explaining improvements in income distribution (Atkinson 2000). In recent years, however, several authors have highlighted the importance of institutional and social factors, formerly ignored in empirical studies, as determinants of income distribution. For example, Atkinson (1997) emphasizes the role of institutional determinants of wages and employment and of macroeconomic variables such as the interest rate and the income share of the factors of production in explaining recent trends of income inequalities among developed countries.[23] Similarly, Tanzi (2000) also stresses the role of social norms and institutions in determining the distribution of income, including labor contract legislation, traditional rental contracts, norms about marriages, rules about inheritance, and the existence of positional rents or "social capital." This new perspective stresses the importance of policies generating and redistributing human capital as having a large significant effect on income distribution.

Democracy can be seen as a part of the institutional framework that enables the needs and demands of the population to be heard and taken into account by the government. The effects of democracy on income inequalities are still unclear. On one hand, a stronger political representation or a better organization of the poor (e.g., through unions) could allow for more active and systematic redistributive policies and so result in a reduction of income inequalities; on the other hand, a democratic society does not necessarily represent the interests of all constituents equally. Thus, plausibly, a democratic society may be less able to address income inequalities than an authoritative system.[24] The empirical evidence so far appears to be divided. It is therefore too early to claim that democracy re-

---

22. For example, Ebel and Yilmaz challenge de Mello's (2000) result that decentralization increases the ratio of fiscal deficit to GDP, Davoodi and Zou's (1998) result regarding the negative effect of fiscal decentralization on growth, and Oates's (1985) result about the positive effect of decentralization on government size.

23. These determinants are presented as alternative explanations for the observed increase of income inequality between the late 1970s and early 1990s in a group of developed countries, including the United Kingdom, France, Germany, Italy, Japan, and the United States. That the real rate of return has increased explains, in part, why the share of capital income has also gone up during the period. Therefore, it explains how the owners of capital, the nonpoor, have benefited in relative terms.

24. For a review of alternative hypotheses about the effect of democracy on income distribution, see Sirowy and Inkeles (1990).

duces income inequality.[25] In any case, some authors have pointed out that, given the clear correlation between development and democracy, it may be difficult, if not impossible, to separate the effects of both variables on income inequality.[26]

Among other institutional determinants, two studies have partially addressed the effect of fiscal decentralization on income inequalities. Durham (1999) argues that econometric studies about income distribution typically suffer from specification bias because they do not control for a complete array of relevant institutional factors such as political regime, left government partisanship, unionization of labor markets, and fiscal decentralization. Beramendi (2003) follows a similar strategy to Durham's but stresses the potentially endogenous relationship between income inequalities and fiscal decentralization. Several other empirical studies analyze the effects of other institutional variables on income distribution. For example, Chu, Davoodi, and Gupta (2000) find a significant but small negative effect of the ratio of direct to indirect taxes on income inequality, and Gupta, Davoodi, and Alonso-Terme (1998) find that corruption increases income inequalities.

The empirical literature has put special attention on the mutual dependence of economic growth and income distribution. In earlier years, it was thought that causality ran exclusively from economic growth to income distribution. This relationship has been described—with considerable success—by the Kuznets (1955) hypothesis, which states that growth initially results in more unequal distributions of income but that once the benefits of development are available to a larger share of the population, the inequalities tend to diminish, and growth leads to a more equal distribution of income. The intuition is simple and is based on income distribution changes being due to the mobility of workers seeking higher compensations. In early stages of development, wealth is concentrated in a small group of people, and those who manage to increase their personal income become part of the still small high-income group,[27] augmenting the relative concentration of income and thus the overall level of inequality. Once development has spread (because, for example, a higher labor demand leads to increases in wage rates) and the poor represent a smaller share of the population, additional shifts of individuals toward the higher income groups tend to reduce overall inequality. A distinctive implication of the Kuznets hypothesis is that there is a level of development after which income distribution tends to become

---

25. Sirowy and Inkeles (1990) survey a dozen papers, from which seven offer support to a negative effect of democracy on inequality and five provide findings for a null or positive effect. More recently, Barro (2000) reports a negative but insignificant coefficient, and Reuveni and Li (2003) find a negative and significant effect of democracy on income inequality.

26. See Sirowy and Inkeles (1990), Perotti (1996), and Durham (1999).

27. Kuznets explains this trend by describing the shift from the agricultural sector to the non-agricultural sector, stressing the importance of industrialization and urbanization in economic development.

Figure 11.1
Log of per Capita GDP and Gini Coefficient: The Kuznets Curve Under the Gross and
Disposable Income Measures of Inequality

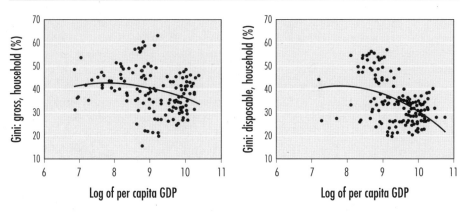

more equal. Empirical evidence has provided some support for this hypothesis, and the Kuznets curve has even been referred to as an empirical regularity (Barro 2000), but still there is no consensus about its validity.[28] In figure 11.1, two scatter plots show the relationship between the (logarithm of) per capita gross domestic product (GDP) and the Gini coefficient, one considering only gross income measures and the other only disposable income measures.[29] In both cases, the Kuznets hypothesis seems to be partially supported by the available data.

Population growth might also affect income inequalities by reducing the relative average income of those demographic groups growing faster, usually the poor.[30] In the context of intercountry inequalities, Firebaugh (1999) explains

---

28. In addition to Barro (2000), recent evidence can also be found, for instance, in Thornton (2001). Deininger and Squire (1998), however, find no support. Vanhoudt (2000) supports the Kuznets hypothesis after controlling for growth fundamentals such as the investment share in human, physical, and knowledge capital. Vanhoudt suggests that these variables help improve the measure of the level of development provided by the per capita GDP. A review of the historical importance of the Kuznets hypothesis in social sciences is provided by Moran (2005).

29. The per capita GDP figures were obtained from the Penn World Table, PWT6.2, Heston, Summers, and Aten (2006).

30. This point is also significant for international comparisons because developing countries usually have much faster rates of population growth than developed countries. According to our data (using the 60 countries in the data set), population in developed countries grew at an average rate of 0.70 percent per year, whereas in developing countries the average rate was 1.30 percent. Moreover, excluding from the developing group the countries from Europe and Central Asia, the average growth rate for developing countries reached 1.96 percent.

the positive relationship between population growth and the age dependency ratio, which measures the relationship between dependents over working-age population. If population growth is concentrated in low-income groups, a higher age-dependency ratio can be associated with increased inequalities. Similarly, rates of population growth might be negatively related with the proportion of population over 65 years old;[31] this population has, on average, lower but less unequal income than the working population. Thus, a higher proportion of retirees will likely be associated with lower income inequalities.

The urban versus rural distribution of the population will also tend to affect income distribution because per capita income within urban areas is generally higher and usually its distribution is more unequal than in rural areas. Urban inequalities could plausibly be either lower or higher than urban/rural inequalities, however, so the sign of the effect of urbanization on income distribution is uncertain. According to Kuznets (1955), though, economic development is associated with higher urbanization,[32] so inequalities would likely increase when urbanization (and development) rates are low and rising, and they would be reduced in more advanced stages of urbanization due to the overall rise in average income.[33]

Several studies have shown a negative, and usually significant, relationship between education, measured as enrollment rates or years of schooling, and income inequalities.[34] Given that educational attainment is related to income and that low education is highly correlated with poverty, we should expect to find less inequality in societies with high levels of education (Tanzi 2000). In addition, a higher level of human capital also means that the share of labor income in the total tends to be higher and that labor income tends to be more equally distributed than capital income. The link between the increasing share of the labor share in national income and the reduction of inequalities has been stressed by Atkinson (1997, 2000) and Tanzi (2000).

Other relevant variables discussed in the literature are openness to trade and inflation. One approach to predict the effects of trade openness on income distribution is given by the Stolper–Samuelson theorem, according to which the

---

31. Population over 65 years is also correlated with the fertility rate. Perotti (1996) explains the link between these two variables in the context of income distribution.

32. Indeed, in our sample, the correlation coefficient between the log of per capita GDP and urban population is 0.756.

33. See also Perotti (1996).

34. Chu, Davoodi, and Gupta (2000) control for secondary enrollment rates and find negative effects on income inequality, but with varying degrees of significance. Barro (2000) finds that primary schooling significantly reduces inequalities, secondary schooling is not significant, and higher education significantly increases inequalities.

abundant factor in the economy, or the one defining the comparative advantages of a country, is the main beneficiary of trade liberalization. Because unskilled labor is relatively scarcer in developed countries and more abundant in developing countries, income inequalities will be expected to increase in the first group of countries and to decrease in the second group. A second view of the effect of openness on income distribution is that trade liberalization mostly benefits the rich because they are better able to take advantage of the new opportunities offered by globalization. The empirical evidence is mixed, and both predictions have recently received support.[35]

Inflation leads to a transfer from those with higher propensity to consume, or less ability to save, to those who are able and willing to substitute future for present consumption. In such a context, devaluations of the exchange rate as well as high market premiums that are reflected in higher price levels would be associated with increasing income inequalities (Bahmani-Oskooee, Goswami, and Mebratu 2006). A parallel argument applies to the real interest rate, which can be interpreted as a cost for net borrowers and a benefit for net lenders. Note that the effect of openness to trade and inflation, however, would mostly be reflected in Gini coefficients measured in terms of consumption and would have less visible effects on Gini measures based on gross or disposable income.

EXPLORING THE RELATION BETWEEN FISCAL DECENTRALIZATION AND INCOME DISTRIBUTION

Although the literature addressing the determinants of income distribution is abundant, it is still unclear which is the proper set of factors determining income inequalities. The interest here is in what additional role fiscal decentralization may play in income distribution. Therefore, to identify the role of fiscal decentralization properly, it is important to control for the effect other variables (as discussed above) may have on income inequalities. At the same time, however, the effect of fiscal decentralization is likely to be influenced by two other variables: the level of per capita GDP and the size of the government. First, the level of development is a key factor explaining market outcomes in the labor markets, and it is also related to the strength and quality of institutions, the preferences for decentralization, and the capability of the government to pursue redistributive policies. Second, the size of the public sector, measured as the share of government on real GDP per capita, provides a reference of the relative importance of expenditure decentralization in the context of the national economy and thus

---

35. Barro (2000) finds a positive and significant effect of trade openness on income inequality, which seems more pronounced in poor countries. Reuveni and Li (2003) find a negative and significant effect.

its actual potential to reduce income inequalities.[36] A high level of expenditure decentralization would not mean much if the government has a minor presence in the economy, whereas relatively low expenditure decentralization would still have a great potential to influence income distribution if the government is an important actor in the economy.

Figure 11.2 plots the trends observed in the relationships between decentralization and the disposable income measure of the Gini coefficient for four observation subsamples. The data used in this case correspond to the same observations of disposable income measures of Gini coefficients used in table 11.1 and figure 11.1, which includes 175 observations for 48 countries. For the purposes of figure 11.2, the data are ordered separately by the level of GDP and the size of government;[37] then, in each case, the data are separated into two subsamples such that we distinguish (1) the observations with low per capita GDP from those with high per capita GDP (plots 1a and 1b); and (2) the observations with a small government size from those with a big government (plots 2a and 2b).[38]

The relationship between expenditure decentralization and income distribution appears to vary quite significantly when the data observations are divided according to "low" and "high" per capita GDP, where low is defined as those values under the median and high as the values above the median. For the subsample of observations under the median per capita GDP, increasing expenditure decentralization appears to be associated with lower inequalities. In contrast, expenditure decentralization seems to be uncorrelated to the Gini coefficient for those observations with a per capita GDP over the sample median.

When the data are separated according to the size of government, a higher degree of expenditure decentralization also seems associated with lower income inequalities. Plots 2a and 2b of figure 11.2, however, show that for a given level of expenditure decentralization the average income inequalities are lower for

36. The government share of real GDP per capita can be measured as the value of final goods and services purchased by the government, excluding the funds allocated among social security and welfare recipients, which might be excluded from an econometric analysis of the effects of fiscal decentralization on income distribution for two reasons. First, social spending will likely depend on the distribution of income; thus, the size of government would become endogenous, and the estimation procedures would be unnecessarily complicated. Second, the effect of fiscal decentralization on income distribution may plausibly be channeled through social spending; thus, an explicit consideration of these funds might underestimate the true effects that fiscal decentralization has on income inequality.

37. The expenditure decentralization data were obtained from Government Finance Statistics (IMF), and the data on the government share in GDP were obtained from the Penn World Table, PWT6.2. See Heston, Summers, and Aten (2006).

38. The median values correspond to a per capita GDP of US$15,465 and a government share of 18.5 percent.

Figure 11.2
Expenditure Decentralization and Gini Coefficient Measured by Disposable Income:
Trends Under Subsamples of Observations

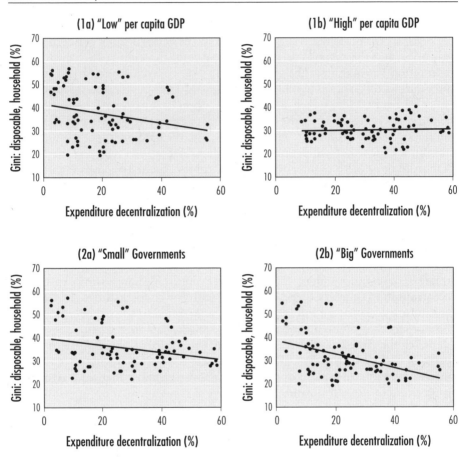

the group of observations with relatively bigger governments (those above the median).

These observations suggest that fiscal decentralization has a positive effect on income distribution and that this effect might vary with certain characteristics of a country, such as the level of development and the total size of the government sector. To test the existence of these relationships, however, we must use the appropriate econometric tools. This task goes beyond the scope and the space available here. In Martinez-Vazquez and Sepulveda (2007), we conduct the econometric analysis of this question. There we find, after controlling for the endogeneity of fiscal decentralization and specific country effects, that decentralization increases income inequalities when government represents a small share of the GDP but that, as the size of government increases, decentralization turns out to have a positive and significant effect on income distribution. Therefore, there seems to be a critical size of the government at which the distributive effects of decentralization turn to positive and thus fiscal decentralization might be expected to improve income distribution. We do not have an immediate clear intuition for why the effect of decentralization is so dependent on the size of government, but it is possible that certain government policies only become effective after they reach some minimum size in terms of GDP. Supporting this interpretation is that the only significant effects of decentralization on income distribution are apparent when a disposable income measure of the Gini coefficient is used in the analysis.

Conclusions

Although fiscal decentralization and income distribution have been the subject of extensive separate attention in the literature, the effects of decentralization on income distribution and how distributional issues may affect the decentralization process have been the subject of little theoretical or empirical research thus far. The goals here are to draw up a conceptual framework for the different ways decentralization relates to income distribution and to set up the bases of an empirical framework by exploring the empirical literature on income distribution.

Even though economic theory has traditionally advised against the involvement of subnational governments in redistribution policies, in practice they do intervene to varying extents. Decentralization, however, is more likely to affect income distribution through the behavioral changes it induces in the location of inputs of production and the indirect effects that decentralization may have in macroeconomic variables and institutions (e.g., growth, the size of government, and the composition of public expenditures), which, in turn, are known to affect income distribution. Moreover, the central government can also use a decentralized structure to channel redistributive policies; remarkable examples are public employment and equalization transfers. Theory, for the most part, offers conflicting implications, however, and so the sign and magnitude of the influence of many factors on income distribution are difficult to predict.

The empirical literature provides some suggestive results about the determinants of income distribution: the level of development, education, population growth, age-dependency ratio, urbanization, democracy and left partisanship, corruption, trade openness, and so on. The empirical findings, however, are not very consistent, and there is still no agreement about the proper set of variables explaining the differences in income distribution across countries. In particular, few studies have explored the potential role fiscal decentralization may play in income distribution. The theoretical links between decentralization and income distribution appear to be quite numerous and complex, and they are often likely to work in opposite directions. Therefore, it is not possible a priori to anticipate what the effect of fiscal decentralization on income distribution may be; the *net* effect is largely an empirical question.

A large panel with data on Gini coefficients and measures of fiscal decentralization from a variety of countries was used in this analysis, and we find, in the aggregate, suggestive evidence of a statistical relationship between those variables. In addition, findings from Martinez-Vazquez and Sepulveda (2007) reveal that, after controlling for the endogeneity of fiscal decentralization and specific country effects, decentralization leads to greater income inequality when government represents a small share of the GDP. As the size of government increases, though, decentralization turns out to have a positive and significant effect on income distribution. Clearly, much more research is needed to arrive at a better understanding of the relationship between decentralization and income distribution.

REFERENCES

Akai, N., and M. Sakata. 2002. Fiscal decentralization contributes to economic growth: Evidence from state-level cross-section data for the United States. *Journal of Urban Economics* 52:93–108.

Alesina, A., R. Baqir, and W. Easterly. 2000. Redistributive public employment. *Journal of Urban Economics* 48:219–241.

Alesina, A., S. Danninger, and M. Rostagno. 2001. Redistribution through public employment: The case of Italy. *IMF Staff Papers* 48(3):447–473.

Arze, J., J. Martinez-Vazquez, and R. McNab. 2005. Decentralization and the composition of public expenditures. International Studies Program Working Paper 05–01. Andrew Young School of Policy Studies, Georgia State University, Atlanta.

Atkinson, A. 1997. Bringing income redistribution in from the cold. *Economic Journal* 107:297–321.

———. 2000. The changing distribution of income: Evidence and explanations. *German Economic Review* 1(1):3–18.

Bahl, R., J. Martinez-Vazquez, and S. Wallace. 2002. State and local choices in fiscal redistribution. *National Tax Journal* 55(4):723–742.

Bahmani-Oskooee, M., G. G. Goswami, and S. Mebratu. 2006. Black market premium and income distribution. *Journal of Developing Areas* 39(2):17–28.

Barro, R. 2000. Inequity and growth in a panel of countries. *Journal of Economic Growth* 5(1):5–32.

Barro, R., and X. Sala-i-Martin. 1991. Convergence across states and regions. *Brookings Papers on Economic Activity* 1:107–182.

Beramendi, P. 2003. Political institutions and income inequality: The case of decentralization. Discussion Paper SP II 2003–09. Berlin: Wissenschaftszentrum.

Borras, S. 2003. Questioning market-led agrarian reform: Experiences from Brazil, Colombia and South Africa. *Journal of Agrarian Change* 3(3):367–394.

Borras, S., and T. McKinley. 2006. The unresolved land reform debate: Beyond state-led or market-led models. Policy Research Brief 2. International Poverty Centre, United Nations Development Programme.

Brennan, G., and J. Buchanan. 1980. *The power to tax: Analytical foundations of a fiscal constitution*. Cambridge: Cambridge University Press.

Breuss, F., and M. Eller. 2004. Fiscal decentralization and economic growth: Is there any link? CESifo DICE Report. *Journal of Institutional Comparisons* 2(1):3–9.

Brown, C., and W. Oates. 1987. Assistance to the poor in a federal system. *Journal of Public Economics* 32:307–330.

Chu, K., H. Davoodi, and D. Gupta. 2000. Income distribution and tax and government social spending policies in developing countries. United Nations University, World Institute for Development Economics Research Working Paper 214.

Davoodi, H., and H. Zou. 1998. Fiscal decentralization and economic growth: Cross-country study. *Journal of Urban Economics* 43(2):244–257.

de la Fuente, A. 2002. Convergence across countries and regions: Theory and empirics. Unitat de Fonaments de l'Analisi Economica and Instituto de Analisis Economico Working Papers 555.02.

de Mello, L. 2000. Fiscal decentralization and intergovernmental fiscal relations: A cross-country analysis. *World Development* 28(2):365–380.

Deininger, K., and H. Binswanger. 1999. The evolution of the World Bank's land policy: Principles, experience, and future challenges. *World Bank Research Observer* 14(2):147–176.

Deininger, K., and L. Squire. 1996. A new data set for measuring income inequality. *World Bank Economic Review* 10:565–592.

———. 1998. New ways of looking at old issues: Inequity and growth. *Journal of Development Economics* 57(2):259–287.

Durham, B. 1999. Econometrics of income distribution: Toward more comprehensive specification of institutional correlates. *Comparative Economic Studies* 41(1):43–74.

Ebel, R., and S. Yilmaz. 2003. On the measurement and impact of fiscal decentralization. In *Public finance in developing and transitional countries: Essays in honor of Richard Bird*, J. Martinez-Vazquez and J. Alm, eds., 101–120. Cheltenham, UK: Edward Elgar.

Feld, L., G. Kirchgässner, and C. Schaltegger. 2003. Decentralized taxation and the size of government: Evidence from Swiss state and local government. CESifo Working Paper 1087. Center for Economic Studies, University of Munich.

Firebaugh, G. 1999. Empirics of world income inequality. *American Journal of Sociology* 104(6):1597–1630.

Fiva, J. 2006. New evidence on the effect of fiscal decentralization on the size and composition of government spending. *FinanzArchiv / Public Finance Analysis* 62(2):250–280.

Gordon, R. 1983. An optimal taxation approach to fiscal federalism. *Quarterly Journal of Economics* 98(4):567–586.

Gramlich, E. 1993. A policymaker's guide to fiscal decentralization. *National Tax Journal* 46(2):229–235.

Gupta, S., H. Davoodi, and R. Alonso-Terme. 1998. Does corruption affect income inequality and poverty? IMF Working Paper No. 76. Washington, DC: International Monetary Fund.

Heston, A., R. Summers, and B. Aten. 2006. Penn World Table Version 6.2. Center for International Comparisons of Production, Income and Prices at the University of Pennsylvania, Philadelphia.

Hodler, R., and K. Schmidheiny. 2006. How decentralization flattens progressive taxes. *FinanzArchiv / Public Finance Analysis* 62(2):281–304.

Kuznets, S. 1955. Economic growth and income inequality. *American Economic Review* 45:1–28.

Marqués, J. M., and J. Rosselló. 2004. Public employment and regional redistribution in Spain. *Hacienda Pública Española / Revista de Economía Pública* 170:59–80.

Martinez-Vazquez, J. 2001. The impact of budgets on the poor: Tax and benefit incidence. International Studies Program Working Paper 01–10. Andrew Young School of Policy Studies, Georgia State University, Atlanta.

Martinez-Vazquez, J., and R. McNab. 2003. Fiscal decentralization and economic growth. *World Development* 31(9):1597–1616.

———. 2006. Fiscal decentralization, macro-stability and growth. *Hacienda Pública Española / Revista de Economía Pública* 179(4):25–49.

Martinez-Vazquez, J., and C. Sepulveda. 2007. Fiscal decentralization and income distribution. International Studies Program Working Paper 22. Andrew Young School of Policy Studies, Georgia State University, Atlanta.

Moran, T. 2005. Kuznets's inverted U-curve hypothesis: The rise, demise, and continued relevance of a socioeconomic law. *Sociological Forum* 20(2):209–244.

Musgrave, R. 1959. *The theory of public finance.* New York: McGraw-Hill.

Oates, W. 1968. The theory of public finance in a federal system. *Canadian Journal of Economics* 1(1):37–54.

———. 1972. *Fiscal federalism.* New York: Harcourt Brace Jovanovich.

———. 1985. Searching for Leviathan: An empirical study. *American Economic Review* 75(4):748–757.

———. 1993. Fiscal decentralization and economic development. *National Tax Journal* 46(2):237–243.

OECD. *See* Organisation for Economic Co-operation and Development.

Organisation for Economic Co-operation and Development. 1999. Taxing powers of state and local government. *Tax Policy Studies* 1. Paris: OECD. Organisation for Economic Co-operation and Development.

Pauly, M. 1973. Income redistribution as a local public good. *Journal of Public Economics* 2:35–58.

Perotti, R. 1996. Growth, income distribution, and democracy: What the data say. *Journal of Economic Growth* 1(2):149–187.

Reuveni, R., and Q. Li. 2003. Economic openness, democracy and income inequality: An empirical analysis. *Comparative Political Studies* 36(5):575–601.

Rodden, J. 2002. The dilemma of fiscal federalism: Grants and fiscal performance around the world. *American Journal of Political Science* 46(3):670–687.

Rodden, J., G. Eskeland, and J. Litvack. 2003. *Fiscal decentralization and the challenge of hard budget constraints.* Cambridge: MIT Press.

Rodden, J., and E. Wibbels. 2002. Beyond the fiction of federalism: Macroeconomic management in multitiered systems. *World Politics* 54(4):494–531.

Rondinelli, D. 1981. Government decentralization in comparative perspective: Theory and practice in developing countries. *International Review of Administrative Science* 47(2):133–145.

Sauer, S. 2006. The World Bank's market-based land reform in Brazil. In *Promised land: Competing visions of agrarian reform,* P. Rosset, R. Patel, and M. Courville, eds., 177–191. Oakland, CA: Food First Books.

Sewell, D. 1996. "The dangers of decentralization" according to Prud'homme: Some further aspects. *World Bank Research Observer* 11(1):143–150.

Shah, A. 1999. Fiscal federalism and macroeconomic governance: For better or for worse. In *Fiscal decentralisation in emerging economies: Governance issues*, K. Fukasaku and L. de Mello, eds., 37–54. Washington, DC: Organisation for Economic Co-operation and Development.

Sirowy, L., and A. Inkeles. 1990. The effects of democracy on economic growth and inequality: A review. *Studies in Comparative International Development* 25(1): 126–157.

Stegarescu, D. 2005. Public sector decentralization: Measurement concepts and recent international trends. *Fiscal Studies* 26(3):301–333.

Stigler, G. 1957. The tenable range of functions of local government. Joint Economic Committee, Federal Expenditure Policy for Economic Growth and Stability, 85th Cong., 1st Sess., 213–219.

Tanzi, V. 2000. Os determinantes fundamentais da desigualdade, pobreza e crescimento. In *Distribuicao de riqueza e crescimento economico*, Estudo NEAD 2, E. Teófilo, ed., 153–172. Brazilia: Ministério do Desenvolvimento Agrário.

Thornton, J. 2001. The Kuznets inverted-U hypothesis: Panel data evidence from 96 countries. *Applied Economics Letters* 8(1):15–16.

Treisman, D. 2000. Decentralization and inflation: Commitment, collective action, or continuity. *American Political Science Review* 94(4):837–857.

United Nations University, World Institute for Development Economics Research. 2005. World Income Inequality Database, ver. 2.0a.

Vanhoudt, P. 2000. An assessment of the macroeconomic determinants of inequality. *Applied Economics* 32(7):877–883.

Wildasin, D. 1994. Income redistribution and migration. *Canadian Journal of Economics* 27(3):637–656.

COMMENTARY
Christine P. W. Wong

Jorge Martinez-Vazquez and Cristian Sepulveda examine the causal linkages—in both directions—between fiscal decentralization and income distribution, a subject, the authors argue, that has received insufficient attention in both the academic and policy arenas. Their endeavor is interesting and ambitious, with clear policy relevance.

Around the world, the trend toward fiscal decentralization is increasing, with reforms to devolve fiscal powers to local governments under way in many countries.[1] At the same time, many of these same countries are intent to stem or reverse the deterioration in income distribution that has occurred since the 1980s. Determining whether these two policy thrusts are producing consistent effects that reinforce each other or opposite and offsetting effects is of great interest.

Of course, extensive academic research and political debate has been done on both fiscal decentralization and income distribution as separate issues. A substantial amount of research has also explored the relationship between fiscal decentralization and income distribution, usually via third variables such as the effect of decentralization on the size and composition of public expenditures, welfare programs, or poverty reduction. Other studies have considered the effect of decentralization on the level and source of government revenues, on tax structure, and on the nature of interjurisdictional competition among local governments, and even others have examined the effect of decentralization on the accountability of local government officials and the potential of local/elite capture as well as the administrative capabilities of subnational governments. Finally, a good deal of work has been done on the effects of fiscal decentralization on a variety of macroeconomic outcomes such as economic growth, macroeconomic stability, the size of government, public expenditure composition, and regional inequalities. Much of this past research is ably surveyed and critiqued here. Indeed, one contribution of Martinez-Vazquez and Sepulveda's study is its systematic survey of the existing literature on the topic, both theoretical and empirical, that takes stock of different approaches attempted and their findings. This survey comprises the first third of the chapter and is a valuable reference source for all students of fiscal decentralization.

Moving beyond these past studies, in chapter 11 Martinez-Vazquez and Sepulveda propose a systematic approach to a conceptual framework for the different ways in which decentralization relates to income distribution as well as how distributional issues may affect the decentralization process itself. Having surveyed the theories, they conclude that "it seems extremely difficult, and likely

---

1. See, for example, World Bank (2005).

incorrect, to allege a priori that fiscal decentralization per se has any predictable effect on income distribution. There are too many dimensions and channels by which fiscal decentralization may improve or worsen the distribution of income" (this volume, p. 285). They then turn to testing the linkages empirically. Using a large dataset with 175 observations for 48 countries between 1971 and 2000, they find that, after controlling for the endogeneity of fiscal decentralization and specific country effects, decentralization seems to lead to greater income inequality when government is small (as a share of the gross domestic product). As the size of government increases, decentralization begins to produce a positive and significant effect on income distribution.

This interesting and potentially important finding could point to some dynamic in the process of fiscal decentralization that dominates all other effects—be they social, institutional, or political—to produce similar outcomes in income distribution. If this finding is robust, it could be the basis for a "Martinez-Sepulveda curve" for fiscal decentralization that is akin to the well-known and widely accepted Kuznets curve in predicting broad outcomes in income distribution!

The problem, though, is that measuring fiscal decentralization is not easy, and using expenditure decentralization as a proxy—the most commonly used measure—presents many difficulties. Although acknowledging the limitations of the data, the authors bravely soldier on, arguing that more nuanced data for international comparisons is difficult to find.

As a complex phenomenon, fiscal decentralization is conducive neither to simple description nor measurement. In this sense, it differs substantially from income or distribution measures used in the Kuznets curve. First, the presumption that expenditure decentralization is matched by, or associated with, revenue decentralization and transfers does not hold uniformly across countries. In fact, World Bank (2005) finds that incoherence among the different components of the fiscal system (expenditure and revenue assignments, transfers and borrowing) tends to be the rule rather than the exception in East Asian countries undergoing fiscal decentralization in recent years. With transfers financing a growing portion of subnational expenditures around the world (Bahl and Wallace 2004), expenditure decentralization may also be increasingly delinked from decision-making autonomy at the subnational level, thus complicating the attempt to identify causal relationships between fiscal decentralization and social outcomes such as income distribution.

These difficulties can be illustrated with the experience of China since the early 1980s, where any correlation between expenditure decentralization and income inequality would surely have been spurious. Figure 11C.1 illustrates the sensitivity of the choice of proxy for measuring fiscal decentralization in China. Under a major reform program introduced in 1994, revenues were dramatically recentralized, while expenditure assignments were left unchanged. In this case, very different scenarios occurred on the expenditure and revenue sides. Moreover, as the reform shifted revenue-sharing from pooled sharing to a partial tax assignment basis, with no equalization transfer to offset fiscal disparities,

Figure 11C.1
How to Choose a Proxy for Fiscal Decentralization: The China Case

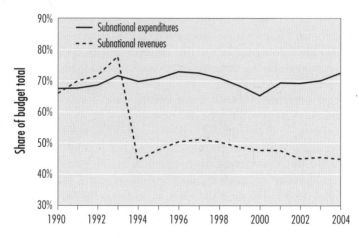

Source: Wong (2007a).

inequalities across local governments grew dramatically in the Chinese fiscal system after 1994. This trend has moderated somewhat since 1998, when the central government began to target transfers at improving equalization (Wong 2007a, 2007b). These changes could not be neatly represented by a single measure, nor, one suspects, could the fiscal decentralization experiences of many other countries.

REFERENCES

Bahl, R., and S. Wallace. 2004. Intergovernmental transfers: The vertical sharing dimension. International Studies Program Working Paper Series. Andrew Young School of Policy Studies, Georgia State University, Atlanta.

Martinez-Vazquez, J., and C. Sepulveda. 2008. Fiscal decentralization and income distribution. In *Fiscal decentralization and land policies*, G. K. Ingram and Y-H. Hong, eds., 277–301. Cambridge, MA: Lincoln Institute of Land Policy.

Wong, C. 2007a. Can the retreat from equality be reversed? An assessment of redistributive fiscal policies from Deng Xiaoping to Wen Jiabao. In *Paying for progress in China: Public finance, human welfare and changing patterns of inequality*, V. Shue and C. Wong, eds., 12–28. London: Routledge.

———. 2007b. Fiscal management for a harmonious society: Assessing the central government's capacity to implement national policies. British Inter-university China Center Working Paper Series 4. http://www.bicc.ac.uk/WorkingPapers/Christine Wong/tabid/431/Default.aspx.

World Bank. 2005. *East Asia decentralizes*. Washington, DC: World Bank.

12

Public and Private School Competition and U.S. Fiscal Federalism

Thomas J. Nechyba

Within the United States and around the world, an increasing focus has been placed on the potential of school competition to improve student outcomes. Such competition can take many shapes and is present in one form or another almost everywhere. The debate is therefore not about whether competition should play a role in primary and secondary education; rather, it is about what form of competition can most effectively achieve particular policy goals. The necessary policy analysis is complicated by such factors as the existence of peer externalities, the role of land markets in "pricing" access to schools, and the many possible ways of financing schools through both public and private means.

The fundamental question common to all debates on school competition revolves around appropriate ways of rationing access to the scarce resource of seats in different schools. In many settings, market prices are relied upon to ration such access, but a pure reliance on prices in education markets may inherently disadvantage children from poorer households and may not appropriately account for social benefits that the price system might ignore. The absence of prices in markets (like those involving most public school systems), however, does not imply the absence of a rationing mechanism itself. Such a mechanism can be explicitly designed or can emerge endogenously in a variety of ways, but it is always there. Understanding the underlying rationing mechanism is key to understanding the effects of different forms of school competition.

In the United States, rationing access to schools takes three different forms. First, access to traditional public schools has typically been rationed through the setting of school district and neighborhood boundaries that assign families in particular residential locations to particular public schools. Such access therefore involves rationing through housing markets. Second, conditional on having chosen a place of residence, families often can choose between the local public school to which they are assigned or a private school located within reasonable commuting distance. Access to private schools, then, largely involves rationing through tuition pricing and admissions policies that may be aimed at creating the "right" peer group. Finally, an increasing number of "choice experiments" within the public school system have emerged recently. In some areas, they have involved the emergence of charter and magnet schools that operate alongside traditional (neighborhood-based) public schools. In other areas, "choice" has been extended to all public schools. Because access to such "choice" schools is not priced, some explicit mechanism determines who is allowed into a choice school whenever such a school has more applicants than seats. Access to these schools is therefore rationed through assignment mechanisms. These mechanisms are typically based on parental preferences that are fed into an algorithm with elements that define priority classes (such as "walk zones" and sibling preferences) and elements that break ties through lotteries.

How do these three rationing mechanisms give rise to different forms of school competition? How do they affect the larger economy in which schools operate? The results referenced in this chapter are drawn from research that has analyzed school choice within a model in which households choose where to live, what school to attend, and how to vote on public school spending. This model provides a useful framework because it permits comparisons of different policies and rationing mechanisms in an environment in which the most salient features of education markets are taken into account—including the important role played by housing and land markets—as well as the role of nonfinancial inputs in education production. In this discussion, the main features of this model, together with some preliminary simulations, are introduced first, followed by a discussion of the effect of two historically dominant rationing mechanisms on residential choices: rationing through housing markets and rationing through tuition and admissions policies. The effect of increased private school competition on public school quality depends critically on the dimensions along which private schools compete, and this subject is discussed next. The term *school quality* here refers to parental perceptions of school quality, which may include, but are far from limited to, the narrow definition of test scores so often employed in the literature. The analysis then turns to the issue of nonresidence-based public school competition, which involves rationing through explicit assignment mechanisms, and compares such public school competition with traditional private school competition. Building on these insights, a natural extension of recent public school choice initiatives is proposed, an extension that offers pathways for private schools to compete within the same framework as new "choice" public schools. Such a system would permit localities to achieve a more appropriate balance between the three different rationing mechanisms that operate in education markets, which becomes even more compelling when more realistic models of school competition (that build on insights from other social sciences) are taken into account.

A Benchmark Framework for Thinking About U.S. School Competition

Two separate literatures suggest that school competition in the United States is shaped by two primary factors: (1) the bundling of household residential and public school choice; and (2) the importance of both financial and nonfinancial inputs into school production.[1] Together, these factors enable the coexistence of good and bad public schools within a system that offers nominally "free" access to all public schools. Without the bundling of housing and schooling, there would be no mechanism to keep public school quality (that is, parental perceptions of school quality, not only test scores) from equalizing as parents choose the best available "free" public school.[2] In the presence of this bundling, however, equilibrium housing prices ration access to housing markets in good school districts and thus price access to public schools in ways that cause lower-income households to "choose" worse public schools. Even in the presence of such rationing through housing markets, though, public school quality could be fully equalized by equalizing school spending if only financial inputs mattered to what parents perceive as school quality. Given the overwhelming evidence that school quality—whether measured by test scores, parental perceptions, or any other metric—is not equalized solely through financial inputs, nonfinancial inputs must play an important role.

---

1. The first literature in public and urban economics, summarized in Epple and Nechyba (2004), begins with Oates (1969) documenting the strong capitalization of school characteristics into housing prices. More recent contributions by Black (1999) and others have refined this approach through the use of regression discontinuity models that document sharp differences in housing prices on different sides of neighborhood school boundaries (for otherwise identical houses). An increasing number of discrete choice models document more directly the importance of public schools and other amenities in residential location decisions (Bayer, McMillan, and Reuben 2005; Epple and Sieg 1999; Nechyba and Strauss 1998). The second literature on education production functions has investigated the extent to which various measurable inputs translate into academic achievement or other student outcomes. Although considerable recent evidence suggests that inputs related to per-pupil spending (such as class size) have some effect on student achievement (Angrist and Lavy 1999; Krueger 1999), this evidence remains subject to controversy (Burtless 1996; Hanushek 2002). Furthermore, increasing attention has focused on nonfinancial inputs such as peer quality, parental monitoring, and nonrandom teacher assignments (Nechyba 2006).

2. In fact, theoretical models of public/private school choice that do not model housing markets typically assume a single quality for all public schools based on public school quality having to equalize in the absence of housing markets that ration such access. See, for instance, Epple and Romano (1998).

These nonfinancial inputs are often lumped together under the label "peer effects." Such effects may indeed arise if peers directly influence one another in classrooms. Nonfinancial inputs, though, can emerge and be correlated with parental income through a number of alternative channels. Higher-income parents may invest more in "home production" of various child characteristics (Gronau 1980), thus freeing schools to focus on producing greater academic achievement. They may play a larger role in monitoring public schools and inducing improved performance by teachers and administrators (McMillan 2000). In addition, given the general sense that children from higher-income families are "easier" to teach, public school systems may reward "good" teachers with assignments in higher-income public schools (Loeb and Page 2001). Nonfinancial inputs that matter (and that may be lumped under the category "peer effects") can therefore include parental inputs and teacher quality. When such inputs are correlated with parental income (as the data suggest they are) and access to public schools is priced through the housing market, good and bad public schools coexist, even if financial inputs are equalized.

The empirical framework in this chapter therefore includes an explicit housing market and a school production process sufficiently rich to incorporate roles for both financial and nonfinancial inputs. A full description of the technical details of the model can be found in a series of previous papers (Nechyba 1997a, 1999, 2000, 2003a, 2003b), but the basic elements are as follows. The model begins with three school districts characterized by overlapping housing quality distributions that are calibrated to the distributions observed in average low-, middle-, and high-income New Jersey school districts in 1990. At this time, the New Jersey school system consisted of largely traditional residence-based public schools in geographically small districts.[3] Each district provides a public school open to any family living in the district, with the level of per-pupil financial inputs in each district determined through voting on local property and state income taxation.[4] The level of nonfinancial inputs in each public school is determined endogenously by the income and child ability characteristics of families that attend

---

3. Several hundred school districts in New Jersey are divided equally into low-, middle-, and high-income districts. The average characteristics of each category of districts are then used in the calibration, with house quality distributions inferred from housing price distributions. The calibration method implies that the distribution of house quality captures both house and nonschool-related neighborhood qualities such as crime rates and environmental conditions.

4. The model can be run for a purely decentralized (property tax financed) system, a purely centralized (state income tax financed) system, or any hybrid system involving local property tax funding supplemented by a state aid formula. Previous theoretical and simulation evidence suggests that local governments in the model will choose local property taxes, whereas state governments use state income taxes (Nechyba 1997b), which matches well to what is generally observed. The benchmark version of the model is calibrated using the New Jersey financing formula.

the school,[5] with families choosing a house and simultaneously either the local public school or an alternative school not linked to residential location. Families differ in their income and peer quality level, but they share the same underlying preferences for housing, consumption, and school quality.[6]

In the initial benchmark models, school quality s for a given school emerges from the combination of financial and nonfinancial inputs. In other words, parents observe both financial and nonfinancial aspects of schools as they determine which schools are better than others. To be more specific,

$$s = x^{(1-\rho)}q^\rho \quad \text{with } 0 \leq \rho \leq 1,$$

where x is the per-pupil spending level in the school, ρ is the weight put on nonfinancial inputs relative to financial inputs in school production, and q is the average peer quality. (In later models, this production function is changed to incorporate other factors.) The structural parameter ρ is then calibrated to yield the empirically observed level of private school attendance in the data.[7] Because the data used to calibrate the model are from 1990, private schools represent the only viable alternative to public schools. In public schools, the level of each of the two input types emerges as described above, with financial inputs resulting from a political process and nonfinancial inputs arising from parental choices of housing and schools. Private schools, on the other hand, are assumed to set tuition rates (equal to per-pupil spending) and minimum "peer quality" standards that survive competitive pressures. Thus, the model assumes for now that private schools are able to compete against "free" public schools by directly controlling nonfinancial inputs through admissions policies, an option not open to public schools, which are legally required to accept all students who reside within the school district.

---

5. A household's peer quality is assumed to result from a Cobb–Douglas aggregation of household income and child ability, and the average peer quality level in the school represents the nonfinancial input level to the school. Parental income and child ability, which, as suggested by the data, are imperfectly correlated, are assumed to play equally strong roles in forming the peer quality of the child. In addition, sensitivity analysis suggests that the results reported here are not qualitatively sensitive to altering the relative role of parental income and child ability in constructing peer quality measures.

6. The model contains 2,500 different household types. Preferences are assumed to take a Cobb–Douglas form, with exponents in the underlying utility function calibrated to yield empirically relevant levels of housing consumption and (majority-rule-determined) school spending.

7. Excessive weighting of financial inputs results in the absence of any private school sector in the model, whereas excessive weighting of nonfinancial inputs results in too large a private school sector. Thus, the level of private school attendance observed in the New Jersey data determines the relative weights of financial and nonfinancial inputs (as captured by ρ).

Table 12.1 reports simulation results using this framework under three different public school financing methods. First, results that mirror the New Jersey financing formula (of 1990) are reported in the initial columns. All variables expressed in dollar or percentage terms are observable in the data, with the housing, production, and preference parameters of the underlying model calibrated to replicate those values.[8] The second and third sets of columns report simulations of the new equilibrium that is predicted by the calibrated model if public funding were changed to be either fully decentralized or fully centralized.

The main message from table 12.1 is that policy decisions over the details of public school financing systems can only be analyzed within the context of the economic environment in which these decisions are implemented. To the extent to which the public system is subject to the two factors introduced above—that is, to the extent to which it rations access through housing markets and is affected by nonfinancial inputs that are correlated with parental income—substantial differences in public school quality emerge under any public financing system, even those that fully equalize financial inputs. Although these simulations suggest that a move away from purely decentralized school financing has reduced inequalities across public schools, it also suggests that average school quality declines under greater centralization, as explored in Nechyba (2003a, 2003b).[9] The underlying economic environment faced by traditional public school systems therefore places severe limits on what can be accomplished through changes in public school financing mechanisms.

To be more precise, changes in public school financing systems can alter the level and distribution of per-pupil spending across public schools, but they have little effect on the spatial segregation of households across districts and thus do not substantially affect the distribution of nonfinancial inputs across schools. As long as housing markets ration access and sort families into public schools, nonfinancial inputs continue to be distributed through essentially the same mechanism. Put differently, if nonfinancial inputs are related to how families select schools under residence-based rationing, public school finance reforms are unlikely to alter the distribution of nonfinancial inputs in any significant way.

---

8. Most of these values come very close to matching the corresponding values in the data. For details, see Nechyba (2003a, 2003b).

9. Under state financing, the median voter in the state determines per-pupil funding. Under local financing, on the other hand, the median voter in each district determines the spending level in that district. If we assume that we can approximate the median voter in each case as the median income household (in the relevant jurisdiction), it is then implied that average per-pupil spending in the state is determined by the *median* income household under state financing and by the *mean* income household under local financing. Although income distributions are skewed to the left, the median income in the state is lower than the mean income, implying a drop in average school spending under centralized financing.

Table 12.1

Baseline Simulation Results

	Decentralized System Plus New Jersey State Formula			Decentralized Local Property Tax			Centralized State Income Tax		
	Low-Income District	Middle-Income District	High-Income District	Low-Income District	Middle-Income District	High-Income District	Low-Income District	Middle-Income District	High-Income District
Per-pupil spending[a]	$6,652	$7,910	$8,621	$5,000	$7,326	$10,215	$7,195	$7,195	$7,195
Peer inputs[b]	0.2684	0.4701	0.6521	0.2613	0.5142	0.6404	0.2826	0.5469	0.6470
School quality[c]	69.96	100.00	126.30	59.47	100.23	132.45	74.72	102.23	110.73
Average spending[a]		$7,753			$7,731			$7,195	
Average quality		99.58			100.42			96.47	
District income[a]	$31,120	$46,216	$65,863	$29,725	$50,262	$63,212	$29,891	$51,309	$62,000
Property values[a]	$117,412	$205,629	$292,484	$123,224	$211,729	$294,825	$118,486	$226,345	$316,308
% private	20%	22.5%	12.5%	30%	20%	10%	22.5%	17.5%	15%

[a]Expressed in 1990 dollars.
[b]Index of peer-quality inputs arises from aggregation of household peer quality normalized to lie between 0 and 1.
[c]School quality index normalized to equal 100 for the middle-income district under the New Jersey formula.

The Effect of Two Forms of Rationing on Local Economies

The simulations reported so far have incorporated two of the three rationing mechanisms discussed earlier: (1) rationing into public schools through housing markets; and (2) rationing into private schools through tuition and admissions policies. A further look at how the combination of these rationing mechanisms affect local urban economies, and with it the distribution of nonfinancial inputs into different schools, is now in order. Understanding these impacts leads to an examination of the third type of rationing that has emerged since the 1990s within some public school systems: rationing school access through explicit assignment mechanisms based on parental preferences.

Table 12.2 presents a series of hypothetical simulation exercises using the same calibrated model used in table 12.1. The table's first row assumes away the existence of public schools, thus removing price distortions from the bundling of housing and schools. Under this simulation, households therefore choose housing

Table 12.2
School Finance, Private Schools, and Residential Segregation

Private Schools Allowed?	Public School Financing	Average District Income			Average District Property Value	
		Low-Income District	High-Income District	Ratio	Low-Income District	High-Income District
Yes	None	$25,700	$67,325	2.62	$158,327	$266,474
No	Local property tax	$17,628	$85,925	4.87	$101,683	$392,402
	State income tax	$19,875	$81,075	4.08	$102,086	$387,549
Yes	Local property tax	$29,725	$63,212	2.13	$123,224	$294,825
	State income tax	$29,891	$62,000	2.07	$118,486	$316,308

independent of schools, with segregation across districts arising solely from the different housing quality distributions in the three districts. The simulation is not meant to be a serious policy proposal; rather, it allows us to establish the levels of income segregation and housing price differences that would exist in the absence of any policy distortions. For instance, the table suggests that the expected average income in the high-income community is 2.62 times the average income in the lowest-income community when households choose housing from existing housing stocks, without considering any bundling of housing with school access.

The next two rows of table 12.2 reverse the experiment by replacing the private school sector with a residence-based public school system, either decentralized and financed through property taxes or centralized and financed through state income taxes. Both types of public school systems dramatically increase the segregation across district boundaries, with the ratio of average income in the high-income district to average income in the low-income district rising by 55 to 85 percent. The bundling of public school access with housing markets thus introduces a significant segregating force into the local economy, depressing housing prices in low-income districts and inflating them in high-income districts.

Finally, the last set of rows in table 12.2 allows the private school market to coexist with the public school system. With the same underlying housing market, the mere introduction of private schools then dramatically decreases the level of residential segregation across school districts because private school attending, relatively higher-income households are not as willing to pay a housing price premium for good public schools in higher-income districts.

Private schools in the model therefore not only enjoy the competitive advantage of being able to shape their nonfinancial inputs through tuition and admissions policies, but they also have an implicit advantage: they can permit households to unbundle their housing decision from their school choice. In a residence-based public school environment where housing prices are depressed in low-income districts (because of bad public schools), the implication is that private school attending households will tend to live in lower-income districts than they would if there were no public school distortions in the housing market. These households also tend to have incomes above the community average and thus raise the average community income. Unbundling school choices from housing choices therefore appears to have a much greater effect on residential location and segregation patterns than does varying the method of public school financing (i.e., central versus local, income tax versus property tax). This unbundling tends to have a desegregating effect within the urban economy, whereas residence-based public school systems by themselves have the opposite effect.

So, for cities that are concerned about the segregation of poor residents within cities from wealthier residents in suburbs, there is a strong incentive to introduce policies that allow parents to unbundle housing and schooling choices. To the extent to which higher-income parents choose suburbs for schools, such unbundling would result in an inflow of higher-income residents into cities. In fact, this point became one of the major arguments in favor of increasing school choice in the 1990s debate over Milwaukee's choice-based reforms.

Public School Quality and Private School Competition

The prediction that private school markets reduce residential housing segregation does not, however, imply that they reduce the variance in nonfinancial inputs across schools. In fact, if private schools compete by selecting among applicants (and thus control their nonfinancial inputs), they will "skim the cream" off the public system, leaving the public system as a whole with fewer high-achieving peers, fewer parents who monitor public schools, and fewer good teachers. Unless there is some counteracting force, average public school quality must fall with an increasingly active private school market. Simulations in Nechyba (1999, 2000, 2003a, 2003b) furthermore suggest that this decline in average public school quality, accompanied by a modest decline in the variance of public school quality, has higher-income districts suffer a greater loss of nonfinancial inputs.[10]

Although a decrease in urban residential income segregation may, in itself, be desirable, few would advocate altering school policy solely to change the residential location patterns in cities, particularly if the effect on public schools would be negative. At this point, however, the model has deliberately excluded any of the potentially positive aspects of increased competition that are cited by school reformers. In particular, no allowance has been made for the possibility that public schools might, all else equal, perform better in a more competitive environment, nor has the model considered the possibility that pedagogy or curriculum could

---

10. In some instances, predicted public school quality actually rises in the poorest district as the private school sector becomes more active because the increase in local tax bases, combined with the decrease in public school attendance within the district, raises per-pupil spending, even though the political constituency for school spending within the district falls with higher private school attendance (Nechyba 1999).

be targeted more effectively if the variance in child abilities within a school narrows.[11] It is useful to consider some simple ways in which such factors could be included in the model and then to return to a final, but more complex, channel through which competition might operate.

The structure of the underlying model permits us to include additional competitive effects and trace their effect through the full general equilibrium model, but it also requires a recalibration of the model so that it will still be able to replicate the data. In our benchmark model thus far, we assumed that the primary competitive advantage private schools have over public schools is that they are able to "cream skim" nonfinancial inputs from public schools. As other competitive advantages for private schools are introduced, the model has to be recalibrated so as to avoid overpredicting private school attendance. For instance, if we assume that private schools are more efficient at translating inputs into school quality, the model would predict more private school attendance than is observed in the data unless we reduce the "cream-skimming" advantage assumed for private schools thus far. So, when a second competitive advantage is introduced, the first has to be reduced in magnitude as the model is recalibrated to match the data. The stronger the second advantage is, the weaker the first has to become. One advantage of using this kind of structural model is that it disciplines the researcher in terms of how strong different potential channels can be and still permit the model to replicate the data under current school finance institutions.

To illustrate the range of possible effects of private school competition on public school quality, two possibilities may be considered: (1) a "resource efficiency" advantage for private schools; and (2) a "pedagogical targeting" advantage. In each case, the assumption of cream skimming on the part of private schools is maintained, but the magnitude of this competitive advantage is reduced to make it approximately equal in magnitude to the second private school advantage that is introduced. In the case of "resource efficiency," it is assumed that private schools operate on the efficient frontier of translating inputs into school quality, whereas public schools operate inefficiently but become increasingly efficient the more private school competition they face. In the case of "pedagogical targeting," it is assumed that, for any average level of nonfinancial inputs within a school, the lower the variance in the peer quality of the households within the school, the greater the quality schools are able to produce.

---

11. Chubb and Moe (1990), for instance, argue that competition reduces rent seeking in the public system, and Hoxby (2000) suggests that competition tends to raise performance and lower costs (though it should be noted that these results are the subject of some controversy [Hoxby 2007; Rothstein 2007]). A considerable literature on peer effects within classroom—and particularly on whether or not a greater variance in abilities within classrooms benefits some children—is still evolving (Nechyba 2006). That literature, particularly within economics, typically takes pedagogy and curriculum as exogenous, however. It also fails to consider whether strategic adjustments in pedagogy and curriculum might be made within competitive environments if the distribution of student characteristics changes.

To be more precise, we assume an underlying school production function

$$s = \phi x^{(1-\rho)} q^{\rho},$$

where, as before, s is school quality, x is per-pupil spending, and q is average "peer quality." Until now, $\phi = 1$ has been implicitly set and ρ was set to provide a sufficiently strong peer effect to allow private schools to compete using their cream-skimming advantage. When "resource efficiency" is introduced, ϕ remains 1 for private schools, but it falls to $(1 - \lambda PUB^2)$ for public schools, where λ is calibrated (conditional on ρ) to replicate the observed levels of private school attendance and PUB is an endogenous variable equal to the fraction of the population attending public school. If ρ remains as in the earlier benchmark case, then $\lambda = 0$. As the cream-skimming advantage falls through a decline in ρ, the value of λ has to increase in magnitude. Under pedagogical targeting, on the other hand, $\phi = (1 - \mu\sigma)$, where σ is the variance in peer quality within the school. In the results reported in table 12.3, ρ is set to half its previous value under both the resource efficiency and the pedagogical targeting scenarios, implying that the cream-skimming effect has been reduced by half.

The strong residential segregation and housing price predictions of public and private school markets (in table 12.2) remain largely unaffected as different

Table 12.3
Private School Competition and Public School Quality

	Voucher Amount[a]	$0	$1,000	$2,500	$4,000	$5,000
				Public School Quality[b]		
Cream Skimming Only	Low-Income District	69.96	68.05	65.82	39.83	[c]
	Middle-Income District	100.00	98.80	89.43	78.93	44.59
	High-Income District	126.30	120.22	112.96	93.19	80.27
Cream Skimming + Pedagogical Targeting	Low-Income District	70.36	76.46	80.55	81.61	76.85
	Middle-Income District	100.00	101.52	104.96	105.99	101.55
	High-Income District	131.05	130.11	129.67	131.74	127.02
Cream Skimming + Competitive Resource Efficiency	Low-Income District	65.72	67.42	69.81	71.08	71.74
	Middle-Income District	100.00	101.83	104.90	107.68	109.75
	High-Income District	124.64	126.96	128.23	131.24	132.59

[a] Expressed in 1990 dollars.
[b] Indexed to be equal to 100 in middle-income districts in the absence of vouchers under the assumption of pure cream skimming by private schools under the 1990 New Jersey financing system.
[c] Public school ceases to exist.

competitive advantages for private schools are introduced and therefore are not reported separately here. Instead, it is useful to focus on the effect of private school competition on public school quality under different assumptions about the nature of private school advantages. One convenient way to do so is to introduce different levels of private school vouchers into the model, assuming decentralized local school funding under the 1990 New Jersey state aid formula.[12]

Table 12.3 reports the effect on an index of public school quality as private school markets become more active through the introduction of different levels of private school vouchers. As in table 12.1, the public school quality index is normalized to be equal to 100 in the middle-income district under the benchmark model in which cream skimming is the primary private school advantage (aside from allowing parents to unbundle their housing and schooling choices). In the first three rows of the table, the decline in public school quality under increased private school competition is illustrated for the case in which private schools compete by removing nonfinancial resources from the public system. Given that the set of such nonfinancial resources is fixed, competition for them, in essence, creates a "tragedy of the commons," with private schools using their advantage to remove high-quality resources from the common pool that would otherwise end up in public schools.[13]

The next two sets of rows in table 12.3 each introduce a different private school advantage while reducing the importance of cream skimming proportionately. In each set of simulations, the cream-skimming advantage of private schools is reduced by half, with pedagogical targeting (in the middle rows) and resource efficiency (in the final rows) making up for this loss. Together, these simulations suggest that it is plausible for private school competition to increase public school quality to the extent to which private schools are not competing primarily by shifting nonfinancial resources from the public to the private system (i.e., to the extent to which there are sufficient competitive channels that raise productivity rather than compete for a fixed pool of resources). The positive effect on public school quality from greater private school competition could, of course, become even larger if the "cream-skimming" advantage were reduced further. The main message here is simply that competition can be akin to a zero-sum game when schools

---

12. A "private school voucher" in these simulations is a lump sum amount made available to any family for the purpose of paying for a portion of private school tuition in a private school chosen by that family.

13. When peer quality is interpreted strictly as child ability, the pricing of peer externality within private schools can, under some circumstances, nevertheless be efficiency enhancing (Epple and Romano 1998). Even when it is efficiency enhancing, though, the public school system inevitably must suffer as high-ability peers are attracted to private schools. In the model used here, explicit pricing of peer quality is not permitted; thus, it is assumed that private schools will charge the same tuition to all students, implying that the efficiency-enhancing effect of externality pricing does not emerge.

compete for a common resource pool, but can also be a positive-sum game when schools are forced to compete in more productive ways.[14]

Nonresidence-Based Public School Competition

As mentioned earlier, competition between schools can take many forms, with different forms resulting in different ways students are rationed into schools (and different ways in which nonfinancial resources are rationed with students). A primary reason often offered for not fostering private school competition through public policy is that private schools will divert resources from public schools, thus reducing public school quality. In virtually all simulations of the effect of private school vouchers, such diversion of resources is solely in terms of nonfinancial inputs (as in the cream-skimming simulations above), with per-pupil funding in public schools typically remaining constant or increasing with use of private school vouchers.[15] The primary concern about private school competition then boils down to how such competition rations students (and the nonfinancial inputs that come with them). Thus, advocates for school reform often favor increased public school competition but oppose private school competition because public schools are typically not permitted to explicitly select students, whereas private schools can.

Although public school competition has traditionally taken the form of interdistrict school competition (with rationing through housing markets), a number of new innovations that foster greater competition between public schools, with rationing of students taking place at least partially outside housing markets, have gained favor. Such public schools do not charge tuition, so when a school is oversubscribed, it may use a lottery mechanism to determine who is admitted. Rarely, however, is the rationing mechanism entirely driven by lottery. Rather, the assignment algorithms typically take into account parental preference rankings of schools and define a priority system in which applicants in higher-priority categories are treated preferentially; a lottery can then be used to break ties when necessary.

The most common priority categories are whether the household lives within the "walk zone" of the school and whether a sibling is already in the school. The greater the geographic area around the school that is included in the walk zone and the greater preference given to those living within that zone, the more the public school represents a traditional residence-based public school. Likewise,

---

14. The concern about schools competing for nonfinancial resources or peer quality is not limited to private school competition. Fiske and Ladd (2000), for instance, document how such competition can emerge in primarily public school choice systems when inadequate attention is paid to this possibility.

15. The change in public school quality in the first set of cream-skimming simulations of table 12.3, for instance, is almost entirely due to a drop in nonfinancial inputs in public schools. One exception is that per-pupil funding in low-income districts actually increases with vouchers because they are primarily used in lower-income districts, by households that nevertheless continue to pay taxes for local public schools.

the smaller the defined walk zone and the lower the preference for living within that zone, the more seats in the school are unbundled from residential location choices. Thus, by varying the size of the area included in the walk zone and the degree of preference given to those living within the area, public school competition can result in as little as no rationing through housing markets (when there is no walk zone) and as much as full rationing through housing markets (when the walk zone is defined sufficiently large that all seats are filled with children from within this priority category). Put differently, traditional residence-based public school competition can be partially or fully replaced by nonresidence-based public school competition by altering the role walk zones play in public school assignment processes. The traditional residence-based school system can therefore be thought of as a special case of a more general public school choice system in which walk zones play a role in the assignment mechanism.

An increasing number of cities are choosing public school competition systems in which walk zones play some, but not the only, role in public school assignments and are thus moving away from the "corner solution" of making walk zones the only criterion for school assignments. In such cities, parents are asked to provide preference rankings of public schools. These rankings are then used to fill the seats in public schools, with preference given to children who fall in high-priority categories (e.g., walk zones, sibling preferences). The precise assignment algorithms that derive the allocation of students to schools from parental preference orderings have been studied in some detail by economists. Some algorithms (such as, for instance, those used in Charlotte-Mecklenburg, North Carolina) are such that parents have an incentive to misrepresent their true preferences, and the resulting matches of students to schools is unlikely to be optimal. Others (such as those used in Boston and New York) are deliberately designed to be strategy proof, giving no incentive to parents to "game" the system and ensuring an optimal allocation of students across schools.[16]

Given the multitude of ways in which nonresidence-based systems of public school competition can be designed, it is difficult to find compelling ways to introduce them into our model and produce additional insights. Some general

---

16. Such strategy-proof assignment mechanisms were first suggested and developed by Abdulkadiroglu and Sönmez (2003) and have since replaced less efficient mechanisms in several cities (see Abdulkadiroglu, Pathak, and Roth 2005; Abdulkadiroglu et al. 2005). The inefficient and nonstrategy-proof mechanisms these new mechanisms are replacing tend to fill up the seats in good schools with applicants in high-priority categories. Parents with either low lottery numbers or in lower-priority categories therefore have an incentive to not rank their most preferred school—a school that was likely filled before they had a chance to apply—truthfully. Instead, they may attempt to "game" the system by ranking a second or third school more highly, aiming for a more realistic chance of getting into a good, if not the best, school. Preliminary evidence suggests that higher-income parents were "better" at gaming these systems. Reported preference rankings changed dramatically when new strategy-proof mechanisms were implemented.

conclusions that follow from the earlier-mentioned simulations, however, may be drawn. (1) To the extent to which such public school competition relies heavily on walk zone priorities, it is no different than traditional residence-based public school competition and thus produces all the same capitalization and segregation effects with the accompanying rationing of nonfinancial resources through housing markets; (2) To the extent to which walk zones do not play a prominent role in such public school competition, the system unbundles housing and schooling choices much as private schools do, with similar effects on capitalization and desegregation in housing markets; (3) Under public school rationing mechanisms with little reliance on walk zone priorities, the competition between public schools cannot easily be based on cream skimming because all public schools must accept the assignment from the assignment algorithm and thus cannot "choose" from an applicant pool. Therefore, the nature of the competition that arises is likely to be similar to that in the second and third set of rows of table 12.3, with generally positive effects on public school quality.[17]

Integrating Decentralized Public and Private School Competition

The ideal of public education is to guarantee access to quality education to all children regardless of background, and this ideal is often in mind when comparing "public" education to "private schools." This ideal has led many to caricature public schools as "accepting everyone for free" and private schools as "rationing access to the privileged." Once we explicitly recognize that traditional public school systems in the United States have rationed access through housing markets and have thus limited access to good public schools to those who can afford housing that provides access to those schools, however, it becomes evident that public schools do not live up to the "ideal" of "accepting everyone for free." Similarly, although there are undoubtedly private schools that screen applicants carefully and provide access only to the privileged, many private schools (such as parochial schools in many U.S. cities) are open to most applicants and are hardly exclusive to the privileged. The caricatured distinction between public and private schools is therefore quite artificial, with many private schools in inner cities coming closer to the public school ideal than many rather exclusive suburban public schools in high-income neighborhoods.

In light of this fact, it is puzzling that many draw such sharp distinctions between fostering greater (nonresidence-based) public competition and greater private school competition. Both categories share much in common: they permit households to unbundle their housing and schooling choices, and they permit competition on efficiency or pedagogical grounds. What appears to separate them

---

17. Evidence on the performance of nontraditional public schools is still evolving, although much of it focuses narrowly on test scores. At this point, some charter schools succeed at raising scores and others do not, but parents appear to be significantly more satisfied.

is that private schools typically ration access in part through tuition and admissions policies, whereas nonresidence-based public schools ration access through assignment algorithms that involve some element of randomization. Put differently, the rationing mechanism used by private schools may (and, in some instances, surely is) used to cream-skim nonfinancial resources from a fixed common pool, even though the randomization element of nonresidence-based public school rationing explicitly prohibits such cream skimming.

With the nationwide move toward increased nonresidence-based competition in the public sector, a natural bridge has emerged. This bridge may permit an evolution of a more inclusive school system that contains elements of traditional public school competition, "new" nonresidence-based public competition, and private school competition to the extent to which private sector schools choose to participate in the system. "New" public schools (such as charter schools) are already attempting to do what some private schools do: make more efficient use of resources while targeting pedagogy and curriculum in ways that are appealing to a subset of households. States have determined per-pupil funding for such schools, but the assignment mechanism prohibits these schools from competing primarily through cream skimming. If a private school were willing to accept the same per-pupil level of state funding and to participate in the same assignment mechanism as that which governs the rationing of students to schools in the public system, there appears to be no reason to view that private school differently than a charter school that is attempting to compete within the public system.[18]

Advocates of increased private school competition argue that cream skimming is, in fact, not the primary channel through which private schools compete with "free" public schools; rather, they believe that private schools are simply more efficient at using resources and better at matching pedagogy and curriculum to the needs of particular subsets of children. If true, opening existing systems of nontraditional public school choice to private schools on the same terms (i.e., the same per-pupil funding level and the same assignment mechanism that governs nonfinancial inputs) ought to appeal to private schools. By making acceptance of the assignment mechanism a condition of receiving public funding, this way of fostering private school competition removes the fundamental objection made by public school competition advocates.

Even more competition (that is not based on cream skimming) could be introduced by making the private schools' decision of whether to participate in the system more continuous; that is, rather than asking private schools to participate or not participate, the system could permit a private school to partially

---

18. One concern often raised relates to children with special education needs that make them inherently more expensive to educate. This concern, however, applies equally to public and private school competition. Because states already have developed formulas for assessing per-pupil costs to such cases, one solution is to simply provide additional per-pupil funding that accompanies such students.

participate and provide public funding (at charter school per-pupil levels) only for the subset of seats within a private school that the school agrees to fill through the common assignment mechanism. This system would, for instance, permit parochial schools to reserve some seats for parishioners who pay tuition while opening other seats to interested parents (who would not be charged tuition, but would instead be funded publicly).

Such a system seems like a natural next step in the evolution of choice-based school reform. The previous insights suggest that the form of competition fostered under this kind of system has many attractive features that emerge from combining the three forms of rationing. First, by permitting a role for walk zones, the system does not eliminate the role of residence-based admissions. Although the rationing through housing markets that comes with such walk zones gives rise to capitalization and income segregation, it becomes problematic only when walk zones are defined to be so large that they create entire enclaves or communities (as is the case in a purely residence-based public school system). If walk zones are kept relatively small, the system therefore maintains many of the benefits of local school ownership that comes with residence-based systems, without producing the larger segregation that becomes problematic. Second, the nonresidence-based rationing (based on parental preferences and lotteries) that is introduced into the system is deliberately designed to foster "healthy" competition (based on greater resource efficiency or better matching of students to schools) rather than "unhealthy" competition for scarce nonfinancial inputs. That is true for both public schools and private schools, to the extent they choose to participate in the system. Third, those private schools that view selection of students (and the nonfinancial inputs that come with them) as sufficiently important to keep them from obtaining public funding are not subsidized in the system, thus eliminating the fear that cream skimming drives the competition induced through public funding. In fact, if anything, the increased number of both public and private schools competing for students would tend to decrease the number of private schools that can rely primarily on cream skimming as their competitive advantage. The proposed system thus maintains a role for all three forms of rationing of students into schools while giving flexibility to localities to determine the appropriate balance given the particular local circumstances (for instance, by setting the size of walk zones differently in different cities).

Horizontal Versus Vertical Differentiation

Although much of the economics literature treats school quality as a concept that allows us to rank schools hierarchically, other social sciences suggest that a particular school may be "high quality" for some but not for others. In the language of industrial organization, economists often emphasize the vertical differentiation between good schools and bad schools, leaving aside the issue of potential horizontal differentiation between different schools that set different objectives, objectives that represent good matches for some children but not for others. The focus on vertical differentiation is natural when one thinks of all schools—such as all traditional public schools—as aiming to achieve the same objective loosely referred to as "academic achievement," and this focus is reinforced in an environment of "accountability" where very particular aspects of education production are measured to the exclusion of others. It is less natural, however, for parents who are searching among, for instance, private schools, where such searches typically focus on the right "match" of school characteristics to child characteristics. Thus, parents may choose between two schools they consider equally "good," but where one school is "better for their child" than the other.[19]

The simplest way to model such horizontal differentiation is to specify child "types" in addition to child "abilities." As before, child abilities and parental income produce the peer quality characteristic of a household. A child's "type," on the other hand, determines how well a particular school "type" matches a child's characteristics, with closer matches resulting in higher school quality as experienced by this particular child. A school then chooses a "type" (of curriculum or pedagogical approach) and uses financial and nonfinancial inputs to produce quality targeted at this type. Specifying types is conceptually different from the "pedagogical targeting" previously discussed, where it was simply assumed that lower variance in (hierarchical) child abilities within a school raises school quality (all else being equal). Put differently, the pedagogical targeting modeled in the previous section is a special case in which a child's "type" is equal to her "ability." The intent here, however, is to recognize horizontal differences between children and model them as "types," while continuing to acknowledge that for any child "type," there exist many different (vertical) ability differences.

To be more precise, suppose that child types, denoted τ, can fall anywhere between 0 and 1. A school of type t then produces quality $s_{t\tau}$ for a child of type τ in accordance with the production function

$$s_{t\tau} = \phi_{t\tau} x^{(1-\rho)} q^\rho,$$

where $\phi_{t\tau}$ is a function that increases as the difference between t and τ shrinks. Children of different types therefore experience the same school differently, opening the door for horizontal differentiation between schools. At the same time, a school of a particular type with the same distribution of child types is better able to produce "quality" if it has more financial and nonfinancial inputs available.

In a residence-based public system in which all public schools are of the same type, the ability of private schools to horizontally differentiate themselves becomes yet another possible—and even more promising—competitive advantage for private schools. Incorporating this advantage into the model again disciplines

---

19. Akerlof and Kranton (2002) explore this idea in rich detail in work that draws heavily on insights from sociology. Such insights place emphasis on concepts like "identity," with children identifying as certain types and schools creating local cultures that match some identities better than others. When this match is close, the school is more able to achieve academically.

us to recalibrate the cream-skimming advantage by lowering the value of ρ (so that the model predicts private school attendance levels accurately). When the cream-skimming advantage is lowered by half (and replaced by this new horizontal differentiation advantage), the predicted effect of increased private school competition on public school quality is then again similar to the second and third sets of rows of table 12.3. The average public school quality rises even when public schools do not explicitly respond to competition because the students exiting the public system are those who are most different from the public school type (and thus the students who experience the lowest school quality in the public system). At the same time, without some response by the public system (whether in terms of increased resource efficiency, increased pedagogical targeting, or strategic horizontal differentiation), those students who remain within the public system would suffer a decrease in quality because the students who exit to private schools are also students with higher peer quality characteristics.

Although simplistic, this model of horizontal differentiation suggests additional ways in which the integration of public and private school competition might create substantial new educational opportunities. Parents would attempt to create matches between child types and school types as they express their preferences for schools, and assignment mechanisms that prohibit cream skimming would tend to keep competition from being based on competition for peer characteristics. More general models of horizontal differentiations, particularly those that draw on a rich sociological literature on the matches of school identities with individual child identities (Akerlof and Kranton 2002), suggest even more subtle ways school entrepreneurs can generate horizontally differentiated schools for the benefit of children who themselves are choosing participants in the education production process. Under a system that minimizes the opportunities for schools to compete through cream skimming, horizontal differentiation offers a promising channel for competitive pressures in education. At the same time, opportunities for competition to evolve in this fashion are likely to be limited by the extent to which participation in the public funding system entails excessive requirements of conformity to particular uniform standards.

Conclusions

Any mechanism that allocates resources in the absence of prices must be based on some nonprice rationing mechanism. Traditional public school systems in the United States have relied heavily on housing markets to ration resources and students to schools, thus creating a system of publicly funded schools that are quite heterogeneous in quality. Private schools have existed alongside this public system, with such schools using a combination of (tuition) prices and admission policies to ration access. These two rationing systems have resulted in some schools that cater to high-income clienteles, whether in exclusive suburban public schools, in high-tuition, elite private schools, or in others (both public and private) that admit a more economically diverse set of students. With a wave of new publicly funded "choice" schools that have developed rationing systems that rely less on housing markets, the distinction between private and public schools has become even more blurred, thus opening the possibility of shaping policy that treats most public and private schools as part of a single system.

This analysis has drawn on insights regarding the effect of the previously dominant rationing mechanisms used in public and private schools to suggest one possible way of integrating private and public competition. It was noted that all systems are subject to competitive forces because scarce resources are rationed in education markets and that the true debate is therefore not as much about whether competition should play a role in education, but, rather, about what form such competition should take. Competition becomes less desirable to the extent to which it results in efforts to compete for scarce (typically nonfinancial) resources from a common pool. Such competition can become a zero-sum (or even a negative-sum) game. It becomes more desirable to the extent to which it fosters innovation, raises resource productivity, and creates better matches of schools to children. Both the traditional residence-based public school competition and cream-skimming private school competition have strong elements that fall into the former type of less desirable competition (although there is also evidence that both contain elements of the latter). New policies that limit the schools' ability to cream-skim while putting into place incentives to innovate hold the promise of fostering more socially integrated housing markets while creating better and more diverse opportunities for school children.

The move toward greater (nonresidence-based) choice, including a move toward integrating larger segments of "private" schools into public funding (as suggested here), also carries implications for U.S. fiscal federalism as it relates to school financing. With the unbundling of residential and school choices, the local property tax becomes a less obvious candidate for such financing, with more central income and sales taxes taking its place. Although decisions on how financial and nonfinancial inputs are used therefore become more decentralized under greater (nonresidence-based) choice, the actual financing of schools may well become more centralized. This change would open avenues for ensuring greater equity of appropriate per-pupil funding while simultaneously strengthening local control, where "local" increasingly means parents, not local school boards.[20]

------

20. A system that integrates public and private schools in ways suggested in this study would also require some state-level oversight for two reasons. First, the public needs to be ensured that equal access through assignment mechanisms are indeed in place. Second, the state must enforce some standards that all participating schools must meet. Setting such standards would require finding a balance between fostering innovation and ensuring some uniformity in some dimensions. (For instance, one would surely want a system in which the Ku Klux Klan cannot set up a school that receives public funding.) In many ways, the current system in many cities and states is already evolving mechanisms for addressing such potentially undesirable outcomes as they struggle with what types of charters to approve for charter schools and what types of exemptions from typical public school rules such schools will receive.

Even though a system such as the one envisioned in this chapter provides straightforward mechanisms to ensure greater equity in per-pupil funding, more equality of opportunity to access good schools, and increased incentives for innovation, it does not lend itself to simple predictions about how the composition of schools will change. The current system is one with high degrees of racial, socioeconomic—and, to some extent, religious—segregation, but some would fear that the kind of system suggested will increase such segregation (as it has in some charter schools). Although that is a possibility, it is by no means a certainty. If a system such as the one proposed here indeed opens the doors to greater horizontal differentiation between schools, it would open the door to a new metric along which children would segregate into schools, a metric that may have no particular correlation with race, class, or religion. Schools may, for instance, differentiate on pedagogy, on subject emphasis, and on extracurricular activities, and preferences for such school features will no doubt cross the typical lines of race, class, and religion. The more the system permits schools to innovate in these dimensions, the more it introduces a force orthogonal to the usual segregating forces that cause concern. At the same time, certain disadvantaged minorities have consistently felt underserved in public school and may indeed initially segregate to provide a "safe haven" for their children, a haven that directly addresses the particular needs such families believe are currently being ignored. Such segregation has occurred in some charter schools that are specifically targeted at minority children from households that are disaffected with traditional public school options. Although this practice may, at least in the short term, result in increased racial segregation across schools in some areas, one cannot equate it with the forced segregation systems of the past. In fact, denying opportunities for minority parents who are ill-served in the traditional system to establish schools that more directly address their concerns may be the very reason traditional public schools are not meeting the needs of such families.

REFERENCES

Abdulkadiroglu, A., P. Pathak, and A. Roth. 2005. The New York City high school match. *American Economic Review Papers and Proceedings* 95:364–367.

Abdulkadiroglu, A., P. Pathak, A. Roth, and T. Sönmez. 2005. The Boston public school match. *American Economic Review Papers and Proceedings* 95:368–371.

Abdulkadiroglu, A., and T. Sönmez. 2003. School choice: A mechanism design approach. *American Economic Review* 93:729–747.

Akerlof, G., and R. Kranton. 2002. Identity and schooling: Some lessons for the economics of education. *Journal of Economic Literature* 40:1167–1201.

Angrist, J., and V. Lavy. 1999. Using Maimonides' rule to estimate the effect of class size on scholastic achievement. *Quarterly Journal of Economics* 114:533–575.

Bayer, P., R. McMillan, and K. Reuben. 2005. An equilibrium model of sorting in an urban housing market. NBER Working Paper 10865. Cambridge, MA: National Bureau of Economic Research.

Black, S. 1999. Do better schools matter? Parental valuations of elementary education. *Quarterly Journal of Economics* 114:577–599.

Burtless, G., ed. 1996. *Does money matter? The effects of school resources on student achievement and adult success.* Washington, DC: Brookings Institution Press.

Chubb, J., and T. Moe. 1990. *Politics, markets and America's schools.* Washington, DC: Brookings Institution Press.

Epple, D., and T. Nechyba. 2004. Fiscal decentralization. In *Handbook of regional and urban economics*, vol. 4, V. Henderson and J. Thisse, eds., 2423–2480. Amsterdam: North Holland.

Epple, D., and R. Romano. 1998. Competition between public and private schools, vouchers and peer group effects. *American Economic Review* 88:33–62.

Epple, D., and H. Sieg. 1999. Estimating equilibrium models of local jurisdictions. *Journal of Political Economy* 107:645–681.

Fiske, E., and H. Ladd. 2000. *When schools compete: A cautionary tale.* Washington, DC: Brookings Institution Press.

Gronau, R. 1980. Home production—a forgotten industry. *Review of Economics and Statistics* 62:408–416.

Hanushek, E. 2002. Publicly provided education. In *Handbook of public economics*, vol. 4, A. Auerbach and M. Feldstein, eds., 2045–2141. Amsterdam: North Holland.

Hoxby, C. 2000. Does competition among public schools benefit students and taxpayers? *American Economic Review* 90:1209–1238.

———. 2007. Does competition among public schools benefit students and taxpayers? Reply. *American Economic Review* 97(5):2038–2055.

Krueger, A. 1999. Experimental estimates of education production functions. *Quarterly Journal of Economics* 114:497–532.

Loeb, S., and M. Page. 2001. Examining the link between teacher wages and student outcomes: The importance of alternative labor market opportunities and non-pecuniary variation. *Review of Economic Studies* 82:393–408.

McMillan, R. 2000. Competition, parental involvement and public school performance. *National Tax Association Proceedings* 150–155.

Nechyba, T. 1997a. Existence of equilibrium and stratification in local and hierarchical public goods economies with property taxes and voting. *Economic Theory* 10:277–304.

———. 1997b. Local property and state income taxes: The role of interjurisdictional competition and collusion. *Journal of Political Economy* 105:351–384.

———. 1999. School finance induced migration patterns: The case of private school vouchers. *Journal of Public Economic Theory* 1:1–46.

———. 2000. Mobility, targeting and private school vouchers. *American Economic Review* 90:130–146.

———. 2003a. Centralization, fiscal federalism and private school attendance. *International Economic Review* 44:179–204.

———. 2003b. School finance, spatial income segregation and the nature of communities. *Journal of Urban Economics* 54:61–88.

———. 2006. Income and peer quality sorting in public and private schools. In *Handbook of economics of education*, vol. 2, E. Hanushek and F. Welch, eds., 1327–1368. Amsterdam: North Holland.

Nechyba, T., and R. Strauss. 1998. Community choice and local public services: A discrete choice approach. *Regional Science and Urban Economics* 28:51–74.

Oates, W. 1969. The effects of property taxes and local public spending on property values: An empirical study of tax capitalization and the Tiebout hypothesis. *Journal of Political Economy* 77:957–971.

Rothstein, J. 2007. Does competition among public schools benefit students and taxpayers? A comment on Hoxby (2000). *American Economic Review* 97(5): 2026–2037.

COMMENTARY
Helen F. Ladd

Not surprisingly, in light of his extensive prior work on school choice, Thomas Nechyba has written a clear and methodologically sophisticated paper about competition between public and private schools. The theoretical modeling and simulation in his study and the general equilibrium aspects of his approach are of particular interest.

The U.S. focus of Nechyba's model and related discussion, however, is worth highlighting. Within this model, private schools are clearly distinct from public schools, as is the case in the United States but not in other countries. This difference reflects, in part, the establishment clause of the United States Constitution. This clause calls for the separation of church and state and makes it unconstitutional to provide public funding directly to religious private schools, which account for the bulk of private schools in the United States. Further, consistent with U.S. policy and practice, the public schools in Nechyba's model are not permitted to charge tuition.

The situation is quite different in other countries (Plank and Sykes 2003). In Australia, for example, the government provides significant funding for private schools, with Catholic schools currently receiving about 50 percent of their funding from the federal government and another 20 percent from state governments. In New Zealand religious private schools were incorporated into the public school system in the 1970s, and the reforms of the late 1980s encouraged all public schools to charge fees. In post-apartheid South Africa, the government made an explicit decision to permit school governing bodies to charge fees and allowed those fees to differ across schools with the goal of trying to keep as many middle-class children—black or white—in the public school system. The concern was that, without the power to charge fees that could be used to hire additional teachers, many high-quality public schools that had formerly served only white students but now were expected to serve a more diverse group of students would decline in quality, which would induce students to shift to the private sector (Fiske and Ladd 2004).

As a result of these cross-country differences, the main thesis of Nechyba's analysis—that it may be time to consider public and private schools as part of a single education system—is not as relevant to other countries as to the United States. Nonetheless, his study presents at least four ideas that are more generally relevant to school choice and decentralization and that deserve further attention and comment.

School Quality and Peer Quality

Studies from around the world confirm that perceptions of school quality depend not only on public inputs, but also on the profile of the students in the school, which is a key element in Nechyba's model. Whether considering perceptions of school quality in Chicago, Chile, or New Zealand, it is clear that parents care not only about schools' inputs and programs, but also about what is here referred to as peer quality.

As Nechyba correctly emphasizes, this observation is important. It implies that equal public spending per pupil does not translate into equal school quality. Actually, the situation is even more complicated than he indicates. Equal public spending does not even translate into equal quality inputs because, for any given teacher salary level, the more qualified teachers are likely to prefer to teach in schools with more advantaged students. Parental concerns about peer quality also imply that competition can have negative effects on the education system. If the competition among schools primarily takes the form of schools trying to skim the most educationally advantaged students, it becomes a zero-sum game, with the outcome being more segregation or polarization of students across schools. This outcome has been documented, for example, by Fiske and Ladd (2000) for New Zealand.

Unbundling Residential and School Choice Decisions

The common use of geographic school assignment zones in the United States has led to a bundling of the decision of where to live with where a child goes to school. I agree with Nechyba that it would be desirable to unbundle these two decisions both because the bundling exacerbates the residential segregation that would occur in any case and because low-income or minority families typically have less residential choice than high-income families.

Among the ways to unbundle residential and school choice decisions are intradistrict or interdistrict choice programs within the public school system. These programs could provide special schools of choice within the public school system, such as magnet schools or charter schools, and give students the financial power through school vouchers to select a private school. Or, as in other countries, such programs could provide direct financial support to private schools.

Choice, however, is not the only way to mitigate some of the problems that accompany bundling. Another strategy is to override geography and assign students so that low-income students are relatively evenly spread across schools, as is currently done, for example, in Wake County, North Carolina.

Potential Positive Effects of Competition

Another major idea in Nechyba's study is that competition among schools can, at least in theory, generate positive productivity effects. Nechyba incorporates three such effects into his model. One potential positive effect would arise if the schools of choice are more efficient than traditional public schools and, through competition for students, are able to induce the others to be more productive. Another would arise if schools, because of the lower resulting variance in the ability distribution of students within schools, could tailor their programs more effectively to students' needs. Finally, choice and competition would generate benefits if the result was a better fit between the educational strengths of students and the schools they attend.

The question, though, is how significant these effects are likely to be in practice. My reading of the extensive literature on the productivity effects of competition is that, although they are probably not negative, they are, at best, quite small. Further, on the variance question, my research on choice and competition in New Zealand indicates that competition made it possible for schools serving the most advantaged students to reduce the variance in student intakes by attracting students who were all college bound, but did the reverse for the schools serving the more disadvantaged students. Such schools had to offer broad and relatively unfocused curricula in an attempt to attract students (Fiske and Ladd 2000). The argument that school choice will improve outcomes by providing a better fit for students with differing educational strengths is quite plausible. A problem arises in the context of states or countries with strong achievement-based accountability standards, however, because those standards tend to lead to a single dimensional ordering of schools.

Minimizing the Negative Effects of Competition

Nechyba correctly notes that any school choice program should be designed to maximize the positive forms of competition and minimize the unproductive aspects, namely the cream skimming. To do that, he argues that if private schools are brought into the U.S. public funding system, they must agree not to charge any additional tuition and must follow any admissions rules applicable to public schools.

One issue is whether private schools in the United States would be willing to meet those requirements. My sense, based once again in part on my research in New Zealand, is that many would not because most private schools cherish the right to select their students.

Another issue is whether even those constraints are sufficient to lead to desirable outcomes in practice. Charter school research sheds some light on this issue because these schools, some of which are former private schools, are explicitly subject to the limits that Nechyba would impose on private schools in the context of his model. My coauthored research based on charter schools in North Carolina suggests that when racial considerations are involved, the outcomes are often far from positive. In particular, our research shows that charter schools in North Carolina not only reduce student achievement and increase the black-white test score gap, but also increase the racial isolation of black students (Bifulco and Ladd 2007). The greater racial isolation, we show, results from asymmetric preferences of charter school families by race. Although black charter school families would prefer to put their children in schools with about half whites and half blacks, white charter school families would prefer schools that are less than 20 percent black. The result is many charter schools that are virtually all black.

Thus, when racial considerations are incorporated into choice models, the results may well be far less positive than indicated by Nechyba's simulations. As is the case with all simulations, the power of the results rests on the validity of the underlying assumptions and the completeness of the model on which they are based. Given the relevance of race to discussions of school choice in the United States as well as in many other countries, the absence of race in Nechyba's model could be a potentially significant shortcoming.

Finally, this study raises an additional set of issues that could profitably be the subject of further analysis on the topic of fiscal decentralization. As educational policy makers around the world continue to shift operational authority to the school level, it would be useful to conduct more research into the nature and form of the intermediary institutions needed to ensure that schools have the capacity to undertake those responsibilities.

REFERENCES

Bifulco, R., and H. F. Ladd. 2007. School choice, racial segregation, and test-score gaps: Evidence from North Carolina's charter school program. *Journal of Policy Analysis and Management* 26(1):31–56.

Fiske, E. B., and H. F. Ladd. 2000. *When schools compete: A cautionary tale.* Washington, DC: Brookings Institution Press.

———. 2004. *Elusive equity: Education reform in post-apartheid South Africa.* Washington, DC: Brookings Institution Press.

Plank, D. N., and G. Sykes, eds. 2003. *Choosing choice: School choice in international perspective.* New York and London: Teachers College Press.

13

Community Associations: Decentralizing Local Government Privately

Robert H. Nelson

Not often in U.S. history does a major new social institution appear,[1] but the rise of the private community association since the 1960s represents just such an event. In 1970 about 1 percent of all people in the United States lived in a community association, a category that includes homeowners associations, condominiums, and cooperatives. Today, amazingly enough, that figure is approaching 20 percent, or 60 million people (Community Associations Institute 2007). This growth partly reflects that, from 1980 to 2000, about half the new housing built in the United States was subject to the private governance of a community association (Nelson 2005b). In many rapidly growing parts of the United States today, almost all new housing, other than small-scale infill development in older areas, is being built within the legal framework of a community association.

The majority, about 55 percent of community association housing units, are found in homeowners associations that typically provide services and regulate land use within a neighborhood of single-family homes (Community Associations Institute 2007). About 40 percent of housing units are in condominiums that can range from a single multifamily building to a full neighborhood encompassing diverse housing types. Cooperatives are the third type of community

---

1. Private community associations are not exclusively a U.S. phenomenon. In fact, the condominium form of housing ownership was imported to the United States from Latin America in the early 1960s. Worldwide, community associations are now rapidly spreading.

association, having about 5 percent of total association housing units, and are most likely to consist of a single building in a large city with multiple occupants. In both homeowners associations and condominiums, the housing units are individually owned, but common areas are subject to the collective private governance. In cooperatives the entire facility is collectively owned, but individuals hold legal rights to occupy their units.

The rise of the private community association in the United States can be compared in social scope and significance with the rise of the private business corporation in the late nineteenth century. Both transformed an existing U.S. property system, one that had long been based on individual ownership, into a new system of collective private rights. Both established new forms of private governance as means of collective decision making: the rise of systems of business and residential "private politics" to add to the traditional "public politics" in U.S. collective life. Within the U.S. federal system, state governments have assumed the responsibility for chartering and overseeing both business corporations and community associations. Finally, partly because of the resulting increased private economic and political power, the rise of the business corporation years ago and the rise of the private community association in recent decades have both proven to be socially and politically controversial and contentious.

Recognition of the full social importance of private community associations has been slow in developing in the United States. Several valuable studies have been done (Dilger 1992; Foldvary 1994; Gordon 2004; McKenzie 1994; U.S. Advisory Commission on Intergovernmental Relations 1989), but, other than the law journals, the academic literature is relatively scant. Part of the problem is that community associations have been most visible in the most rapidly developing parts of the United States (which happen to be distant from many leading U.S. centers of learning). Another significant problem is a shortage of data. The U.S. Census of Governments, for example, regards a community association as a form of private activity outside its scope and collects essentially no information on the rapidly growing place of community associations in the U.S. system of local governance. The Census of Housing collects a bit more, but it is still minimal. It is no exaggeration, however, to say that private community associations are transforming the basic organization of local governance in the United States, achieving a major decentralization of local government privately (Nelson 2005b).

In the nineteenth century, good government at the local level in the United States was considered to mean consolidated government. In 1898, for example, the current City of New York was created by combining five separate boroughs into one much larger, centralized political unit. Chicago, Baltimore, and many other U.S. central cities were the result of wide annexations (Jackson 1985). In the first half of the twentieth century, however, the tide began to turn. Small suburban governments increasingly resisted being swallowed up by larger central cities. By the mid-twentieth century, the familiar northeastern and midwestern pattern of today was well established: a large central city surrounded by numerous small suburban municipalities, many with no more than a few thousand people. Today, reflecting this decentralized model of suburban local governance in the public sector, the Chicago metropolitan area includes 569 general-purpose local governments; the Detroit, St. Louis, and Cleveland areas, exhibiting the same basic pattern of public-sector suburban decentralization, have 335, 314, and 243 local governments, respectively.

Today, the basic manner of organizing local governance in the United States is once again changing. In California, Florida, Texas, Arizona, Nevada, and other rapidly growing areas, the rise of the private community association is central to the new urban models. In such places where private community associations have proliferated, the small suburban municipality of the Northeast and Midwest is an endangered species. Local government in the public sector is not disappearing altogether, but it is taking new forms. On a neighborhood scale, the regulation of land use and the provision of "micro" common services such as garbage collection, street cleaning, and private security patrols are being undertaken privately by community associations (McCabe and Tao 2006). Local governments in the public sector are then increasingly left to focus on wider responsibilities of a regional scope such as water and sewer systems, arterial highways, rapid transit, courts of law, and other responsibilities that involve significant economies of scale or otherwise are best provided at a regional and, even, a full metropolitan scale.[2]

In the newly evolving U.S. system of local governance, the two key players in the public sector are powerful county governments and large suburban municipalities. Strong county governments have become the principal instrument of local public governance in unincorporated areas, sometimes covering much of a metropolitan area. In those areas that have been incorporated, counties share these responsibilities with large municipalities, what Lang and LeFurgy (2007, 129–130) have labeled the new municipal "boomburgs" of the South and West. These large, new suburban municipalities typically have nonpartisan elections and part-time mayors, leaving daily oversight of municipal affairs to a professional city manager. The scope of responsibilities is less than those of the old central city and suburban municipalities of the Northeast and Midwest, and the municipal administrative staff is correspondingly reduced. In one extreme case, given a smaller number of service responsibilities, the municipality of Weston, Florida—home to 70,000 residents—has contracted out almost all the municipal functions, leaving the local city government in the hands of a total of three employees. All these changes are further accompanied by a sharp decentralization of the microfunctions of local government to the individual neighborhood level, now carried out by private community associations and financed by association assessments. Thus, the new urban

---

2. In terms of physical and administrative character, schools could be provided locally in a highly decentralized manner, but in much of the United States they have nevertheless long been consolidated into larger regional systems of public education in counties and special school districts.

local governance model is a novel blend of public government on the larger scale and private government on the smaller scale.

Because of the long lifetime of urban housing and infrastructure, the specific character of any metropolitan area is highly path-dependent. Moreover, community associations are created at the time of development and are seldom found in areas—typically built before the 1960s—with separate ownership of each unit. In such areas, the retroactive establishment of a community association would require the unanimous consent of every property owner, which is almost always a practical impossibility. As a result, the new metropolitan trends are most visible in newly developing and rapidly growing metropolitan areas such as Las Vegas, which had a population of 139,126 in 1960, but which grew to 1.9 million in 2007.

As a particularly fast-growing part of the most rapidly growing state in the nation, and thus a place where the weight of the past is minimal, Las Vegas offers a prototype of the evolving new U.S. patterns of local governance. In contrast to the many hundreds of public municipalities typically surrounding central cities in the Northeast and Midwest, there are only 13 general-purpose local governments in the public sector in the Las Vegas metropolitan area. Almost all metropolitan Las Vegas falls within one county, Clark County. The county includes large, unincorporated sections (including most of the famous "Vegas strip"), where the county is the principal instrument of local governance. In three large, incorporated municipalities—the City of Las Vegas (population of 575,000), Henderson (256,000), and North Las Vegas (202,000)—governing responsibilities are shared with Clark County.

At the same time, much of the traditional role of local government is now private. Although there are some older Las Vegas neighborhoods where local land use controls were established as a municipal function many years ago, in almost all newer developments the regulatory protection of neighborhood quality has now been taken over by private community associations. They also provide many services and perform other neighborhood-level tasks. As Lang and LeFurgy (2007, 129–130) note, "The bottom line . . . is that every new North Las Vegas development now has some form of common-interest development," and these community associations have become "critical . . . to the basic functioning" of the system of local government throughout much of the metropolitan area.

In Phoenix, another rapidly growing metropolitan area that has largely taken shape in recent decades, similar governing patterns are on display. Despite having a total population of 3.3 million, there are only 34 general-purpose local governments in the public sector, compared with 318 in an older metropolitan area of almost the same population, Minneapolis–St. Paul. Much of the governing responsibility in the Phoenix area is exercised by two large and powerful counties, Maricopa County and Pinal County. The Phoenix metropolitan area also includes the incorporated City of Phoenix and seven other large, incorporated suburban boomburgs. These eight municipalities are home to fully 80 percent of the total Phoenix metropolitan population, a much higher percentage than a similar number of the largest municipalities surrounding a typical central city in the Northeast or Midwest. As in Las Vegas, private community associations have proliferated in the Phoenix metropolitan area, assuming land use regulation and common service responsibilities at a neighborhood scale that in the Northeast and Midwest have remained largely in the public sector.[3]

A Private Tiebout World

This transformation in the system of local government is a matter of large changes both in substance and in form. The formal privatization of local government is discussed later. The decentralization and privatization of metropolitan governance began at least informally, however, well prior to the rise of the private community association. The numerous suburban municipalities surrounding the central cities of the Northeast and Midwest, although nominally public, might also be described as de facto private governments.[4] As Lang and LeFurgy (2007, 124, 127) comment, traditional suburban governance, as they examined it recently in Bergen County in the northern New Jersey suburbs of New York City, is characterized by "strong municipal and weak county governance," including separate provision by each municipality of its own schools, amounting to a system of "de facto private" education encompassing Bergen County. The best Bergen County public schools, found in upper-middle- and upper-income suburbs where entry is strictly limited by zoning, are comparable to higher-quality private schools in the nation.

Not only the schools, but the entire system of local government—including dozens of municipalities in Bergen County, none larger than 50,000 in population—are, for most practical purposes, largely private. Thus, as Lang and LeFurgy (2007, 127) observe, most municipalities in Bergen County, often containing 5,000 or fewer residents, "are essentially run as private clubs," whatever the formal appearances of being "public" might be. They are, in fact, similar to the private community associations in the more newly developing parts of the United States. Or, as Lang and LeFurgy (2007, 127) comment, many Bergen County municipalities "could easily be accommodated in just one phase of a master-planned community in the West." Las Vegas and Phoenix today are witnessing a newly explicit and official legal recognition of the past informal privatization of local governance that occurred earlier in the twentieth century in the Northeast and Midwest.

---

3. Even in the Northeast and Midwest, private community associations are now also widespread in the farthest outer suburbs, the newest and most rapidly growing parts of these older metropolitan areas.

4. For example, University of Virginia law professor Richard Schragger (2003, 1835, 1852) states that U.S. suburban municipalities in the twentieth century had "essentially become privatized," resulting in a new "political economy of privatized local government."

A number of urban scholars—often with training in economics—have recognized the essentially private character of the small suburban municipality. One of the earliest and most famous depictions of this metropolitan governance pattern was that of Charles Tiebout (1956). Tiebout noted that the traditional problems of organizing the production of public goods at a national level did not apply in the case of the system of local government in the United States, at least not as it was evolving in mid-twentieth-century America, with hundreds of suburban governments surrounding the typical central city. Given such large numbers of small municipalities and a metropolitan area of any significant size, purchasers of housing had a wide range of individual choices. They could select a particular municipality that provided the set of public services they wanted in light of the level of property and other taxes that would be required to pay the costs. It was, in fact, similar to buying other ordinary consumer goods and services in the marketplace: a housing purchaser would act to maximize his or her overall consumptive benefits subject to an income constraint.

Housing was a bit complicated in that a single choice involved a range of housing features, neighborhood amenities, and location characteristics, but this aspect did not distinguish housing in principle from other forms of consumption. An automobile, for example, represents a practical means of transportation, a statement of personal image, a level of safety, and other relevant features of consumption. If all transaction costs were assumed to be zero—an assumption made in most economic analyses in the 1950s when Tiebout was writing—the system of local government would, in fact, reach a perfect equilibrium equivalent to a competitive market outcome for other ordinary goods and services, as described in the conventional economic theory.

In such a perfect metropolitan equilibrium, as Tiebout (1956, 420–421) thus explained, "the allocation of resources [by local municipal governments] will be the same as it would be if normal market forces operated" to determine municipal service and taxing levels. Even allowing for some imperfections in the workings of the suburban market for municipal service provision, "the solution will approximate the ideal 'market' solution." In establishing the market equilibrium, "the act of moving or failing to move [from a given municipality] is critical." In the suburban "market" for municipal services, instead of visiting a store or other location away from home to make a purchase, the decision to stay or leave "replaces the usual market test of willingness to buy a good and reveals the consumer-voter's demand for public goods. Thus each locality has a revenue and expenditure pattern that reflects the [private] desires of its residents." In fact, it reflects them as accurately as individual consumer purchases made in a grocery store or other conventional market setting.

As an economist, Tiebout applauded the resulting effective privatization of the local governance system as it could be found in the U.S. metropolitan areas of the 1950s. In effect, even though it was an approximation, this implicit privatization of local government allowed the market methods of a capitalist economic system to be extended into yet another area of American life, something that previously had been thought to be impossible because of the intrinsically "public" character of all governmental service provision. Other observers, however, were less sanguine. Around the same time Tiebout was writing, Charles Haar, a Harvard law professor, addressed critically the workings of the same system of privatized local governance as he found it in New Jersey (and as Lang and LeFurgy still find it little altered today in Bergen County). Haar (1953, 1036, 1063), criticizing a decision of the New Jersey Supreme Court upholding the exercise of strong municipal zoning powers, wrote that "the preservation of expensive homes . . . apparently becomes a proper function if suitably dressed up as a zoning ordinance." Even as the workings of the land use system were harmful to the poor, "the New Jersey Court substituted shibboleths for reasoning and used liberal shibboleths to attain an illiberal result," according to Haar.

Committed to greater income equality in American life, progressive critics such as Haar were, in essence, deploring the distributional consequences of the country's evolving de facto private system of suburban municipal governance, the very same result that Tiebout was so enthusiastic about. In effect, neighborhood environmental quality, neighborhood common service provision, and other local collective amenities were being socially allocated in much the same manner as ordinary private goods and services in the market. Just as the rich can drive a Mercedes-Benz and go to French restaurants, the poor drive used Chevrolets (or now Toyotas) and eat at McDonald's. With the workings of zoning and other elements of the evolving system of local suburban governance, the rich could also live in a Scarsdale, leaving the poor to live in the Bronx. It was the American way, and the private market system now extended to encompass the collective use of neighborhood land. Indeed, that was why zoning and the other elements of this decentralized suburban system have, since they emerged in the first half of the twentieth century, proven so popular with the public.

Another concern of progressives such as Haar was that a privatized system of local governance would obstruct the wider metropolitan planning and land use control they had long advocated. If it was a question of use of market methods or public planning and control in organizing the metropolitan land system, most urban planners and lawyers of the 1950s and 1960s—and many still today—assumed that the wide range and the complexity of physical and economic interactions among land uses in a large metropolitan land system would defy market resolution. The private land market, they believed, would be hopelessly inadequate as the basic organizational device for the metropolitan economy.

As capitalism generally proved unexpectedly vital in the last decades of the twentieth century at the national economic level, however, in urban economies it was, in practice, the visions of the economists such as Tiebout that mostly prevailed. For the most part, the zoning and other powers of small autonomous municipalities in the suburbs withstood the many progressive challenges. The resulting privatization of local government is now being extended—on an even smaller geographic scale, in many cases—to the newly developing neighborhoods of the U.S. South and West. The difference is that there is no longer an informal and partially disguised privatization; it is now up front and official, the result of the rise of the private community association since the 1960s.

Reconciling "Public" and "Private"

Tiebout spawned a successor group of economists—and of legal theorists inspired by the teachings of the law and economics movement—who in the 1970s and 1980s cleaned up some of the details of his theoretical model and recommended a set of zoning and other reforms to reflect a more explicit recognition of the actual private character of suburban governance. In 1975 economist Bruce Hamilton clarified the crucial role that zoning regulations played in keeping out unwanted land uses, acting informally in the exclusionary capacity of a conventional private property right (a collective private right in this case). Since the late 1970s, another economist, William Fischel (1978, 1985, 2001), has carried this line of analysis much further, exploring comprehensively in his many writings the workings of zoning as a de facto collective private property right and other aspects of the effectively privatized system of suburban municipal governance in the United States (see also Nelson 1977). Within the legal profession, law professors Dan Tarlock (1972) and Robert Ellickson (1977) characterized zoning in the 1970s with new accuracy as an internal redistribution of neighborhood property rights and suggested making these rights transferable with monetary payments—in effect, buying and selling zoning and nuisance protection rights—as a step toward enhanced metropolitan land efficiency (and, to some extent, equity).

On the whole, these efforts have had more scholarly influence than practical consequences. The legal mills grind slowly, and the task of transforming the official law of zoning and municipal governance to the evolving Tiebout–Ellickson–Fischel reality was daunting. Significant changes in local governance were occurring, but the most important public-sector ones had to be legally camouflaged. To acknowledge formally the de facto private realities, a virtual revolution in the public forms of the law in these areas was required. Perhaps equally difficult, an explicit acknowledgment of the practical failures of the progressive urban governing vision—at least as this vision had been applied in matters of zoning and local government—was also required. In the academy, moreover, this progressive vision still generally held sway in urban planning schools, in law schools, among students of urban politics, and elsewhere, even at the end of the twentieth century.

In the legal community, instead of facing the evolving private realities, widespread obfuscation prevailed, sustained in the courts by the ritual recitation of a set of legal myths and fictions. A particular characteristic of land law is that the outward forms tend to depart significantly from the accepted common practice. Indeed, such disparities have long attracted notice and commentary among legal scholars; in Great Britain, for example, altogether outmoded feudal elements of the land laws survived as a matter of form until well into the nineteenth century and even, in some cases, into the twentieth century (Pollock 1979 [1896]). When change does come to land law, it is commonly by means of brand-new institutions that do not as much challenge directly as supplant the old practices. Such has been the case with the rise of the private community association in the late-twentieth-century United States. Now, in the newly developing areas of the South and West, these associations have officially acknowledged the long-standing private character of neighborhood-level suburban governance.[5]

A Coasian Analysis

Unlike Tiebout, Ronald Coase, a leading figure of twentieth-century economics and winner of the Nobel Prize in 1991, has written little about the system of local government. Nevertheless, his 1937 article, "The Nature of the Firm"—a main reason he received his Nobel—raised issues that are also relevant to understanding the nature of local government in the United States today. In the article, Coase (1937) explored the reasons for the growing role of the private business corporation in the U.S. economy, a role that had become widely evident by the 1930s. As Coase noted, large parts of the U.S. economy were found outside the marketplace and instead were governed by the internal private planning and management of the business corporation. In some ways, this reality seemed at odds with the core message of mainstream economics that the market is the most efficient method of economic organization.

Coase explained, however, that all economic activity—whether in the market or in a single, large organization—involves transaction costs. Evidently, based on the evidence of the U.S. economy, the private business corporation—at least up to some large size that often encompassed many thousands of employees spread among many plants and other manufacturing operations across the country—was an efficient way of economizing on transaction costs. It would simply have been too cumbersome, and otherwise costly, to organize such complex production and distribution systems through individual sales and price agreements in the market, among potentially hundreds, or even thousands, of independently owned economic agents. Together with other writings, Coase's insights in this regard eventually led to the rise of the "new institutional economics" in the 1970s. This movement has since radically altered the understanding of the basic workings of markets among American economists (Furubotn and Richter 1997).

---

5. As a student of urban affairs who received his professional economic training in the late 1960s at Princeton University (where Bruce Hamilton and William Fischel were fellow economics graduate students at the time), my own economic contribution in the spirit of Tiebout—with less attention to the theory and a greater emphasis on legal and other institutional details of the zoning system—is Nelson (1977). I concluded by recommending the substitution of collective private rights for a gravely flawed zoning system, which is not too far from what has since happened in newly developing areas of the United States (not to suggest that there was any causal connection).

If local government in the United States, at least at the neighborhood level in the suburbs, has now become a private good, it is subject to a similar analysis. The same kinds of questions Coase asked arise in the "market" for private neighborhoods today. Why have collective forms of housing ownership largely replaced the traditional individual home ownership of the past? Among forms of collective ownership, why is the small suburban municipality of the mid-twentieth century now losing out? How large should a collectively owned and managed private neighborhood be, and what factors limit the size of such neighborhood governing units? Why not simply have a single, large government that could closely plan for and thus better coordinate land uses throughout every part of a full metropolitan area, including all its neighborhoods?

A system of strictly individual housing ownership would not, in itself, preclude actions to maintain overall neighborhood quality. Bargaining could still take place among individual homeowners within a neighborhood, including monetary transfers from one neighbor to another as compensation for desired actions and to limit negative neighborhood externalities. Or, a developer could establish covenants on all individually owned neighborhood properties in advance, thus limiting the future actions of the homeowners. Such covenants were, in fact, widely employed to protect neighborhood quality in the early 1900s. By the second half of the twentieth century, however, the collective instrument of the community association was rapidly replacing those older, private covenant regimes.

In a Coasian framework, this success of private governance will be understood as a way to minimize transaction costs when providing neighborhood services and neighborhood environmental amenities. Enforcement of covenants, for example, was burdensome and unreliable because it depended on individual owners to bring legal actions against any neighborhood parties who might be violating the covenants. Large expenses might also be imposed on the legal system if the resolution of every covenant dispute among property owners had to rely on the courts.

Another land tenure based on individual ownership is the rental model, whereby a developer, in the pursuit of private business profits, might rent individual housing units to tenants. This governing system is one of "private neighborhood dictatorship" by landlords who have received voluntary renter consent (at least for the term of the lease).[6] The renters are then not burdened with the potentially significant responsibilities to participate in democratic neighborhood governance. Day-to-day, the lowest transaction costs of neighborhood management are likely to be found under such a landlord/renter tenure. Indeed, emphasizing the savings in political time and effort of residents—and the efficiencies of having a single, responsible decision maker—some observers have argued that

---

6. Although usually the case, this tenure arrangement is not necessarily a for-profit venture. For example, public housing projects lease apartments to renters.

large rental projects will be the economically optimal ownership form for organizing a neighborhood environment (MacCallum 2002).

There were, in fact, many such large rental projects in the past, but, as collective ownership with private neighborhood democracy has come to dominate the
housing market, fewer are being built today. There has, however, been little economic research thus far to explore the relative total transaction costs of the various
individual and collective systems of housing ownership and why rental housing is
losing out. As such investigations are undertaken, important factors in explaining the preference for ownership versus rental tenures should be the role of home
ownership within a person's investment portfolio and the prospect of achieving
home equity gains as part of a broader investment strategy (Fischel 2001).

Transaction Costs: Small Municipalities Versus Community Associations

As noted, the small suburban municipality is, for most practical purposes, an
alternative form of "private" land tenure, one that will involve its own forms of
transaction costs. The municipal form of privatization, though, has also been losing out to the private community association. Following a Coasian line of analysis, it would seem that a private community association lowers the transaction
costs of neighborhood organization and management. Although no precise calculations can be offered here (and few are available in the literature), it is possible,
at least, to identify the qualitative factors that will influence relative transaction
costs of small municipalities in comparison to community associations.[7]

In municipalities, there are two main governance models: the town council/
mayor and the town council/city manager. (Numerically, the latter type is most
common.) In a community association, by comparison, legal authority lies with an
association board of directors elected by the property owners, which may choose
to delegate the operational responsibilities to a private management firm. With
some important differences, this arrangement resembles the council/town manager system of a municipality. (One difference, for example, is that the dismissal of
the private manager and administrative staff of the community association—firing
the management firm—would likely involve considerably fewer transaction costs
than the dismissal of a municipal city manager and all the civil service.)

Compared with a small suburban municipality, a community association—
officially a private entity—will usually have more flexibility of organizational
structure and operation, and thus wider ability to act to minimize transaction
costs. A community association, for example, has wider discretion in assigning
voting rights; most associations assign the rights to unit owners, but a private
association can (and some do) also give renters the right to vote. Associations

---

7. One attempt to address such matters is found in Fennell (2004).

can search for the "optimal" voting scheme among many private constitutional possibilities. Municipalities, however, are tightly bound by the one person/one vote requirement imposed by the United States Supreme Court (*Avery v. Midland County*, 390 U.S. 474 [1968]). This requirement creates the possibility that renters, if they become numerous enough in a municipality, might alter the neighborhood initial contract to impose rent controls or take other steps adverse to owner interests. As a result, property owners relying on municipal protections could be faced with large transaction costs in enforcing the neighborhood contract, perhaps leading them to organize politically to protect their private ownership interests, including in some cases "political bribes" to buy off renter votes. Alternatively, property owners may simply direct more of their investments outside the housing area.[8]

The level of "social capital" might be higher, and transaction costs therefore lower, in neighborhoods that are able to gather together a more homogeneous group of homeowners. A strong neighborhood culture, based on a powerful set of shared norms that help to reduce internal transaction costs, is more likely in the private setting of a community association (Ellickson 1991). Although municipalities can achieve substantial homogeneity of owner incomes through the exercise of their zoning powers, in other respects they have less authority than a private community association to set personal entry requirements. For example, community associations of senior citizens (one unit owner must be 55 years old or older) have proliferated across the United States. It would be difficult—and perhaps legally impossible—for a public municipality to maintain a similar age restriction, though. In general, although the Fair Housing Act (the federal law prohibiting racial and other forms of discrimination in the buying and selling of housing) applies to private community associations, private governments will have a greater legal flexibility to work to establish a neighborhood common culture that minimizes transaction costs.[9]

---

8. The differences between a small suburban municipality and a private community association are not necessarily an intrinsic—and thus fixed—characteristic of the law. Indeed, to a large extent, they are the product of past court decisions. In the future, courts could, in concept, modify the legal status of suburban municipalities to loosen current municipal restrictions and grant greater freedom of operation, more resembling the flexibility of today's private community association. It seems that it has been easier and faster, however, simply to transfer local government from the official "public" status to "private" status. From this perspective, the rise of private community associations can be seen as a legal device that has made possible a rapid and efficient increase in the flexibility and freedom of operation of local governments in the United States.

9. Admittedly, this new and evolving area of the law is subject to considerable future legal uncertainty. It can at least be argued that, in the case of a community association established for religious purposes (a "residential church"), the courts should interpret freedom of religion to prohibit the interference of public governments with discriminatory actions that reflect the pursuit of genuine neighborhood religious purposes. See Nelson (2005a).

A private neighborhood can typically regulate free speech, including the posting of signs, in ways that would be constitutionally impermissible in a public municipality. If most private neighborhood residents object to such signs, the transaction costs that would otherwise be incurred in buying out (through formal or informal means) those who want to put up the signs would be reduced. It might be suggested that basic constitutional rights should not be surrendered under any circumstances. In small enough social units, however, a right to discriminate is widely accepted in American society. Is there anything objectionable in a small neighborhood limited to Italians, or Baptists, or unmarried residents, or people under age 30? As neighborhoods become smaller and more intimate in size, the private legal status of a community association will give courts wider flexibility to make appropriate judgments on such matters.

The different legal statuses of a small municipality and a private community association will produce different transaction costs when it comes to the initial organization of a neighborhood collective governance regime. A suburban municipality in the public sector is established through each state's legal procedures for municipal incorporation, usually based on a simple majority vote of the residents. Hence, in the public sector, it is typically impossible for a developer to establish a particular system of neighborhood governance in advance as part of the overall development "sales package." If the incoming neighborhood residents subsequently wish to have an incorporated municipality, they will have to work through the procedures for municipal incorporation on their own, normally involving major uncertainties and large internal organizing costs among the residents. Of course, it is also possible that an existing municipality already encompasses the boundaries of the development. In that case, though, another transaction cost problem arises: usually, the municipal boundaries will not correspond to the new development boundaries. Thus, neighborhood collective decision making could end up outside the hands of the owners and other residents themselves, potentially requiring complex political negotiations with many other neighborhoods in the same municipality.

A private community association, by contrast, can tailor the boundaries of the neighborhood government precisely to fit the geographic requirements of a new development. As part of the development process, the developer prepares the declaration of a community association—the neighborhood "private constitution"— that becomes part of the marketing plan for the entire neighborhood project. In this way, the specific form of neighborhood government becomes a private market item itself, subject to developer calculations designed to maximize profits (Barzel and Sass 1990; Boudreaux and Holcombe 1989). The transaction costs for a neighborhood establishing its own distinct system of governance can thereby be substantially reduced privately.

Municipal incorporation, however, will enjoy a decisive transaction cost advantage in at least one circumstance: organizing a new regime of collective governance in an existing neighborhood of individually owned homes. Municipal incorporation in such circumstances will usually be possible with a favorable simple majority vote of the neighborhood's resident voters.[10] By comparison, after the fact of development, the private establishment of a new community association in an existing neighborhood would require the unanimous consent of the property owners, which is likely to be a practical impossibility.[11] This issue, of course, does not arise with brand-new housing developments that establish a private government in advance and then require every incoming buyer, as an initial condition of purchase, to agree to the terms of the community association declaration in the usual manner of establishing a community association.

Long-Term Neighborhood Contracting

Following Coase's seminal contributions, the new institutional economics has explored the important organizational consequences of the frequent need for long-term contracting in the business world (Williamson 1975). If one business party must make a large investment now and the benefits depend on the actions of a second party well in the future, there may be a strong incentive to integrate the two parties into a single firm. Otherwise, if the two were operating as independent agents in the market, the second might end up with the future bargaining power to capture most of the total investment value. This problem could, in concept, be solved by a long-term market contract, but it might be difficult to foresee all future contingencies and incorporate them formally in an enforceable legal contract.[12] Instead, such issues may be best resolved with a minimum of transaction costs by keeping all current and future activity within one business unit.

Similar issues arise in the residential housing market, partly because, compared with most other forms of consumption, a housing purchase has long-term economic consequences. Many people buy a home with the expectation of

---

10. In many cases, of course, multiple neighborhoods may be included in the same municipality. In this case, a particular neighborhood can obtain collective controls through the simple majority vote of the wider municipal legislature (normally reflecting the expressed wishes of the neighborhood residents). When zoning was first widely employed in the United States in the 1920s, it was often established in this manner in older neighborhoods that had previously been under systems of individual home ownership. Without the exercise of zoning coercive powers, it would have been impossible to establish any system of collective controls in such neighborhoods.

11. State legislatures, admittedly, could enact new laws to make it easier to retrofit a private community association in an existing neighborhood of individually owned homes with less than unanimous consent. In that case, it might then be possible to create a community association with a favorable vote of, say, 75 percent of the property owners (and the remaining 25 percent would be legally required to join as well). I make such a proposal in Nelson (2005b, part IV).

12. Even if the large number of possible future contractual issues can be accurately foreseen, the costs of spelling out so many future contingencies in adequate detail for legal purposes may itself be prohibitive.

remaining there for many years, perhaps even decades. As a result, it is usually impossible to foresee every neighborhood situation that might come up. Without a well-specified contract, it may be necessary to leave considerable discretion to a future neighborhood decision-making process, however it may be structured. This process may have to be put in place, and the decision-making rights of future unit occupants well established, in the initial neighborhood contract.

Specifying and maintaining this decision-making process can be a particular problem in the landlord/rental form of land tenure. Incoming occupants of new homes who expect to live in a neighborhood for many years may want contracts that spell out the outcomes of many future long-term contingencies. That specificity may not be possible with the traditional serial renegotiation of short-term rental agreements. Renters can always move out at the end of the lease, but each turnover has potentially high transaction costs. Landlords, for their part, may be unwilling to commit to very long-term leases whose full contractual consequences are unclear and whose terms may be difficult to change. In short, the particularly high transaction costs of long-term contracting in this legal setting may discourage wider use of the landlord/renter form of land tenure.

Under the collective land tenure of the small suburban municipality, the municipal legislature will have the authority to revise neighborhood land use regulations, common service levels, and other terms of neighborhood governance by simple majority vote of the residents. Hence, even leaving aside the complication that potentially multiple neighborhoods may be politically involved within the same municipality, many neighborhood property owners may be exposed to newly revised neighborhood contracts that may be opposed by as many as 49 percent of fellow property owners. A private community association could, in concept, follow the same municipal voting rule, but it has greater institutional flexibility to fine-tune its neighborhood recontracting procedures. Indeed, rather than a simple majority vote as in municipalities, most community associations require high supermajority votes—typically 66 or 75 percent—to change the land use regulations or otherwise amend the declaration. Many also require still higher approval percentages for "foundational" changes.

The exact voting requirement chosen will reflect two types of costs. One, the transaction costs of renegotiating a neighborhood contract, will be higher as the approval percentage is increased above 51 percent. Another form of transaction cost can be described as the "losing side" cost, whereby the burdens are borne by those who oppose a particular change but whose preferences are overridden by the collective decision and thus who end up in an inferior position. This latter cost will decline as the voting requirement increases toward unanimity. In 1962 Buchanan and Tullock famously analyzed this issue in a general way in *The Calculus of Consent*. They showed that there will be an optimal voting rule, normally lying somewhere between a simple majority (minimum negotiation costs) and unanimous consent (minimum "losing side" costs).

Unlike the circumstances analyzed by Buchanan and Tullock (in which the losers had no choice but to accept the final collective decision), it is possible for a losing homeowner to exit a neighborhood. Despite the resulting upper bound this sets on individual "losing side" costs, though, the option of moving somewhere else may not be much comfort for many homeowners. For those who have made large commitments to an existing circle of friends and otherwise have strong connections to their existing neighborhood, the greater constitutional flexibility of a private community association in setting an optimal neighborhood rule for recontracting may be a significant advantage. Probabilistically, the freedom to select their own supermajority voting rule may reduce their expected long-run transaction costs.

Community association rules commonly regulate exterior paint colors, shrubbery placement, driveway use, fences, and, in fact, almost any detail of a property's exterior. That few public municipalities have such all-encompassing neighborhood controls is an indication that the overall transaction costs of collective decision making may be lower in the private community association. Having less confidence in the future reliability and predictability of their own neighborhood regulatory regimes—or, as one might say, facing higher transaction costs to obtain greater contractual security—municipal residents may choose to put less at risk in terms of the extent of future neighborhood controls.

Payment of Compensation

Although many community associations have taken advantage of this wider flexibility of constitutional design and practice—a consequence of their official private legal status—further gains of this kind may be realized. Admittedly, developers of community associations would need to show greater creativity in the future, rather than simply adopting the boilerplate declarations of previous associations. Community associations are a fairly new development in American life, however, and further progress along a learning curve is to be expected.[13]

One example of a potentially valuable private innovation is the greater use of monetary compensation in resolving neighborhood disputes and in negotiating neighborhood agreements in general. This practice would again follow the thinking of Coase (1960), who argued many years ago that market incentives could resolve private externality issues without the direct involvement of government, as long as the private legal rights were well defined and the rights were freely transferable according to the wishes of the holders. Thus, if I wish to plant a tree that diminishes the sunlight reaching my neighbor's property, the two of us in a Coasian setting can be expected to strike a bargain. If I have the initial right to plant the tree and my neighbor wants to block it, he or she will have to offer a large enough payment to dissuade me from going forward. Conversely, if

---

13. I explore a wide variety of possible improvements in the private governance systems of community associations in Nelson (2005b, part V).

the neighbor legally must agree to the tree, I will then have to offer a sufficient payment to compensate for any negative externalities the neighbor experiences. Either way, as long as the legal rights are clearly specified, free private bargaining between me and my neighbor will achieve an efficient result.

At present, however, few community associations recognize in their declarations the possibility of any such forms of Coasian bargaining. A unit owner who wants to paint his or her property green, against the current rules of the association, has no option, say, to offer $10,000 to the association in exchange for a waiver of the house-color rules. Ellickson (1973), among others, argues that greater legal flexibility in this regard—both in community associations and in other private settings—might yield more flexible and satisfactory internal neighborhood outcomes, significantly enhancing overall economic efficiency in the land market.

In one particularly important case, a land developer might offer to buy out an entire community association (the entire package of neighborhood rights) and transform the use of land at the entire neighborhood site.[14] Owing to changed economic circumstances, the site might have become much more valuable than in its current use. Few community associations, however, anticipate in their declarations the possible full buyout of the entire neighborhood even if it could be a large win-win proposition all around, creating large profits for the developer and large financial gains for unit owners. This defect should be remedied in future new declarations of community associations, and states may have to address the matter legislatively for older associations that now lack such provisions.

State Oversight

Although community associations have wider private flexibility of operation than small municipalities, they are also subject to significant state oversight. Like a business corporation, a community association is chartered under a state law that may include various requirements relating to the structure of association governance and other internal matters. Other state laws typically include significant further requirements. Many states, for example, require as a matter of consumer right that developers must make relevant information about the financial status of community associations available to prospective unit owners. In Florida a community association and unit owner are required to enter into nonbinding

---

14. A recent example involving a trailer park in Palm Beach County attracted considerable media attention. Although not a conventional community association, the residents of Briny Breezes had many years ago established a collective ownership. With land values rising rapidly in that part of Florida, a developer offered more than $500 million for the full park area. Eighty-two percent of the residents voted to accept (66 percent was required for approval), yielding around $1 million per household. Under the agreement, the owners had up to two years to vacate the park. See *South Florida Sun-Sentinel* (2007).

arbitration prior to initiating any court action. In one widely noted 2006 case (*Committee for a Better Twin Rivers v. Twin Rivers Homeowners Association*, 383 N.J. Super 22 [App. Div.]), a New Jersey appeals court, departing from the precedents in most states, limited the rights of community associations to control the placement of political signs within the common areas. In 2007, however, the New Jersey Supreme Court overturned that decision, thus illustrating the many uncertainties with respect to the future legal rules for community associations. In California, after a long debate, brand-new community associations were denied the right to exclude pets (older associations with such rules already in place were grandfathered).

A particularly complicated transaction for many community associations is the transition from developer control to unit owner management. To protect the developer's rights, unit owners do not normally take full control of community association management until a significant share—most often 75 percent—of the units have been sold and occupied. Early in the history of community associations, however, there were problems with developers locking in management contracts and taking other measures that unit owners subsequently found objectionable. After turning over the project, litigation alleging developer defects in construction often followed. In hopes of reducing these types of transaction costs, states have established rules to define developer and association rights.

In addition, states increasingly oversee many aspects of the routine internal decision making of community associations (separate state laws may apply to homeowners associations and to condominiums). Community associations are required to hold annual meetings for the election of board members and the conduct of other business. Access to board meetings, as well as access to information relating to the operations of the community association, is generally guaranteed under state law as a matter of unit owner right. Florida condominium law requires that annual budget increases greater than 15 percent must be approved by a vote of all unit owners, if 10 percent of owners sign a petition requesting such a vote. Some states are now moving to limit the foreclosure options of community associations in dealing with unit owners delinquent on payment of their assessments or otherwise in violation of association rules.

In 1982 the National Conference on Uniform State Laws published a model law for common-interest developments, recommending that states oversee various details of community association operation. For example, the model law suggested that states establish a quorum requirement of 20 percent for meetings of all the unit owners and of 50 percent for meetings of the board of directors. In general, a community association's private status is relative. State governments are increasingly involved with overseeing community association affairs. State oversight should reflect, among other things, a balance of transaction cost considerations. With clear state rules, developers can operate according to a well-established standard and need not commit unnecessary resources to creating individualized rights regimes for each community association. A common statewide standard will reduce the information burdens and monitoring costs of prospective and current unit owners as well. The negative side, however, is that such state limitations may impede developers and individual neighborhood groups that wish to tailor collective property rights to particular circumstances and preferences. Ill-conceived state regulations may force all community associations to adopt inefficient rules that impose unduly high transaction costs on neighborhood residents and otherwise frustrate their collective wishes.[15]

Indeed, the greater danger at present may be an excess of state oversight of community association workings. States increasingly seem inclined to micromanage even the small details of community association life. Small vocal minorities within community associations may be willing to incur significant costs trying to influence state legislatures, whereas larger silent majorities of unit owners may be deterred from political involvement by the usual free-rider disincentives to collective action.

One option is to make more state requirements a default option for community associations. Certain core developer and unit owner rights would be established for all community associations uniformly. Beyond that, an association might be granted wide latitude to establish its own private governance regime as long as the collective rights are clearly defined in the initial declaration. If the declaration is silent on a crucial matter, however, a uniform state rule would then come into play. A backup rule is needed because the transaction costs to restructure a collective property rights regime that initially failed to address an important governance issue may be high.

Since the late 1960s, a large law and economics literature has addressed in a general way the definition and oversight of property rights in society. A main goal in specifying rights is to minimize transaction costs as well as meeting equity and other social aims. To date, however, this literature has not given much attention to private community associations.[16] Future research might contribute to this area valuably, including giving attention to the proper oversight role of state government.

Taxation of Community Association Property

Under federal tax law, the profits of a business corporation are taxed as corporate income, whether they are later distributed as dividends or not. Then, any dividends received by shareholders are taxed again as individual income, resulting in double taxation. Economically, the rationale for taxation of both business profits

---

15. In Florida, where state oversight is particularly detailed, one provision of state law had the effect of requiring variable cable television charges within many condominiums based on the square footage of each unit. Florida unit owners complained that hookup charges should instead be the same for each condominium unit. To make this simple change, the state legislature in 1998 had to revise the law.

16. A few authors have begun such explorations. See Fennell (2006).

and distributed dividend income has long been doubtful.[17] In the face of strong economic criticisms, the political durability of corporate double taxation may reflect that many Americans are ambivalent about the prominent role of large business corporations in American life. They are willing to tolerate these corporations because of the major contributions the companies make to the U.S. economy. In return, however, Americans want corporations to pay some form of penance—higher taxes—to compensate for their special legal privileges (limited liability, for example) and the wide private powers in society they are allowed to possess.

In a much different way, private community associations are also subject to double taxation, conceivably for similar implicit reasons. Many community associations deliver common services that are also provided by a municipality (or local county) in other areas of the same jurisdiction (where there are no community associations). The association unit owners end up paying twice, first in the form of private assessments to cover the costs of their own services and second through property taxes to pay service delivery costs elsewhere in the public sector.[18] Like double taxation of corporate dividends, this situation creates a potentially inefficient set of incentives, artificially discouraging private provision and encouraging public provision of local services. In jurisdictions of mixed public and private governance, for example, double taxation creates a strong incentive for service provision in the public sector, even if community association provision may be more efficient.

Equally important is that double taxation of community associations creates a strong incentive for local public jurisdictions in rapidly growing areas to require that all new development must occur within the legal framework of a private community association. If all housing in the jurisdiction is located within a community association, there need be little or no public service delivery at all (at least of the micro kinds of services associations typically provide); there will also be no cross transfers of funds from private to public service recipients and thus no double taxation. Indeed, in areas such as Las Vegas and Phoenix, large county and municipal governments are doing precisely that: requiring, formally or informally, all new housing developments to have a community association.

Some people, however, may object to the tight collective land use controls of a community association. Other people will have other reasons for not wanting to live in a community association. It would be preferable to allow the two main forms of collective land tenure—the small suburban municipality and the private

---

17. If the capital gains tax is less than the dividend tax, as has often been the case in the United States, there will be a strong financial incentive for corporations to retain earnings for reinvestment, stimulating the further concentration of the U.S. business sector. This situation is virtually the reverse of antitrust goals.

18. Adding to the private disadvantage, municipal taxes are deductible under the federal income tax, but community association assessments are not.

community association—to compete on an even playing field. They might even coexist within the same large county jurisdiction as alternative forms of neighborhood collective governance. Some people would then choose to live in a small municipality and others in a private community association, according to their specific preferences. As described above, these two tenure forms each have their own levels of transaction costs along with other advantages and disadvantages. If double taxation were eliminated, the resolution could simply be left to a competitive process.[19]

One way to eliminate double taxation is for local governments in the public sector to provide compensation if a community association provides privately a service that is provided publicly in other areas of the same jurisdiction. At least a few public jurisdictions do provide such compensating payments. In New Jersey, state law requires them for some types of local services. As in other aspects of community association life, however, there has been little research on this subject, including the issue of the difficulty—the likely level of transaction costs incurred—in calculating appropriate compensation payments.

In connection with the writing of this chapter, the Community Associations Institute distributed a questionnaire to its membership seeking greater knowledge of the extent of double taxation and any compensating payments from local public governments being received by associations. Unfortunately, given several constraints, there was no assurance that the sample collected was representative, and the response rate was low (further research may be possible).[20] Nevertheless, the information obtained from 127 respondents may be of some interest. If only suggestive, the main findings were that only a few associations (about 10 percent of the respondents) are receiving compensation, many more would like to receive compensation, some associations are not concerned (they may provide few services or be located in areas where associations already dominate the landscape), and double taxation is an important political issue for about half of all associations.[21] About one-quarter of the associations surveyed paid property taxes on the common elements, in addition to the personal tax payments for the individually owned units within the association.

---

19. Admittedly, to achieve a level playing field for resolving the efficient form of land tenure competitively, some additional tax issues may have to be addressed. Individual home ownership, for example, receives significant tax advantages, especially the deductibility of mortgage interest payments. A result is a bias against rental forms of land tenure, although it is partially compensated for by business tax advantages available to real estate investments.

20. Part of the problem reflected the membership system of the Community Associations Institute (members are individuals) and the difficulty of distributing questionnaires to community associations rather than to individual members. Further survey efforts will be needed to establish a more reliable information base.

21. Additional survey details are available from the author.

Conclusions

The system of local government in the United States is being transformed by the rise of the private community association. Local government in the public sector is increasingly limited to large county and municipal governments—and also sometimes large special districts—that assume responsibilities of a regional and metropolitan scope. The regulation of land use to protect neighborhood environmental quality, and the delivery of small-scale neighborhood services, is increasingly the responsibility of a private government. In the most rapidly growing parts of the United States in the South and West, the small suburban municipality in the public sector, historically the dominant collective ownership mode for Northeast and Midwest neighborhoods, is disappearing.

Previous studies have described these new patterns of governance, but little literature is available to understand the full reasons for such changes. This chapter has offered several hypotheses relating to the magnitude of transaction costs under alternative forms of land tenure. Table 13.1 summarizes expected key transaction cost advantages and disadvantages of private community associations relative to municipal governments in the public sector. The analysis here, however, is conceptual. A large research agenda remains; the specific levels of transaction costs associated with rental housing, small suburban municipalities, private community associations, and potentially other individual and collective instruments of neighborhood governance need to be studied in greater detail. It may also be possible to reduce the transactions costs associated with each tenure form by appropriate institutional redesign of the precise legal status of that tenure.

Table 13.1
Relative Transaction Costs

Transaction costs of . . .	Private Community Association	Small Municipality
Establishing new collective controls in existing neighborhoods	Higher	Lower
Fine-tuning voting rules for special neighborhoods	Lower	Higher
Using monetary compensation in neighborhood disputes	Lower	Higher
Tight controls over aesthetics	Lower	Higher
Changing use rules	Higher	Lower
Changing community management	Lower	Higher
Collecting taxes/assessments	Higher	Lower
Installing gates	Lower	Higher
Defining social environment (e.g., senior citizen community)	Lower	Higher
Avoiding double taxation	Higher	Lower

REFERENCES

Barzel, Y., and T. R. Sass. 1990. The allocation of resources by voting. *Quarterly Journal of Economics* 104(August):745–771.

Boudreaux, D. J., and R. G. Holcombe. 1989. Government by contract. *Public Finance Quarterly* 17:264–280.

Buchanan, J. M., and G. Tullock. 1962. *The calculus of consent: Logical foundations of constitutional democracy.* Ann Arbor: University of Michigan Press.

Coase, R. H. 1937. The nature of the firm. *Economica* 4(November):386–405.

———. 1960. The problem of social cost. *Journal of Law and Economics* 3(October): 1–44.

Community Associations Institute. 2007. Factsheet. www.caionline.org/about/facts.cfm.

Dilger, R. J. 1992. *Neighborhood politics: Residential community associations in American governance.* New York: New York University Press.

Ellickson, R. C. 1973. Alternatives to zoning: Covenants, nuisance rules, and fines as land use controls. *University of Chicago Law Review* 40(Summer):681–782.

———. 1977. Suburban growth controls: An economic and legal analysis. *Yale Law Journal* 86(January):385–511.

———. 1991. *Order without law: How neighbors settle disputes.* Cambridge, MA: Harvard University Press.

Fennell, L. A. 2004. Contracting communities. *University of Illinois Law Review* 2004:829–896.

———. 2006. Properties of concentration. *University of Chicago Law Review* 73(Fall): 1227–1297.

Fischel, W. A. 1978. A property rights approach to municipal zoning. *Land Economics* 54(February):64–81.

———. 1985. *The economics of zoning laws: A property rights approach to American land use controls.* Baltimore: Johns Hopkins University Press.

———. 2001. *The homevoter hypothesis: How home values influence local government, taxation, school finance and land-use policies.* Cambridge, MA: Harvard University Press.

Foldvary, F. 1994. *Public goods and private communities: The market provision of social services.* Brookfield, VT: Edward Elgar.

Furubotn, E. G., and R. Richter. 1997. *Institutions and economic theory: The contributions of the new institutional economics.* Ann Arbor: University of Michigan Press.

Gordon, T. M. 2004. *Planned developments in California: Private communities and public life.* San Francisco: Public Policy Institute of California.

Haar, C. 1953. Zoning for minimum standards: The Wayne Township case. *Harvard Law Review* 66:1051–1063.

Hamilton, B. W. 1975. Zoning and property taxation in a system of local governments. *Urban Studies* 12(June):205–211.

Jackson, K. T. 1985. *Crabgrass frontier: The suburbanization of the United States.* New York: Oxford University Press.

Lang, R. E., and J. B. LeFurgy. 2007. *Boomburbs: The rise of America's accidental cities.* Washington, DC: Brookings Institution Press.

MacCallum, S. H. 2002. The case for land lease versus subdivision: Homeowners' associations reconsidered. In *The voluntary city: Choice, community, and civil society,*

D. T. Beito, P. Gordon, and A. Tabarrok, eds., 371–400. Ann Arbor: University of Michigan Press and the Independent Institute.

McCabe, B. C., and J. Tao. 2006. Private governments and private services: Homeowners associations in the city and behind the gate. *Review of Policy Research* 23(6):1143–1157.

McKenzie, E. 1994. *Privatopia: Homeowner associations and the rise of residential private government.* New Haven: Yale University Press.

Nelson, R. H. 1977. *Zoning and property rights: An analysis of the American system of land use regulation.* Cambridge, MA: MIT Press.

———. 2005a. In defense of religious neighborhood associations. *Philosophy and Public Policy Quarterly* 25(Fall):10–15.

———. 2005b. *Private neighborhoods and the transformation of local government.* Washington, DC: Urban Institute Press.

Pollock, F. 1979 [1896]. *The land laws.* Littleton, CO: Fred B. Rothman & Co.

Schragger, R. 2003. Consuming government. *University of Michigan Law Review* 101(May):1824–1857.

South Florida Sun-Sentinel. 2007. Briny breezes votes to sell itself. January 11.

Tarlock, A. D. 1972. Toward a revised theory of zoning. In *Land use controls annual,* F. S. Bangs, ed., 141–152. Chicago: American Society of Planning Officials.

Tiebout, C. M. 1956. A pure theory of local expenditures. *Journal of Political Economy* 64(October):416–424.

U.S. Advisory Commission on Intergovernmental Relations. 1989. *Residential community associations: Private governments in the intergovernmental system.* Washington, DC: Advisory Commission on Intergovernmental Relations.

Williamson, O. E. 1975. *Markets and hierarchies: Analysis and antitrust implications.* New York: Free Press.

COMMENTARY
Robert W. Helsley

Robert Nelson offers a legal, political, and institutional analysis of the rise of the community association in the U.S. system of governments. The community association is a residential form of a "private government," a voluntary, exclusive organization that supplements (and sometimes supplants) public spending and public regulation. Residential private governments (also known as homeowner associations and common interest developments) are typically established by developers to further the interests of property owners in the communities or neighborhoods that they create. Recent estimates indicate that there were 231,000 residential private governments in the United States in 2002, housing approximately 57 million people, or about 20 percent of the population. Data from the American Housing Survey indicate that 9 percent of all households, and 28 percent of households in newly constructed housing, paid fees to a residential private government in 2001. Thus, as Nelson emphasizes, the rise of the residential community association represents a substantial innovation in the institutions of local government.

Nelson sees the community association as a vehicle for decentralizing the "microfunctions" of local government to the individual neighborhood level, often under the umbrella of a large county government. There are two general aspects to this decentralization. The first concerns the decentralization of service provision, especially security, sanitation, common facilities, and some infrastructure, including roads. The second, more controversial aspect involves the decentralization and extension of land use regulations, accomplished through covenants, codes, and restrictions (CCRs) embedded in property deeds. Many of these regulations are clearly designed to exclude some potential residents (see Helsley and Strange 2000). According to McKenzie (1996, 4), activities that have been prohibited by CCRs include "flying the flag, delivering newspapers, parking pickup trucks in the driveway, kissing outside the front door, using one's own back door too much, building fences, painting the exterior certain colors, having pets, working from one's home, marrying people below a certain age, and even having children." These supplementary regulations apparently result in higher levels of neighborhood quality; although they seem oppressive, they have survived the test of the marketplace.

Nelson also asks if the rise of the community association should be seen as an extension of the broad twentieth-century trend toward smaller, independent suburban municipalities offering choice in the spirit of Tiebout and therefore as a continuing trend toward privatization in the local public sector. A great deal of heterogeneity in demand clearly survives the Tiebout sorting mechanism, and this heterogeneity is one force behind the rise of the community association. Private government allows high-demand consumers to supplement public provision and public regulation. The growth of private government also seems to be encouraged by the cost advantage associated with private provision (through contracting out) for many services. A third important factor may be the fear (real and imagined) of crime: gating is an important aspect of many residential private governments. Privatization, however, is not synonymous with jurisdiction choice; the methods of provision and finance are also important. As noted, private governments tend to contract out for the services they provide. They are also self-financing, generally through the imposition of membership fees.

The central contribution of Nelson's paper is a Coasian or transaction costs treatment of the advantages of community associations over other organizational forms at the local level. Nelson identifies a number of potential advantages associated with the community association form, including lower costs of establishing and enforcing covenants on individual property owners, especially where long-term contracts are required; lower costs of neighborhood organization and management, especially the costs of dismissing staff; greater discretion in assigning voting rights and selecting voting rules; higher levels of social capital in more homogeneous neighborhoods; and greater flexibility in the establishment of community boundaries. This transaction cost approach to the study of local government form and structure is, in my view, interesting and potentially important.

Let me conclude by discussing a few other economic issues that have been addressed in the academic literature on private government. At a conceptual level, a key issue has been the effect of private government on the traditional public sector. Consider a population of heterogeneous consumers who differ in their most preferred levels of a public service, where public and private provision are perfect substitutes in the eyes of consumers. The public sector chooses a level of provision to maximize welfare of the entire population, while the private government simultaneously chooses a provision level to maximize the welfare of its members only. Provision is financed through user fees in either case. In this setting, Helsley and Strange (1998) show that the Nash equilibrium features "strategic downloading"—the public sector partially withdraws from provision of the service. Cheung (forthcoming) finds evidence of strategic downloading in the interaction between public and private governments in a panel of California communities.

A second general issue concerns the welfare effects of private government. If the presence of private government changes public spending, both members and nonmembers will be affected. In the Helsley and Strange model, even with "strategic downloading," private government members receive more of the public service (due to the private supplement) in equilibrium, whereas nonmembers receive less. If members (high demanders) want more than is publicly provided and nonmembers (low demanders) want less, both of these groups may be better off. However, consumers in the middle of the distribution are generally worse off—they are faced with a choice between too much and too little of the public service. Private government may be welfare enhancing, but it is not a Pareto improvement.

Finally, a third general issue concerns the effect of private government on the spatial distribution of activity, economic and otherwise. That is perhaps most apparent in the study of so-called gated communities. Helsley and Strange (1999) show that gating in one community diverts crime to other areas, which may help explain the tendency for many communities in an area to gate at similar points in time. In the language of industrial organization, gating expenditures are "strategic complements" for competing developers. Gating (like other forms of policing) may also lead to deterrence if it reduces the payoff to criminal activity. Because of the diversionary externality, however, there is generally too much gating in equilibrium. If there are multiple equilibrium levels of crime in a community, a passive (i.e., nongated) community may even be tipped into a high-crime outcome by gating in other, neighboring areas.

REFERENCES

Cheung, R. Forthcoming. The interaction between public and private governments: An empirical analysis. *Journal of Urban Economics.*

Helsley, R. W., and W. C. Strange. 1998. Private government. *Journal of Public Economics* 69(2):281–304.

———. 1999. Gated communities and the economic geography of crime. *Journal of Urban Economics* 46(1):80–105.

———. 2000. Social interactions and the institutions of local government. *American Economic Review* 90(5):1477–1490.

McKenzie, E. 1996. Homeowner association private governments in the American political system. Papers in Political Economy 75. University of Western Ontario.

14

Increasing the Effectiveness of Public Service Delivery: A Tournament Approach

Clifford F. Zinnes

Why is it that in most developing countries one finds extremely low-quality public service delivery, even when supported by donor aid or development assistance (World Bank 2005)? In fact, there is almost universal agreement that donor aid itself has not been particularly effective (Collier 2003; Easterly 2006; Espina and Zinnes 2003; World Bank 1998). Slowly, national governments and the donor community alike have come to realize that the problem is not primarily one of insufficient funding.[1] Rather, the root of the problem of public service delivery in particular, and of aid effectiveness in general, is institutional.

Drawing on advances made in microeconomics beginning in the 1980s, the new institutional economics (NIE)[2] has radically deepened our understanding of institutions. By institutions, we now mean a set of rules, strategies, payoffs, players,

---

1. Sachs (2005) argues that a significant increase in funding is a central part of the solution. See Easterly (2006) for a rebuttal. This chapter supports the top-down view of Sachs that tournaments need referees and the bottom-up view of Easterly that solutions (and incentives for them) must be local and that large dollops of aid are unnecessary.

2. Especially developments in game theory, agency theory, transaction cost economics, and the economics of information. See Furubotn and Richter (1999).

and player beliefs. Thus, the term *institution* may refer to culture, norms, markets, firms, government, organizations, contracts (including between donor and recipient, regulator and service provider), and legislation. NIE analyzes the institutional problem as one of misaligned incentives that result from a set of agency and contracting issues associated with the horizontal and vertical relations.

Based in part on these insights, public service delivery designers are paying ever greater attention to governance, monitoring and evaluation, performance indicators, public participation, and participatory development (Williams and Kushnarova 2004). Below, we use NIE to assess an emerging class of "tournament"-based public service delivery approaches that promises to improve on the lackluster performance of conventional methods. In such "games," beneficiary groups, which are often subnational governments (SNGs), act as teams and "play" against each other in interjurisdictional competition (IJC) under explicit predefined rules and rewards—both pecuniary and in-kind—to achieve the best implementation of a particular project. The greater the amount of cooperation within the team (the SNG and its constituents), the more likely its chances of winning or placing. Eliciting cooperation through competition allows the tournament approach to avoid the perverse incentives that often hamper intervention effectiveness.

Of particular interest is not only how successful the outcomes of past IJC-related applications have been across a variety of sectors, issues, and circumstances, but their sustainability, that is, whether the initiative remains successful, especially once the sponsor's involvement has ended. If sustainable, it is crucial to determine how portable a project is (replicability) and whether it might work at different sizes of implementation (scalability). Portability refers to the potential for implementing the initiative using a different group of players with similar characteristics, such as a set of jurisdictions in a different region of the same country, or even in a different country.[3]

Consider briefly a sponsor's conundrum.[4] It wishes to provide assistance or funds to recipients in a foreign environment and in a way that meets its multidimensional objectives. Issues of control and monitoring that reflect principal-agent problems (Murrell 2002), however, often may manifest themselves hierarchically through the "chain of command" from the central government organizations down to the SNGs, where interventions are susceptible to unanticipated breakdowns or even failure. Matters are not helped on the local public service delivery

---

3. Scalability and scale are not the same thing. Scale refers to the minimum size required for a successful application.

4. The word *sponsor* rather than *subnational government* or *donor* is used to underscore that the mechanisms upon which this work focuses apply to most nonmarket initiatives organized by an outsider.

side because relations between service providers and consumers are generally intermediated by government agencies. Likewise, how can a ministry of finance or a sponsor avoid adverse selection and separate serious from frivolous local requests for revenue grants or assistance? In other words, how can an SNG signal to a sponsor its seriousness to engage in high-level efforts? Historically, sponsors have responded to these dilemmas in several ways,[5] including the use of indicators and engaging in conditionality, although the latter has a poor track record (Collier, Guillaumont, and Gunning 1997; Svensson 2003).

At the same time, as understood in the public finance literature (Oates 2002), IJC often occurs naturally as states, municipalities, and even countries compete in a tacit, decentralized way to attract business investment and new citizens with high human or financial capital.[6] In this game, jurisdictions use tax holidays, regulatory and immigration exemptions, publicly paid-for amenities and infrastructure, and even subsidies, often creating a race to the bottom. The push toward devolution and decentralization worldwide may also be considered as applications that use IJC principles. As seen below, IJCs may occur between any set of institutions, including intragovernmental ministries, intergovernmental organizations, and private volunteer organizations (NGOs), schools, hospitals, and even water companies and cultural manifestations (including religious establishments). In each case, the initiator—be it a donor, government department, or civil society organization—bases an intervention on an incentive mechanism within a game that explicitly or implicitly has players, rules, strategies, beliefs, and payoffs.

It is therefore natural to ask if there is a way to design sponsor interventions so as to economize on the sponsor's operational and informational inadequacies.[7] Research (Brook and Petrie 2001; Collier 2003; Kremer 2003; Zinnes and Bolaky 2002) suggests that the answer may lie in harnessing the power of incentives rather than in trying to fight them. Such incentives would encourage the players in SNG reform or in the aid game to use their asymmetric local knowledge in a way aligned to sponsor's objectives, which, in turn, would require that the recipient have a predominant role in both problem, as well as solution, identification. Although experience is growing with these innovative applications, the writings describing them and lessons learned from them are scattered across several disciplines. In fact, a comprehensive assessment of their

---

5. For a review of aid mechanisms and aid effectiveness, see Martens et al. (2002), Svensson (2003), and World Bank (1998).

6. Even earlier, Tiebout (1956), in pointing out how residents sort themselves by matching own-preferences with neighborhood characteristics, illustrated "voting with one's feet" and essentially set the stage for an analysis of IJC and, thus, our present work.

7. There is also the complementary approach of designing better institutional incentives within a sponsor to align the objectives of the bureaucracy to development effectiveness (Collier 2003; Ostrom et al. 2001; Zinnes and Bolaky 2002).

performance does not appear to exist,[8] although the theory essentially has already been developed.[9]

Based on a careful reading of the innovation and experimentation that the failure of aid effectiveness has spawned (Espina and Zinnes 2003), I have proposed elsewhere (Meagher and Zinnes 2004) an approach that holds promise. Called prospective interjurisdictional competition (PIJC), it brings together several desirable, yet tested, incentive-compatible mechanisms. The prospective design of the PIJC in which all players know the rules of the game in advance ensures that the donor can construct race-to-the-top and not race-to-the-bottom competition. First, though, it is necessary to assess the broader applicability of PIJC, both to encourage improvements in SNG service delivery and to improve the effectiveness of development assistance.

The following sections identify the components of the tournament approach and introduce examples of actual applications as detailed in Zinnes (2008); present a framework to analyze the PIJC approach from an institutional perspective; assess how PIJCs stand up to actual experience in terms of performance, sustainability, scalability, and initial conditions; and consider the role of future research.

The PIJC Approach

At its core, the PIJC approach offers a way for potential beneficiaries to signal through their performance their seriousness to achieve the sponsor's objectives and their ability to take advantage of sponsor funds that carry opportunity costs. To gain a better sense of the approach, it is helpful to briefly examine the steps in a PIJC application and then review some existing examples.

STYLIZED STEPS OF A PIJC APPLICATION
Although in practice one can often simplify or even skip some steps depending on the initial conditions[10] and objectives, a full PIJC might comprise the following steps.

Set Objectives   The sponsor (e.g., central government) makes the objective(s) explicit, such as the case in which the central government desires to reduce corruption within municipalities in a target region.

---

8. Steffensen (2007), however, reviews performance-based grants internationally, and Frey and Eichenberger (1999) analyze functionally overlapping jurisdictional competition for public service delivery.

9. See Green and Stokey (1983), Lazear and Rosen (1981), and Nalebluff and Stiglitz (1983).

10. *Initial conditions* are any country characteristics present at the start of the project that might influence outcomes. Such characteristics may be institutional (cultural, religious, legal/legislative, governmental), economic (policy as well as organizational, wealth, income, industrial, agricultural), political, social, geographic, historical, or financial, for instance.

Set Tasks   The sponsor identifies a list of tasks, each of which either fulfills or contributes to the objectives: reduction in time and effort to acquire start-up, construction, and operating permits; public declaration of senior officials' assets, presumptive permitting, independent oversight office, anonymous telephone hotline, transparent dissemination of new regulations and budget allocations, and so forth. Ideally, the objective(s) and tasks would derive from focus groups of key stakeholders, surveys of the targeted population and their decision makers, and a sponsor's independent assessments.

Set Priorities   The sponsor assigns weights to each task or activity to reflect their importance to achieving the specified objective. Unlike the standard approach of sponsors where they use their extensive knowledge and experience to dictate which, how, and when tasks are to be done, PIJC takes the more recent community-driven approach (Platteau 2005). Here, the sponsor sets final objectives and the methodology to measure outcomes (indicators) and offers a graduated scale of technical assistance during the tournament; the sponsor does not dictate how each player is to achieve their own outcomes. Because the tournament already motivates players do their best, they will optimally draw on their own idiosyncratic local knowledge and sponsor recommendations in their efforts to win.

Develop Rating System   The rating system comprises an outcome indicator for each task and the aggregation methodology to compute the score of each objective from their underlying respective tasks.[11] In addition, the sponsor may establish minimum thresholds of acceptable performance. Data come from pre- and posttournament surveys as well as from statistics already being collected by the government or other official agencies. To be maximally motivating, the indicators and methodology should be simple enough so that all stakeholders and players can fully understand them and view them as feasible and legitimate. During the actual tournament period of the PIJC, players—in this case, municipalities—would compete to amass as many points as possible by allocating their efforts across a subset of tasks (or reforms) of their choosing on the aforementioned list, subject to time, budget, collective action constraints to the community, and based on their collective preferences. This demand-driven approach is efficient from an allocation standpoint: only the communities can know their own cost functions and preferences, and only the donor can know its own (marginal) valuations of the proposed tasks. Likewise, because communities played a role in the identification of activities, and because participation is voluntary, reforms

---

11. A tournament may have multiple objectives, such as improving investment-related rules, administrative procedures, budgeting, and service provision. Here the weights are assigned to the objectives, not the tasks, which gives the municipality greater latitude in choosing the objectives to pursue, with the weights reflecting sponsor preferences.

occur with the cooperation of representatives of the population of potential players. In short, the tournament has legitimacy.

Provide Technical Assistance   Municipalities exhibiting evidence of striving to achieve tasks would be offered assistance throughout the tournament, although concentrated during the first half. The technical assistance is an input to the improvements sought, not an end in itself. Given the large number of players (municipalities) the tournament motivates, one should provide assistance in a way that reduces the transaction costs. Examples include workshops attended by representatives of each player group (where continued attendance depends on demonstrating player seriousness through reform action) and use of the Internet to offer an easy way for hundreds of project stakeholders to receive technical information, stay informed on tournament activities, self-report performance (for NGO tracking), and facilitate inter- and intracommunal sharing of reform experience.

Design Tournament   The sponsor identifies the eligible municipalities and creates the rules of the game: how players may compete, the length of play, and when events occur (e.g., the baseline and follow-up surveys) as well as how to amass the points on the rating system. This key component establishes the necessary incentives for the overall project to function. Because most municipalities engage in the reforms but only winners receive significant funding, the tournament provides a massive leveraging of the sponsor's funds,[12] limited local knowledge, and monitoring effort.

Determine Rewards   Although the main benefit of competing is surely the fruits of reform, additional targeted incentives are often required to overcome principal-agent and coordination problems, as well as to compensate decision makers bearing idiosyncratic risk that they cannot otherwise spread or insure against. The reward schedule should cover winning and placing municipalities as well as those meriting "consolation" (exceeding a task threshold). These rewards may be in the form of access to more substantial technical assistance, cofinancing for firms in the municipality, and free investment and trade promotion (including foreign travel for some municipal officials).

Plan Strategic Communications   Such a plan is extremely important for the success of the enterprise. First, it must create public awareness—and, one hopes, interest—in the PIJC, both prior to and during the tournament. Second, because one of the PIJC's most powerful rewards is the public relations it generates for the locality and its politicians, it is critical that credible and effective means are

---

12. Zinnes (2008) provides an algebraic exposition of how this leveraging works.

provided for broad dissemination of who the winners, placers, also-rans, and laggards are, and that the participating public know that in advance.

Integrate Evaluation (Optional)   A monitoring and evaluation (M&E) plan is now becoming a part of donor projects (Kusek and Rist 2004), as epitomized by Millennium Challenge Corporation (2006) (MCC) practices. Due to the requirement that the PIJC have rigorous and nonmanipulable performance measures and that there are a relatively large number of players, it is relatively easy to design—and make known to all stakeholders—a prospective, rigorous M&E plan in a PIJC application.[13] M&E has several benefits. Ideally, a PIJC is repeated many times. This eventuality strengthens its incentive properties as well as spreads the fixed costs of development across more reform. Impact evaluation facilitates the improvement of later PIJCs. Likewise, sponsors are often interested in the scalability, replicability, and sustainability of their interventions; prospective impact evaluation offers a reliable prediction of whether the PIJC will have these properties. Finally, because PIJC success depends on the quality of calibration (of task selection, scoring methodology, reward structure, play time, etc.) in-tournament monitoring—especially during a pilot—allows the PIJC to be adjusted.

PIJC EXAMPLES

Local Government Reform Initiatives   Zinnes (2008) describes cases in which a donor has used a local government tournament as a means to both encourage local reform efforts and allocate its aid. In the case of Russia, for example, as a major component of a fiscal reform loan, the World Bank has run a tournament in which 89 regions compete for budget support of US$6 million to US$9 million each by implementing a range of reforms and administrative improvements, such as extending budget coverage, making local tax law more transparent and consistent with federal legislation, improving expenditure management, strengthening information and audit functions, and improving debt management. Quantitative targets (indicators) are used to ensure transparency and objectivity. Thus far, 15 regions have won. The Russian government has been so impressed with the results that it has committed its own budget funds through 2008 to run three more tournaments.

The United States Agency for International Development (USAID) funded the IRIS Center at the University of Maryland to design and run a certification

---

13. The main challenges are to identify a control group that is free of contamination and to ensure that the control group includes some players who wanted to participate, but were not allowed to. The latter group is required to avoid confounding positive performance effects of the tournament with self-selection effects (where only better performers would enter the tournament and weaker ones would stay out). A common concern raised against randomized trials in public policy despite their ubiquitous use in health and education sectors is the political acceptability of the exclusion requirement for randomization. This concern is discussed in detail elsewhere (Azfar and Zinnes 2003; Duflo 2005).

competition to encourage further deregulation of administrative barriers degrading the business environment in Romania. Simple indicators were used to focus local efforts to address five specific impediments. Most efforts required effective private-public partnerships for success. Out of the 80 municipalities in the country, 29 actively took part, and 4 cities "won." Here, rather than pecuniary rewards or extra donor technical assistance, winners received unprecedented publicity and acknowledgment that they viewed as a valuable signal to outside investors of their business friendliness (and that mayors appreciated as political capital).[14]

In Honduras, USAID funded the design and implementation of a competition among municipalities to carry out reform tasks in the areas of good governance, sustainability, commitment to maintain and attract investment, and absorptive capacity for future technical assistance. Out of the 298 municipalities in the country, 35 were deemed eligible to compete. Their past performance was then measured against seven indicators. Municipalities that scored the highest on the aggregation of these indicators—what USAID called the "sustainability quotient"—won a rich array of technical assistance. Here again, the mayors specifically pointed to the political capital they believed winning would confer.

The World Bank is also running a project in nine Nigerian states to strengthen local government use of federation transfers (Terfa, Inc. 2005) by including local government areas (LGAs) as beneficiaries in the other components of the World Bank's International Development Association (IDA) and Global Environmental Facility grant-funded technical assistance program.[15] This project component grades participating LGAs according to a scorecard, with eight indicators and their subindicators, to assess LGA commitment to effective service delivery (looking at administrative efficiency, budget and financial appraisal, and overall financial integrity) and responsiveness to rural communities (Terfa, Inc. 2005, 4-1). This initiative is especially interesting because it focuses on poverty reduction and on scaling up (Terfa, Inc. 2005, 1-7).

Revenue Sharing   The trend in fiscal federalism and decentralization in general has brought to the fore the question of how national and lower-level revenue sources are to be shared. Although the literature is extensive on this matter,[16] among the conclusions are that "successful decentralization cannot be achieved in the absence of a well-designed fiscal transfers program" and that "the role of [such] transfers in enhancing competition for the supply of public

---

14. USAID is currently conducting a procurement to address governance in Bolivia by running a PIJC (USAID 2006).

15. The World Bank program is called the Local Empowerment and Environmental Management Project.

16. See Bahl and Linn (1992), Oates (2005), and Shah (1998) for a review and assessment.

goods should not be overlooked" (Shah 1998, 32). For example, "in Mexico, South Africa and Pakistan, federal revenue sharing transfers finance up to 99% of expenditures in some provinces" (Shah 1998, 31).

Several of these cases of revenue sharing or intragovernment transfers may be viewed as a type of PIJC.[17] In these cases, jurisdictions are aware that their transfers will depend on recent or expected performance. For example, in South Africa "the central government has implemented a conditional grant aimed at providing incentives for reform of urban services for large cities after having devolved powers to city governments" (Ahmad, Devarajan, and Khemani 2005, 21). Moreover, the role of the donor in the PIJC is taken up by oversight committees (Bolivia), provincial finance commissions (Pakistan), or grant commissions (e.g., Australia, India, and Nigeria).[18]

Steffensen (2007) provides an in-depth operational analysis of performance-based grants to SNGs. He surveys many known developing country examples[19] in which "performance-based grants (PBGs) provide incentives for [local governments] to improve their performance by linking the access to and size of the release of grants with their performance in pre-determined areas" (Steffensen 2007, 10; emphases omitted).[20] PBG objectives include improving administrative performance, organizational learning, and accountability; bringing funds on-budget; and streamlining/coordinating donor support (Steffensen 2007, 11). The implication is that such grants supplement the objectives of other grants; they are not used to fund core services or recurrent costs. According to Steffensen, the purpose of PBGs depends on level of development: they start with process-oriented (institution building[21]) targets and later focus on sector output targets (e.g., quality of urban service delivery). He classifies them into single and multisector grants, where the latter offers greater latitude to SNGs to choose how to invest. Like the

---

17. On the other hand, the literature on the design of equalization grants (e.g., Martinez-Vazquez and Boex 1999) does not seem explicitly to advocate using revenue sharing to stimulate expenditure effectiveness competition among recipients. Of course, no such ambiguity exists on the raising of revenues, for which competition among SNGs should be avoided at all cost.

18. See Faquet (2000), Ahmad, Devarajan, and Khemani (2005, 23), and Martinez-Vazquez and Boex (1999, 39), respectively.

19. Examples include Uganda, Kenya, Tanzania, Nepal, Bangladesh, and Sierra Leone, with projects under way in Sudan, Ghana, Philippines, Cambodia, Indonesia, and the Solomon Islands.

20. This country experience seems to belie Bahl and Linn's observation that "the threshold level of economic development at which fiscal decentralization becomes attractive appears to be quite high" (1992, 385).

21. Examples include good governance, accountability, and financial management; participatory development planning and budgeting; resource mobilization; expenditure management; audit reports; and transparency.

arguments in Zinnes (2008), he notes that PBGs (1) allow "spending where performance is good and absorption capacity is available, and where funds are not misused" (Steffensen 2007, 12; emphases omitted); and (2) can be used to create "a balance between adherence to national targets and ensuring local autonomy/efficiency" (Steffensen 2007, 15).

At the same time, efforts to improve accountability and governance, especially at the subnational level of government, have led to the expanded adoption of performance-based budgeting, defined in Moynihan (2003) as the allocation of fiscal resources based on the achievement of specific, measurable outcomes. Their similarity to the PIJC is seen by observing that they involve (1) expenditure allocation decisions upon which lower levels compete (the budget lines, so to speak); (2) strategic planning in which core tasks and government goals are identified; and (3) performance information upon which to manage and measure performance. Moreover, the last item is often explicitly made available for communication to the general public and is happening in "some U.S. states, such as Missouri and Virginia, [to] provide extensive performance data on government Web sites to increase accountability to the public" (Moynihan 2003). The same happens in European Union (EU) member countries because the European Commission explicitly links part of its budget support to performance (World Bank 2005, box 11.7). Closely related to revenue sharing are municipal development funds used by international donors, which we briefly examine below in our discussion of donor grant programs.

Dissemination and Signaling   Perhaps the second most prevailing use of PIJC (after donor grant programs) is jurisdictional recognition awards, such as blue-ribbon city competitions.[22] Here, we only mention the Ford Foundation's promotion of the Galing Pook Foundation in the Philippines. This program was established in 1993 with the hope of stimulating a response to the then new Local Governance Code. The foundation runs a tournament with the goal of "building the capacities of local government units by disseminating, popularizing and replicating" best practices of awardees (Galing Pook Foundation 2005). The winners of the tournament are determined through a multilevel screening process. The only reward for winning is national recognition and publicity, which municipal politicians covet. Since 1993 when it was established, almost 3,000 local governance programs have competed, 175 of which have won some category of recognition.

Donor Country Allocations   At least two multilateral aid agencies use a quasi-PIJC approach to allocate their financial resources at the country level. The IDA uses a complex set of 16 public expenditure management indicators to evaluate progress on Highly Indebted Poor Countries (better known by its acro-

---

22. Zinnes (2008) describes 10 such awards.

nym, HIPC) areas and in its setting of country allotments (IDA 2005). The MCC conducts a veritable tournament by only offering to work with countries that score above the median for their group on 16 governance-related indicators. The hope is that the lure of substantial funds—for example, US$300 million in the case of Mongolia's proposed compact—will create a consensus of special interests within a country to focus on good governance. Many (Boone and Faguet 2002; Collier 2003; Easterly 2002; Svensson 2003) are essentially calling for donor aid to be disbursed in a more competitive fashion with greater recognition of opportunity costs and based on effectiveness. Ironically, with the two exceptions just noted, most of the competition in the market for aid is among the donors fighting for the attention of recipient country governments. Finally, some donors have been looking retroactively at how they have been allocating assistance (World Bank 1998) and even within their own programs. A particularly revealing example is found concerning the International Labor Organization, where the requirement that performance exceed the median for projects in the program meant that this evaluation activity had a tournament structure (see Zinnes 2008, box 2).

Donor Grant Programs   Many donors run grant programs aimed at every development sector imaginable and are too numerous to list. Structured as a tournament, these programs often aim at encouraging experimentation. Some encourage civil society to engage in service provision or public participation of oversight of local government. Others aim to encourage technology transfer and collaboration between recipient and donor countries. Still others seek to discover new approaches to perennial problems, such as the Development Marketplace of the World Bank (Wood and Hamel 2002).

One type of donor grant program of particular interest is the municipal development fund. These funds are related to the revenue-sharing applications discussed above, but they tend to focus on nonrecurrent, capital investment.[23] The World Bank was one of the early adopters of this instrument in the form of the urban infrastructure fund (UIF), launching its first in 1979. According to Annez, Huet, and Peterson (2008, i), UIFs can "provide finance to improve a range of urban services, not just one sector, such as water and sanitation." A UIF mimics several aspects of a PIJC. First, a UIF is demand-driven, "leaving flexibility for local beneficiaries to set their priorities" (Annez, Huet, and Peterson 2008, i). Second, a UIF takes advantage of local knowledge by "using local institutions to do the work of identifying, appraising, and channeling finance to sub-national entities (municipalities, local utilities, or community groups) on behalf of the [donor]. This arrangement makes it feasible [for the donor] to reach beyond the

---

23. Annez, Huet, and Peterson (2008) discover that many UIFs were often unable to disburse the desired amount of funding when interest rates exceeding the cost of capital were applied. The most successful UIFs were grant-based.

major capitals or business centers . . . to fund much smaller sub-projects, suited to . . . smaller cities and towns" (Annez, Huet, and Peterson 2008, i). Third and foremost, this ability to reach down simultaneously to a much larger group, together with the limited funds of a UIF, means that the UIF provides grants competitively to the best (according to the social objective of the specific project) or at least upper tail of the recipient proposals it receives. This makes the grants a payoff in a tournament, with the recipient proposal representing the strategy and action in the "game."

Charter Schools   Charter schools are intended to revitalize and improve the effectiveness of public schools (O'Reilly 2000, 19) by using market mechanisms such as school choice plans. Although they receive public funding, each school is autonomous and has a unique charter (O'Reilly 2000, 20). The license of charter schools must be renewed every five years and requires that the charter school typically exceed the average score of the traditional public schools in standardized testing. Chile permits Catholic schools access to public education financing to compete against public schools; Canadian provinces allow choice among public and private schools for the receipt of their property tax dollars (Shah 1998, 32).

Proposal-Stage Potential Applications   By now, it should be clear that the potential range of applications of the PIJC concept is broad. The richness of the approach continues to be tested, however, as proposals submitted to donors (and their reactions) attest. The Foreign Agricultural Service of the U.S. Department of Agriculture considered a proposal to organize a series of agricultural subsector competitions among counties (*rayons*) in Uzbekistan (Zinnes, Hansen, and Miller 2005) to improve the local institutional and technical support environment along the consumption-production chain. The Bangladesh National Women Lawyers' Association proposed to the U.S. Department of State to introduce a set of tasks focused on the problems of trafficking in persons for local officials and NGOs to improve local provision of law enforcement and social services.[24] The minister of education of the Federal Republic of Nigeria requested a proposal for running a tournament among higher education institutions in Nigeria to empower local collaborative efforts, including from business, to overcome local obstacles to school performance.

Why none of these proposals has yet been implemented raises interesting questions. Are the applications inappropriate? Were the proposals poorly designed? Was there political resistance in the recipient country, or were the donor institutions intellectually or organizationally unprepared? Although it is unlikely that a single common reason caused their rejection, donor tepidness probably played a key role. The institutional incentives in donor agencies encourage risk

24. This description has been paraphrased from Cadwell (2005).

aversion, in spite of an official position to the contrary. Donor agencies are reluctant to innovate, especially if one cannot point to a prior implementation.

An Institutional Analysis of PIJC

The PIJC approach can be seen more clearly by breaking it down into analyzable components. First, a breakdown allows us to assess those components that have already been applied so that the effect of jointly implementing them together as part of a single PIJC application can be inferred. For example, governance indicators[25] have been used extensively by donors and governments alike, donors are turning to output-based contracting (Brook and Petrie 2001; OECD 1999), governments to PBGs (Steffensen 2007), and competition is being used via grant programs to better target assistance and even to identify sources of innovation for the sponsors themselves (Wood and Hamel 2002). Second, just as economists study the perfect competition model to understand the effect of the inevitable real-world deviations from it, it is possible to examine those full or partial PIJC applications that do exist and observe which components are absent or additional and whether they mattered for success (or failure). Toward these two ends, it is useful to draw on Zinnes (2008), who examines a dozen PIJC applications, several of which were briefly described earlier. To start, it is necessary to consider some of the concepts that underpin the analysis.

PIJC CONCEPTUAL ISSUES

As pointed out previously, IJC is well known in the literature of public finance economics (Oates 2002). In its usual form, localities and even countries compete against each other, typically for business investment. Singapore has successfully competed against Hong Kong and other countries with good port access and quick cargo transit. Cities compete on the basis of the quality of their infrastructure to hold the Olympic Games. Here, competition has led to a "race to the top" in which jurisdictions claim to offer more highly educated workers or better amenities. On the other hand, various states within the United States have used tax holidays to lure Japanese car manufacturers to set up plants in their jurisdiction (e.g., Nissan in Mississippi), but at the same time, some fear that developing countries have (unfairly) competed against them by offering less stringent regulation (e.g., the so-called pollution haven hypothesis and no child-labor prohibitions). In such cases, competition can lead to a "race to the bottom."

In the case of a PIJC development delivery vehicle, several ways can be used to ensure that the race is to the top because the competition is prospective; namely, the jurisdictions commit in advance to a set of preestablished ground rules on what to achieve, how to do so, and what the reward structure will be. Thus, the

---

25. Popular examples are Freedom House, Transparency International, ICRG, Polity IV, and the Heritage Foundation.

competition is explicit. Moreover, sponsors and players are able to agree on tasks that should have a positive socioeconomic effect.

In principle, PIJC creates a different kind of motivation than is typical for government transfers or development assistance. Rather than merely serving as a source of funding, training, or information, the competition creates a temporary, stable, institutional environment—the tournament—which acts to bring otherwise suspicious and uncooperative local interests together to pursue common goals, although in active competition with other jurisdictions. A tournament can be defined (Green and Stokey 1983, 350) as a contest in which "reward structures [are] based on rank order"[26] rather than achieving a particular performance.

The PIJC approach rewards outputs, not inputs. The Organisation for Economic Co-operation and Development (OECD) has now recognized the importance of this design element for public-sector modernization, what it calls "governing for performance" (OECD 1999). A host of examples exist for infrastructure provision and operation (e.g., ports, rail, and highways) and service provision (e.g., water provision and rubbish collection). Winning and placing in a PIJC is therefore based on de facto performance, not *de jure* intent. Passing stroke-of-pen reforms, for example, although perhaps necessary to create change, should not generate PIJC points; only measurable results do.[27] This orientation has the added benefit of allowing one to exploit impact evaluation technologies to assess rigorously the extent that the tournament had an effect. This strategy is useful, for example, when a ministry wants to scale up a local PIJC application to the national level.

Tournament incentives can be harnessed in powerful ways. Incentives of this type have become prevalent in a large number of economic settings because of their ability to generate high performance across all contestants, even when organizers have limited information on the capabilities of participants or do not want to set bounds on possible performance levels.[28] Executive compensation, research and development (patent races), college admissions, and agricultural production contracts all have incentive structures that can be classified as tournaments.

Rewards   The PIJC takes advantage of the incentive properties of the tournament by tailoring tasks and rewards to activities that build local political insti-

---

26. Green and Stokey (1983) also investigate the power of tournaments over other incentive devices.

27. In the Morocco example below, stroke-of-pen "reforms" are sufficient to generate increased technical assistance during the tournament.

28. The analysis of the tournament nature of many economic transactions is also richly examined in the experimental economics and mechanism design literatures (Kagel and Roth 1995).

tutions and civil society with the aim of fostering economic development. Besides the benefits of the reforms, the types of prizes are selected to maximize player (stakeholder) interest, that is, from those groups in government, the private sector, and civil society whose actions, risk taking,[29] and cooperation are needed to effect change. The nature of the prizes also depends on the specific reform objectives. In the example of higher education in Nigeria, such prizes might include a job and training center, international study tours for local education administrators, computers for the schools, recreation centers for the students, and, of course, significant media publicity (which local politicians love). Examples for other applications include access to grants or financing and to other benefits to the player's public or private sector.

To elicit high effort among differentially capable competitors, prizes or awards may also be tiered. In the case of Galing Pook in the Philippines, one type of innovation prize is awarded to the first-time municipality winner of the annual event, while a different prize is given to winning municipalities that have also won the previous tournaments (Galing Pook Foundation 2005). In a tournament run by International Child Support (ICS) in Kenya, a two-tiered award system was used, one for "Top-scoring schools" and one for "Most-improved schools" (Glewwe, Ilias, and Kremer 2003). At the extreme, the prize can be a continuous function of performance, an example being the trainer "bonus" in a USAID marketing training initiative for small- and medium-scale enterprises (Azfar and Zinnes 2003).

Perhaps the greatest motivation for a jurisdiction to agree on participating in a tournament is that each jurisdictional unit—whether it agrees to play or not—is graded and publicized. If only those interested in participating would be measured, the result would be an incentive for potential players who would expect to be embarrassed by their indicator scores not to participate. Both Ashbrook and Clement (2001) in the case of Romania, and Meagher and Zinnes (2004) in the case of Morocco, implement this incentive using a system of up to five stars (like the famous Michelin restaurant guide) to identify good business environments. In this way, citizens in each locality have a way to judge how their own institutions are faring relative to their neighbors.[30] Similarly, as part of these projects, an international Web site is set up and promoted so that both domestic parties and foreign investors and donors are able to see which localities are serious about improving their business and investment environment.

---

29. To design a strategy to stimulate high levels of effort (performance) on a given application, a donor should elicit information about the effort (costs) and benefits of player principals and agents. Then prizes should be identified for each level of decision maker, as well as the polity.

30. This innovation highlights an often neglected aspect of indicator use. They are only effective if those who need to act on the information can easily interpret them and also have legal avenues to pursue action.

Scoring   A successful PIJC is one in which a large proportion of the target group of players has engaged in reform efforts. Key is creating a level playing field so that the existence of better or more advanced players doesn't give them an unfair advantage at the start of the tournament or scare off others from choosing to compete. Although the simplest way to address this issue is to select players with homogeneous initial conditions, that may not always be possible if the players are competing across several objectives (or tasks) and starting positions across them are correlated. In these cases, PIJC designers may decide whether the score for a task should be based on either the level of performance achieved (player conditions are homogeneous for the task) or degree of improvement (player conditions are highly heterogeneous for the task).

Harnessing Socially Based Incentives   Three other components of change, often overlooked, are instrumental to the PIJC approach. One is the power of public participation and feedback mechanisms. To ensure that all stakeholders are on board and form a team focused on placing in a tournament, a PIJC requires that commitment devices be used to engage them. Thus, the PIJC approach advocates requiring that public hearings (or their application-specific equivalent) be held as a condition for a tournament task to be registered. Meagher and Zinnes (2004) required that Moroccan municipal mayors sign public statements of their decision to participate after holding such town meetings. Although such mechanisms increase information sharing, they also play a key role in raising the likelihood that outcomes are equitable, which is not ensured even when the tournament rules are fair.

A second underused mechanism is the power of collective action, either through public-private partnerships or with adjacent municipalities. Such devices are particularly useful for small municipalities that cannot achieve economies of scale. Examples include joint purchasing (e.g., fire equipment), joint concessions (trash removal), and industrial park creation. A PIJC may take advantage of this mechanism by requiring that an interjurisdictional task be included in the tournament, either as an item on the menu of eligible tasks or as a required task.

Third, in striving to harness as many incentives as possible while keeping its overall design as simple as possible, the PIJC should also make use of peer and social pressure, sometimes referred to as the "blame and shame" mechanism. Hence, it is critical that all jurisdictions within the target population be measured—and their baseline and end-line results be widely disseminated—for maximum incentive effect. Otherwise, potential participants will simply opt out of playing for fear of having themselves compared with other jurisdictions. This design feature thus leads to greater transparency and freedom of information at the level of the players' constituencies. Moreover, many times members of a jurisdiction will not even be aware of their relative standing otherwise. For example, in the PROPER tournament in Indonesia (Afsah and Vincent 1997), players—in this case large industrial plant owners—were not aware of how bad their environmental profile was.

A TYPOLOGY OF COMPETITION MECHANISMS

At the simplest level, one can distinguish two types of play. Each is predicated on a different degree of information asymmetry between the sponsor and recipient. The contract type, which is easier to understand, is by far the most prevalent and should not be confused with the PIJC approach. Under the contract approach, the sponsor examines each player (e.g., municipality) on a case-by-case basis and determines—with or without local participation—what interventions might be feasible to achieve and then sets those as goals. The jurisdiction is rewarded if the goals are certified as achieved, essentially mirroring conditionality in technical assistance (development loans). This approach involves writing a contract or memorandum of understanding between the sponsor and each jurisdiction. Under this system, each municipality that fulfills the contract must be compensated: one package of sponsor funding stimulates one instance of reform in one municipality. Likewise, the chance of a jurisdiction winning depends only on its own efforts, not on actions undertaken by other jurisdictions.[31]

Under the relativist approach, the sponsor acknowledges not knowing what jurisdictions are capable of achieving and lets a tournament among them set the standards.[32] The approach builds on two ideas. The first is that with enough players, the gamut of what is feasible to achieve, given the resources and skill sets available, is observable. The second idea is that competition encourages excellence. Thus, those who do the best provide an indication of what was feasible at the start[33] (i.e., trace out the production possibility frontier). A variant of the pure relativist approach is the preferred modality for a full PIJC. It combines the contract approach, by insisting that participants meet certain thresholds on key indicators as a necessary condition to win, and the relativist approach, by using a tournament to sort potential winners, placers, and others.

As argued in Zinnes (2008), a more concrete and useful way to classify the underlying incentive mechanisms employed by IJCs is as follows.

Simple Certification   Simple certification assesses players against a pre-established performance benchmark. The sponsor, players, or outside organizations may disseminate or refer to how players fared for their own organizational purposes. The results of the certification process may therefore (1) affect player

---

31. A variation of this approach is when the benchmark is set by examining past performance of a cohort of jurisdictions, together with an assessment of current idiosyncratic local conditions.

32. Benchmark (or "yardstick") competition is an example of the relativist approach.

33. This indication is not just an information asymmetry between the sponsors and the players. Generally speaking, the players themselves will not have a good idea of what performance is possible by their group.

reputation by, for example, being a good place to do business, which might attract investors; (2) lead the player's constituency to demand changes or strengthen support of the player; or (3) make the player eligible for participating in a follow-up activity offering attractive benefits (e.g., access to donor financing).

Pecuniary Certification   Pecuniary certification is the same as simple certification, but once certified, the player is guaranteed a pre-announced tangible reward.

Pure Tournament   Although all eligible players may compete, only those with the N best performances (where N is announced in advance) win the rewards. Here, the winning score is endogenous and not known in advance.

Mixed Tournament   A tournament is used to allocate rewards (e.g., investment financing), and pecuniary certification is used for incentive compatibility to encourage weaker or less confident players to compete in the tournament. It does so by offering a consolation prize to players whose performance was inadequate to win but exceeds some minimum threshold. A mixed approach can mitigate risks of using one approach. For example, a tournament approach used alone may risk winners not having achieved a high enough performance for the donor to view the project as cost effective; a certification approach used alone may risk low participation (bar set too high) or too little effort by those participants who could have achieved much more (bar set too low).

In theory, there are two main differences between approaches. The first is whether the performance bar is absolute or relative, that is, whether winning depends on a player's performance relative to others or whether the actions of others are irrelevant. The second is whether the contest can be open-ended (certification) or must be limited to a fixed time interval (tournament). On the other hand, either approach can use indicators that measure levels of performance (requiring only an end line) or improvements in performance (requiring both baseline and end line). Either mechanism can have a participatory design focus, include an evaluation using randomized trials, be designed with a baseline measurement followed by a finish line benchmark (or only the latter). In both cases, the project may deliver technical assistance before, during, and/or after the benchmarking period. Both mechanisms can have a design based on prospective or retrospective incentives and, independently, score either inputs or outputs. Hence, in theory neither mechanism design is inherently more time consuming to run, other things being equal. Moreover, mixing the three core mechanisms essentially forms a continuum of incentive design options.

DECOMPOSITION OF PIJC INCENTIVE MECHANISMS
Because only a few PIJC donor tournaments have actually been implemented, there is limited experience on their performance and necessary conditions for success. We address this limitation for evaluation by decomposing a generic PIJC

application into its constituent incentive mechanisms and then by assessing the experience with the substantial number of mechanism-specific applications that do exist.

A PIJC contains mechanisms that increase the legitimacy of reforms. Here, the jurisdictions themselves participate in creating the menu of reforms from which they may then choose a subset of individual reforms to implement, thereby encouraging their active engagement in the competition. PIJC approaches also increase intervention legitimacy over conventional project designs because individual jurisdictions can usually opt out. In addition, particularly in the case of tournaments, the incentives are designed to overcome coordination problems so as to allow the sponsor and recipients to take advantage of commonly held goals. Likewise, the technical assistance a jurisdiction receives during the tournament is demand driven. On one hand, it is left to the jurisdiction to decide whether to participate in particular technical assistance workshops; on the other hand, the sponsor requires the jurisdiction to fulfill certain intermediate output conditions to be eligible for additional amounts of technical assistance during the tournament.

Because legitimacy is not the same as equity, how can we be sure the poorest can reach the winner's circle if, as is likely, the poorest are the worst performers and also have the worst governance? PIJCs not only are built around fair and transparent rules of the game but also contain design opportunities to ensure equity of outcomes, if desired. For example, one can ensure a level playing field either by limiting eligibility to a homogeneous group or by using relativist scoring (measure improvements, not levels),[34] select objectives targeting an equity objective,[35] and apply strategic advertising and training to galvanize "recalcitrant laggards."[36]

Being based on competition, a PIJC also contains mechanisms that work toward increasing the allocative efficiency and cost-effectiveness of the intervention. For example, the tournament mechanism encourages efficient efforts from participants. We say "efficient" because a player's effort is endogenously determined by the size of the rewards (both indirect benefits, due to the reform per se, and direct rewards from the sponsor) and the privately valued costliness of effort expended by the player.

Likewise, a tournament mechanism per se ensures tremendous leveraging of donor funds. First, marginal transaction costs are lower because the sponsor need not conduct protracted and expensive bilateral contract negotiations with each jurisdiction. Second, the fixed rewards budget stimulates reform efforts across

---

34. If the emphasis on demonstration effects in decentralization is to be believed, diminishing returns to improvements are then implied, which provides an advantage to the poorest performers under relativist scoring.

35. An example is per capita income of the lowest quartile or the adoption of particular accountability measures.

36. Pradhan, Kaiser, and Ahmad's (2007) term for those with the worst governance.

a larger number of players compared to the standard donor agreement where the donor commits to a similar amount, but for each player unit. For example, in the case of Galing Pook in the Philippines, the cost of providing financial and nonpecuniary incentives to between 5 and 10 recipient jurisdictions motivated more than 200 jurisdictions to carry out reforms. As Pradhan, Kaiser, and Ahmad (2007, 1) state, "All swimmers in the tournament make progress, not just the ones who come into the victory circle." Third, technical assistance is targeted. On the one hand, it is "laddered" so that the amount and type of technical assistance a jurisdiction receives depends on how far along a predefined schedule of milestones it has moved. Moreover, technical assistance is provided only to those jurisdictions that meet reform-dependent thresholds of performance (output).[37] This output-based technical assistance focus is strengthened by the requirement described above in which technical assistance is demand-driven. Thus, unlike most of the literature on output-based aid (e.g., Smith 2001), which focuses on efficient delivery by linking payment to performance, PIJC applications contain mechanisms that ensure beneficiary preferences will guide the nature of the services actually provided.

A series of articles in the 1980s (Green and Stokey 1983; Lazear and Rosen 1981; Nalebluff and Stiglitz 1983) come closest in the theoretical literature to investigating the efficiency issues considered here, whether tournaments, certification, or direct contracts. They underscore the importance of uncertainty and of who bears the risk of the tasks. (This line of thought goes further by considering the issue from the perspective of both the team playing against other teams and the decision maker playing against other stakeholders within a team.)

These articles start by identifying two sources of (additive) risk, the idiosyncratic efforts of the player and the common shock affecting all players. Among their results, they find that when the common shock "is sufficiently diffuse"—for example, an unexpected piece of new national legislation impacting all players— "then the optimal tournament dominates using independent contracts" (Green and Stokey 1983, 352). In other words, if jurisdictions believe that the results of their efforts could be adversely affected by actions outside of their control, tournament incentives will be more powerful than certification incentives in motivating reform. They also find that if the number of players is sufficiently large, a player's rank in the tournament is sufficient information for the sponsors to know the player's output level net of the common shock (Green and Stokey 1983). That is, a tournament design is an effective way for sponsors to discover what performance is feasible in the volatile environment found in most recipient countries.

A third set of mechanisms ensures the incentive compatibility of the PIJC, the property that the incentives facing the players and created by the PIJC are such

---

37. There is an increasing applied literature on output-based approaches to economic development that is now becoming more common in a raft of applications. See Brook and Petrie (2001) for many examples.

that they align player objectives (and therefore efforts) to those of the sponsor. As we have seen, that is possible (1) by giving the beneficiary a real role in selection of project goals, tasks to achieve them, and assistance they would require; (2) by strengthening institutional governance; and (3) by explicitly providing in-kind, pecuniary, or reputational rewards for those who would otherwise bear net costs from the intervention, either because as decision makers they assume direct political risks or because the project produces positive externalities.

Add that players self-select to participate in a PIJC and we see that a major benefit of this feature is the minimal need for the sponsor to monitor reform efforts on-site because the players themselves have an interest in the success of the activity. This situation is in stark contrast to the conventional one in which donors spend considerable time and expense monitoring recipient actions.[38]

Incentive compatibility has yet another consequence. It helps to overcome the tremendous information asymmetry existing between sponsors (and their foreign consultants) and local recipients; that is, critical project know-how is "impacted" with the recipient. Impacted means that it cannot be transferred to others; rather, it can only be indirectly drawn upon through the execution of its (local) owner's skills. Under the incentive-compatible design of a PIJC, the sponsor creates a situation in which the players have their same interests and therefore no longer needs to extract the recipients' local know-how or micromanage local implementers with such know-how. Likewise, recipients have the incentive to apply their own idiosyncratic private information through their efforts in the interest of the intervention.

As these various components suggest, the PIJC draws heavily on what is now called participatory development. In fact, it is even more powerful because the IJC strongly encourages intrajurisdictional cooperation. That is especially the case when jurisdictions differentiate themselves ethnically, religiously, politically, or even simply jurisdictionally (e.g., "our hometown football team is better than their hometown team"). In other words, a jurisdiction-based tournament tends to harness social capital, leading to collective action and using the power of peer pressure to mitigate free riding. Moreover, PIJCs can change how disparate interests within a community view the merits of collective action, consensus building, and decentralization itself.[39]

Perhaps the most concrete, and commonly employed, of mechanisms comprising a PIJC application is the use of actionable indicators and benchmarking.

---

38. This result suggests an added benefit of nonpecuniary rewards over pecuniary ones: the incentive for "elite capture" in repeated contests is probably lower because (1) winning is of limited value if a tournament's reputation is poor; and (2) past winners and present players have an incentive to blow the whistle on cheating.

39. Smoke (this volume) finds this paramount, claiming that the key challenge to decentralization is changing attitudes about how the public sector works. He urges a less formulaic application, exactly the orientation PIJC takes.

"Actionable" should be stressed because it is important that players know their own actions will directly affect indicator values and also trust that the benchmarks are correct, which would be less likely if they were purely conceptual.

A PIJC applied to local jurisdictions may be seen as an application of decentralization or the exercise thereof. For example, as described above for the cases of human rights and of local governance, the PIJCs were designed to encourage local governments to exercise statutory rights already legislated but not applied. This situation is akin to a physical therapist exercising the limb of a patient with functional, but atrophied, muscles. Likewise, winners of the PIJC generate—and demonstrate—innovative solutions to problems probably being faced by most of the other players, just like a good decentralization. Although in theory this scenario could occur with any donor intervention, in a PIJC as in decentralization there are large numbers of applications of the same intervention, thereby generating much more variation in experience and the greater likelihood for replicable lessons.

The structure of the PIJC uses the mechanism of what economists call a separating equilibrium to reduce adverse selection. In other words, the incentive design of a PIJC splits jurisdictions in two: one group that is serious about carrying out reform is encouraged to participate in the PIJC (and draw upon sponsor resources), and another group that is not interested in reform (but still desirous of sponsor resources) is encouraged to opt out of the tournament. Participation in the tournament allows members of the former group to signal to outsiders, sponsors, and investors alike, that they are serious about improving their performance targeted by the PIJC.[40] Winning permits even stronger signaling, which tournaments take advantage of in their rewards structures.[41]

A final aspect of the PIJC is its use of the outside coordinator/referee, that is, an institution all players can trust to enforce the rules of the game, objectively assess the winners, and deliver the promised rewards.[42] For example, Eastern European countries at the start of transition trusted the European Union (EU) to deliver the goods promised—EU accession. This enormous potential payoff had the effect of focusing minds and leading disparate interests within a country to

---

40. In particular, it is important not to discourage suitable reform candidates from participating because the tasks or the tournament design appear too daunting. On the other hand, the lure of rewards should not be used to encourage those not interested in reform to either game the system or cheat. I thank Johannes Linn for this observation.

41. Debbie Wertzel (private communication) suggests that such certification, if related to creditworthiness, would really draw SNG attention because it might allow it to tap international credit markets. In this example, a PIJC reward costs the sponsor almost nothing.

42. Despite Afonso and Guimarães Ferreira's (2008) concern, there is no contradiction here with Shah's (1998) view of SNGs as the origin of legitimacy of power. Rather, we can interpret SNGs as ceding the central government the statutory role of tournament referee, with the choices of tasks selected at the discretion of the SNGs.

cooperate (e.g., Poland). As the reliability of the EU's promise of accession has recently been called into question, so too has its role as a focal point and outside coordinator of reform effort. As another example, any foreign "expert" will tell you that half the benefit of their presence in the field is to act as an objective referee among competing ideas of local (real) experts.

In summary, the conditions under which alternative incentive mechanisms might be preferred are the following. The conventional approach is most appropriate when there are few recipients who need substantial help, when objectives require limited idiosyncratic local information, and when rigorous evaluation is not desired. Certification approaches are preferred when adequate performance is more important than achieving highest feasible performance, when the sponsors have a clear idea of what feasible performance levels are, when there are potentially many recipient-players, and, in the case of pecuniary rewards, when the sponsors have a flexible budget or clear idea of the number of likely certifications. Tournament approaches, on the other hand, should be preferred when a scarce resource needs to be allocated to the best performers, when systemic exogenous shocks are a concern, when there are potentially many recipient-players, and when the donor has a poor idea of what level of performance is achievable. Finally, PIJC may be seen as a mixture of pecuniary certification and tournament. Like a tournament, it prospectively offers awards and prizes to a limited number of contestants for achieving the best performance on a set of tasks. Like a pecuniary certification, it offers consolation prizes to contestants who exceed a preset threshold of performance.

An Assessment of Applications to Date

In Zinnes (2008), I evaluate the practicality and performance of actual PIJC by assessing a dozen projects from the World Bank, USAID, the Government of Indonesia, UNIDO, and the Ford Foundation. The framework emulates the way economists use the perfect competition model to understand the effect of the inevitable real-world deviations from it. For each existing PIJC application, I compare what components are absent or additional relative to the stylized full model presented here and determine whether these components mattered for the application's observed success or failure. We can then identify lessons learned how each incentive mechanism: (1) affects project effectiveness and sustainability; (2) makes idiosyncratic demands on a country's initial conditions; (3) contains prospects and limitations for scaling up; and (4) presents obstacles for implementation (including cost and time). Although a surprising number of existing projects use some form of certification, tournament applications are rare.

EFFECTIVENESS OF APPLICATIONS TO DATE

Looking at the effectiveness of certification approaches, it can be observed that projects that were able to build on social or cultural norms within the target region and that were able to communicate the meaning of the certification were

382	Clifford F. Zinnes

more successful than those that weren't communicating well, even if the former projects offered no specific pecuniary rewards. Examples include the PROPER large-firm environmental performance rating system in Indonesia (Afsah and Vincent 1997) and, to a lesser extent, the Public Services Report Card project in Jharkhand, India (Public Affairs Foundation 2004).

On the other hand, projects that were not able to enforce strict quality control on their certification—typically due to engaging in precertification rather than output-based certification (e.g., Senegal Literacy Project[43])—were less successful than those that were (Romania Fast and Simple Project). Likewise, poor dissemination of the certification scores weakened their incentive effects, contributing further to lost project impacts (e.g., both aforementioned projects). Instituting multilevel certification appears to have been more economically efficient, where feasible, than a single certification level because it increased participation.

Regarding the project effectiveness of tournament approaches, projects that offered salient rewards and adequate technical assistance during the competition—such as the Russia Fiscal Reform Project (World Bank 2006) and the Kecamatan Development Program (KDP 2005) project in Indonesia—did better than those that didn't. Programs based on repeated tournaments (in fact, certifications, too)—for example, Galing Pook—that maintained the quality of their reputations resulted in awarded activities having both a demonstration effect (on other municipalities) as well as a participation effect (more players would participate in the next tournament round). On the other hand, a tournament in which competition is based on indicators of past performance had a much weaker incentive effect (e.g., *Mancomunidades* in Honduras, Nigerian Scorecard Project) than those based on performance during the competition (e.g., Russia Fiscal Reform Project). Where rewards were insufficiently specific, their incentive impact was not commensurate with their implementation costs (e.g., USAID's R4).

Regardless of the core mechanism(s) applied, it seems that none works properly unless the right components are present simultaneously. For example, having a reward with no benchmarking, or benchmarking without a reward, made a huge difference to project effectiveness. Several of the certification projects may have achieved more had they included extra PIJC components, which would have been feasible to add had designers wanted to. The Romania Fast and Simple project would have had greater success had rewards been brighter and more salient. An evaluation component would have increased the cost-effectiveness of the Senegal Literacy Project. The *Mancomunidades* project would have achieved a much greater effect had it followed the prospective design of a PIJC. Instead, the project design opted for retrospective "competition"; that is, rewards were given on the basis of performance that had taken place prior to the time the project's incentives could have an effect.

---

43. See Nordtveit (2004) or Zinnes (2008) for project details.

We also find that weaknesses in projects adopting the tournament approach did not seem to be intrinsic to the mechanism; rather, they were the result of shortcomings in a specific application's design or implementation. For example, the mediocre performances of the USAID R4 system and the World Bank's Nigerian Scorecard Project were not due to the use of a tournament approach, but to the lack of sufficiently bright rewards.

Finally, it is useful to consider how the additional complexity of PIJC designs affects their feasibility. As argued above, much of the extra complexity is due not to inherent differences in design but to the historical lack of sponsor interest in outcomes when they applied conventional approaches. Hence, for a fair assessment, it is necessary to sustain the degree of sponsor interest in outcomes, the number of jurisdictions to reform, and the tasks to achieve. Stated this way, it appears that conventional sponsor approaches and those using PIJCs have no inherent differences in complexity for task selection, indicator design and data collection, or impact evaluation.

Significant differences in complexity and cost do exist for other design elements. Under a conventional approach, the contracting of the sponsor-recipient agreement must take place for each jurisdiction. Thus, a special study of each jurisdiction is required to identify what it is likely to achieve and how, what idiosyncratic assistance it will need to do so, and what it could absorb after the reform (the reward). Because the sponsor has a limited technical assistance (TA) budget and typically works directly with the SNG in situ, the sponsor must decide whether to accept a TA budget spread thin to cover all jurisdictions or to bear the much higher costs of providing TA to all jurisdictions, regardless of their interest.

Under a PIJC approach, once the tasks are set, only a set of game instructions are needed. It is up to each jurisdiction to decide whether to play, in which case it submits precommitment documentation (generally after organizing public meetings), adding complexity on the recipient's side. The recipient must then decide which strategy to use and which TA workshops to attend. Moreover, because there is no "big brother donor" dictating what to do or when, the PIJC requires local initiative and, ideally, a team captain, which the reward structure has been designed to encourage. This reward schedule, however, is an additional complexity for the sponsor to calibrate and test. On the other hand, the intensive in-project monitoring for compliance, which conventional approaches require, is unnecessary under a PIJC. Likewise, a PIJC requires an investment in public relations both before and during the contest, to stimulate participation and interest, as well as afterward, to disseminate performance (the "praise or shame" incentive). Finally, although conventional approaches set time limits for reform performance, in practice these are not time consistent and are typically extended, in some cases several times. That cannot happen under a tournament structure because a race needs a "finish line," but it is possible under certification.

For all these reasons, conventional approaches grow more expensive to run than PIJCs as the number of jurisdictions increases. Tournaments, however, require more training to explain the rules of the game to the players. Although their calibration and testing would seemingly make tournaments more complex than conventional approaches, that idea is misleading because it ignores the high transaction costs of jurisdiction-by-jurisdiction negotiation, contracting, and monitoring. With neither approach being dominant in cost-complexity space, it will depend on the initial conditions and the application as to whether absorptive capacity limits, on either the sponsor's or recipient's side, have been reached.

EFFECT OF INITIAL CONDITIONS ON APPLICATIONS TO DATE

From the case study applications discussed above, we may draw some likely inferences about the effect of initial conditions on PIJC outcomes. Although there are only a few core incentive mechanisms, in the cases reviewed successful application critically depends on the idiosyncratic tailoring of the game to the variation of local conditions. Thus, participatory approaches must be used to establish and calibrate game tasks, size and schedule of rewards, nature of TA, and public relations campaigns (including how to disseminate performance results). In short, attention to initial conditions is of paramount importance. An adequate legislative and regulatory framework must already be in place if PIJC applications are to encourage (exercise) their de facto local-level implementation. Likewise, local public finance laws need to be sufficiently decentralized and business laws sufficiently modern to permit pecuniary rewards for jurisdictions and their officials.[44] Cultural conditions upon which to build cooperation are required because players are teams. The teamwork needed to effect change generally required a culture of an active civil society or motivated senior local officials. Although PIJCs require less sponsor monitoring than conventional projects, incentives for local oversight were required to combat a culture of corruption.[45] The culture should either expect or appreciate their officials having the political will to overcome "measurement reticence."[46] There needs to be an initial indigenous desire for change because the PIJC only encourages collective action.[47]

Sponsors, on the other hand, must be willing to commit to an extended performance period, which is a function of the type of reform contemplated. Moreover, they must be institutionally able to withhold benefits from players not meeting the award criteria (maintain a "hard budget" constraint). Hardest of all, sponsors must carefully evaluate their other in-country programs to ensure that

---

44. One World Bank employee cleverly suggested as an alternative more holidays as a reward to government officials.

45. For example, in the Russia Fiscal Reform Project, the ministry of finance had incentives to control creeping corruption at the SNG level.

46. The "fear" of having one's performance quantitatively tracked.

47. Of course, one might be able to conduct a project first to educate the target population on the need for change.

players are not distracted, or game incentives diluted, by the presence of other significant contemporaneous assistance from the sponsor.

Incentive mechanism design is also constrained by initial conditions. For example, use of intangible (e.g., signaling or reputational) rewards requires that a sufficient breadth of media dissemination exists to reach the target population. Likewise, lack of reliable official data, especially on the local level, may constrain the choice of the preferred performance indicators.[48] Finally, to prevent collusion, a design based on level of performance requires that a sufficient number of homogeneous players along the relevant dimensions exists.

These conditions may seem quite demanding. The experience from past applications, however, suggests that need not be the case. The applications examined do run the gamut developmentally, although sponsors needed to choose the site, ambitiousness, and speed (Smoke 2008) of their applications appropriately. For example, the competition in Morocco focused on rural municipalities and excluded any big cities.

SUSTAINABILITY OF APPLICATIONS TO DATE

It is important to distinguish between the sustainability of the institution (program) running the distribution mechanism (game) and the sustainability of the projects or activities it stimulates. Of course, if a program is conceived as a one-time enterprise, only the latter is of interest.

Program Sustainability   Casual experience suggests that people eventually lose interest in "games," be they children or staff offered recognition incentives. Does experience with jurisdictional competition agree? In the case of projects with longer-duration setup time, there is some evidence of donor fatigue. In the case of USAID's R4 initiative, incentives were nebulous due to the vague reward structure and the large role exogenous factors could play on indicator outcomes. In the case of UNIDO's Moroccan PIJC, the time taken for planning (two years) permitted unrelated politics at UNIDO to change its priorities and abort the initiative.

We do not find evidence for fatigue in the case of well-run and -designed contest programs. Such programs create their own legitimacy and reputational momentum. For example, to date the Galing Pook competition has run for twelve years and does not even involve a pecuniary prize. The Indonesian government's PROPER initiative has run since 1995 and has spawned copycats domestically and internationally. The World Bank's KDP project ran for five years and has continued to this day despite a regime change in the country. Part of the reason is that, unlike the challenge of motivating a specific person on one's staff, a fixed incentive in a repeated game with jurisdictions as players confronts different

---

48. Although PIJC-specific data collection adds to costs, that is less a concern in repeated games. SNGs may also have additional uses for the data, especially if the technical assistance in its collection leads to an ongoing data program.

individuals, just like in any league sport. Local government officials change over time, and beneficiaries of different project activities are rarely the same; consider, for example, those who would benefit from a red-tape reduction activity versus from a literacy campaign activity.

The alternatives to allocation by contest are formulas and discretionary selection. Probably the main determinants of sustainability for the allocation method are its administrative efficiency and the effectiveness and equity of its outcomes. Although formulas are surely the most administratively efficient, their fairness generally depends on the quality of the "democratic" political process issuing approval. The motivations for discretionary selection (sole sourcing)—aside from corruption—tend to be speed and cheapness of contracting. Donors do not appear to have such institutional concerns, but central governments, which often run revenue allocation programs annually, require administrative efficiency. Steffensen (2007) shows that even in developing countries performance-based allocation is possible if properly regularized.[49] Formulas and sole sourcing, however, are much less likely to lead to economically efficient outcomes compared with competitive allocation processes (e.g., grant competitions). Hence, sustainability of the allocation mechanism boils down to how these elements get weighted in a government's adoption decision.

Regarding our case studies, we find that mechanism sustainability depends on the organizer's commitment to the continued quality of its reputation, which, in turn, requires the long-term credibility of the referee. Such commitment is relatively easy if a foreign donor stays engaged, as in the case of Galing Pook and the Ford Foundation. When there is only a local referee, care must be taken to avoid loss of mechanism reputation from creeping corruption, especially when a pecuniary prize is at stake. I see no evidence, however, that constituencies of "losing" jurisdictions feel "punished" as feared by Afonso and Guimarães Ferreira (this volume). For example, the Russia Fiscal Reform project (World Bank 2006) specifically states that such a consequence was not the case. A possible reason is that any level of reform achieved was itself a benefit, regardless of whether a player won. It also appears that the most effective incentive mechanisms are those run by an organization outside the one whose behavior is to be modified (e.g., compare Jharkhand Report Cards to USAID R4 programs). Finally, when pecuniary rewards are involved, it seems that mechanism sustainability after the sponsor's departure depends on finding other funders of the rewards and operational running costs. In cases in which the activity has been deemed successful during the sponsor period, the government may step in (e.g., Russia Fiscal Reform, KDP, Galing Pook).

---

49. Missing from the analysis here, as well as Steffensen's, is the multiperiod nature of funding. For example, budget allocations are annual, but capital projects require multiyear funding commitments.

Project Activity Sustainability   Of greater importance for sustainability than the competitive element are the presence of local ownership, long-term gains that can be captured locally, and the degree to which PIJC outcomes can reach the poor. From the case studies, it seems that the sustainability of projects funded through a tournament was greater when using output-based, rather than input-based, performance rewards (e.g., Russia Fiscal versus Nigerian Scorecard) and when it was possible to award intermediate rewards for achieving concrete project milestones (tasks required on the way to fulfilling project deliverables).[50] Better sustainability also seems linked to the degree to which participation was voluntary and initial project goals were aligned to existing preferences in the target population. Finally, higher sustainability was more likely if the structure of rewards, whether offered directly or generated indirectly, led to both private and public capture of benefits.[51]

SCALABILITY AND REPLICABILITY OF APPLICATIONS TO DATE
As in the case of sustainability, a distinction can be made between process and funded activity.

Process Scalability   An important consideration relates to the fixed costs of running the process. For example, the MCC now appears to be at full capacity with its current level of staffing and would not likely be able to increase the number of compacts it manages without substantial additional hiring. Variable cost considerations are easier for organizations to address. For example, to expand the Galing Pook project could simply entail finding additional peer reviewers, with no expansion in permanent staff or facilities necessary.

Regarding scaling up the number of activities a tournament-based approach can handle, most of the projects selected exhibited good within-country scalability qualities. KDP in Indonesia and investment promotion in Morocco provide two examples that help explain why. In KDP, more activities were easily handled by simply replicating the game structure in an additional *kecamatan*. In Morocco, because tournaments were designed for the provincial level, it was possible to simply increase the number of provinces—either simultaneously or sequentially—running (separate) tournaments. A more powerful way to scale up the number of jurisdictions in a contest is to "nest" tournaments. In this case, it is pre-announced to players that a simultaneous "super" tournament will be conducted by computing the average scores of jurisdictions in each province. The

---

50. Perhaps such sweeteners encouraged greater participation by tempting the weaker players to compete.

51. The Galing Pook game used speaking tours for proactive officials and investment promotion for the town.

province with the highest average score is declared the winner. This design also encourages the provincial governments to find reforms to implement that would help their lower-level jurisdictions attain higher scores on their tournament tasks. Note that we do not propose to scale up a tournament by having more provinces compete in the same tournament. This is because the greater the mutual anonymity of players (e.g., greater distance reduces knowledge of competitors), the weaker the social and psychological forces of teamwork and local pride may be.

Regarding replicating funded activities in other countries, many of the initial conditions required for a successful mechanism implementation may also be viewed as scalability requirements. Moreover, each of the incentive mechanisms described here appears feasible to adjust to fit local conditions. One can vary the complexity of the tournament benchmark indicators, require more or fewer tasks, offer different reward structures (number, value, intermediate bonuses), and modify the number of eligible jurisdictions allowed to compete per tournament. The degree of success in making these adjustments depends on the level of local participation in designing the intervention and the amount of pilot testing and calibration done in advance.

Activity Scalability   Activity scalability should be distinguished from process scalability. In the Senegal Literacy program, scalability is straightforward: simply expand the number of districts for which firms can offer services. In the case of KDP, however, what does scalability mean in the case of a winning village building a bridge (although replicability in this case is clear)? What does it mean if a winning SNG engages in administrative reform as a result of a tournament? Although replicability is a characteristic of activities implemented through a tournament, scalability is generally better assessed at the process level, as discussed above.[52]

AREAS FOR FURTHER RESEARCH

Putting aside the actual substance of the reform, several remaining implementation challenges need to be overcome in order to have a successful PIJC. One area concerns the calibration of optimal rewards and their structure. First, the project designer must decide whether to base the competition on achieving the highest level of performance or the largest incremental improvement in performance. Or, should there be one set for best performers and one set for best improvers (Duflo 2005)? How the latter is a more effective incentive when players are heterogeneous has been previously discussed. Beyond that, however, is the question of determining the number of winning positions to offer and the size of each reward, given the number of players and their heterogeneity. A similar question concerns the need to add certification thresholds in a tournament and the level at which to

---

52. On the other hand, one could analyze whether the number of hospital patients treated via SNG health expenditures is more or less easily scaled up under PBGs or under other funding allocation methods.

set them. Larger than necessary rewards can be distracting and encourage corruption, whereas insufficiently sized rewards risk attracting too few players.

Closely related to the structure of rewards is how to set the number of players and their individual size so as to have the most effective tournament possible. The Russia Fiscal Reform Project had 7 jurisdictional players; the Morocco project anticipated 80. Many factors must be taken into consideration, and some research-based guidance on this matter would be helpful.

The standard way to resolve these questions has been with focus groups, rules of thumb, and inferences from experience elsewhere. It now seems possible, however, to augment focus group tests by using a pilot survey and even to take greater advantage of laboratory experiments. Developing a standard set of field instruments in this regard would be worth pursuing.

Tournaments and certification in particular depend on good preplay public relations and postplay dissemination of results. How does one prepare the public to collaborate? How does one introduce the tournament concept into a particular cultural environment? What forums does one convene to bring together disparate interest groups within a jurisdiction in order to stimulate team formation? What scope is there to use the Internet and remote education technologies to reduce the cost of providing commonly needed reform TA during a tournament? There are many ways, as well as media, from which to choose. The field of strategic communication is certainly growing, and more research would be useful on its application to the design of reputational awards for maximum incentive effect in tournaments and certification. Part of the success of the PROPER project in Indonesia is owed to its clever use of communication in the design of the measurement metric. Mastery of these issues may also help to develop techniques to overcome the problem of political reticence of having one's performance measured.

In considering how far the PIJC might go, Pradhan, Kaiser, and Ahmad (2007) raise a rather profound question. They ask whether a government/donor could use a PIJC to change initial conditions (i.e., create hard budget constraint and weaker elite power). Although only experience will tell, evidence exists for such changes. In both the Morocco and KDP projects, players have exuded exuberance over their changed attitudes toward local-level collective action. Likewise, the PROPER has been lauded—and imitated—for changing attitudes about environmental responsibility. The Russia Fiscal and Moroccan projects both included hard budget constraints as one of the tasks to achieve, with the former project being successful.

In a different context, Kanbur (2006) raises some interesting collateral issues which have bearing on PIJCs. He asks how to increase donor accountability and how to apportion credit and blame when an intervention has mixed-team players as, for example, in his original case, a joint partnership environment. He also worries about such issues when dealing with vested interests and when donor, government, and team member contributions may be subject to fungibility of funds. He rightfully suggests that one must pay more attention to overall impacts rather than individual contributions. Ironically, vis-à-vis the donor, fungibility is much more of a problem for conventional project designs, where the donor takes on a more direct role in guiding outcomes and in decision making. In the types of incentive mechanisms presented here, the donor is forced to take a hands-off approach once the parameters of the game are established. Regarding apportioning blame and praise when the player comprises separate local entities, teamwork is what matters, and the players themselves will know whom to blame or praise. Moreover, each party's agreement to play on the team presupposes the party's acceptance of the risks and rewards.

Conclusions

An assessment of the case studies in Zinnes (2008) reveals that competition-inducing designs have the potential to generate more cooperation and collective action than those based on noncompetitive approaches. Likewise, we see that much scope exists for incorporating "information-lite" incentive mechanisms into decentralization, service delivery, and public finance reforms as well as into donor initiatives. Central governments want to increase their international competitiveness and reduce poverty. Poor public service delivery weighs heavily on both and, worse, also weakens the legitimacy of central governments' attempts to raise the revenues to address the situation. Some are turning to varying degrees of decentralization, but local understanding and experience have made these attempts somewhat de jure. Our analysis suggests that PIJC may offer a chance to exercise the new powers decentralization confers to local administrations, although it is an empirical question whether political patronage can be overcome with the right reward schedule. On the other hand, the almost nonexistent feedback channel between aid recipient and donor funder (the taxpayer) contributes to the poor track record of development assistance, and the institutional incentives facing donors need to be changed to encourage more ambitious and innovative projects. For those sponsors now interested in leveraging their assistance by becoming "advocates for change," PIJC offers a potentially powerful way for them to do so.

REFERENCES

Afonso, J. R., and S. Guimarães Ferreira. 2008. Commentary on Zinnes's "Increasing the effectiveness of public service delivery: A tournament approach." In *Fiscal decentralization and land policies*, G. K. Ingram and Y-H. Hong, eds., 395–397. Cambridge, MA: Lincoln Institute of Land Policy.

Afsah, S., and J. Vincent. 1997. Putting pressure on polluters: Indonesia's PROPER Program. Case Study for Harvard Institute for International Development. Asia Environmental Economics Policy Seminar, March. Harvard University, Cambridge, MA.

Ahmad, J., S. Devarajan, and S. Khemani. 2005. Decentralization and service delivery. Policy Research Working Paper 3603. Washington, DC: World Bank.

Annez, P. C., G. Huet, and G. Peterson. 2008. Operational lessons for the urban century: Urban infrastructure funds in World Bank lending operations 1979–2006. Washington, DC: World Bank. Mimeo.

Ashbrook, A., and C. Clement. 2001. A local government competition to improve the business environment in Romanian counties. USAID Task Order. Mimeo.

Azfar, O., and C. Zinnes. 2003. Improving the effectiveness of technical assistance through the use of prospective evaluation procedures. Task Order 7, SEGIR/LIR PCE-I-00-97-00042-00. Washington, DC: USAID.

Bahl, R., and J. Linn. 1992. *Urban public finance in developing countries*. New York: Oxford University Press.

Boone, P., and J-P. Faguet. 2002. Multilateral aid, politics, and poverty. In *The global crisis in foreign aid*, R. Grant and J. Nijman, eds. Syracuse, NY: Syracuse University Press.

Brook, P., and M. Petrie. 2001. Output-based aid: Precedents, promises, and challenges. In *Contracting for public services: Output-based aid and its applications*, P. Brook and S. Smith, eds., 3–11. Washington, DC: World Bank.

Cadwell, C. 2005. Bangladesh local government accountability project protecting the rights of persons vulnerable to trafficking. Grant proposal to the Department of State, Bureau of Democracy, Human Rights and Labor Human Rights and Democratization Initiatives in Countries with Significant Muslim Populations.

Collier, P. 2003. Making aid smart: Institutional incentives facing donor organizations and their implications for aid effectiveness. Task Order 7, SEGIR/LIR PCE-I-00-97-00042-00. Washington, DC: USAID.

Collier, P., S. Guillaumont, and J. Gunning. 1997. Redesigning conditionality. *World Development* 25(9):1399–1407.

Duflo, E. 2005. Field experiments in development economics. Paper prepared for the World Congress of the Econometrics Society, University College, London, August 24.

Easterly, W. 2002. Tired old mantras at Monterey. *Wall Street Journal*, March 18.

———. 2006. The big push déjà vu: A review of Jeffrey Sachs's *The end of poverty: Economic possibilities for our time. Journal of Economic Literature* 44(1): 96–105.

Espina, C., and C. Zinnes. 2003. Institutional incentives within USAID: How do they affect project outcomes? IRIS Forums Discussion Paper, F5-1, Task Order 7, SEGIR/LIR PCE-I-00-97-00042-00. Washington, DC: USAID.

Faquet, J-P. 2000. Does decentralization increase government responsiveness to local needs? Decentralization and public investment in Bolivia. Discussion Paper 999. Centre for Economic Performance, and Development Studies Institute, London School of Economics.

Frey, B., and R. Eichenberger. 1999. *The new democratic federalism for Europe: Functional overlapping and competing jurisdictions*. Northampton, MA: Edward Elgar.

Furubotn, E., and R. Richter. 1999. *Institutions and economic theory: The contribution of the new institutional economics*. Ann Arbor: University of Michigan Press.

Galing Pook Foundation. 2005. *Galing Pook Foundation: A tribute to innovation and excellence in local governance.* http://www.galingpook.org/index.htm.

Glewwe, P., N. Ilias, and M. Kremer. 2003. Teacher incentives. Department of Economics, Harvard University, Cambridge, MA. Mimeo.

Green, J., and N. Stokey. 1983. A comparison of tournaments and contracts. *Journal of Political Economy* 91(3):349–364.

IDA. *See* International Development Association.

International Development Association. 2005. Update on the assessments and implementation of action plans to strengthen capacity of HIPCs to track poverty-reducing public spending. Prepared by the International Monetary Fund's Fiscal Affairs Department and the World Bank's Poverty-Reduction and Economic Management Network. http://www.imf.org/external/np/pp/eng/2005/041205a.pdf.

Kagel, J., and A. Roth, eds. 1995. *The handbook of experimental economics.* Princeton, NJ: Princeton University Press.

Kanbur, R. 2006. The economics of international aid. In *Handbook of the economics of giving, altruism and reciprocity,* vol. 2, *Applications,* S-C. Kolm and J. M. Ythier, eds. Amsterdam: North Holland.

KDP. *See* Kecamatan Development Program.

Kecamatan Development Program. 2005. Kecamatan Development Program information package. KDP Secretariat in PMD, Ministry of Home Affairs, Government of Indonesia, Jakarta.

Kremer, M. 2003. Institutions, aid and development assistance. Task Order 7, SEGIR/ LIR PCE-I-00-97-00042-00. Washington, DC: USAID.

Kusek, J., and R. Rist. 2004. Assessing country readiness for results-based monitoring and evaluation systems. *PREMnotes* 87. Poverty Reduction and Economic Management. Washington, DC: World Bank.

Lazear, E., and S. Rosen. 1981. Rank-order tournaments as optimum labor contracts. *Journal of Political Economy* 89(5):841–864.

Martens, B., U. Mummert, P. Murrell, and P. Seabright. 2002. *The institutional economics of foreign aid.* Cambridge: Cambridge University Press.

Martinez-Vazquez, J., and J. Boex. 1999. Fiscal decentralization in the Russian Federation during transition. International Studies Program Working Paper 99-3. Andrew Young School of Policy Studies, Georgia State University, Atlanta.

Meagher, P., and C. Zinnes. 2004. The use of inter-jurisdictional competition to strengthen the investment climate: A field guide and application to Morocco. United Nations Industrial Development Organization Investment Promotion Office of Bologna, Italy. Final Report. Mimeo.

Millennium Challenge Corporation. 2006. Homepage of the Millennium Challenge Corporation, Washington, DC. www.mcc.gov.

Moynihan, D. 2003. Performance-based budgeting: Beyond rhetoric. *PREMnotes* 78. Poverty Reduction and Economic Management. Washington, DC: World Bank.

Murrell, P. 2002. The interaction of donors, contractors, and recipients in implementing aid for institutional reform. In *The institutional economics of foreign aid,* B. Martens, U. Mummert, and P. Murrell, eds., 69–111. Cambridge: Cambridge University Press.

Nalebluff, B., and J. Stiglitz. 1983. Prizes and incentives: Towards a general theory of compensation and competition. *Bell Journal of Economics* 14(1):21–43.

Nordtveit, B. H. 2004. Managing public-private partnership: Literacy education in Senegal. Africa Region Human Development Working Paper Series 72. Washington, DC: World Bank.

Oates, W. 2002. Fiscal and regulatory competition: Theory and evidence. *Perspektiven der Wirtschaftspolitik* 2(4):377–390.

————. 2005. Toward a second-generation theory of fiscal federalism. *International Tax and Public Finance* 12(4):349–373.

OECD. *See* Organisation for Economic Co-operation and Development.

Organisation for Economic Co-operation and Development. 1999. Performance contracting: Lessons from performance contracting case studies and a framework for public sector performance contracting. PUMA/PAC (99)2, Programme on Public Management and Governance. Paris: OECD.

O'Reilly, R. 2000. Charter schools: The search for community. *Peabody Journal of Education* 75(4):19–36.

Ostrom, E., C. Gibson, S. Shivakumar, and K. Andersson. 2001. Aid, incentives, and sustainability: An institutional analysis of development cooperation. *Sida Studies in Evaluation* 1(February).

Platteau, J-P. 2005. Institutional and distributional aspects of sustainability in community-driven development. In *Evaluating development effectiveness*, vol. 7 of World Bank Series on Evaluation and Development, G. Pitman, O. Feinstein, and G. Ingram, eds., 275–298. New Brunswick, NJ: Transaction Publishers.

Pradhan, S., K. Kaiser, and J. Ahmad. 2007. Comments and talking points on "Harnessing inter-jurisdictional competition to increase the effectiveness of socio-economic development initiatives" by Clifford Zinnes. Wolfensohn Center for Development. Washington, DC: Brookings Institution. Mimeo.

Public Affairs Foundation. 2004. Benchmarking public service delivery at the forest fringes in Jharkhand, India: A pilot citizen report card. Public Affairs Foundation Discussion Paper. October, unnumbered. Bangalore, India.

Sachs, J. 2005. *The end of poverty: Economic possibilities for our time.* New York: Penguin.

Shah, A. 1998. Balance, accountability, and responsiveness: Lessons about decentralization. World Bank Policy Research Working Paper Series 2021. Washington, DC: World Bank.

Smith, W. 2001. Designing output-based aid schemes: A checklist. In *Contracting for public services: Output-based aid and its applications*, P. Brook and S. Smith, eds., 38–68. Washington, DC: World Bank.

Smoke, P. 2008. Local revenues under fiscal decentralization in developing countries: Linking policy reform, governance, and capacity. In *Fiscal decentralization and land policies*, G. K. Ingram and Y-H. Hong, eds., 38–68. Cambridge, MA: Lincoln Institute of Land Policy.

Steffensen, J. 2007. Performance based grant systems: Using grants as incentives— Concept and lessons learned. PowerPoint slides presented at the World Bank, Washington, DC.

Svensson, J. 2003. Why conditional aid does not work and what can be done about it? *Journal of Development Economics* 70:381–402.

Terfa, Inc. 2005. Scorecard assessment of rural local governments in nine states of Nigeria, vol. 1. Consultant Report produced for Africa Region Department. Washington, DC: World Bank.

Tiebout, C. M. 1956. A pure theory of local expenditures. *Journal of Political Economy* 64(5):416–424.

United States Agency for International Development. 2006. Support to democratic systems and governance in a changing environment in Bolivia. RFTOP 511-06-029, July 20. Washington, DC: USAID.

USAID. *See* United States Agency for International Development.

Williams, V., and I. Kushnarova. 2004. The public sector governance reform cycle: Available diagnostic tools. *PREMnotes* 88. Poverty Reduction and Economic Management. Washington, DC: World Bank.

Wood, R. C., and G. Hamel. 2002. The World Bank's innovation market. *Harvard Business Review* (November) reprint RO211H:2–8.

World Bank. 1998. *Assessing aid: What works, what doesn't, and why.* New York: Oxford University Press.

———. 2005. *The world development report 2004: Making services work for poor people.* Washington, DC: World Bank / Oxford University Press.

———. 2006. Report and recommendation of the president of the International Bank for Reconstruction and Development to the executive directors on a fiscal federalism and regional fiscal reform loan in the amount of $US120 million to the Russian Federation, Report P7504-RU. Washington, DC: World Bank.

Zinnes, C. 2008. *Tournament approaches to policy reform: Making development assistance more effective.* Washington, DC: Brookings Institution.

Zinnes, C., and A. Bolaky. 2002. Harnessing the power of incentives: An NIE framework for increasing aid effectiveness. Task Order 7, SEGIR/LIR PCE-I-00-97-00042-00. Washington, DC: USAID.

Zinnes, C., J. Hansen, and R. Miller. 2005. Harnessing local initiatives to stimulate the growth of free-market agriculture in Uzbekistan. Proposal submitted to the Foreign Agricultural Service of the U.S. Department of Agriculture by University Research Corporation, Inc., and the College of Agricultural and Resource Economics, University of Maryland. Mimeo.

COMMENTARY
José Roberto R. Afonso and Sérgio Guimarães Ferreira

Clifford Zinnes proposes a new approach to increasing the effectiveness of public service delivery. Given such a general goal, it is useful to consider this problem from a pragmatic view, adding elements of political economy to the analysis, identifying problems on a case-by-case basis, and adopting a more proactive approach. In other words, one can "learn by doing." In his introduction, Zinnes (this volume, p. 360) states, "The greater the amount of cooperation within the team, . . . the more likely its chances of winning or placing. Eliciting cooperation through competition allows the tournament approach."

Zinnes deserves credit for analyzing this question from a mechanism design perspective. It is an excellent starting point and leads to a new approach called prospective interjurisdictional competition (PIJC), which "brings together several desirable, yet tested, incentive-compatible mechanisms. The prospective design of the PIJC in which all players know the rules of the game in advance ensures that the donor can construct race-to-the-top and not race-to-the-bottom competition" (this volume, p. 362).

Interjurisdictional competition is a natural companion of decentralization. It occurs in a situation in which each federate unit independently decides a tax or expenditure policy. Potentially, it always exists because it is the consequence of differences among jurisdictions, not necessarily of intentionally promoted discrepancies, and there are no two identical government units in the world. One cannot, in all cases, presume to know whether fiscal competition is welfare enhancing or welfare reducing. A general inference is that the answer depends on several factors. Prominent among them are (1) the objectives of competing governments; (2) the competition's "prize"; (3) how the governments compete; (4) the behavior of economic agents, especially their mobility in response to fiscal stimuli; and (5) the characteristics of the economic environment, particularly the possibility of interjurisdictional externalities arising from government actions.

An economic analysis can be employed to comment on the PIJC strategy defended by Zinnes. As Zinnes proposed, the idea of introducing private incentives to make recipients act in accordance with donors' expectations is potentially interesting, especially concerning foreign aid. It is important, however, to be careful when applying this concept to intergovernmental fiscal transfers.[1]

This comment expresses the authors' opinions and not those of the institutions to which they are bonded. We would like to thank Beatriz Meirelles and Ricardo Figueiró for assistance.

1. There is a glitch with the temporal framework of the proposal: it is necessary to decide in advance about the grant of a loan or a fiscal transfer based on a performance that can only be measured after. The main issue is the central government's decision to believe in the local authorities' promise of fulfilling the presented plan, after they have received the financial resources. It is a subjective decision-making process.

Empirically testing the effects of institutional reforms in countries (or states or municipalities) poses an important problem: those reforms are endogenous. For instance, introducing monetary incentives for teachers generally weakens cooperative behavior; if cooperative behavior does not impose sufficient resistance to reform, it may be because teachers are already performing with high (not low) effort.

In the case of grant distribution reforms, central governments require a commitment of efficiency from local public good providers (instead of "buying" voting services in the congress through "bribing" representatives from local oligarchies). Unfortunately, most of the time most of the intergovernmental transfers are earmarked and linked to central government tax revenues. Reforming such a mechanism by replacing it with a tournament or even something less based on outcome (and more on input) requires a strong political alliance.[2] Moreover, legal tradition does not favor innovation such as incentive-driven grants or pay.[3]

Another concern is the design of intergovernmental transfers. Care must be taken not to deal with any kind of transfer, credit or fiscal, and financial intergovernmental relationship as if it were an extra, a favor from one government to the other, from the "donor governor." This reasoning and further proposals may be extended to the so-called ad hoc grants and voluntary transfers, that is, funds that are transferred at the free will of those who transfer them. They cannot be applied without due caution and explanation to regular transfers such as revenue sharing, however. Because transfers are tax-revenue sharing, aimed at balancing insufficient self-generated tax revenues by local governments, central governments (and also the intermediate governments) should not be seen as donors of financial resources.[4] The donor-recipient logic is only applicable to voluntary transfers or to transfers linked to some programs, when the central (or state) government transfers the financial resource to achieve a specific policy result. Here, the highest level of government may (and should) require more efficient public service delivery by the recipient governments.

At the Lincoln Conference, participants conjectured the following crucial predicament: What if the recipient government doesn't win the new tournament? Should the central government stop transfers to public schools? Should school

---

2. In the case of Brazil, states and municipalities are members of the federation at the same level of hierarchy.

3. Another Brazilian example: Some states recently experimented with attaching school grants to performance. Some judges, however, interpreted the performance-based grants as unfair differences in wages, and the program was terminated. In other cases, the wage premium may be considered a permanent increase in job pay. In a nutshell, the judicial system is generally a big obstacle to implementing incentive-driven mechanisms.

4. In revenue-sharing transfers, the upper tiers of government do not own the financial resource. In the case of federations and even of unitary decentralized countries, those funds collected by other and higher levels of government especially appointed that function should be considered revenues.

lunch be cut? Should medical assistance be denied to the sick? If the poorest regions don't receive federal transfers, poor performance of the local manager (or decision maker) results in punishment of the entire community. The penalty in the case of losing the tournament should fall only on the decision maker, never the beneficiary population. The population cannot be punished, in any case.[5] Zinnes's response is, "The implication is that such grants supplement the objectives of other grants; they are not used to fund core services or recurrent costs" (this volume, p. 367).

This approach can be interpreted in a more pragmatic manner, considering the specific circumstance of each case rather than treating it as though it were a mechanical process. There is enormous diversity among countries and jurisdictions: countries that are similar geographically, economically, or socially may have very different assignments of tax authority and expenditure responsibilities, among others differences.[6] Various questions can be raised regarding the definition of benchmarks and comparisons among countries and the ability of indicators to measure what they purport to measure, often resulting in more of a qualitative analysis of decentralization due to the nature of the reform process. What happens in practice tends to be different from what is projected in theory.

Last but not least, one experiment of tournament has been going on in Brazil, namely the incentive for donations to municipal and state CDCAs (Councils for the Rights of Children and Adolescents), established in the 1992 Estatuto da Criança e do Adolescente, ECA (Statute for the Child and Adolescent). According to this law, individuals can divert up to 6 percent and companies up to 1 percent of their annual income taxes to municipal and state funds (managed by local governments). In practice, it is a vertical transfer from the central government to state and local governments selected by the tax payer. However, probably because the projects registered under such committees are not attractive enough, donations have been very small. In other words, tax payers have preferred handing taxes to the central government when voting with their pockets.

REFERENCE

Zinnes, C. F. 2008. Increasing the effectiveness of public service delivery: A tournament approach. In *Fiscal decentralization and land policies*, G. K. Ingram and Y-H. Hong, eds., 359–394. Cambridge, MA: Lincoln Institute of Land Policy.

5. In his chapter, Zinnes mentions some publicity mechanisms that would constrain policy makers' behavior. Although fiscal and managerial transparencies are always desirable, transfers to basic social programs should not be cut off because of a manager's poor performance.

6. Regarding proposals for technical assistance, this point is crucial, but, facing limited resources, may cause the program to be overly expensive and hence not cost effective. Obviously, training is a nice by-product of the experiment. Sometimes, however, there are strong constraints on the availability of human capital in local governments. In many developing countries, local government jobs are generally low paying, and individuals with few skills are often selected for them.

CONTRIBUTORS

Editors

GREGORY K. INGRAM
President and CEO
Lincoln Institute of Land Policy

YU-HUNG HONG
Fellow
Interdepartmental Programs
Lincoln Institute of Land Policy, and
Visiting Assistant Professor
Department of Urban Studies
and Planning
Massachusetts Institute of Technology

Authors

EHTISHAM AHMAD
Advisor
Fiscal Affairs Development
International Monetary Fund

ROY BAHL
Member of the Board of Directors
Lincoln Institute of Land Policy, and
Regents Professor of Economics
Andrew Young School of
Policy Studies
Georgia State University

GIORGIO BROSIO
Professor
Department of Economics
University of Turin

LUIZ DE MELLO
Senior Economist
Department of Economics
Organisation for Economic
Co-operation and Development

WILLIAM A. FISCHEL
Professor
Department of Economics
Dartmouth College

SHELBY GERKING
Galloway Professor of Economics
Department of Economics
University of Central Florida

JORGE MARTINEZ-VAZQUEZ
Professor of Economics and Director
International Studies Program
Andrew Young School of
Policy Studies
Georgia State University

DANIEL P. MCMILLEN
Professor
Department of Economics and
Institute of Government and
Public Affairs
University of Illinois at Chicago

THOMAS J. NECHYBA
Fuchsberg-Levine Family Professor
and Chair
Department of Economics
Duke University

ROBERT H. NELSON
Professor
School of Public Policy
University of Maryland

398

CRISTIAN SEPULVEDA
Research Associate
International Studies Program
Andrew Young School of
Policy Studies
Georgia State University

HILARY SIGMAN
Associate Professor
Department of Economics
Rutgers, The State University of
New Jersey

LARRY D. SINGELL JR.
Professor and Head
Department of Economics
University of Oregon

PAUL SMOKE
Professor of Public Finance and
Planning, and Director
International Programs
Robert F. Wagner Graduate School
of Public Service
New York University

VITO TANZI
Consultant
Inter-American Development Bank

SALLY WALLACE
Professor of Economics and
Associate Director
Fiscal Research Center
Andrew Young School of
Policy Studies
Georgia State University

CLIFFORD F. ZINNES
Senior Fellow, The IRIS Center
Department of Economics and
Affiliate Faculty
School of Public Policy
University of Maryland

Commentators

JOSÉ ROBERTO R. AFONSO
Economist
National Development Bank, and
Researcher
University of Campinas

MAUREEN L. CROPPER
Professor
Department of Economics
University of Maryland

ROBERT D. EBEL
Deputy Chief Financial Officer and
Chief Economist
Office of Revenue Analysis
Washington, DC

DENNIS EPPLE
Thomas Lord Professor of Economics
Tepper School of Business
Carnegie Mellon University

LEE ANNE FENNELL
Professor
University of Chicago Law School

RONALD C. FISHER
Dean
The Honors College and
Professor
Department of Economics
Michigan State University

SÉRGIO GUIMARÃES FERREIRA
Economist
National Development Bank, and
Professor
Instituto Brasileiro de Mercado de
Capitais, Ibmec

ROBERT W. HELSLEY
Watkinson Professor for
Environmental and Land
Management
Sauder School of Business
University of British Columbia

HELEN F. LADD
Edgar T. Thompson Professor of
Public Policy Studies and
Professor of Economics
Sanford Institute of Public Policy
Duke University

PAUL BERND SPAHN
Professor and Executive Director
House of Finance
University of Frankfurt

LAWRENCE SUSSKIND
Ford Professor of Urban and
Environmental Planning
Department of Urban Studies
and Planning
Massachusetts Institute
of Technology,
and Vice Chair
Program on Negotiation
Harvard Law School

CHRISTINE P. W. WONG
Senior Research Fellow
Contemporary China Studies
School of Interdisciplinary Area
Studies and Said Business School
University of Oxford

JEFFREY S. ZAX
Professor
Department of Economics
University of Colorado at Boulder

INDEX

Abdulkadiroglu, A., 318*n*
academic achievement: public school competition and, 308, 322, 322*n*; racial integration and, 330
accountability: of local governments, 24–25; of local revenue systems, 49; participation and, 49; of subnational governments, 24, 81
actionable indicators, 380
Addison, T., 46
affordable housing. *See* low-income (affordable) housing
Afonso, J. R. R., 14, 367*n*, 381*n*, 387, 395–97
Afsah, S., 375, 382
age-dependency ratio, 293
Ahlin, H., 94
Ahmad, E., 6–7, 38, 39, 39*n*, 47, 73–102, 105
Ahmad, J., 19*n*, 38, 39*n*, 51, 367, 367*n*, 378, 378*n*, 389
Ahmed, S. J., 42
aid programs. *See also* donor aid; conditions for success of, 360–61; design of, 361–62; donor country allocations, 369; donor grants, 369–70; ineffectiveness of, 359, 362; new institutional economics and, 359–60
air pollution: decentralization and, 208–11, 216–17; as environmental measure, 200; gross domestic product (GDP) and, 210; state and federal policy and, 199
Akai, N., 70, 97, 98, 283*n*
Akerlof, G., 322*n*, 323
Akron, Ohio, 132*t*
Alabama: employer relocation incentives, 226, 228, 230–31, 231*t*, 232, 233; school expenditures, 146*t*; toxic waste disposal taxes, 180
Albany, New York, 132*t*
Alberini, A., 174, 185
Albino-War, M., 82
alcohol sales, 94, 96
Alesina, A., 247, 282
Alm, J., 39*n*, 227
Alonso-Terme, 291
Ambrosiano, F., 74, 81, 82*n*
American Housing Survey, 356
Anderson, N. B., 141, 225
Angrist, J., 307*n*
Annez, P. C., 369*n*, 370
antidevelopment policies: in California, 129–30; in Loudoun County, 119, 123
antisnob zoning laws, 128–29

antitrust law, 125
aqueous cleaners, 191
Argentina, 23, 201*n*, 248
Arizona, 147*t*, 334
Arkansas, 146*t*, 179
Arz, J., 281
Arze del Granado, J., 32*n*, 96
Asian OECD countries, 76
assessment ratios, 43
Association of Local Government Authorities of Kenya, 57
Aten, B., 292*n*, 295*n*
Atkinson, A., 290, 293
Atlanta, Georgia, 132*t*
Auerbach, A., 224
augmented Dickey-Fuller (DF) tests, 257*n*, 261–62, 263*t*
Australia, 106, 201*n*, 367; environmental policy, 213*t*; government funding of private schools, 328; intergovernmental relations, 77*t*; net worth-to-GDP ratio, 253*f*, 257; taxation, 289
Austria, 106, 106*n*, 201*n*; environmental policy, 213*t*; intergovernmental relations, 77*t*; taxing powers, 82*t*
automobile capital investment, 228–29
Autonomous Communities (AC), 86*n*
"autonomous" revenues, 290
autoregressive distributed lag (ADRL) model, 264
Avery v. Midland County, 343
Azfar, O., 365*n*, 373

Bahami-Oskooee, M., 294
Bahl, R., 5–6, 43, 44, 45, 51, 52, 219, 279*n*, 303, 367*n*
Balaguer-Coll, T., 92
Baltagi, B. H., 257*n*, 261*n*
Baltimore, 125, 132*t*, 333
Banfield, E., 119
Bangladesh, 367*n*
Bangladesh National Women Lawyers' Association, 370
Banta, S., 70
Baqir, R., 282
Baquero, M., 50
Barankay, I., 87, 87*n*, 89, 106
Bardhan, P., 38, 39*n*, 47
Barrett, S., 202
Barro, R., 284, 291, 292, 292*n*, 293*n*, 294*n*
Bartholomew, J., 174
Bartik, T., 225
Barzel, Y., 344

ABOUT THE LINCOLN INSTITUTE OF LAND POLICY

The Lincoln Institute of Land Policy is a private operating foundation whose mission is to improve the quality of public debate and decisions in the areas of land policy and land-related taxation in the United States and around the world. The Institute's goals are to integrate theory and practice to better shape land policy and to provide a nonpartisan forum for discussion of the multidisciplinary forces that influence public policy. This focus on land derives from the Institute's founding objective—to address the links between land policy and social and economic progress—that was identified and analyzed by political economist and author Henry George.

The work of the Institute is organized in four departments: Valuation and Taxation, Planning and Urban Form, Economic and Community Development, and International Studies. We seek to inform decision making through education, research, demonstration projects, and the dissemination of information through publications, our Web site, and other media. Our programs bring together scholars, practitioners, public officials, policy advisers, and involved citizens in a collegial learning environment. The Institute does not take a particular point of view, but rather serves as a catalyst to facilitate analysis and discussion of land use and taxation issues—to make a difference today and to help policy makers plan for tomorrow.

The Lincoln Institute of Land Policy is an equal opportunity institution.

LINCOLN INSTITUTE
OF LAND POLICY

113 Brattle Street
Cambridge, MA 02138-3400 USA

Phone: 1-617-661-3016 x127 or 1-800-LAND-USE (800-526-3873)
Fax: 1-617-661-7235 or 1-800-LAND-944 (800-526-3944)
E-mail: help@lincolninst.edu
Web: www.lincolninst.edu